GRIEVANCE GUIDE

Fourth Edition

WITHDRAWN

by the

BNA Editorial Staff

BNA
BOOK

THE BUREAU OF NATIONAL AFFAIRS, INC., WASHINGTON, D.C.

1972

Printed in the United States of America

Library of Congress Catalog Card Number: 72-91597

International Standard Book Number: 0-87179-147-1

INTRODUCTION

This book takes up the problems that employers, unions, and workers encounter in the day-to-day business of living under a union contract, using awards handed down by impartial arbitrators as examples. The cases selected are those thought to illustrate general principles having application in many bargaining situations. Awards based on complex or unusual factual situations or interpreting highly unusual contract language have not been included.

KEEP THESE POINTS IN MIND—

Arbitrators are not bound by precedents. Their job is to give their best judgement as to the meaning of particular contract language. So the fact that one umpire decided a case in a particular way does not necessarily mean that another umpire would do so in a similar case. However, arbitrators *do* take note of rulings handed down by their fellow umpires.

No two contracts are exactly alike. Small differences in language may make all the difference in the outcome of a dispute. So check your contract carefully in deciding whether a particular ruling might apply in your situation.

The meaning of a contract clause may be determined in large part by the actions of the parties. Consider your own past practice, and what has taken place in contract negotiations, in deciding whether a particular ruling might apply.

The fact that management or union conduct is permitted by contract does not necessarily mean it is permitted by law, and vice versa.

Table of Contents

Table of Contents—Contd.

Grievance Procedure Problems

Any grievance procedure, whether union or nonunion, formal or informal, is subject to problems of interpretation and application in dealing with actual cases. Arbitrators' rulings under union grievance procedures may provide guidelines for handling some of these problems, even where unorganized employees are involved. Rulings on some of the more frequent problems are summarized below.

──────────**PROBLEMS OF APPLICATION**──────────

Enforcement of Time Limits

Promptness is one of the most important aspects of grievance settlement. Failure to settle grievances with dispatch is sure to lead to adverse employee reaction.

Opinions differ, however, on the best method to insure promptness in grievance handling. While many agreements provide time limits for taking complaints to the grievance procedure as well as time limits for processing grievances through the various steps of the procedure, other agreements contain no such procedure. Some feel that time limits provide a safeguard against stalling and the backlogging of stale complaints. Others, on the other hand, believe that fixed time limits encourage an uncooperative party to stall to the maximum time limit and also may bar meritorious grievances that should be settled for the sake of good employee relations. In the final analysis, prompt settlement of grievances probably depends more upon the attitude of the parties than upon the terms of the contract grievance procedure.

If the agreement does contain clear time limits for filing and prosecuting grievances, failure to observe them generally will result in a dismissal of the grievance if the failure is protested. (27 LA 157, 26 LA 732, 25 LA 225)

But the time limits may not be strictly enforced under certain circumstances, such as where—

● Both parties have violated the contract with respect to the grievance procedure. (9 LA 595)
● The employer waived the time limit violation by recognizing and negotiating a grievance without making a timely objection. (49 LA 147, 49 LA 214, 28 LA 398)
● The existence of the grievance wasn't known until some time after the event occurred. In such cases, arbitrators usually hold that the time limit did not begin to run until the individual became aware of, or should have become aware of, the existence of a grievance. (26 LA 501, 24 LA 268, 24 LA 141, 23 LA 21)
● The act complained of is repeated from day to day. Such "continuing violations" are treated as giving rise to continuing grievances. (49 LA 1028, 49 LA 480, 28 LA 424, 27 LA 262)

By-passing First Step

Unions may seek to by-pass the first-line supervisor in the grievance procedure because of his lack of authority with respect to matters of general management policy. Arbitrators, under certain circumstances, may permit this if the grievance is of a general nature (e.g. veterans' vacation rights), which can be resolved only at high union-management levels.

EXAMPLE: A union's failure to follow the first and second steps of a contract's grievance procedure didn't bar arbitration of its grievance protesting the employer's refusal to pay increased contributions to the health and welfare fund. Such a "general policy" grievance is not adaptable to the procedures set up for handling individual grievances, an arbitrator said. (Advance Window Cleaning Co., 43 LA 695)

As indicated above, many contracts state that certain grievances, usually described as "general" or "policy" grievances, do not have to be submitted to lower-level stages of the grievance procedure.

Absence of Time Limits

Usually if the contract sets no time limit for presentation, a grievance which does not antedate the contract may be filed at any time during the contract. (3 LA 327) A contract which merely limits processing time without imposing a time limit on the initial filing of grievances has been held to require "reasonable promptness" in submission of grievances, as well as in processing. (12 LA 311)

Right to Union Representation

Unions and management frequently disagree on whether employee grievances should be taken directly to the foreman or first to the union steward and then to the foreman.

Management may argue that better relationships are fostered if the individual employee and the foreman discuss the grievance alone first. Bringing in the steward at this stage may tend to make the gripe appear more serious than it really is and may inhibit an early settlement, it is argued.

Unions, on the other hand, may argue that the steward should be in at the start. The employee may need his assistance and moral support to ensure recognition of his rights. Management may even benefit from an early screening by the union to weed out grievances that lack merit.

In discipline cases, some arbitrators have held in effect that unless the contract provides otherwise, an employee has no absolute right to have a union representative present during the investigation stage prior to the actual filing of charges or assessment of discipline against the employee. Thus, a worker is not necessarily entitled to have his union steward present when he is called in to his supervisor's office to explain his side of the story. (29 LA 646, 28 LA 179)

However, where a grievance questioned management's distribution of overtime, the grievant was held to have the right to union representation during a meeting with his foreman to discuss the grievance. (27 LA 892)

In any event, arbitrators generally recognize the employee's right to union representation at least commencing with the first step of the grievance procedure.

Grievance Investigation

Many agreements give non-employee union representatives the right of reasonable access to the plant to investigate grievances. But it has been held that such provisions do not give union representative "the right to roam the plant at will" and that it would be a clear violation for the union to use the opportunity to engage in organizational activities. The employer is entitled to know the subject of the grievance for which the outside union representative seeks entry to the plant. (11 LA 1147)

But, another arbitrator observed, an employer has no right to deny access on the basis of his unilateral determination that the grievance was not bona fide. (23 LA 317)

Where a contract grants employees the right to take leave during working hours for union business, the company is entitled to know more than simply that the requested leave is for union business. (32 LA 589)

Individual Presentation of Grievances

Under the Taft Act, individual employees are given the right to bypass their union representatives and present their grievances to management on their own. But it has been held that this does not require the employer to deal with the employees individually; the law merely gives them permission to present grievances. Management can insist upon dealing through the union which represents the employees, it was held. (Administrative Decision of NLRB General Counsel, Case No. 317 (1952), 30 LRRM 1103)

In any event, even where an employer is willing to deal with the employee who brings in his grievance on his own, the law requires the employer to observe these two conditions:

● The bargaining agent must be given a chance to be present at the adjustment of the grievance.

● The adjustment must not be inconsistent with the terms of the collective bargaining contract.

The latter condition poses obvious dangers to the employer who deals directly with an employee regarding a grievance, since the union may file refusal-to-bargain charges if it feels that the individual settlement is inconsistent with the bargaining agreement.

For more information on the Taft Act's rules on handling grievances, see LABOR RELATIONS, Section 34.

Pay for Grievance Time

The extent to which stewards are entitled to pay for time spent adjusting grievances depends upon the particular contract language or past practice of the parties involved. Arbiters have ruled as follows:

● Where the contract specified that union representatives were to be paid for time spent conferring with management, an arbitrator held that grievance preparation, including time spent examining company records, should not be done on company time, except where the presence of a company representative was necessary or whether the amount of time involved was relatively slight. (16 LA 734)

● Where stewards were to be paid for time spent "in regular or special meetings with management," stewards were held not entitled to pay for time spent in grievance meetings that extended beyond their regular working hours, where surrounding circumstances made it clear that the parties had intended to limit the pay to time spent in meetings during working hours. (43 LA 730)

If a company is required to pay stewards for time spent processing grievances, it probably can impose reasonable reporting requirements. For example, a company was held entitled to adopt a new rule requiring stewards to notify their supervisor before leaving their work station and to clock out and clock in for the period of time away from their station. (44 LA 463)

Under the Wage-Hour Act, the status of time spent adjusting grievances may be regarded as working time for the purpose of determining when overtime pay is due. As a general rule, such time is presumed to be working time unless a contrary intention appears from the collective bargaining contract or the parties' past practice. (See WAGES AND HOURS, Section 93.)

POLICY GUIDE

When you take a grievance to arbitration, you may be setting the stage for a costly proceeding. If you "go for broke" and take the deluxe arbitration model, you will be faced with per diem charges from the arbitrator, your lawyer, and a court reporter. In addition, you may be billed for travel expenses for the arbitrator, the lawyer, or the court reporter. You also will have to pay for time lost by company representatives in preparing for the hearing and by employees who appear at the hearings.

APPLICATION OF POLICY

Cost-saving Tips

In view of this potential for sizeable charges, you might want to consider ways of holding down expenses. Some cost-saving suggestions include—

● Don't rent a hotel room for the hearing if it is possible to hold the hearing in the company conference room.

● Don't use a court reporter unless you really need one. Usually a transcript isn't essential unless the case is extremely complicated or technical.

● In the old stand-by type of case, involving discipline, seniority, job classifications, and like issues, consider whether you wouldn't be just as well off training your own representatives to present the case rather than hire a lawyer.

● Consider using a relatively new arbitrator. New arbitrators are in less demand than the old pros and therefore charge smaller fees. At least in the routine cases, there is a high degree of predictability no matter who hears the case.

● In any event, find out the arbitrator's fee in advance. Also find out his policy on billing for travel time.

● Settle as many facts as possible with your opponent before the hearing starts. This will cut both hearing time and the arbitrator's study time.

● Consider dispensing with a written opinion if the case turns mainly on matters of fact. (But many employers still feel that a written opinion in the long run saves time and money, particularly where basic issues are at stake, by making it easier to understand and explain the decision.)

● Avoid indiscriminate citations of other awards. You don't help yourself by citing cases that are easily distinguishable, and you only add to the arbitrator's study time.

● Avoid futile fights about arbitrability if all you really mean is that the grievance lacks merit.

● Be considerate of the arbitrator's time. If you fail to keep hearing dates or ask for postponements on short notice, you will be charged for it one way or another.

● Find out what you can about the arbitrator before you select him—otherwise you may have to pay to educate him on your time.

Company-Union Cost Sharing

> BASIC PATTERNS SURVEY

Expenses of arbitration are considered in 86 percent of arbitration clauses, according to a BNA survey of representative union contracts. The vast majority of these (95 percent)

4

specify that the expenses of the impartial arbitrator are to be shared by the company and the union. Under most of the rest, the loser pays; but in some cases, the assessment of cost is left to the discretion of the arbitrator or the company is required to foot the whole bill. ⟵

Just Cause for Discipline

A basic principle underlying most disciplinary procedures is that management must have "just cause" for imposing the discipline. This standard often is written into union contracts or read into them by arbitrators. Even in the absence of a contract, it sums up the test used by employees in judging whether management acted fairly in enforcing company rules.

While the definition of "just cause" necessarily varies from case to case, one arbitrator has listed these tests for determining whether a company had just cause for disciplining an employee:

► Was the employee adequately warned of the consequences of his conduct? The warning may be given orally or in printed form. An exception may be made for certain conduct, such as insubordination, coming to work drunk, drinking on the job, or stealing company property, that is so serious that the employee is expected to know it will be punishable.

► Was the company's rule or order reasonably related to efficient and safe operations?

► Did management investigate before administering the discipline? The investigation normally should be made before the decision to discipline is made. Where immediate action is required, however, the best course is to suspend the employee pending investigation with the understanding that he will be restored to his job and paid for time lost if he is found not guilty.

► Was the investigation fair and objective?

► Did the investigation produce substantial evidence or proof of guilt? It is not required that the evidence be preponderant, conclusive, or "beyond reasonable doubt," except where the alleged misconduct is of such a criminal or reprehensible nature as to stigmatize the employee and seriously impair his chances for future employment.

► Were the rules, orders, and penalties applied evenhandedly and without discrimination? If enforcement has been lax in the past, management can't suddenly reverse its course and begin to crack down without first warning employees of its intent.

► Was the penalty reasonably related to the seriousness of the offense and the past record? If employee A's past record is significantly better than that of employee B, the company properly may give A a lighter punishment than B for the same offense (42 LA 555)

GUIDELINES

Additional Guidelines

In addition to the checklist outlined above, another arbitrator indicated that these guidelines are "well accepted":

● The employer should enjoy reasonable discretionary powers to prescribe rules of conduct.

● The employer should publicize these rules either by direct publication or by consistent enforcement.

● The employer should apply his disciplinary policies "seriously and without discrimination."

● The employer should regard industrial discipline as corrective—not punitive.

● The employer should avoid arbitrary or hasty action when confronted with a situation.

● The employer should evaluate each situation in the light of the employee's disciplinary record.

● The employer should tailor the punishment to fit the crime. (48 LA 336)

Disciplinary Ground Rules

Another arbitrator listed the following criteria generally applied by arbitrators in evaluating the justness of discipline:

Equal treatment — All employees must be judged by the same standards, and the rules must apply equally to all. This does not mean, however, that the same penalty always must be given for the same offense.

Rule of reason—Even in the absence of a specific provision, a contract protects employees against unjust discipline and permits a challenge to any company procedure that threatens to deprive employees of their rights.

Internal consistency—The pattern of enforcement must be consistent, whether a company disciplines on a case-by-case basis or uses a rule book.

Personal guilt—Even though two employees are involved in the same act of misconduct, the same penalty need not be meted out to each. Such things as prior disciplinary records may be considered. (47 LA 1104)

Disciplinary Procedures

Every company is forced at some time or other to administer discipline, but there are good ways and bad ways of doing it. A study of many successfully administered policies reveals this pattern:

▶ Company rules are carefully explained to employees. This is especially important in the case of new employees. Indoctrination courses, employee handbooks, bulletin board notices, and many other forms of bringing rules to the attention of employees, are used.

▶ Accusations against employees are carefully considered, to see if they are supported by facts. Witnesses are interviewed, their statement recorded, and careful investigation made to see that both sides of the story are available and fairly presented. Circumstantial evidence is kept to a minimum in judging the facts, personality factors and unfounded assumptions are eliminated.

▶ A regular "warning" procedure is worked out and applied. Sometimes *all* warnings are in writing, with a copy handed to the employee and one filed in the employee's record in the personnel office. Sometimes first warnings are *orally* delivered, but a written record of the warning is filed away. Warnings are given for all except the most serious offenses—those which management has made clear will call for immediate discharge.

▶ Some companies bring the union into the discipline case early in the procedure. Copies of warning notices go to the union. The union is given advance notice of other disciplinary action which management intends to take. Sometimes the action is held up until the union has time to make its own investigation.

▶ Before disciplinary action is taken, the employee's motive and reasons for the violation of rules are investigated. Then the penalty is adjusted to the facts—whether the employee's action was in good faith, partially justified, or totally unjustified.

▶ Before disciplinary action is taken, the employee's past record is taken into consideration. A good work record and long seniority are viewed as factors in the employee's favor, particularly where a minor offense is involved, or where it is a first offense. Previous offenses are not used against the employee unless he was reprimanded at the time they occurred, or warned that they would be used against him in any future disciplinary action.

▶ Companies make sure that all management agents, and particularly first-line supervisors know the company's disciplinary policies and procedures, and carefully observe them. This is particularly important in the case of verbal warnings, or informal reprimands.

▶ Discipline *short of discharge* is used wherever possible.

STANDARDS OF FAIRNESS

In ruling on the fairness of discipline for such offenses as insubordination, misconduct, absenteeism, and poor work, arbitrators do not concern themselves merely with whether the workers involved are guilty. They also examine the procedures followed by the company in punishing the workers and the nature of the punishment itself. If they feel that a worker wasn't given a fair shake, or that the wrong sort of penalty was imposed, they will refuse to uphold management disciplinary action.

POINTERS—

▶ Unless the contract says otherwise, the company has the right to make new rules without consulting the union. But the union can protest a rule it considers unfair through the grievance procedure. Moreover, the company may have a *legal* obligation to bargain on new plant rules.

▶ Once established, rules must be enforced impartially; established disciplinary procedures also must be followed.

▶ While company rules don't necessarily have to be posted, umpires agree that workers must be informed of the existence and nature of the rules if they're to be expected to observe them.

—————————————— GUIDELINES ——————————————

Right To Adopt Rules

It is generally agreed that management is authorized to make and to post any rules of conduct that are not inconsistent with the collective bargaining agreement. (11 LA 689, 7 LA 150)

Once promulgated the rules may be subject to challenge through the grievance procedure as contrary to the contract or as arbitrary, unfair, or discriminatory. (28 LA 583, 10 LA 113)

While management's right to make reasonable rules is recognized, particular rules may be voided if they are vague and ineffective (27 LA 717) or arbitrary (27 LA 99).

Even reasonable rules have been held unenforceable if they (1) have not been brought to the attention of employees (18 LA 866), (2) infringe unduly upon an employee's private life (18 LA 400), or (3) are applied discriminatorily (26 LA 934).

Consistent Enforcement

Where management has winked at violations of a rule, it should announce its intention to require observance of the rule before it hands out heavy penalties. This is especially true where the rule applies to conduct that, unlike stealing or assaults on supervisors or co-workers, isn't inherently objectionable. Lax enforcement of rules may lead employees reasonably to believe that the conduct in question is sanctioned by management. (20 LA 342, 21 LA 729, 28 LA 65, 42 LA 87, 46 LA 161)

This does not mean that the same discipline must be meted out to each individual in a group, even where each is equally culpable. Such things as prior disciplinary and work records may be considered. (47 LA 1104)

While arbitrators have no jurisdiction to pass upon management's treatment of its supervisors, they may set aside penalties imposed upon rank-and-file workers if supervisors who were guilty of the same offense are let off free or given lesser penalties. Thus, when both a supervisor and a worker were cleared of the offense, the umpire found management guilty of double standards when it reinstated only the supervisor. (39 LA 823)

Pay for Time Spent in Disciplinary Interview

Is a worker who is being questioned or interviewed to determine possible disciplinary action entitled to pay for the time spent in this way? At least one arbitrator has ruled that workers could not be docked for the time spent in disciplinary interviews held on company time. Both management and the worker stand to profit from such interviews, he pointed out, and there is no reason why the employee should have to suffer a monetary loss. (Bethlehem Steel Co., 19 LA 261)

Furthermore: Another arbitrator ruled that workers should be paid for time spent in a disciplinary conference held on their off time. In this instance, the workers were called in on a Saturday, so the arbitrator awarded them four hours' pay for the time spent in conference under the call-in pay provision of the contract. (Bethlehem Steel Co., 21 LA 579)

Staggered Penalty

Where management penalizes a group of workers by suspending them, can it stagger the suspensions so that the workers aren't all off at the same time? Several arbitrators have ruled that management has the right.

In one case where workers struck in violation of the contract, the arbiter reasoned that if management suspended everyone at once, the result would be a work stoppage, the very thing the disciplinary action was intended to penalize. (United States Steel Corp., 40 LA 598) Another umpire came to a similar conclusion, adding that although management wasn't free to schedule the discipline "at its convenience" any time after the stoppage, it was entitled to reasonable latitude in deferring the time of the suspensions. (Bethlehem Steel Co., 39 LA 686)

UNION'S ROLE IN DISCIPLINARY PROCEEDINGS

Notice to Union

Where a contract calls for notice of disciplinary action to be given to the union, arbiters are likely to require strict compliance with such a provision. They operate on the theory that a worker's rights are seriously abridged if the union is not given a chance to get in on the ground floor.

Even if the disciplined employee clearly was guilty of misconduct, the penalty may be mitigated if the union wasn't given proper notice. Thus one arbiter ordered a discharged employee reinstated without back pay where the company failed to adhere to the contractual requirement of consultation with the union over discharges. (Hayes Mfg. Corp., 17 LA 412) Another umpire ruled that a company that had failed to comply with notice requirements had to give an employee pay for time lost between the date of his discharge and the date of the first grievance meeting, even though his discharge was for just cause. (National Lead Co., 13 LA 28)

Moreover: Where it has been the company's custom and practice to give notice of disciplinary action to the union, even though the contract did not require it, one arbitrator ruled that the discharge of a worker without notifying the union was improper. (Coca-Cola Bottling Co., 9 LA 197)

Challenging New Rule

A union lost any right to challenge the discharge of a worker for violation of a new plant rule forbidding drinking during lunch breaks, when it did not protest when the rule was posted, and arbiter ruled. A worker was caught drinking on his lunch break and was fired. The arbiter denied the union's grievance, holding that management was justified in enforcing a new rule which it considered had full union support. (International Pipe & Ceramics Corp., 44 LA 267)

Union's Right to Disciplinary Forms

The personnel forms management develops are its own business and ordinarily need not be given to the union, one umpire has ruled. He suggested, though, that this rule may not hold where a form is used in imposing discipline.

EXAMPLE: When an employer developed three new personnel forms to replace a single reprimand form, the union demanded that it be given a copy whenever one of the forms was used. Management was willing to supply one that was to be used solely for reprimands, but it refused to fork over one used to record attendance and changes of address or one entitled "Employee Performance & Conduct Memo."

The umpire said the employer had the right to develop his own forms without any discussion or negotiation with the union. And if a form was to become merely part of management's records, he added, the union had no more right of access to it than management had to union records. He noted that the employer had an established practice of supplying reprimand, and he said he considered this a sound practice. So he concluded that the new reprimand form had to be given to the union whenever it was used; the Performance & Conduct Memo had to be supplied only if used as a reprimand; and the attendance and change of address form could be withheld altogether. (Harshaw Chemical Co., 32 LA 86)

Union Representation During Investigation

If a contract gives employees the right to union representation when disciplinary action is taken against them, do they also have the right to have a union official on hand when the employer is conducting preliminary investigations held prior to disciplinary action? Arbiters are divided on this question. Some feel that employees have the right to union representation during preliminary investigations on the theory that this is the beginning stage of a grievance. (Independent Lock Co. of Alabama, 30 LA 744)

On the other hand: Some take the position that union representation isn't required unless the employee actually is charged with an offense, or until the beginning of the investigation. Suspension pending this investigation is upheld. (Sperry Rand Corp., 49 LA 1245)

Union Representation Waived

Under a contract giving a disciplined employee the right to representation, what happens if the employee is not in the plant when he's discharged or other discipline is imposed? Arbiters generally hold that representation requirements are waived if the employee is absent when action is taken against him or if the penalty is imposed via mail or telegram. (Lyon, Inc., 24 LA 353; E. J. Kress Box Co., 24 LA 401)

The type of penalty assessed for wrongdoing usually is either a temporary suspension or discharge. A temporary suspension, or "disciplinary layoff," results in loss of pay (and sometimes seniority) for the period of suspension and mars the employee's record. When an arbitrator reinstates a discharged employee without back pay, the end result is not unlike suspension.

Warnings are a lesser type of discipline. Failure to warn an employee of the consequences of violating a rule is one of the most frequent reasons given by arbitrators for setting aside disciplinary layoffs or discharges.

Management may be on shaky ground if it attempts to use types of penalties other than warnings, suspensions, and discharge.

GUIDELINES

Discipline other than Discharge

The fact that a contract gives the right to discharge for cause or mentions certain offenses that are grounds for discharge usually doesn't mean that management may not impose lesser forms of discipline. Under the principle that the greater includes the lesser, arbitrators have upheld management's right to impose degrees of penalties.

But if a contract specifies a procedure of progressive discipline, such as warnings, suspension, and discharge, arbitrators may not uphold management's right to apply other types of penalties, particularly if such measures contravene other provisions of the contract. Thus, arbitrators have held that employers had no right to apply the penalties of denial of a promotion (9 LA 47), denial of holiday pay (16 LA 317, 13 LA 126, 25 LA 332), loss of seniority (30 LA 519), denial of incentive earnings (29 LA 512), and forcing public apologies (22 LA 528).

EXAMPLE: When an employee went for his paycheck, the payroll clerk was carrying on a personal telephone conversation. The employee waited 10 minutes, then broke the connection to get the clerk's attention. She complained about his conduct, and he was told to apologize. When he refused, he was fired.

The employee was unnecessarily rude to the clerk, the umpire figured, since he could have attracted her attention in some other way. But a short layoff would have been adequate discipline, he said, for the offense was minor and the clerk's conduct irritating. The company's attitude, the umpire found, put the employee on the spot; he was required to say he was wrong when he felt he wasn't.

The company's action, the arbiter held, was out of line. (Magnavox Co., 28 LA 449)

Warnings

Arbitrators in general seem to feel that some form of warning should precede a discharge, except where the employee is guilty of serious misconduct such as stealing or drunkenness on the job. (17 LA 334, 3 LA 181)

A warning is particularly important where a worker has been let off lightly for past offenses and management intends to crack down on future offenses. A discharge for a "last-straw" offense probably will be set aside unless the worker was warned previously that he would be dealt with more severely. (23 LA 284, 29 LA 599)

Progressive Discipline

For most offenses, management is expected to use a system of progressive discipline under which the employee is warned or given disciplinary suspensions before being hit with the ultimate penalty of discharge. A common pattern is: oral warning, written warning, disciplinary layoff, and discharge.

But management isn't bound by a progressive-discipline formula in cases of serious offenses. Some offenses, such as stealing, loan-sharking, or drunkenness on the job, are regarded as so serious that no specific warning or prior disciplinary action need precede discharge. Employees are presumed to know that such serious offenses will lead to discharge. (27 LA 768)

If progressive discipline were to apply to every case, one arbitrator noted, an employee who brutally assaulted his foreman or a fellow employee would get off with a simple warning slip if it were only his first offense. Thus, he held, the schedule of penalties spelled out in the contract was intended to apply to the offenses referred to and other violations of specific contract provisions and was not intended to apply to other offenses, including serious infractions of plant rules. (48 LA 457)

As one arbiter explained:

"The policy of progressive discipline does not mean that for any given employee each penalty must necessarily be more severe than the immediate preceding one, regardless of the offense involved. . . . What progressive discipline does mean is that progressively more severe penalties may be imposed on each given employee each time any given offense is repeated.

"Progressive discipline also means that after a specified number of offenses, regardless of whether the offenses are identical or not, the company may have the right to discharge the given employees.

"Both of these . . . interpretations of progressive discipline avoid the inequitable meting out of discipline, and at the same time serve the dual purpose of progressive discipline, namely, the discouragement of repeated offense by employees and the protection of the right of the company to sever completely its relationship with any employee who by his total behavior shows himself to be irresponsible." (17 LA 230)

Double Jeopardy & Delays

It is a well recognized principle that discipline should be reasonably prompt and that a penalty, once announced, should not be increased absent evidence that the offense was more serious than it looked at first.

The principle of double jeopardy has been applied by arbitrators to prohibit the imposition of two successive penalties for the same offense, such as a recorded warning and a suspension. (12 LA 129, 13 LA 551, 18 LA 86, 24 LA 356)

One arbitrator pointed out, however, that the legal "double jeopardy" rule assumes that a full hearing has been held and that disclosures at that hearing are the basis for the penalty imposed. But "normal industrial plant disciplinary procedures" do not contemplate the kind of hearing which is the basis of the legal rule, he pointed out. He upheld the discharge of employees who already had received a layoff for participating in a wildcat strike where evidence obtained after the layoff showed that they were leaders in the strike. (13 LA 611)

Court and company penalties—The fact that an employee has paid a fine or served a jail sentence for acts committed in connection with his employment doesn't preclude management from imposing discipline for the same acts. An arbitrator, however, may consider the legal punishment in determining the severity of the penalty imposed by management. (26 LA 836)

Delays—Management may delay in imposing a penalty for a reasonable time, but arbitrators sometimes find that excessive delay is almost the same as double jeopardy, since an employee then has the threat of the penalty hanging over him for months. (28 LA 874)

It has been held that an employee is entitled (1) to expect full discipline within a reasonable time, and (2) to assume that the penalty received is the complete one. (8 LA 234, 9 LA 606, 12 LA 344)

Demotion as Discipline

Many arbitrators disapprove of demotion as an ordinary tool of discipline. It permits unequal penalties for similar offenses, they reason, and may have side effects more drastic than the intended punishment, as where a demoted employee subsequently loses his job because of the change in his seniority status. (42 LA 252)

Other arbiters, however, have allowed demotions for such matters as carelessness and negligence, poor work attitudes, and incompetence. But in such cases approval frequently is grounded on the theory that the demotion is not really a form of discipline but an adjustment required by the employee's inability to do his job. (See 12 LA 266, 17 LA 328, 18 LA 457, and the chapters on "Poor Work," beginning at p. 203:501.)

EXAMPLE: An employee who had worked for a supermarket chain for about 14 years had served two long stretches as head of a meat department. Each time he had been demoted to cutter, first class, for unsatisfactory performance. Nevertheless, he talked the company into giving him another shot at running a department. He was told at that time, however, that he would have to maintain a satisfactory profit margin.

Although the company couldn't point to specific defects in the employee's subsequent handling of the department, his profit margin consistently was below the all-store average, was below his predecessor's average, and was, in fact, the worst of any of the company's 40 stores. After 14 weeks of this, the employee was warner in writing; a week later, the picture not having improved, he was demoted.

An arbitrator upheld the demotion, but he clearly did not view it as discipline. Instead, he treated the employee's 15 weeks as a department head as a trial period during which he had failed to demonstrate his ability to handle the job. (Hart's Food Stores, Inc., 43 LA 934)

Discharge v. Resignation

Where the facts and circumstances are such as to lead management reasonably to conclude that intent to resign exists, the matter may be treated as a resignation even though the individual never actually stated his intent to quit. (30 LA 225, 26 LA 786, 25 LA 608)

However, if intent to resign is not adequately evidenced or if a statement of intent to resign is involuntary or coerced, an alleged resignation will be treated as a discharge and subject to the usual tests of "just cause."

The fact that an employee leaves work without permission because of dissatisfaction or upset over something that has occurred doesn't necessarily mean that you are justified in treating him as a voluntary quit. Arbiters have held that the test is whether the employee intended permanently to sever his connection with the company. As one arbitrator stated:

"The overwhelming w e i g h t of

authority holds that there is no voluntary quit by reason of an employee's refusal to perform work to which he is assigned. Unless some affirmation of an intent to quit the job is manifested by the employee, the employer's subsequent refusal to let the employee continue his status constitutes a discharge rather than a resignation." (24 LA 522; see also 41 LA 913, 921)

Rescinded Resignations

An employee who voluntarily quits loses his status as an employee, it is generally recognized. Therefore, if he subsequently tries to rescind the resignation, the decision as to whether to accept the retraction is considered to be within the sole discretion of management. (40 LA 469, 29 LA 700)

In one case an arbiter refused to reinstate an employee who quit rather than take a demotion, even though the demotion was found to be a contract violation. The fact that an employee may have a grievance, the arbiter said, doesn't alter or justify a resignation or prevent the individual from losing his employee status by quitting.

On the other hand, some arbiters have held that extenuating or mitigating circumstances may justify a departure from "rigid" application of the general rule. One arbiter said that there is "at least substantial authority" for the proposition that a resignation may be withdrawn if the withdrawal is prompt and the company has not been seriously prejudiced by the employee's conduct. He required a company to take back a 10-year employee who quit in a huff at the prospect of what he considered to be an unjust demotion but who cooled off almost immediately and asked to be retained.

Proving Misconduct

IN BRIEF

In most disciplinary cases, and particularly in discharge cases, the burden is on management to prove the guilt or wrongdoing, particularly where the contract requires "just cause" for discharge. (29 LA 781, 29 LA 525, 26 LA 562, 24 LA 401)

Usually the degree of proof required is a preponderance of the evidence (28 LA 65, 27 LA 486, 24 LA 401) or "clear and convincing" evidence (27 LA 148, 8 LA 261). But a higher degree of proof frequently is required where the alleged misconduct is of a kind recognized and punished by the criminal law or is regarded as morally reprehensible. In such cases, the common-law standard of "proof beyond a reasonable doubt" has been required. (25 LA 906, 24 LA 804, 21 LA 832)

GUIDELINES

After-the-Fact Evidence Gathering

When management discharges or disciplines an employee, it should have enough facts in hand at the time of the action to establish "just cause." Efforts to build up a good case by extensive research after a grievance is filed generally will be a waste of time, since arbitrators usually hold that management's case must stand or fall on the basis of facts it had at the time it acted. (12 LA 108, 10 LA 117, 1 LA 153)

Lie Detector Tests

Arbiters generally have been reluctant to uphold discipline based on the results of lie detector tests.

Some arbiters have held that test results can be given no weight whatsoever in determining guilt. Granting that such tests are used extensively in government and industry, one arbitrator said, the fact remains that most courts have ruled them inadmissible as evidence in criminal and civil cases. The same rule should apply to arbitration proceedings, he said. (38 LA 779; see also 44 LA 709, 45 LA 1155)

Other arbitrators have held that test results may be considered as a "factor of evidence" but may not serve as the sole basis of proof. (39 LA 470, 39 LA 893, 43 LA 450)

Others have said that an employee's refusal to submit to a test cannot be used against him, especially where the company is fishing for a guilty party among a group of employees and hasn't yet accused anyone. (32 LA 44, 39 LA 470)

One arbitrator set forth these guidelines on the use of lie detector tests in cases involving dishonesty: The company could offer these tests to employees on a voluntary basis when there was a reason to suspect them of dishonesty and could consider the failure to take a test as an additional possible factor in determining whether to proceed with discharge action. However, where the company had nothing else to go on but an employee's unwillingness to take a test, it could not use this factor as a basis for discipline. (39 LA 1121)

One arbiter, however, upheld a discharge for refusal to cooperate in the investigation of a theft where the missing articles were found in the employee's car and he refused to offer a satisfactory explanation or to take a test. (26 LA 362)

Handwriting Expert

Arbitrators have accepted testimony of handwriting experts and have based their awards principally on such testimony. On one such case, involving the discharge of an employee for allegedly writing and posting three obscene notices slandering female employees, the arbitrator ignored the employee's refusal to take a lie detector test, holding that he was within his rights in so refusing. But he relied on the testimony of a handwriting expert in upholding the discharge. He noted that the examiner's qualifications as an expert were substantial and that his identification of the employee as the author was both positive and firm. (39 LA 125)

Use of 'Bugs,' TV Surveillance

Suspension of a telephone operator for poor work performance was upheld by an arbitrator, where supervisors used a multiple listening device to monitor her performance. Discipline needn't be limited to eyewitness observation by supervisors, it was held. (45 LA 689)

Use of a TV surveillance system was knocked down by another arbitrator, but only on the ground that installation of the cameras was a substantial enough change in working conditions to require negotiation with the union. The umpire did not completely close the door to the use of closed circuit television as a tool of supervision. For one thing, he rejected the union's claim that this constituted an unlawful invasion of privacy or spying.

In ruling that the TV system had to go, the arbitrator relied heavily on the fact that the company failed to show any particular need for or benefit to be derived from the system. (44 LA 563)

Unnamed or Biased Accusers

Some arbitrators have refused to sustain discipline based on charges by persons whom the employer either refused to identify or to produce at the arbitration hearing. (24 LA 538, 22 LA 320, 13 LA 433) But where a discharge was based on the report of a professional "spotter" employed to detect irregularities, an arbitrator held the company did not have to produce the spotter at the hearing, since this would have destroyed his effectiveness. (23 LA 362)

Biased accusers—When co-workers accuse an employee of misconduct, management should check to see if they have ulterior motives for making their accusations. The testimony of biased witnesses most likely will be discounted by arbiters.

EXAMPLE: An employee was discharged for being a goof-off. Two of his fellow workers said they'd rather clock out and go home than be assigned to work with this employee because of his habit of wandering off and leaving them to shoulder the whole load.

It so happened that one of these employees was a brother-in-law of the discharged employee's foreman and the other was a neighbor of the foreman. The discharged employee on an earlier occasion had turned in the foreman for being intoxicated on the job.

The arbitrator didn't put any store in the testimony of the foreman's allies, but relied instead on the testimony of other employee's who said they'd never had any trouble working with the discharged employee. (Scientific Data Systems, Inc., 53 LA 487)

Absenteeism

Absenteeism

It has been held consistently that chronic or excessive absenteeism is just cause for discharge. The real problem has been to determine when absenteeism is excessive. No general rules can be laid down, but arbitrators consider such factors as these: the length of time during which a worker's attendance record has been bad, the reasons for his absences, the nature of his job, the attendance records of other workers, and the company's attempts to correct the problem.

Before sustaining a discharge for absenteeism, an umpire probably will require that these factors be present:

▶ The company must have a clear disciplinary policy on absenteeism known to employees.

▶ The policy must have been applied fairly and consistently.

▶ The worker must have been given fair warning that he faced discharge unless his attendance record improved.

A special form of absenteeism, lateness, also is taken up in this section.

─────────────────**GUIDELINES**─────────────────

REASONS FOR ABSENTEEISM

In balancing the employee's right to job security against management's right to expect a reasonable degree of job attendance, the result frequently turns on whether the reason offered for the absence is justifiable or not. Some of the problems in striking this balance are discussed below.

Chronic Illness

Even if the reasons offered for each individual absence seem proper, employees may be disciplined for excessive absenteeism, if the absences become so frequent as to render the employee's services of little or no value to the company (39 LA 187, 23 LA 663, 18 LA 869, 15 LA 593). It is generally felt, however, that employees should be put on notice and given an opportunity to improve before the discharge penalty is invoked.

It may be relatively easy for a company to justify a discharge for excessive absenteeism where the employee has had frequently recurring illnesses for short periods over a long period of time showing symptoms of psychosomatic origin or chronic bad health. On the other hand, it may be more difficult for it to justify the termination of an employee with several genuine illnesses, each lasting a long time. (36 LA 1042)

Management's case for justifying a

discharge will be strengthened if it has sought through counseling, warnings, and health care to rehabilitate the employee. But the fact that the final absence would not by itself support discharge is immaterial, so long as the company has given adequate warning.

The test is whether the employee's attendance has fallen below the acceptable range for an unreasonable period of time. In determining this, management may consider the employee's previous attendance record, his length of service, his desire to be a faithful employee, his efforts to improve, the nature of the absences the extent to which they exceed the norm, the effect upon efficiency and morale, and the prospects for the future. (41 LA 551)

EXAMPLE: A company discharged an employee who had been absent because of illness 14 or 15 weeks out of a six-month period. In upholding the discharge, an arbitrator said: "No plant can operate profitably unless it can depend on fairly regular attendance of employees. A n y situation which results in or tends toward unprofitable operations is against the best interests not only of the company but of the employees themselves." (Celanese Corp. of America, 9 LA 143)

Alcoholism

Alcoholism now is looked upon as an illness, and many companies have developed programs aimed at spotting and rehabilitating alcoholics. But management isn't obligated to retain indefinitely an employee whose alcoholism keeps him from delivering on a regular basis.

EXAMPLE: An employee had been warned on numerous occasions concerning his attendance. Lack of improvement resulted in a seven-day disciplinary suspension. This was followed by more counseling concerning the seriousness of his absenteeism and his drinking problem, and finally by a 30-day suspension pending discharge with the understanding that he would be given "one more chance" if he committed himself to the state alcoholic hospital and successfully underwent treatment. After temporarily getting "on the wagon," the employee subse-

quently fell off with the result that he lost a week from work and woke up in the state hospital again. The company finally decided to discharge him.

Refusing to set the discharge aside, an arbitrator said that when a "last-chance" agreement has been reached, another chance must rest entirely within the company's discretion. If he were to rule otherwise, it might jeopardize the chance of other employees to obtain reinstatement on the same condition, he noted. (Mohawk Rubber Co., 47 LA 1029)

Imprisonment

In determining the propriety of discipline for an absence caused by a jail sentence, a number of factors may be taken into consideration. These include the duration of the absence, the nature of the act causing the confinement and the effect the employee's reinstatement would have on plant morale, the ease or difficulty of having the absent employee's duties performed by others, and the employer's past practices with respect to absenteeism generally and to arrest-caused absences specifically.

Arbiters are by no means unanimous in their attitude toward absence caused by confinement in jail. Some hold that it is just cause for discharge, while some say that it is a sufficient excuse for absence. In between are those who hold that it isn't necessarily one or the other and that disposition depends on the circumstances. Among the circumstances strongly to be considered, one arbiter listed (1) the employee's length of service, (2) his prior disciplinary record, and (3) his record for dependability (32 LA 545).

EXAMPLE: An employee with 37 years of service was arrested in a local movie house on a morals charge. He was held in a jail a couple of days before being released, and later was tried, convicted, and sentenced to a year and a day in prison. Upon his release, he began receiving treatment from doctors and psychiatrists toward elimination of the "sociopathic personality disturbance, sexual deviation," that had landed him in jail. The company decided to terminate him permanently.

While conceding that the employee was mentally ill and that his illness had manifested itself in a way that was repugnant and unlawful, an arbitrator directed his reinstatement. The illness didn't impair his ability to do his job, the arbiter noted, and the company hadn't shown that it couldn't be eliminated or substantially improved by medical treatment. Nor was it shown that the employee's absence had affected the efficiency of his department or had significantly increased the company's insurance charges. And aside from sheer speculation, there was no basis for finding that his return would result in bad feelings or tensions in his department. All of this, plus his spotless employment record of 37 years, convinced the arbiter there was not just cause for charge. (U.S. Steel Corp., 41 LA 460)

Religious Beliefs

Management's right to discipline an employee for absences caused by his religious beliefs is complicated by the ban on religious discrimination in Title VII of the federal Civil Rights Act and by similar bans in many state FEP laws.

Guidelines issued by the Equal Employment Opportunity Commission call for employers to make reasonable accommodations to the religious needs of their employees when this can be done without undue hardship to the business. In one case, a federal court found that an employer violated the ban on religious discrimination by firing a worker who refused to work on Sunday or to find a replacement because of his religious convictions.

Weather Conditions, Riots, etc.

On occasion, bad weather, civil disturbances, or other outside conditions make it difficult for employees to report to work. A survey conducted by BNA and the American Society for Personnel Administration suggests that most companies that remain open in this situation dock the pay of hourly-paid employees who are unable to report, but that at least some of the salaried workers aren't penalized if the excuse is reasonable.

'Personal Business'

Employees at times are reluctant to disclose their reasons—good or bad—for wanting to take time off from work. To avoid unpleasant situations, employers frequently are willing to accept personal business as a valid excuse for absences in some situations.

But when a company decided to crack down on absenteeism because of suspected abuses, an arbiter held that it could require employees to come up with something more than "personal business" as an excuse for absences. It is appropriate in such cases, the arbiter said, for the company to inquire into the *general* nature of the business without invading the privacy of the employee's personal affairs.

Since it would be next to impossible to prescribe a set formula covering every situation, the arbitrator advised, each personal absence should be diagnosed and treated separately. (47 LA 225)

This case-by-case approach generally is followed by arbiters. For example, "personal reasons" were held an acceptable excuse where the employer ordinarily accepted that excuse, even though the disputed absence occurred on the day before a scheduled vacation (31 LA 386). On the other hand, suspension of an employee was held justified where all he would say was that he had been "out of town" (12 LA 47).

The extent of an employee's prior absences may have a bearing on the extent to which management may probe into the reason for an absence.

EXAMPLE: An employee, with a record of extensive absenteeism and failing to call in or give explanation for his absences, gave as an excuse for a one week's absence that he had been out on "personal business." Because this explanation was considered inadequate, he was asked on several occasions to come up with a more substantive explanation. When he failed to do so, he was terminated. Only then did he explain that the reason for his absence was a highly personal situation involving domestic difficulties which he found embarrassing to make public.

If the employee hadn't had the poor past record of unexplained absences, the company might have been in the position to give him the benefit of the doubt, an arbitrator said. But in view of his record, a request for an explanation was justified. (Mead Corp., 51 LA 1121)

NOTIFICATION OF ABSENCE

Company rules usually require both notice to the employer when the employee is going to be absent and a justifiable excuse for such an absence. Notice alone, without a good excuse, doesn't fulfill the employee's obligation. On the other hand, a good excuse for the absence doesn't necessarily justify an absence without notice.

Lack of Notice

If employees are expected to give notice of their absences, a failure to attempt to meet this requirement normally will justify discipline, regardless of the merits of the reason for the absence.

EXAMPLE: An employee was allowed one day's leave to aid her sister who had been involved in an accident in a distant city. She remained with her sister for a week, however, in order to care for the sister's children. Although the situation justified the employee's absence, she still was required to notify the company, an arbiter ruled in upholding discipline. (National Rose Co., 43 LA 1066)

Defective Notice

If an employee makes a good-faith effort to comply with the notice requirement, but is unable to do so, he is more likely to be treated leniently. But a sincere effort at compliance should be demanded.

EXAMPLE: An employee was taken ill shortly before the time he was to leave for work. Having no telephone, he asked a fellow employee to transmit the message to management. The message never arrived.

An arbitrator credited the employee with an honest effort to meet the notice requirement. The employee's obligation is met, the arbitrator said, when "he employs a means of reporting that is, under all circumstances, reasonable and calulated, in all probability, to result in actual receipt of the notice." (Goodyear Clearwater Mills, 11 LA 419)

EXAMPLE: An employee who wanted to overstay his vacation mailed a letter to this effect to the employer at the end of his originally scheduled vacation period. The company's rule specified that absence without notice "for three consecutive working days" meant termination. The employee's letter was mailed within the three day period, but the employer didn't receive it until later.

The employee didn't meet the notice requirement, an arbitrator held. The employer must actually receive notice within the three-day period. (Lear Sieglar, Inc., 48 LA 276)

OTHER ABSENTEEISM PROBLEMS

Special absenteeism problems, apart from the issues of excuse and notice, are discussed below.

Overstaying Leaves, Vacations

Vacations, layoffs, and leaves of absence often give rise to absenteeism problems when employees report back late. Arbitrators tend to judge these situations as they would any other other absenteeism case, with particular attention to the reason for the absence and the consistency of the company's enforcement of rules against leave-stretching.

EXAMPLE: An employee did not return to work until one week after the end of her scheduled two-week vacation. She claimed that she couldn't get transportation back from the distant place where she spent her vacation unless she waited for her husband to finish his three-week vacation.

Discharge of the employee for violating the company's rules was upheld by an arbitrator. He was of the opinion that she probably had deliberately chosen not to return to work on time. In any event, she had demonstrated an irresponsible attitude toward her job. (Packaging Corp. of America, 42 LA 606)

EXAMPLE: In another case where an employee overstayed her vacation by a week, an arbitrator found that her excuse was good enough to warrant reducing her discharge to a suspension without pay. Her reason for her absence was an attempt to save her marriage, which the arbitrator felt weighed against the employer's need for her presence. (Vellumoid Co., 41 LA 1129)

Past Leniency

The fact that management has been lenient with an employee in the past doesn't necessary bar it from resorting to discharge if he persists in his misconduct. A decision to give an employee a break in hopes that he will straighten out will not later be held against management by an arbitrator. But where management, over an extended period of time, gives only lip service to a rule of conduct, arbiters will insist that discharge be preceded by effective notice that the rule will be enforced.

EXAMPLE: In an effort to get a delinquent employee to mend his ways, management sent him a total of five "final" warnings over a three-year period. It finally decided to terminate him.

Overruling the discharge, an arbitrator noted that the "final" warnings all read exactly alike. Thus it wasn't surprising that the employee didn't think anyone actually was concerned about his absences. If somewhere along the the line management had let the employee know that it meant business, either by specific warning or disciplinary suspension, then discharge for subsequent absences probably would have been upheld. Instead, management had completely nullified the effectiveness of its warnings by repeatedly threatening discharge and then taking no disciplinary action. (Limestone Greer Co., 40 LA 343)

Absence on Usual Day Off

When management schedules work on a Saturday, holiday, or other day that normally is not a working day, it usually runs into a higher degree of absenteeism than usual. Arbiters are agreed, however, that, as a general principle, the right to schedule work belongs to management, except to the extent that this right has been specifically limited by contract.

Even where a contract gives employees the right to decline to work on a Saturday or holiday, arbitrators usually have held that once an employee accepts an assignment to work on such an overtime day, his duty to the company is the same as it would be on a regular work day. (11 LA 947, 12 LA 770, 29 LA 672)

Insubordination

The offense of absenteeism often is compounded by insubordination where employees after being denied permission to take time off, take the time anyway. Arbitrators usually find just cause for discipline in such cases. (43 LA 1070, 24 LA 593)

TARDINESS

While not as serious an offense as an absence without excuse or notice, tardiness is properly a subject for discipline. Since the reported cases commonly involve discipline of employees for a combination of absenteeism and tardiness, it would appear that the employee who is guilty of one is likely also to be guilty of the other. As with absenteeism, a program of progressive discipline (e.g., counseling, warning, suspension) generally is viewed as the proper way to encourage a delinquent employee to mend his ways. But, also as with absenteeism, excessive and consistent tardiness can reach the point of rendering an employee no longer suitable for employment.

When Does Tardiness Begin?

Can employees be counted tardy if they are not at their work stations at the time the contract says the workday starts, even though they clock in on time?

EXAMPLE: Under a contract that failed to specify whether the workday began at the time clock or at the work station, an arbiter held, management had no right to fire a worker for tardiness because he didn't clock in before the beginning of his shift.

According to the contract, the "standard day shift" ran from 7:30 a.m. to 4:00 p.m. The Company construed this to mean that workers had to be at their work stations by 7:30, and it issued a notice stating that they'd be considered late if they failed to clock in before then. A worker who persisted in clocking in exactly at 7:30 was given a written warning. He appealed the matter to a union-management committee but was turned down. Eventually he was discharged on three counts, one of which was tardiness.

The arbitrator, noting that the company bore the burden of proof, decided that the charge of tardiness wouldn't stand up. Nothing in the contract, he pointed out, established whether the parties intended the workday to begin at the time clock or at the work station: therefore there was no basis for the company rule. For either the grievance committee or the arbitrator to "interpret" the contract on this issue would actually be an amendment to the contract, and therefore improper, the umpire concluded. (Pacific Air-Motive Corp., 28 LA 761)

Tightening Rules on Tardiness

If it becomes necessary for a company to adopt stricter rules on tardiness, are there any limitations on the penalties it can impose? One arbitrator has taken the position that a new set of rules on tardiness must be judged not only on their merits but also by how they compare with past practice. Applying this reasoning, he refused to approve a rule that departed radically from past practice.

EXAMPLE: After trying a number of approaches to the problem of tardiness, a company finally laid down a rule stating that an employee would be discharged if he was tardy 12 times in a 12-month period.

An umpire held that this rule was arbitrary and unreasonable. Looking at past practice, he found that none of the rules promulgated by the company in the past eight years had provided for discharge without prior warning. Moreover, the penalty of discharge had never been invoked on the basis of as few as 12 instances of tardiness in a 12-month period. It sometimes may be okay to define "chronic tardiness" in terms of a fixed number of instances of tardiness, the arbiter said, but in his view it was unreasonable to do so where the number of instances of tardiness was reduced from the number allowed in the past, where notices were not issued to the employee, and the rules made no provision for a graduated system of penalties. (The Maccabees, 27 LA 99)

Similarly: Another umpire ruled that a company had no right, after signing its first contract, to start docking workers for tardiness. Nobody had ever been docked for tardiness before the contract was signed. Further, the company had agreed that no clause in the contract would be interpreted to "imply a lowering of the working conditions heretofore existing."

The arbiter found the contract language of special significance, since it was a first contract, and said it granted the workers all rights, privileges, and benefits they previously enjoyed plus the new ones in the agreement. He concluded that to start docking for tardiness after the contract became effective was a lowering of previously existing conditions. (Hellenic Lines, Lte., 39 LA 31)

But a reasonable rule on discipline for tardiness was upheld by another arbiter as not conflicting with employee rights under a union contract. (U.S. Steel Corp., 44 LA 829)

IN BRIEF ────────────────────────────────────

Arbitrators rarely upset discipline for refusal to carry out orders given by a properly designated representative of management. To protect his job, a worker should obey an order he questions and then file a grievance. The principal exception to this rule is that a worker need not carry out an order that would require him to endanger health or safety—his own or that of other workers.

POINTERS—

▶ A supervisor's instructions must be very clear; they must be understood by the employee to be an order; the supervisor must clearly state the penalty for failure to comply. Failure to respond to a supervisor's inquiries as to whether the employee would like to do a certain task is not insubordination.

▶ Merely protesting an order is not insubordination and normally would not be cause for discipline if not carried too far. Also, *failure* to carry out an order is usually a less serious offense than *refusal* to carry out one.

▶ Refusal to perform overtime is in a special category. Arbiters generally hold that, if the contract is silent on the point, a company may require workers to put in overtime work. But they say that the company's demands must be reasonable and that workers' reasons for not wanting to work must be considered.

▶ The use of objectionable language to supervision often is cause for discipline. But where salty language is commonplace in the plant, it may not be ground for discharge.

▶ Union representatives acting in their official capacity normally are not subject to discipline for insubordination.

──────────────────── **GUIDELINES** ────────────────────

THE RULES IN GENERAL

Before they will sustain a discharge for insubordination, arbitrators generally require that two tests be met:

▶ Very clear instructions were given by a supervisor to the employee.
▶ Even more explicit warning was given of the consequences to the employee if he failed to comply. (31 LA 575, 38 LA 218, 52 LA 217)

Degrees of insubordination also are recognized. One arbitrator observed: "A man may quietly say that he does not think that he should follow instructions . . .; he may become 'wordly abusive'; or he may engage in open conflict with his supervisor. Each action may, it is true, be generally classified as insubordination; but there is none the less a difference." (31 LA 575)

The definition of dischargeable insubordination also may vary according to the type of employee involved. For example, a professional employee expects to exercise a larger degree of independence and discretion than the assembly-line worker and may assert his rights in this regard in a manner that might be considered insubordinate if exercised by another.

Two Forms of Insubordination

Insubordination cases commonly appear in one of two forms. One type is the willful refusal or failure to carry out a direct order, instruction or company rule. The other is a personal altercation between employee and supervisor, often involving shouting matches, profane or abusive words, and actual or threatened violence.

Discharges have been sustained for abusing a supervisor in foul or threatening language where there have been prior incidents or insubordination (43 LA 864) or where the employee had been warned previously that repetitions of such behavior would result in discharge (44 LA 193, 45 LA 361). On the other hand, where the asserted insubordination did not involve refusal of orders nor affirmative abuse or aggressive defiance but only in excessive argumentation or minor name-calling, lesser penalties have been held appropriate. Thus, a five-day layoff was sustained for belligerently calling a foreman a "goddamned liar" in the presence of other employees (44 LA 254).

And disciplinary discharges have been reduced by arbitrators to reinstatement without back pay when an employee lost his temper in a dispute over a reprimand (44 LA 289 and cases cited therein) or when an employee loudly resisted a supervisor's authority to tell him to stop whistling after several prior requests (41 LA 1176) or when an employee used profane language during a dispute with a maintenance foreman over maintenance work that the employee mistakenly thought was being done without a work order and without proper regard for safety procedures (52 LA 61) or when an employee refused to work overtime and made an obscene gesture to his supervisor (47 LA 175). See also 53 LA 274.

Insubordination by Professional

Since professionals normally operate under only general guidelines or instructions, it may be difficult to prove a claim of dischargeable insubordination in the absence of a clear violation of a specific order.

EXAMPLE: A company that operated a hospital located about five miles out of town and a downtown clinic hired a laboratory technician to work at the downtown clinic. It subsequently had no complaints about her ability or qualifications, which it conceded were "outstanding." But it charged her with repeated violations of laboratory rules and policies. The chief complaint was that she persisted in turning patients away from the clinic and also insisted upon appointments for glucose tests long after the policy of requiring appointments had been abandoned. She finally was discharged for insubordination.

Overturning the discharge, an arbitrator noted that the employee, as the sole laboratory technician at the clinic with her supervisor located some five miles away, had to exercise more independent judgment than might otherwise be required. The physical separation made effective communication difficult and no doubt contributed to a number of misunderstandings.

The arbitrator also concluded that the employee, not being the bashful type, had challenged her supervisor about his policy changes, particularly those which she felt reflected upon her professional competence, and that he, in an effort to maintain harmony, had assured her somewhat ambiguously, that she could continue to use her discretion. (Permanente Medical Group, 52 LA 217)

Refusal to Take Tests

Arbitrators generally agree that a refusal to take a lie-detector test does not amount to insubordination. Their reasoning is often based on the fact that results of such tests generally are not admissible as evidence in courts. (Continental Air Transport Co., 38 La 778; Town & Country Food Co., 39 LA 332)

One umpire ruled that a company's demand that a worker take a lie-detector test was an invasion of the right of privacy and the constitutional right against self-incrimination, even though the worker had signed employment forms agreeing to take such tests. The employment form wasn't agreed to by the union, he found, and as an individual contract couldn't stand up, or else management would be able to impose all manner of work-ing conditions and thus circumvent the union contract. (Lag Drug Co., 39 LA 1121)

However: Refusal to take tests other than lie-detector tests may be considered insubordination. One arbiter held that it was okay to discipline a worker who refused an order to complete an aptitude test, even though he had volunteered to take the test in the first place. If the worker thought he was being treated unfairly, the umpire said, he could have filed a grievance after taking the tests. (St. Regis Paper Co., 40 LA 562)

Refusal To Sign Patent Agreement

A worker should have signed an agreement to turn inventions over to the company, and then have used the regular grievance channels for his protest. The agreement was required of workers in all key classifications. After a five-day suspension for refusing to sign, the worker signed adding that it was being done under protest. This was unacceptable to the company and he was fired. He was subject to discipline for failing to sign without reservation, but discharge was not warranted since the requirement was being challenged by other workers at the time. (Ekco Containers Inc. and Machinists, 43 LA 46)

REFUSAL TO OBEY ORDER

One of the most firmly established principles in labor relations is that an employee must obey supervision even when he disagrees with an order. Generally speaking, an order may be challenged only through the grievance procedure, which was set up to eliminate unseemly disputes at the time an order is given. The general rule often is stated as: "Obey now. Grieve later."

The reason for this rule was stated as follows by the late Harry Shulman: "An industrial plant is not a debating society. Its object is production. When a controversy arises, production cannot wait." (3 LA 781)

Despite the wide acceptance of this rule, it is recognized that in some situations, an overriding right or interest of the employee may require an exception to the general rule. The most frequently recognized exception is where obeying the rule might endanger the employee's health or safety.

Supervisors should make every possible effort to determine an employee's real motive for refusing to comply with an order, especially if the employee expresses fear for his own or someone else's safety.

Insubordination by Service Workers

Although the pressure of dealing with the public may increase the potential for friction, it doesn't warrant abandoning the general rule of "obey now, grieve later," an arbitrator has made clear. He rejected a contention that in the personal service industry the mere declaration by an employee that he is busy or "stuck" exculpates him from complying with the instructions of his supervisors. In this industry, as in others, the arbiter said, the supervisor, not the employee, must be the judge of when and what tasks are to be performed.

It would be destructive of proper employer-employee relations, he said, if the employee were the final judge of what instructions he should follow or honor. (National Lawyers Club, Inc., 52 LA 547)

Hazardous Working Conditions

The leading exception to the "obey now, grieve later" rule arises when an employee has reasonable cause to believe that the work is unusually hazardous, substantially injurious to health, or abnormally dangerous. In such cases, arbitrators hold, the employee may disregard the grievance procedure and refuse to perform the work. The danger must be unusual and not just a normal part of the job for which the employee is being paid, however. (41 LA 888, 44 LA 148, 46 LA 607, 48 LA 788)

But what if the danger exists only in the minds of the employee when in fact the job was safe? Most arbitrators hold that it makes no difference that the employee's fears were groundless. The important thing is that the fears were real to him and that what he feared would have been an unusual danger. The evaluation of the situation necessarily must be a subjective one.

Regardless of whether it turns out later that there was or was not an actual hazard, the employee may not be disciplined if he was "sincere in his belief of danger and so long as he makes a 'reasonable' appraisal of the potential hazards." (41 LA 666)

EXAMPLE: An outside electrician was summoned back to the plant to open two high-voltage switches outside the plant. He was told that an inside electrician would act as his stand-by while he threw the two outside switches. He insisted on an outside electrician, however, and, when given an ultimatum to go ahead with the job, he walked off the job.

In defending its decision to discharge the employee for insubordination, the company argued that an employee who relies on safety factors to justify a refusal to obey orders must demonstrate that a danger actually exists. The arbitrator held, however, that the refusal may be justified by a good-faith fear for personal safety—whether the danger actually exists or not. Finding that the employee's fear was "real" enough, the umpire ordered his reinstatement. (Hercules, Inc., 48 LA 788)

Even if an employee isn't in danger himself, he may be justified in refusing to perform a work assignment out of consideration for the safety of others, it has been held. Thus, an arbiter found a company in error when it disciplined a worker for refusing to work with another worker who performed his job in such a way as to endanger the safety of others. (Midland Structural Steel Corp., 30 LA 38)

Uncomfortable Conditions

Where working conditions are uncomfortable, as distinguished from hazardous (see above), it is generally agreed that the proper method of securing relief is to (1) file a grievance, or (2) request permission to leave. An employee who walks out to protest the heat or the lack thereof normally is subject to discipline, although arbitrators may reduce discharge penalties if they find mitigating circumstances.

EXAMPLE: Seven employees who were working an overtime day told their foreman they were going home on a day when the temperature in the plant approached 100 degrees. Their foreman told them they were making a mistake, but they left nevertheless.

An arbitrator reduced the discharges imposed by management to two-week disciplinary layoffs. He agreed with the company that the employees had violated the well recognized standard of conduct in industry that an employee does not leave his work during a shift—either regular or overtime—without permission. But mitigating circumstances were found here, particularly in the foreman's vague response, which was at best only a half warning. He probably could have forestalled the walkout if he had told the employees that they had a duty to remain and that they would be disciplined if they left without permission, the arbitrator observed. (Phelps Dodge Aluminum Products Corp., 52 LA 375)

EXAMPLE: A woman who claimed extreme nervousness moved her work area farther away from the noisy area of the plant despite her foreman's order to remain until she substantiated her complaint with a doctor's slip. Upholding her discharge, the arbiter found that the woman repeatedly disobeyed orders to stay at her regular work station, ignored a warning of discharge, and "acted with full knowledge of the consequences." (Scripto, Inc., 48 LA 980)

However: A distinction may be made between working conditions that are merely uncomfortable and conditions that are so bad as to make it unreasonable for management to require employees to continue working. The latter type situation was found by an arbiter in a steel fabricating plant where the heat was turned off for renovation during the winter and the thermometer dipped to 20 degrees. Disciplinary suspensions of workers who walked out were set aside by the arbiter. (Berger Steel Co. 46 LA 1131)

Failure To Obey Unreasonable Order

The reasonableness of an order may be taken into account in determining the penalty to be imposed for insubordination. Under the "obey now, grieve later" principle, an employee is supposed to obey a nonhazardous order, even if it is unreasonable. But a discharge penalty for insubordination may be modified if it is found that the rule is not reasonable.

EXAMPLE: A 60-year-old employee was discharged for violating a plant rule which prohibited employees sitting down during their tour of duty. In reducing the discharge to a one-month suspension, the arbitrator said:

"We recognize managements rights to impose plant rules unilaterally. However, to sustain actions taken thereunder, such rules must be within the bounds of reason, considering all the circumstances surrounding their application. The no-sit-down rule in a cement plant where operations are at least semi-automatic and therefore to an extent monotonous, temperatures at least at some spots above normal and floors hard, would seem to go beyond the bounds of reason." (Ideal Cement Co., 13 LA 943)

Refusal To Work Overtime

In the absence of contract language specifically permitting or forbidding management to compel overtime work, arbitrators generally hold that overtime work may be required. But before discipline is imposed for a refusal to work overtime, certain conditions usually must be met:

● The overtime must be reasonable in amount.

● Adequate notice must be given except in emergencies.

● Overtime must be distributed equitably on a departmental basis.

● It must be assigned first to qualified workers who are willing to work extra hours.

● Only if there are not enough willing workers may unwilling employees be required to work overtime. (41 LA 834)

One arbitrator held that employees' refusal to work on Christmas and New Year's Eves was not punishable as insubordination in view of the "peculiar and sacred" place those holidays occupy in the culture and in view of the irretrievable loss that would result if the employees followed the "work now, grieve later" rule. (31 LA 567)

Moonlighters—An employee who holds a second job cannot use this as an excuse for refusing to work overtime. (41 LA 1250) But in a case where management had followed a policy of trying to accommodate overtime assignments to employee wishes, a discharge penalty was reduced, particularly since substitute workers were available to handle the moonlighter's overtime assignment and other employees with the same assignment had been excused. (52 LA 1290)

Violation of Safety Rule

Although employees are the main beneficiaries of safety precautions undertaken by management, the introduction of safety equipment, such as hard hats or safety glasses, frequently is met with stubborn resistance from employees. Even the most forceful selling job may fail to convince all employees of the efficacy of safety rules or equipment.

Arbiters generally have upheld management's right to introduce safety measures and to use the disciplinary stick on recalcitrant employees. Some accommodation may be made, however, for employee misconceptions about the safety rules.

EXAMPLE: An old-time miner objected to a new rule requiring the wearing of safety glasses, complaining that the glasses, in his view, were more hazardous than helpful. After being given several warnings, he was told to wear glasses or else, and he chose the latter.

An arbitrator conceded that management had authority to discharge, after suitable warning, for refusal to comply with the safety-glasses regulation. But because the employee's record was good and his fears apparently were genuine, the arbitrator was moved to permit him to return, but without back pay and provided he pledged to cooperate in the future. (Bunker Hill Co., 43 LA 1253)

ASSAULTS ON SUPERVISORS

An assault upon a supervisor is considered a very serious offense that usually is just cause for discharge, particularly where it would have the effect of undermining employees' respect for management's authority if it went unpunished.

To be considered insubordination, the assault need not occur on company property or during working hours if it is work related and has its roots in the employer-employee relationship. But it would not be considered insubordination if the assault occurs off company property and outside of working hours *and* results from a purely personal matter. A distinction is drawn between the civil law which governs the normal relations between men and the private law of industrial relations which governs job-related relationships.

Job-Related Assault

An assault on a supervisor is considered a sufficiently serious offense as to warrant the discharge of even a long-service employee.

EXAMPLE: A truck driver with 15 years' seniority had a routine safety interview with his supervisor one morning. That evening, he went to the supervisor's home to complain angrily about some comments that had been made during the interview. Without provocation, he struck the supervisor on the head with a blunt instrument.

Upholding the employee's discharge, an arbitrator held that management had the right to take disciplinary action, since the incident was directly related to events in the plant. Although public authority also is available to deal with those who willfully commit assault and battery, this doesn't deprive management of its right to maintain discipline and protect members of supervision from retaliatory action by dissatisfied employees, whether in the plant or away. (U.S. Steel Corp., 35 LA 227)

Mitigating Circumstances

If the company helps create a situation in which personality conflicts are more likely to flare up, it may have to bear some of the responsibility for any resultant outburst. This may lead to a reduced disciplinary sentence for an employee involved in the outburst.

EXAMPLE: A man who had worked for the company 33 years without a prior incident of insubordination got drunk at the company Christmas party and threw the contents of a can of beer in the face of the industrial relations manager while cutting loose with a stream of profanity. As a result, he was given a 30-day suspension.

An arbitrator overturned the penalty and ordered back pay. The offense was not committed during working hours or under conditions of plant discipline, the arbitrator said, and the employee's conduct appeared to be the result of consuming too much alcohol rather that to be connected with the employment relationship. Despite prior incidents of drunken fights at the Christmas party, the company continued to furnish free and unlimited liquor and therefore ran the risk of "predictable consequences." (Hopper Paper Co., 30 LA 763)

Non-Insubordinate Assault

Not every assault upon a supervisor wil be regarded as an act of insubordination.

EXAMPLE: An arbitrator reinstated an employee who was fired after a shoving match with a supervisor. The umpire noted:

● The employee had not failed to obey any order from the foreman.

● The employee didn't know the foreman and was unaware of his supervisory status.

● The employee had an unblemished work record.

● The altercation wasn't a "true fight"; one reason it looked like a fight was that the noise level in the shop forced the men to shout in close proximity to one another. (Libby-Owens Ford Glass Co., 44 LA 493)

Provocation by Supervisor

In defense of a worker's assault on a supervisor, it often is claimed that he was provoked by the improper conduct of the supervisor. Provocation by the supervisor may be considered a mitigating factor but it rarely is held to justify letting the employee go scot free; only extreme provocation would excuse an assault on a management representative.

Sometimes unions claim that management acts unfairly when it disciplines an employee for the assault but takes no action against the supervisor who "provoked" the assault. Arbiters hold, however, that a union has no right to question an employer's relations with his supervisors. The supervisor is not subject to the bargaining agreement, they note, and an arbitrator has no authority to require that he be penalized.

Some arbiters, however, have said that while the decision to impose discipline or not is the employer's, the union may challenge in arbitration, conduct or remarks that undermine the good relations of the parties.

EXAMPLE: In an argument with an employee, a supervisor used the term "Greenhorn," which was generally understood in the plant and community as a derogatory term, reflecting on an individual's foreign background and suggesting one who is considered "stupid, unknowing, and inexperienced." At this point, the employee slugged the foreman on the back of the ear.

In upholding the discharge, the arbitrator noted that regardless of a provocation, the use of physical violence against another person (except perhaps in the case of self-defense) is universally condemned.

While recognizing that he lacked authority to order discipline of the foreman, the arbitrator noted nevertheless that management had the responsibility to do eveything within its power to put an end to the use of racial epithets and other "trigger'" words in places of employment. While

physical violence is reprehensible, the umpire commented, the spoken word can be equally or more devastating. (Pioneer Finishing Co., 52 LA 1019)

ABUSIVE LANGUAGE

Generally arbitrators do not require companies to put up with verbal abuse of their foremen by employees. Use of profane and obscene language by an employee does not necessarily subjct him to drastic discipline, but if such language is used to embarrass, ridicule, or degrade a supervisor, it would be considered an insubordinate act, especially if other employees were present to hear it.

One arbitrator has identified four situations in which abusive name-calling is cause for discipline. They are:

● The employee, instead of executing an order, argues about it and calls the supervisor a name.

● The employee calls his supervisor a name in front of other employees.

● The employee calls his supervisor a name privately but afterward brags to other employees about how he told off the boss.

● The employee calls his supervisor a name privately, is warned by the supervisor, but continues to indulge in name-calling. (35 LA 887)

In some name-calling cases, arbitrators have reduced discharge penalties in view of mitigating factors such as the employee's good work record, common use of profanity in the shop, or reciprocal use of profanity by the supervisor. (25 LA 439, 27 LA 611, 39 LA 58, 661, 849)

But when profanity, obscene, or abusive language is coupled with a refusal to obey an order or other insubordinate act of the employee, arbitrators uphold a discharge or other severe penalty. (26 LA 713)

'Shop Talk'

One defense that may be offered to the use of obscenities or other abusive language in discussions with management is that such language is in common usage in the shop. Arbiters generally accept as valid the contention that words must be judged in their natural setting, although they do not necessarily accept the unions' tolerant views in particular cases.

EXAMPLE: Two employees joined in a discussion between a union steward and a foreman concerning the discharge of another employee. One of the employees, in criticizing the foreman of the discharged, used profanity and in very obscene terms suggested the foreman perform an act of in-

dignity upon himself. The foreman told him he would be given a warning for such language and started to walk away. The employee called after him and repeated the remark with emphasis. Ten to 20 employees were in the vicinity at the time.

In upholding the employee's discharge. an arbitrator conceded that the term used was in common usage in the plant. But, he said, the way in which it was used is the important consideration. Use of the term in ordinary banter may be tolerated, but it is vastly different when such an expression is used in anger and with the intent to degrade and insult the recipient.

The company must maintain the respect of both employees and supervisors, the umpire said; it cannot condone repeated insubordination, such as this, without losing this respect. To permit one employee to be disrespectfully insubordiate, could undermine the morale of the entire work force. (44 LA 864)

Calling Supervisor a 'Liar'

Calling a supervisor a "liar" usually is regarded as a major offense that may warrant the discharge penalty.

A discharge for this offense was upheld even where the employee had an "erroneous impression" which led him to think the supervisor had told an untruth. (3 LA 141)

One employee managed to maintain his job after calling his foreman a "damn liar" only because he had a good past record and because there were no other employees within hearing at the time. Furthermore, there was some evidence that the foreman had first used abusive language. (25 LA 439)

DISRESPECTFUL ATTITUDE

Few things are likely to annoy a supervisor more than the employee who always replies with a flip or sour remark when told to do something. However, it often is difficult to draw a line between defiance or disrespect of the type that undermines discipline and harmless, so-called healthy griping. And it is not at all rare for a supervisor to put up with questionable remarks and then finally to blow his stack.

Perhaps the best approach to handling an employee who repeatedly flirts with insubordination is to pick a period relatively free from stress and warn him calmly but firmly to mend his ways. This should be done in private so as to minimize the risk of inflaming the situation. If a supervisor appears to needle an employee or allows himself to get into a verbal slugging match, an outsider very likely will conclude that both sides were at fault.

Back Talk

Even if a certain amount of grumbling and back talk is tolerated over a period of time, this doesn't preclude management from deciding that an employee finally has gone too far. It may be necessary, however, to warn the employee that management's patience has run out before serious disciplinary action is taken.

EXAMPLE: An employee who had been with the company about 20 years talked virtually all the time, including times when nobody was around. He always insisted on having the last word and almost invariably would go off muttering disapproval when given an order. Twice on one day, his foreman's orders drew "I-know-my-job" retorts. This led to an exchange that culminated in discharge.

An arbitrator reduced the discharge to a 3½-month suspension. The um-

pire conceded that the employee, along with his extremely active tongue, apparently had a persecution complex, and his own special brand of a n y t h i n g-you-can-do-I-can-do-better. But all of this was nothing new to his fellow employees or supervisors. While he had engaged in misconduct on the day of his discharge, his conduct on innumerable occasions in the past might similarly be characterized as objectionable. A slight variation in his 20-year theme shouldn't precipitate anything so drastic as discharge, the umpire said. (Armour Agricultural Chemical Co., 40 LA 289)

Disparaging Management

It is not unheard of for an employee in conversations with his co-workers to make disparaging or disrepectful remarks about a supervisor or about management or the company in general. Normally, such remarks, even if overheard by a supervisor, are not considered grounds for disciplinary action.

EXAMPLE: After a company instituted a crackdown on previously tolerated practices, two employees were overheard making derogatory remarks about the company president. They were discharged for this and for failing to observe the newly instituted rules. On being terminated, one of the employees used profanity in directly addressing the president. Finding little to support the claim

of rules violations, the arbitrator also found the case based on the derogatory remarks to be extremely weak. It wasn't shown that such remarks were uncommon, that the statements were malicious in character, or that they affected morale and productivity.

The only incident where the employer actually was confronted with disrespectful conduct was after he had fired these employees. As this occurred subsequent to the discharge, it could not properly be used as grounds to sustain the discharge. (Top World, 51 LA 1285)

UNION ACTIVITY

In cases involving alleged insubordination by union stewards or an alleged breach of other plant rules, arbitrators generally look to see whether the offense charged was committed when the official was acting in his official capacity or merely as an employee. If the steward was insubordinate as an employee, then the penalty properly is the same as for any rank-and-file employee under similar circumstances.

But where the steward is "on business," the usual requirement of "obey now, grieve later," doesn't apply if the order given is in conflict with the union's rights. This principle has been extended to cases where union officials refused to obey orders in the good faith, but mistaken, belief that the orders violated the contract.

No consensus exists, however, on whether management has a right to discipline a union official where he doesn't act in good faith but rather in knowing disregard of the contract and management's rights. One school holds that union officials have a blanket immunity from discipline by the employer for their official actions, regardless of good or bad faith, and that management's recourse is through the grievance procedure. The contrary view holds that evidence of bad faith destroys the shield usually accorded union officials.

Grievance Investigation

If a steward, pursuant to the contract, seeks permission to leave his job to investigate a grievance, management cannot withhold permission unreasonably. It is not the supervisor's prerogative to decide whether or not the matter in dispute is a legitimate grievance and therefore subject to investigation.

EXAMPLE: A union steward asked his foreman for a pass to investigate the discharge of a probationary em-

ployee. His foreman refused and referred him to the general foreman. The general foreman argued that the discharge of a probationary employee wasn't a grievable issue and told the steward to go back to his job or risk discharge. The steward refused and was discharged.

An arbitrator set the discharge aside. "There is a clear distinction," the umpire said, "between the case of a supervisor telling an employee to go back to his job, and a supervisor telling the union to stop investigating a grievance." When the duly authorized representative of the company told the duly authorized representative of the union to stop investigating a grievance, the company was issuing orders to the union, and it was the steward's duty, as a representative of the union, to insist upon the union's rights. If the steward had been rough, rowdy, belligerent, or insolent in his attitude, some disciplinary action might have been warranted, but that wasn't the case here. (International Harvester Co., 16 LA 307)

Debates with Supervisors

Although a steward has the right to process a grievance energetically and may dispute a supervisor's decision, he may be subject to discipline if he becomes abusive to the supervisor who made the decision.

EXAMPLE: In an argument over a grievance, a foreman and steward exchanged angry words. The foreman then warned the steward that if he continued his display of bad temper "he had better punch his time card and leave." The company subsequently issued the steward a letter of warning because of his conduct toward the foreman.

In upholding the disciplinary action, the arbitrator said: "A steward cannot be disciplined for actively pursuing grievances or presenting his arguments in a positive manner. A distinction must be drawn, however, between presenting arguments in a positive manner and being argumentative. There is a difference between attacking the logic of a decision and attacking the man who made the decision. Moreover, we cannot ignore tone of voice or attitudes. These may be just as important as the words used." (Westinghouse Electric Corp., 38 LA 1226)

MISCONDUCT

INTRODUCTION

The term "misconduct" covers a wide variety of offenses, including destruction of company property, dishonesty, fighting, loafing and sleeping on the job, smoking, intoxication, gambling, subversive activity, leaving the job without permission, and misconduct outside the plant. According to one study, more workers are fired for misconduct of one sort or another than for any other reason.

POINTERS—

▶ Theft and other kinds of dishonesty usually are regarded as cause for discharge. But arbitrators require convincing proof of the worker's guilt, since the impact of a discharge for dishonesty is so great.

▶ Fighting on company property also is a dischargeable offense, except where a worker does no more than is necessary to defend himself.

▶ When it comes to such offenses as being drunk or sleeping on the job, the amount of evidence against the worker is especially important. Umpires agree that a company can't fire a man on the basis of a supervisor's suspicions.

▶ Misconduct occurring away from the plant outside working hours is none of the company's business, arbiters agree, unless it affects the employment relationship in some way.

Particular forms of misconduct and the general principles laid down for management in dealing with them are discussed in the following chapters.

Damaging Company Property

Defacing or damaging property is usually regarded as a serious charge, and most arbiters don't think the value of the property has much bearing on the penalty to be fixed.

If the act is deliberate and there are no extenuating circumstances, they will uphold the discharge penalty. (3 LA 346)

But where the evidence failed to show that there had been wilful or deliberate destruction of company property, an arbiter overturned a discharge even though the damage was costly. (3 LA 403)

The cases of malicious and deliberate acts of vandalism are relatively rare, and management need only to prove malicious intent to justify discharge. Much more common, however, are cases in which company material or machines are damaged through "gross carelessness." (These cases are in the chapter on "carelessness."

GUIDELINES

Malicious Intent

Deliberate damage to company property almost invariably is held to warrant discharge.

EXAMPLE: An employee assigned to placing slats of wood on a conveyor belt was doing the work badly and a company official proceeded to show her how it should be done. Afterwards, however, the employee made a mockery of the job, working with excessive slowness. Finally she pushed some sticks into the machine and one of the chains broke.

In upholding her discharge, an arbitrator said he might have been willing to minimize this incident except for the fact that the employee had a history of unsatisfactory work and had been transferred to the conveyor line as an alternative to discharge

earlier. (Decorative Cabinet Corp., 17 LA 138)

Sabotage

Sabotage, like theft (see below), requires proof beyond a reasonable doubt that the employee willingly and knowingly engaged in the alleged act, rather than that the act resulted from carelessness or negligence.

EXAMPLE: A company had been plagued by frequent breakdowns of a conveyor, caused by foreign objects thrown into the works. Within a six-month period, there had been 43 such incidents. Employees were questioned about one of the breakdowns, which was caused by a small horseshoe-shaped object. One employee reluctantly admitted he had seen another take such an object from a storage bin and put in in his pocket. Although this employee denied committing the sabotage, management fired him.

An arbitrator upheld the discharge, while applying the test of "proof beyond a reasonable doubt." The credibility of the witnesses, the circumstantial evidence, and corroborating testimony indicated the guilt of the discharged employee. (Aladdin Industries, Inc., 27 LA 464)

Dishonesty

Discharge for dishonesty would seem to be an unquestioned right of management. Yet the discharge penalty is reduced or reversed in a high majority of the arbitration cases in this area.

The reason for this is that arbitrators demand a higher standard of proof in these cases and frequently are reluctant to stigmatize an employee as "discharged for theft," with the potential this has for causing a permanent loss of employment.

The evidence required to support a discharge for dishonesty frequently is stated as "proof beyond a reasonable doubt," while a lesser degree of proof, such as "preponderance of the evidence" is accepted in cases that don't involve overtones of moral turpitude. (25 LA 906, 28 LA 65, 48 LA 891)

Because of this reluctance to label an employee a "thief," both management and arbitrators have a tendency to seize upon some other violation of company rules as justification for disciplinary action when in truth the real reason is the suspected dishonesty. This often results in cases where the penalty seems excessive for the offense that assertedly is the basis for the discipline.

GUIDELINES

Falsification of Job Applications

Arbitrators generally agree that discipline is warranted where an employee is shown to have falsified work records or employment forms. However, there must have been more than an oversight or a lapse of memory; a deliberate act with intent to defraud usually must be shown.

Also the present consensus of arbitrators seems to be that after some reasonable period of time, falsification of an employment application should not operate as an automatic cause for discharge. A lengthy period of satisfactory employment should bar a subsequent discharge for falsification provided the facts falsified are not of such a nature as to endanger the present and future employment relationship. (29 LA 192, 21 LA 560, 17 LA 230)

However: Most arbitrators have declined to follow a flat one-year "statute of limitations," but instead prefer a case-by-case approach. (50 LA 161)

False statements on applications

for employment is a dischargeable offense even if the company's rules do not specify such conduct as cause for dismissal. (42 LA 323, 43 LA 233, 55 LA 581)

Misstatement as to the employee's medical history will justify discharge if the employe's physical condition, if known, would have disqualified him for the type of work for which he applied. (39 LA 142, 36 LA 889, 55 LA 581)

Failure to mention prior employers in his application may be cause for discharge, since such information is material for the assessment of the applicant's qualifications (12 LA 207, 34 LA 143, 55 LA 581)

Allowances for minor discrepancies sometimes are made on the theory that it's a natural tendency for a worker to put his best foot forward in applying for a job. Some exaggerations or "puffing" are permitted.

Another consideration used by some arbitrators is whether the employee would have been hired if he had disclosed the true information at the time. In other words, they require that the true facts, if known, would have been a bar to employment.

EXAMPLES: On his employment application, a worker replied "no" to the question "Have you ever had a back injury?" Four years later, in the course of treatment of an on-the-job injury, it was discovered that the employee had had back trouble off and on for 25 years.

A discharge for falsifying the employment application was upheld. While acknowledging that the employee may have answered the way he did because he didn't regard himself as disabled, the arbitrator noted that this meant substituting the employee's judgment for that of the company as to his qualifications for employment. While the company might also have concluded that the employee wasn't disabled so as to disqualify him for employment, it was entitled to have a full and accurate disclosure of all relevant health in-

formation in order to make a judgment. (Zia Co., 52 LA 89)

A worker was improperly discharged for "falsifying his application form" by not listing previous illegal arrests. But, the arbiter continued, even though both arrests were thrown out of court as illegal, the past cannot be erased, and the worker must share some of the blame for his discharge since he failed to make a frank disclosure on his job application. The arbiter directed reinstatement, but without back pay. (American Airlines, Inc., 47 LA 119)

In consideration of a worker's good record and trouble-free period of employment, another arbiter voided discharge for a two-year-old falsification of job application forms. The employee had falsified the reason for leaving a prior job, and had failed to list an arrest. The arbiter directed reinstatement—but without back pay and with the charges and disciplinary suspension to remain a part of his permanent record. (Ward Mfg. Co., 46 LA 233).

Falsifying Work Records

Falsifying records so as to claim credit for work not done is so serious an offense as clearly to justify discharge. It must appear, however, that the falsification was deliberately intended to cheat the company. Where there is room for doubt, discharge likely will be set aside. (38 LA 1157, 47 LA 966, 48 LA 891)

EXAMPLE: A long-service employee was assigned to an on-the-road job where he was required to keep his own time cards. The company heard that he had been out sick for two days in a week for which he put in a time card indicating that he had worked a full week. The employee maintained that his failure to report these days of illness had been an oversight resulting from the fact that he had marked the card in advance to indicate a full week.

An arbitrator reduced a discharge penalty to a long suspension. Other employees indicated that they followed the practice on the road of filling in their time sheets in advance, he noted. Other evidence also was found to support the employee's claim of inadvertent error. (Marion Power Shovel Co., 45 LA 580)

Stealing Company Property

No employee needs a rule to tell him that stealing company property is wrong and that he runs a great risk of losing his job if he is caught. This is true even of items of relatively little value. Companies simply don't want to retain employees who demonstrate they cannot be fully trusted, and management is aware that small thefts can produce great losses if sufficient numbers of people are involved.

Frequently, however, the claim will be made that the employee didn't think an item was of any value to the company or thought it had been thrown away or would be. For that reason, it often is wise to have a clearly stated policy concerning the disposition of scrap, the equipment that may be used or borrowed, and the "sampling" of company products by employees. Perhaps it will not be feasible to cover all possible contingencies, but an established procedure for clearing questionable items may save a lot of grief.

EXAMPLES: After receiving complaints from its subscribers about unwanted solicitations, a telephone company made an investigation and discovered that a maintenance man who collected scrap paper from waste paper baskets had been selling discarded subscriber lists to a person representing himself as a dealer in waste paper. The employee admitted selling the scrap paper, but he insisted he hadn't known this was wrong.

In upholding the discharge, an arbitrator refused to buy the employee's explanation. The amount the employee was being paid obviously was well in excess of the value of the paper as scrap. The secrecy with which the employee operated and the fact that he didn't report this extra income on his tax returns indicated that he knew better, the arbiter said. (New Jersey Bell Telephone Co., 40 LA 533)

However, other arbiters tend to modify discharge penalties where the value of the stolen goods is relatively small and the employee's seniority is relatively long. Thus, discharge was deemed too harsh for taking two cents worth of crackers (33 LA 40), theft of five beers by a long-service brewery worker (29 LA 262), stealing a pair of coveralls by a seven-year employee with a good record (24 LA 549), and pilfering building materials worth about $10 (44 LA 234).

In one case, however, an arbiter upheld discharge for theft of $1.10, even though the employee had been with the company 28 years and had a good record. The arbiter said he might have imposed a lighter sentence if the employee had admitted his mistake. Instead, he had tried to get off the hook by inconsistent, evasive, and implausible statements and sometimes outright falsehood. Such conduct doesn't call for leniency, the umpire said. (43 LA 1218)

Arrests for Thefts

What course of action should you take if an employee is arrested by the police and charged with theft of company property? You're on dangerous ground in relying solely on actions by the police or what happens in court as a basis for discipline. Discharge or even suspension of an employee simply because he has been arrested for a crime connected with his work may be overturned by an arbitrator and is almost sure to be set aside and back pay ordered if the charges are dropped or the employee is acquitted (35 LA 77, 39 LA 859, 39 LA 1242).

On the other hand, where the company has made an inquiry into the facts and has substantial evidence of guilt, discharge has been upheld, despite the fact that criminal charges were dropped. (31 LA 674, 44 LA 711) Moreover, where the company has evidence not used in the court, discharge has been allowed despite acquittal by a court. (32 LA 44, 38 LA 93)

Dress and Grooming

Standards as to what constitutes unacceptable or unsuitable attire are likely to change with the times. In the 1920's, for example, females were not permitted to work in many plants if they wore their hair bobbed. In the 1930's, some plants refused to allow women to work in slacks.

In the late 1950's, on the other hand, a company disciplined a female employee for persisting in wearing a dress after being told to wear jeans. The umpire upheld management's right to set standards for appropriate attire, but overruled the displine, since the posted rule requiring jeans had not been enforced consistently. (28 LA 83)

In the late 1960's, attention turned to male employees and their hirsute adornment—beards, mustaches, sideburns, and long hair. A proliferation of arbitration cases resulted from management's attempts to set standards in this area for its male employees, particularly those who deal with the public.

In dealing with discipline for violation of dress and grooming standards, arbitrators make these points:

▶ The standard must be clear, unambiguous, and consistently enforced.

▶ The standard must be reasonably related to a business need of the company, although it is recognized that "business need" includes the need to keep employees from being distracted by outlandish or overly revealing attire.

▶ The standard must be reasonably attuned to contemporary mores and attitudes toward dress and grooming. As styles change, the standard may have to change.

━━━━━━━━━━━━━━━ **GUIDELINES** ━━━━━━━━━━━━━━━

Proper Female Attire

When it comes to dress codes, management is in an awkward position, particularly at times when styles are changing radically.

> **ASPA BNA SURVEY** >

To learn the reactions of business toward the changes seen in the late 1960's, companies in an ASPA-BNA survey were asked what attitude they would be most likely to take toward employees who sported the new styles. For female employees, see-through blouses were most frowned on by companies. Half the companies said they would forbid them, 17 percent said they would object in extreme cases, and 29 percent indicated they might suggest moderation in individual cases. Large companies were slightly more tolerant than the smaller firms.

Long hair was the most accepted of the new styles, with only 5 percent of the companies absolutely forbidding it. Thirty-five percent of companies, however, indicated that while they had no set policy they might suggest moderation in individual talks. Several companies mentioned that for reasons of safety, hair nets are required on women with long hair who work in production areas.

Mini-skirts and culottes, if they are not extreme, were accepted by 39 percent of the companies. An additional 41 percent indicated that they had no set policy but might suggest moderation in individual talks with employees. Only 6 percent of the companies indicated no objection at all. A blanket policy of forbidding mini-skirts was more common in small companies (21 percent) than in larger ones (7 percent).

Companies seemed to be generally against the wearing of sandals without stockings. Twenty-eight percent absolutely forbid them, and an additional 35 percent indicated that while they had no set policy they might suggest moderation in individual talks.

Companies showed mixed reactions to Afro dress styles. Close to half reported no set policy but said they might suggest moderation through personal talks. One quarter of the companies said they would have no objection to the styles except in extreme cases, while only 8 percent replied that they would have no objections at all. ⟵

New style trends, an umpire said, will inevitably find their way into the work place unless the employer establishes clear, precise, understandable, and reasonable standards. (52 LA 781)

Where a company permitted women to wear shorts, an arbitrator held it was wrong for the company to send two women home for wearing short shorts. The company had been so permissive on the matter of shorts that it could object only if the shorts were indecent or unsafe, it was held. Short or long, the attractiveness (or distractiveness) of shorts depends on the woman who is wearing them, the arbitrator said. (45 LA 1071)

Proper Male Attire

In the late 1960's when beards, mustaches, sideburns, and long hair were becoming relatively common in a wide range of occupations, one arbitrator observed that "in the presence of these changing values, the maintenance of an image, essential to the prosperity of a company serving the public, poses many complications."

In a review of other cases dealing with "hair," the arbitrator noted that these points were made:

● An employee who'd worn a beard on the job for 10 years did not violate a company rule requiring merely that an employee be neat and clean in his appearance.

● The discharge of an airline employee for wearing long (mutton chop) sideburns was upheld since he violated the company's "clean-shaven" rule.

● The discharge of two airline employees who wore shoulder-length hair and beards was sustained as a violation of a company rule stating: "Radical departures from conventional dress or personal grooming will not be permitted."

In the case before him, the arbitrator held that the suspension of an employee wasn't warranted, since, in the umpire's view, his sideburns conformed to a rule requiring "conservative" haircuts. (52 LA 1068)

For executives struggling to arrive at grooming guidelines for employees —especially those who deal with the public—here's what one umpire decided would be appropriate standards:

● Sideburns shall not extend beyond the bottom of the ear.

● Sideburns shall be of uniform width throughout their length, shall be in a straight line perpendicular to the horizontal plane of the head, and be well-trimmed so as to avoid the appearance of being bushy.

● Hair styles should be of such type as to avoid having any part of the ear covered.

● Hair shall be kept neatly trimmed on the sides and in back and shall extend downward on the back of the head no further than a line one-half inch above the collar. (53 LA 126)

ASPA BNA SURVEY

An ASPA-BNA survey on management's reaction to the new clothing and hair styles when worn by their male employees showed the following results:

Mod styles in pants and shirts generally were frowned upon by the companies. Mod clothing was absolutely forbidden by 23 percent of the firms, while an additional 41 percent indicated no set policy but said they might suggest moderation through individual talks. Twenty percent of the companies indicated no objection except in extreme cases, while only 6 percent said they would have no objections at all.

Long hair was only slightly more acceptable. Eighteen percent of the companies indicated that while they had no set policy, they might suggest moderation in an individual talk with the employee. Thirty-nine percent of the companies replied that they would have no objection to long hair except when extreme, while only 2 percent said they would have no objection at all. Six percent would forbid long hair only on those employees who came in contact with the public.

Sandals were absolutely forbidden by 54 percent of the companies. An additional 22 percent replied that while they had no set policy on sandals on male employees, they might suggest moderation to an employee wearing them by having a personal talk with him. Only 5 percent of the firms indicated that they would have no objection at all.

Longer sideburns and the wearing of a mustache were the two changes in men's styles that companies found most acceptable. One quarter of the companies indicated no objection at all, while over half replied that they would have no objection to either except in extreme cases. None of the companies indicated that the wearing of sideburns was absolutely forbidden, and only 3 percent said they would forbid a mustache.

Companies showed mixed reactions on the subject of beards. Thirty-eight percent indicated that they would have no objection to them unless they were extreme, while 13 percent said they would have no objection to them at all. Twelve percent of the companies, however, absolutely forbid the wearing of beards, and an additional 27 percent indicated no set policy but said that moderation might be suggested through individual talks. Nine percent of the companies replied that beards were forbidden only for those employees who came in contact with the public. ▱

Fights and Altercations

Fights, heated disputes, and other disturbances obviously are not conducive to shop efficiency. But some personal friction is bound to arise out of the normal tensions of the work environment.

The code of behavior established in arbitrator's rulings recognizes these considerations. Thus, fighting on the job normally warrants discharge, but no right of discipline (other than a warning) usually is recognized for the normal disagreements and personality conflicts of everyday interpersonal relationships.

Even where fighting occurs, arbitrators have reduced discharges to less drastic penalties when it is shown that the violence was provoked. In such cases, one arbitrator said, a company reasonably could discharge the employee who provoked the assault without discharging the one who finally resorted to violence. (12 LA 682)

In handling nonviolent tensions that arise in the work place, management long ago abandoned the "big stick" technique and adopted instead human relations methods that emphasize teamwork and cooperation. In recent years, however, the human relations approach has come in for criticism as tending to smooth over, rather than deal with, basic conflicts. In many management circles, the vogue is "sensitivity training" and other methods of bringing feelings out into the open where they can be dealt with.

The new emphasis on increasing employee participation and involvement in decisions affecting their jobs means more potentials for conflict, particularly the previously frowned-upon conflicts between an employee and his supervisor. This eventually may lead to a basic shift in attitudes regarding the amount of aggressive behavior that should be tolerated in a work situation.

GUIDELINES

Factors To Be Considered

In cases involving aggressive and abusive conduct by one employee toward another, one arbitrator listed these points to be considered in evaluating disciplinary action:

● The apparent cause for the action (i.e., was it work related?)

● The extent and duration of any violence involved.

● Whether the action was restrained or whether the aggressor gave vent to an uncontrollable temper.

● The type of force used.

● The place of the altercation.

● Its effect upon the morale, safety, and the work habits of other employees.

● Whether the disagreement was a chance occurrence or premeditated.

● Whether a reasonable and prudent employee would have been likely to react in a similar manner.

● The likelihood that animosity between the two participants will subside to the point that they can be expected to work together in a normal relationship.

● Whether the aggressor's misconduct will lead to refusal, reluctance, or inability of other employees to work with him. (52 LA 423)

Fighting Words & Provocation

Mere cursing or the use of obscene and vulgar language in and of itself is not sufficient basis for discipline of an employee, arbiters generally hold. Much depends on the manner and spirit of its use. Such language may be used to lend color to one's remarks, or it may be hurled as slurs and epithets designed to goad or jeer another into a fight.

In deciding whether cursing and using threatening language warrants discipline, a test used by many arbiters is whether the conduct violated reasonable job decorum so as to cause apprehension or reaction in another employee which might hamper production. This test clearly is met where the conduct almost inevitably will provoke a fight.

There can be no provocation sufficient to justify an assault, arbiters emphasize. But provocation may mitigate the penalty for the assault. Mitigation also may be found in the failure of management to head off an impending conflict, such as where it knows of bad blood between employees and fails to take readily available steps to keep them apart.

Determining the Aggressor

In determining what penalty should be imposed as a result of a fight, most arbitrators hold that management should not wholly ignore the right of an employee to defend himself from attack.

Even where the employee lands the first blow, his attack may be held to have been provoked, either by fear of impending assault or by goading from the other employee. Determining the aggressor and apportioning penalties in accordance with degree of responsibility for the disorder then becomes much more complicated.

Management's job is further complicated by the fact that many arbitrators have found a particular penalty to be unjustified because of the employer's failure to make a full investigation. (27 LA 279).

EXAMPLE: An employee who was using an aisle to bring in parts to stack up at the rear of a gas station found his way blocked on two occasions by a Christmas tree that was being set up by another employee. This resulted in some friction between the two employees which ended up with one of them jumping on or shoving the other. The victim of this assault then pulled out a pocket knife, opened it, and told the other worker, "If you hit me, I'll use this knife." After a thorough investigation, management gave a five-day suspension to the worker who pulled the knife.

An arbitrator suggested that a written reprimand should be the maximum penalty in this case. The disciplined employee wasn't the aggressor, in the arbitrator's view. He had been physically assaulted without provocation and took out the knife only under provocation. (Navy Exchange, Naval Station, 52 LA 1142)

Off-Duty Fights

Ordinarily employees aren't subject to discipline for misconduct committed off company premises. But an exception often is made to this general rule in the case of off-duty fights that are job related, particularly where the fight is between a rank-and-file employee and a supervisor. (The subject of assaults on supervisors is covered in the chapter on "Insubordination.")

In upholding the discharge of an employee for a violent assault on another employee, an arbitrator cited the following circumstances as warranting action by management:

● The attack occurred very near the plant at a place where other employees were known to be present.

● It occurred during the scheduled working day.

● It stemmed from activities inside the plant that were a part of the employment relationship.

● Other employees could have been expected to become involved, and did.

● The attack had a disruptive effect upon plant operations, morale, and efficiency. (40 LA 435)

Other arbitrators have noted that the employer has an obligation to maintain order and safety on its premises, which includes more than just the plant. Therefore, discharges have been sustained for assaults on company parking lots and against employees leaving the company premises. (29 LA 820, 30 LA 948, 50 LA 407)

Gambling

Gambling of some type is prevalent in many companies whether it be the relatively innocuous world series baseball pool, the lunch-hour poker game, or an organized "numbers" racket. Here are some of the general principles arbitrators tend to use in passing on cases of discipline for alleged gambling:

► The evidence connecting the employee with gambling must be substantial and convincing. (12 LA 699, 18 LA 938, 39 LA 859, 45 LA 247)

► Discharge is normally too severe a penalty for the first offense of gambling. (12 LA 21, 22 LA 210, 28 LA 97)

► But discharge is appropriate where the employee was connected with an organized gambling racket (13 LA 253, 17 LA 150), engaged in gambling during working hours (16 LA 727), or had been warned previously about gambling (16 LA 727).

► Management's tolerance of world series pools and Thanksgiving turkey raffles does not preclude it from cracking down on employees who are involved in bookmaking or numbers operations. (22 LA 210, 33 LA 175)

GUIDELINES

Nonworking Time

Is it enough to show that an employee was gambling on company property or must you go further and show that he also was using his working time for this activity?

One arbiter upheld the discharge of an employee, suspected of writing numbers, who was accosted by plant guards and found to have "number slips" in his possession. Although he wasn't shown to have engaged in bookmaking on company time, the umpire held that an employee who engages in illegal conduct on company property—even during nonworking hours—is not carrying out his responsibilities as an employee. (29 LA 778)

However: An arbitration board in another case refused to sustain the discharge of an employee who was arrested by city police in the plant during working hours with numbers' slips in his possession and who subsequently pleaded guilty to a gambling charge. The arbitration board felt that clear proof hadn't been presented that the employee had ac-

47

cepted wagers or gambled on company property. (45 LA 247)

Unorganized Gambling

Where unorganized gambling is concerned, arbitrators seem to be reluctant to uphold discharges, except after repeated warnings and progressively strict discipline.

Thus, an arbitrator set aside the discharge of employees for playing poker, even though the game in question had lasted three to four hours during company time. Such "social games" as rummy, black jack, and poker were lunch-time practices, and no employee previously had been discharged for gambling, the arbitrator noted. (3 LA 423)

But a discharge of three employees for poker playing was upheld where they had been warned twice before about gambling on company time and property. (16 LA 461)

Organized Gambling

Where gambling takes organized forms—usually "numbers" or making book on horses—arbitrators take a more serious view of the transgression. But at the same time standards of evidence become more stringent, since charges of moral turpitude or criminal conduct are involved.

Thus, the discharge of an employee for allegedly engaging in the numbers racket on company time and property was set aside where the evidence fell short of "substantial and convincing proof." (12 LA 699)

Garnishment

IN BRIEF

These basic principles are applied by arbiters in garnishment cases:
- The rule must be clear, unambiguous, and well-known by employees.
- The rule must not be unreasonable. (Discharge for a single garnishment is held to be unreasonable.)
- The rule must be applied without discrimination.
- The rule must be predicated reasonably on saving the company from inconvenience, cost, liability, or other serious burdens.

Arbiters tend to give a sympathetic look to garnishment-discharge victims these days. Frequently, extenuating circumstances are found to justify reinstatement. Extenuating circumstances include discharging the debt through bankruptcy, speedily lifting it prior to discharge, lack of knowledge of the debt, a good work record, or loss of income caused by chronic layoffs. (See cases collected and discussed in General Telephone Co. of Wisconsin, 48 LA 1331.)

GUIDELINES

Legal Restrictions

Under a federal law that takes effect July 1, 1970, employers may not discharge an employee for a single wage garnishment. States with laws restricting an employer's right to discipline for wage garnishments include:

California (no discharge because of any one indebtedness prior to court's final order)

Connecticut (no discipline unless garnishments exceed more than seven in one year)

Delaware (no discharge because of garnishment)

Georgia (no discharge for any one garnishment)

Hawaii (no suspension or discharge for garnishments)

Iowa (no discharge for garnishments)

Kentucky (no discharge because any one indebtedness)

Michigan (no discharge if sole cause)

Minnesota (no discharge unless three or more separate garnishments in 90-day period)

Montana (no discharge or indefinite layoffs for garnishment)

New York (no discharge or layoff)

Oklahoma (no discharge unless one or more garnishments have been served twice in one year)

Utah (no discharge for any one garnishment)

Vermont (no discharge unless five or more separate garnishments or unless other substantial contributing causes)

Virginia (no discharge because of and one indebtedness)

Washington (no discharge unless

49

three or more garnishments in 12-month period)

Wisconsin (no discharge for any one garnishment)

Wyoming (no discharge for garnishments)

For further details on the federal and state laws on garnishment, see PAYROLL—PAY POLICIES, Chapter 305 on "The Laws in Brief."

Arbitrators' Rulings

Arbiters are unlikely to disturb a discharge made in accordance with a garnishment rule that has been enforced consistently. Even if there is no specific rule dealing with garnishment, a discharge probably will be upheld if the worker has been warned and has failed to improve.

EXAMPLE: One employee had a long series of claims filed against him by his creditors. He'd been called on the carpet each time and always managed to put off the creditor one way or another. So management had never actually had to make any deductions from his pay. He had been warned, both orally and in writing, that he'd have to put his financial house in order or face severe disciplinary action, but these warnings apparently had been ineffective. Finally the company fired him.

Although the company had no garnishment rule, an arbiter upheld the discharge. Wage garnishment is a proper concern of the employer, he said, even if deductions never have to be made. In that case, for instance,

management was forced to expend much time and effort trying to straighten things out. Since the employee had been given fair warning, the umpire saw nothing improper about the discharge. (Capital Airlines, Inc., 27 LA 358)

However: One arbiter ruled that management had no right to fire a worker whose pay was garnisheed for three weeks in a row under one court order. Workers whose wages were attached were punished by warnings for the first two offenses and discharge for the third. In this case, the arbiter held that three withholdings under one court order could not be considered three separate offenses. (Bagwell Steel Co., 41 LA 303)

Further: A company should investigate the circumstances of a garnishment before taking action to make sure the worker actually is at fault. One arbiter ordered the reinstatement of an employee who had been discharged when the federal government filed a tax levy against her wages. The company had a rule listing garnishment of wages as misconduct punishable by immediate dismissal, but the umpire found that the employee had known nothing about her tax delinquency and was not even responsible for it. (Her estranged husband was.) Therefore the umpire told the company to return the employee to her job with full back pay. (J. D. Jewell, Inc., 32 LA 50; see also American Brass Co., 35 LA 139, Trumbull Asphalt Co., 41 LA 631)

IN BRIEF

In determining how to handle incidents of horseplay on company property, a distinction may be made between joking that involves only a remote possibility of injury and acts that involve a high risk of serious injury. Conduct of the latter type clearly warrants a more serious penalty even if disastrous consequences luckily do not result.

GUIDELINES

Degree of Danger

The distinction between relatively harmless horseplay and conduct that creates serious dangers is indicated in the following cases.

EXAMPLE: For some time, employees had engaged in occasional horseplay when management's back was turned. Most often this took the form of blowing an employee's hat off with an air hose or throwing pieces of hard rubber used in shipping the company's products. On one occasion when the rubber squares were flying, an employee who was struck in the head retaliated by sneaking up behind an employee and dropping a lighted cigarette in his back pocket. After about five minutes, the employee entered a spray booth where highly combustible paints, lacquers, and solvents were used. Fortunately, another employee noticed smoke coming from the victim's back pocket and helped him snuff out the coals. The prankster also dropped a lighted cigarette in the pocket of another employee who also managed to escape injury.

Refusing to set aside the prankster's discharge, an arbitrator noted that his conduct showed a serious disregard for the personal safety of others. In allowing the first employee to walk into the spray booth, the prank-

ster created a serious fire hazard. The second employee was working on a cutting machine at the time the hot-seat was administered. These incidents could not be considered in the same class with the throwing of rubber squares or the misuse of the air hose, the arbitrator said. (Decar Plastics Corp., 44 LA 921)

EXAMPLE: Discipline short of discharge was held warranted where an employee pulled back a supervisor's chair, causing her to fall. The employee's conduct showed a lack of judgment, the umpire found, but it wasn't shown to have been a malicious act. A ten-week suspension without pay, the arbiter concluded, ought to be enough to impress upon the culprit that employees have an obligation to "conduct themselves as mature individuals rather than as light-hearted juveniles." (Fisher Electronics, Inc., 44 LA 343)

Mitigating Circumstances

The importance of an employee's past record also is taken into consideration by arbiters in evaluating the penalty imposed.

EXAMPLE: An employee who was prone to needling other employees had harassed a fellow worker all morning.

In retaliation the other man came up behind the grievant and grabbed him in a bearhug, placing most of his 265 pounds on the grievant's head and shoulders. The grievant thereupon drew a pocket knife and made a slicing motion toward the other worker, for which he was later discharged. In lightening the penalty to reinstatement without back pay, the arbiter noted that the grievant's nearly perfect record of 19 years' service supports the conclusion that he is not a "chronically mean or vicious" person. (Erwin Mills, Inc., 51 LA 225)

Rehabilitative Effect

Discipline short of discharge may be advocated for employees guilty of mild horseplay to see if they can be taught a lesson.

EXAMPLE: A company was within its rights in disciplining a third-shift employee who was guilty of "teasing" his female coworkers by transferring him to the first shift, with attendant loss of his shift differential, an arbitrator said. But for the action to have a rehabilitative value, the arbitrator pointed out, the employee should be given a chance to prove that he profited from the experience. Accordingly, the company was directed to give him another try on the the third shift. (Sobel Metal Products, Inc., 54 LA 835)

Intoxication & Alcoholism

In intoxication cases, arbiters formerly concentrated on the question: Was he drunk on the job? If he was, the discharge usually was upheld.

But now arbiters, like the courts, are beginning to accept the idea that intoxication on the job may indicate that the employee is an alcoholic. If he is, then the feeling is that this should be treated as an illness rather than as simply misconduct.

This doesn't mean that the employee who is caught drunk on the job should get off scot free. But if it appears that he is making a good-faith effort at rehabilitation, his reinstatement may be ordered. Some reasonable assurance against a recurrence must be present, however.

In dealing with alcoholism as a form of illness, management frequently makes sickness, disability, leave of absence, and other benefits available to the alcoholic. Moreover, many companies take positive action to help rehabilitate alcoholics, such as working with units of Alcoholics Anonymous.

GUIDELINES

In cases involving the use and possession of intoxicants, arbitrators have developed the approach that discharge for drinking or drunkenness generally is sustained in these situations:

▶ Frequent absenteeism as a result of drinking.

▶ Drinking on the job combined with other misconduct such as serious improper behavior or material falsification of employment records.

▶ Drinking on the job that results in an inability to perform the work.

▶ Drunkenness or drinking that has a definite destructive effect on the employer's business and/or the morale of other employees.

▶ Chronic alcoholism with no sign of efforts at rehabilitation.

When such factors are not present and where drinking on the job is a first offense, the penalty of discharge often is reduced to some lesser degree of discipline. (49 LA 190, 31 LA 832, 34 LA 14, 35 LA 757, 37 LA 130, 38 LA 1221, 40 LA 717, 41 LA 987, 52 LA 990, 55 LA 1274)

Long continued service usually is recognized as a factor in an employee's favor when determining the appropriate penalty for intoxication. (21 LA 80, 23 LA 245, 24 LA 720, 55 LA 1274)

Drinking and Alcoholism

Not every incident of intoxication on company property demands that the employee involved be treated as "sick" rather than disciplined for misconduct. Unless there is other evidence that the on-premises intoxication or drinking is part of a pattern suggesting alcoholism, management is free to treat the matter as a simple violation of company rules.

While it always helps to have a rule written out, drinking on the job usually is so clear a violation of normal standards of employee conduct as to warrant discipline even in the absence of a written rule. This might not be the case, however, if management in the past has closed its eyes to evidence of on-the-job drinking. Problems of proof also arise in trying to establish that employees were in fact drinking.

EXAMPLE: Although plant rules proscribed possessing or drinking intoxicating beverages on the premises, there had been a problem of employee drinking on the second-shift break. In an effort to crack down on this, two supervisors staked out the plant parking lot during the break and apprehended three employees who had been sitting in the car of a nonemployee. Empty beer bottles were found in the car. The nonemployee signed a statement that the three employees "were drinking beer in my car," but later repudiated it, saying that he initially had signed it only out of fear that he otherwise would be turned over to the authorities.

An arbitrator overturned the discharge of the three employees solely because of the lack of sufficient proof to back up the charges. If the charges had been proved, he noted, the company would have had the right to discharge the men even without a specific rule against liquor on plant property. (Holland Die Casting & Plating Co., 48 LA 567)

However: Where witnesses testified that the employee was inebriated, discharge was upheld without reliance on sobriety tests. (3 LA 146, 181) And where the employer applied his own sobriety test, an arbitrator endorsed the findings even though the employee's standards weren't the same as those used by the courts. (28 LA 289)

Evidence of Intoxication

Where an employee is disciplined for alleged intoxication, a dispute often arises as to the sufficiency of the evidence regarding his state of sobriety. From a review of prior decisions, one arbitrator set forth these principles:

● Mere opinion evidence is not sufficient proof of a drunken condition. The evidence must be sufficiently specific in describing various details of appearance and conduct so that it is clear that the person accused is under the influence of liquor.

● Supervisors who have no medical training nevertheless are capable of recognizing when an employee is intoxicated or under the influence of alcohol if they objectively compare an employee's normal demeanor and work habits with those at the time his sobriety is questioned.

● Results of blood alcohol tests may be accepted as conclusive proof of guilt of intoxication. However, it is not required that management give such a test in order to prove intoxication, since it is recognized that requiring such tests might cause undue delays and disruption of production. (54 LA 145)

One arbitrator quoted the following statement from the National Safety Council on the use of blood tests:

"The results of a chemical analysis should not be the sole criterion upon which an official judgment is based. The results of a chemical test should be employed to confirm conclusions drawn from clinical and physical diagnoses. It is also emphasized that arbitrary deductions based upon the so-called '0.15 percent line demarcation' be avoided." (31 LA 832)

Rehabilitation of Alcoholic

An employee's rehabilitation efforts after a discharge for alcoholism may lead arbitrators to order reinstatement. In two cases, for example, the arbitrators found that just cause for discharge existed at the time it was made. But they held that post-discharge steps taken by the employee constituted mitigating circumstances that could be taken into consideration in their review of the propriety of the penalty. (40 LA 935, 42 LA 408)

But another arbitrator emphasized that while alcoholism is an illness, it is an illness which only the patient can "cure." The discharge of an alcoholic was upheld where the employee had been given repeated opportunities to get the situation under control and had failed too often for the arbitrator to conclude that all would be well if only he was given another chance.

The arbiter did suggest, however, that the employee might be considered for medical leave rather than be fired. But he left this to management's discretion, since it involved a risk which should not be forced upon the company. (44 LA 87)

Off-Duty Drinking

In the normal course of things, the consumption of alcohol after working hours doesn't have a direct impact upon the employer-employee relationship and therefore is outside the reach of management's disciplinary powers. Off-duty drinking is cause for discipline, however, when it results in an employee's reporting for work "under the influence." (41 LA 333)

One arbiter upheld the discharge of an employee for violating a new amendment to a no-drinking rule that extended it to meal-time drinking off company property. In this case, however, the arbitrator pointed out that the union had led the company to believe that it saw an evil in lunch-hour drinking and would support the company in an effort to do something about it. (44 LA 267)

Off-duty drinking also may be cause for discipline where it indicates back-sliding by an employee who has promised to try to bring an alcoholism problem under control.

EXAMPLE: An employee who had been with a company for 25 years obviously had a drinking problem. After issuing s e v e r a l written warnings about his use of alcoholic beverages, the company finally discharged him for being drunk on company property. Subsequently, however, the company agreed to take him back if he promised to stay off alcohol, attend AA meetings on a regular basis, and see his doctor and follow his orders. Nearly a year later, he was observed by company officials drinking beer in a tavern out of working hours. As a result, he was discharged.

An arbiter upheld the discharge. The employment h i s t o r y demonstrated that the employee's consumption of alcohol, whether on company time or not, had a direct impact on the employment relationship, the arbiter said. The employee's attitude indicated that he did not intend to improve his conduct in regard to the use of alcoholic beverages. (Emge Packing Co., 52 LA 195)

Off-Duty Misconduct

The general rule is that an employer may not discipline an employee for what he does off duty. As one arbitrator explained: "To do so would constitute an invasion of the employee's personal life by the employer and would place the employer in the position of sitting in judgment on neighborhood morals, a matter which should be left to civil officers." (45 LA 283)

An exception to this rule permits discipline when the off-duty conduct affects the employer-employee relationship, as in these cases:

▶ The conduct renders the employee unable to perform his job. This may occur when the employee is confined to jail. (39 LA 1165, 33 LA 735)

▶ Other employees refuse to work with the employee. In cases involving discharge for immoral conduct, arbitrators may hinge reinstatement awards upon union assurance that the employee's co-workers have no objection to his reinstatement. (23 LA 229, 22 LA 1, 15 LA 42)

▶ The company is harmed by the off-duty conduct. This includes indirect harm, such as a criminal conviction that jeopardizes the company's public image (35 LA 25, 36 LA 965, 38 LA 1003, 49 LA 117, 53 LA 203), or direct harm, such as working for a competitor (26 LA 401, 34 LA 638).

Running through these exceptions is the guiding principle that the outside activity is subject to discipline if it definitely relates to plant operations. By this it is meant that the misconduct must have arisen out of plant activities or carry with it a serious threat of disrupting the orderly, efficient, or safe conduct of the company's business.

GUIDELINES

Criminal Conviction

If you can prove that an employee's conviction of a crime is detrimental to your public or employee relations, you stand a good chance of having a discharge upheld.

One arbiter, for instance, ruled that the discharge of an employee for his off-duty conduct was fully warranted, since this conduct stamped him as a man capable of resorting to violence and thus potentially dangerous to the safety of other employees. (24 LA 603). Another arbiter also backed the company in discharging an employee for his off-duty behavior where his work with the company required him to enter customer's homes. The umpire termed him a bad risk because of his association with disreputable characters capable of taking advantage of information about customers' homes and because of his contempt for minimum standards of acceptable social behavior. (39 LA 1025)

(Management's right to discipline where an employee is accused of conduct that is immoral or social reprehensible is discussed under a separate heading.)

EXAMPLE: An employee of a gas company was convicted of a charge of embezzlement at a laundromat where he worked part-time. As a result, he was fired by the gas company.

Upholding the discharge, an arbitrator noted that the company was "understandably concerned" about the risk of bad customer and public relations that would flow from knowledge that the man was in the company's employ. The overriding consideration, he said, must be the public nature of the gas company's business and the position of trust that its employees were placed with respect to customers' homes. The fact that this employee didn't have access to the keys to customers' homes wasn't known to the customers, he noted. (New Haven Gas Co., 43 LA 900)

Discipline Pending Trial

Depending upon the seriousness of the crime and its impact upon a company's employee or public relations, management may be justified in suspending an employee pending his trial on charges of criminal misconduct. (29 LA 442, 26 LA 570, 22 LA 851)

EXAMPLE: A driver-salesman for a dairy was one of 10 people arrested in a raid on a night club and charged with Sunday sales of liquor, prostitution, pandering, and conducting obscene exhibitions involving both men and women.

An arbitrator recommended (1) suspension pending trial, (2) discharge if found guilty and sent to jail, and (3) reinstatement if found innocent, or if the charges are otherwise dropped, but to a job in which he would have no contact with customers. Suspension was clearly warranted, the umpire held, because of possible damage to the company's image and good will if it kept the driver on. The driver-salesman's duties necessitated a close personal relationship with customers, he noted, and the seriousness of the charges increased the potential of harm to the company. (Menzie Dairy Co., 45 LA 283)

Several arbitrators have taken the position that a suspension in such circumstances is not properly to be considered disciplinary and is unrelated to a final verdict as to the employee's guilt or innocence. The suspension instead is viewed as an act of self-defense on the company's part to eliminate a potential detriment to or impairment of the company's business. (45 LA 498, 48 LA 391)

Length of Suspension

Some arbitrators have questioned the propriety of a suspension of an employee pending a court trial verdict, where this results in a lengthy loss of employment. In such cases, these arbitrators have suggested, the better course of action is for the company to make its own investigation and decide upon the appropriate disciplinary step.

EXAMPLE: Two employees were indicted by the grand jury for committing criminal acts of violence against nonstrikers during a strike. When they returned to work at the end of the strike, the company suspended them temporarily. The employees emphatically denied the guilt, but several months passed without any indication of the date when they would be brought to trial.

A temporary suspension at the time they returned to work was justified, an arbitrator ruled, since the employer reasonably could conclude that their return at the time would disrupt plant operations. But the suspension shouldn't have continued beyond 60 days without the company's making its own investigation and taking appropriate disciplinary action. (Plough, Inc., 54 LA 541)

Effect of Acquittal

An employer is not necessarily bound by the finding of a criminal court on the guilt or innocence of an employee, arbitrators have held. (53 LA 1279, 54 LA 541)

EXAMPLE: An arbitrator upheld the discharge of an employee for damaging company property, even though a jury had acquitted the employee of the criminal charge of malicious destruction of property. The arbitrator held that the jury's action did not foreclose him from making his own judgment on the evidence presented to him, observing that he did not know what evidence or arguments were presented in the criminal action, what rules of law were applied, and what elements of evidence persuaded the jury to reach the verdict it did. (Chrysler Corp., 53 LA 1279).

Socially Reprehensible Conduct

Management may be presented with a tough decision where an employee is convicted of criminal conduct that is regarded as immoral or repugnant by society. On the one hand, there is the threat to employee and/or customer relations that may be presented by returning the employee to his job. On the other hand, the argument may be made that punishment of the employee should be left to the courts and that the employee shouldn't be placed in "double jeopardy" by loss of employment as well.

In resolving this dilemma, arbitrators tend to weigh the employee's past record against the threat of a recurrence of the misconduct. Thus, an employee who pleaded guilty to a charge of taking indecent liberties with a nine-year-old girl and who spent about eight months in a state mental hospital was given a conditional reinstatement. The employee's record of 16 years' employment without prior incident was cited as some indication that he could continue as a satisfactory employee. The fact that he had been a factory worker was seen as minimizing any adverse affect upon the morale or efficiency of other employees. And, his lack of contact with the public should avoid adverse outside reaction, the arbiter said, which might not have been the case if he had been a retail clerk in a toy store, for example. (Armco Steel Corp., 43 LA 977)

Where an airline purser was arrested once in an altercation arising from his taking picture of nude males in a hotel room, an arbitrator converted a discharge to a 90-day suspension. But when the employee subsequently pleaded guilty to criminal charge involving the photographing of a nude minor, a discharge penalty was upheld. The cumulative effect of these incidents exposed the airline employer to potential damage, the arbiter said, noting that "some people may be given pause in riding planes "under the control of persons who are so inept at managing their own affairs." (53 LA 203)

Some of the considerations that must be weighed in these cases appear in a decision ordering the reinstatement of an employee who sought to return to his job after serving a nine-month jail sentence after being arrested on a morals charge at a motion picture theater. The arbitrator noted these factors:

● The employee had a 37-year, unblemished work record.

● The nature of the offense did not impair the employee's ability to perform his job functions.

● The underlying psychiatric problem that led to the offense did not, in itself, render the employee unfit for further employment.

● Aside from supposition, it was not shown that either supervision or fellow employees would be subjected to resentments or tensions impairing the department's operation if the employee were to be reinstated. (41 LA 460)

Illegitimate Pregnancy

Even granting that society generally disapproves of women who bear illegitimate children, it doesn't necessarily follow that a company will be condemned for retaining such a woman in its employ. On this theory, arbitrators have declined to uphold a policy of discharging unmarried females who become pregnant.

EXAMPLE: A cashier at a supermarket was permitted to continue to work until shortly before the birth of her first illegitimate child. But when she subsequently sought maternity leave for a second pregnancy, management asked her to resign. When she refused, she was fired.

Rejecting the company's claim of damage to its customer relations, an arbitrator noted that customer-employee relations in a supermarket are not as intimate as they are in a small neighborhood grocery. More-over, the first pregnancy apparently didn't injure the company.

He also rejected a claim that the discharge was justified by the possibility that parents might forbid their daughters to work at the store. She was not charged with sexual misconduct on the premises, and there was no evidence that she was a bad influence on the other girls. In fact, the arbiter said, her case might serve to underscore the dangers inherent in illicit sexual relationship. (Allied Supermarkets, Inc., 41 LA 713)

Outside Employment

IN BRIEF

Outside employment may be a cause for disciplinary action in these situations:

▶ Where an issue of dishonesty is raised. An employee who falsely claims sick leave in order to hold down a second job would be subject to discipline or discharge.

▶ Where the outside employment results in poor performance, absenteeism, or tardiness. Here, discipline may be imposed for the poor job performance, and arbitrators generally will not consider outside employment as an excuse. For example, discharge has been held proper where an employee refused to perform regularly scheduled overtime because it interfered with his outside job.

▶ Where the outside employment has a natural tendency to interfere with an employee's work, such as working for a competitor, especially where trade secrets or special skills are involved.

GUIDELINES

False Claims To Cover Moonlighting

Just cause for discharge usually is found where an employee falsely claims sick leave in order to work on his second job. Such cases usually are treated as instances of misconduct akin to dishonesty rather than as simple absenteeism.

Thus, one arbitrator upheld the discharge of a worker who frequently went on sick leave during the harvest season in order to tend to his outside farming job. The company was not required to proceed under the contract provision dealing with absenteeism, which set up a progressive discipline procedure of warnings and lesser penalties prior to discharge, the arbiter said. He noted that application of the absenteeism procedure, which contained a 12-month cutoff on warnings, would result in continual erasure of the discipline each year for the harvest-season absences. (37 LA 254)

However, an employee may be able to escape discipline for working elsewhere while on sick leave if no intent to cheat is involved. For example, just cause for a discharge was held to be lacking where an employee took a second job involving light work while recuperating from a heart attack. The employee had sought to return to his primary job, but both his doctor and the company doctor had recommended against it, and the company also turned down his request for lighter work. The employee's failure to notify the company of his other job and his denial at one point that he was working was held to constitute at most bad judgment, rather than dishonesty. (43 LA 1106)

Similarly, the discharge of an employee who was found tending bar at a local tavern while on sick leave was set aside by an arbitrator on the basis of testimony from the tavern owner and the employee that they

60

were old friends, that the employee was not compensated, and that he often used the tavern as a "second home." (52 LA 918)

Working for Competitor

It is generally conceded that management has the right to bar employees from working for a competitor during their off hours. Such employment not only gives the competitor the benefit of experience provided by the fulltime employer, it frequently does so at bargain-basement prices. Moreover, the employee, whether he intends to or not, may divulge information damaging to the company—trade secrets, new designs, sales figures, etc.

Arbiters insist, however, that employees be warned in advance that such outside work is forbidden. The company normally can't announce such a rule and impose discipline at the same time.

One arbitrator observed that a company had the right to establish its rule against working for a competitor without first consulting with the union. He added, however, that the union had the right to challenge the reasonableness of the rule and its application through the grievance procedure.

In appling such a rule, he commented, a company is not required to establish beyond doubt that damage to the business or financial loss actually has resulted. It is sufficient if the outside employment reasonably suggests that it might lead to disclosure of information or the use of special skills. (39 LA 404)

EXAMPLE: Two workers accepted part-time employment with a company that was in direct competition with their full-time employer. When the latter learned of this, he warned the employees that further such activity would be cause for discharge.

The arbitrator ruled that the employer was justified in barring outside work for a competitor for two basic reasons. First, he said, an employee who engages in such employment gives the competitor the benefit of experience provided by the fulltime employee. Even if the employee takes no cut in pay for the outside work, the umpire pointed out, he likely won't be eligible for fringes as he is in his full-time employment. This means the competitor pays less for the same grade of labor.

Moreover, the employee may damage his full-time employer by divulging information to the competitor— trade secrets, new designs, sales figures, etc. This may happen in a small way whether the employee wishes it or not, and if he sets out to give information to the competitor he can do real harm to his full-time employer, the umpire said.

Nevertheless, the umpire considered the warnings in this case unjustified. Management could put a stop to outside work for a competitor, he said, but it couldn't impose discipline at the same time it gave notice of its policy. (Mechanical Handling Systems, Inc., 26 LA 401; see also Phillips Petroleum Co., 47 LA 372)

Other Conflicting Employment

Even where the second job isn't with a direct competitor, a company still may claim that it inherently conflicts with the employee's responsibilities and obligations to his primary employer. Such an issue frequently has been raised by employers in the publishing industry. Here are some examples of how arbitrators have ruled in these cases:

● A publisher had the right to give one of his reporters a choice between his job with the paper and an outside job as editor of a union weekly that espoused political views contrary to the newspaper's editorial policy. (41 LA 899)

● A publisher didn't have just cause for discharging two circulation managers for operating a local beer tavern. The arbiter rejected the company's contention that a bias against beer exists in a large segment of the community, noting that the sole test of community morals is that which has been crystallized by statute or ordinance into positive mandate. Since dealing in beer is a legal business, the employees weren't engaged in activities of a detrimental nature to the newspaper. (48 LA 931)

● A publisher didn't have the right to order one of his advertising salesmen to quit a night-time job in a local department s t o r e, notwithstanding the publisher's contention that other advertiser-stores might view it as a conflict of interest. As a remedy, the publisher was directed to make the employee whole for wages he lost by relinquishing his part-time employment. (43 LA 273)

● A publisher had the right to fire its drama critic for accepting outside work as press agent for a summer theatre and allowing her name, which was also the name of her column in the newspaper, to be used in promoting the summer theatre. (42 LA 504)

Nonconflicting Moonlighting

Moonlighting that does not involve working for a competitor or other conflicts with the primary job usually isn't regarded as just cause for discharge in the absence of contractual prohibition on outside employment. On the other hand, a company was held to be within its rights when it adopted a rule prohibiting the holding of a second full-time job, on the ground that this would have a natural and obvious tendency to interfere with an employee's work (41 LA 1126). Moreover, outside employment normally will not be considered an excuse for poor performance, absenteeism, tardiness, or a refusal to work overtime.

EXAMPLE: In the course of preparing reprimands to an employee for spoiled work, management bumbled onto the fact that he was a moonlighter. The reprimands were changed to a discharge when the employee refused to give up his second job.

An arbitrator set aside the discharge on the ground that management had insufficient backing for its conclusion that it was injured by his other job. Although his two jobs allowed him only about five hours of sack time a day, his foreman saw no signs that he was suffering from lack of sleep and instead had given him rapid promotions. There also was no showing that he was less efficient or spoiled more work than nonmoonlighters. (37 LA 1095)

Sleeping & Loafing

Discharge is generally acknowledged to be a proper penalty for sleeping on the job as long as there is a plant rule or established practice making discharge the penalty for such an offense. (27 LA 510, 22 LA 498) Even in the absence of a specific rule, discharge is regarded as warranted if the dozing involves any danger to the safety of employees or equipment. (26 LA 472, 21 LA 676, 20 LA 50)

Although discharge may be accepted as a just penalty for sleeping on the job, specific cases often are dealt with as mere loafing, which is subject to a lesser penalty. This is due to the difficulty of determining whether a man is asleep or merely resting with his eyes shut. (27 LA 137, 14 LA 907) The only way to decide may be to awaken him or stand beside him until he awakens. (27 LA 512, 19 LA 380)

GUIDELINES

Penalty for Loafing

Is discharge too severe a penalty for the first offense of loafing on the job? Although management may feel that once a worker is found guilty of loafing he has lost his value as an employee, arbitrators often reduce a discharge penalty and give the loafer another chance.

EXAMPLE: A company's charges against the employee were that he loafed on the job and as a result of his loafing, his work area was not cleaned properly, and he neglected to tend to a bin which ran over and caused loss to the company. Management stated that it had previously realized that he was deficient in his duties and had reinstructed him. When he failed again he was discharged.

The employee was ordered reinstated with back wages, less two weeks' pay for a disciplinary layoff. The arbiter found that the company had reinstructed the employee in his duties but had not specifically warned him at the time of the reinstruction,

as was customary. The arbiter also found that the irregularities complained of were no greater than those of other employees who had been reprimanded or laid off but not discharged. (International Minerals & Chemical Corp., 4 LA 127)

Loafing After Making Incentive Quota

Can a pieceworker be disciplined for loafing the remainder of the day after putting out what he thinks is his quota for the day? One umpire upheld a company's right to punish a worker guilty of this offense.

EXAMPLE: A contract said the company was entitled to expect a full day's work from each employee. It added that workers were expected to turn out at least 60 units an hour and stay at their work stations. The worker in question did 480 units in about 3½ hours and then, after being told he couldn't go home, stood around talking to the worker next to him for the rest of his eight-hour shift. When the company suspended him for this, he argued that his 480-unit output was a full day's work.

The umpire upheld the suspension. The contract, he pointed out, said workers should turn out 60 units an hour; this means 60 units during each hour, he said, not merely 480 units a day. Moreover, the arbiter concluded, even if the worker honestly believed he was right, he should have kept working and filed a grievance. (C & D Batteries, Inc., 26 LA 61)

Penalty for Sleeping

Generally arbitrators have held that where management has strictly enforced no-sleeping rule, the discharge of a worker for violating it is fully justified in principle. In the absence of a specific rule, awards indicate that umpires consider the degree of responsibility of the worker's job and the circumstances under which he was found asleep in deciding what penalty is proper.

In the opinion of one arbitrator, sleeping-on-the-job cases fall into three categories. First there's the worker who's ill or tired for a good reason and who drops off involuntarily while trying to work. Then there's the worker who's been out whooping it up while off duty and who yields to the need for sleep during working hours. Finally there's the worker who makes preparations, hides out, and goes to sleep as a regular practice; people in this group deserve the severest discipline, the umpire said.

In this case a maintenance man was found asleep on a blanket in a remote section of the plant with his shoes off and an alarm clock set to wake him just before the end of his shift. His preparations for sleeping, together with the fact he'd been moonlighting, suggested to the arbitrator that sacking out on company time was a habit with him. The arbiter concluded that his conduct put him into the third class of offenders and that the company was within its rights in firing him. (Collins Radio Co., 30 LA 121)

On the other hand: An arbiter decided that discharge was too severe a penalty for a worker who wasn't feeling well and was found sleeping when no work was available. The arbiter distinguished between this instance and that of sleeping while an unattended machine is running, and thus reduced the penalty. (Nestle Co., 45 LA 524)

Sleeping During Break

Can a worker be disciplined for sleeping during lunch breaks or rest periods? The answer to this question may depend on whether the worker took steps to make sure that he would wake up before the break was over. In one instance where an employee took such measures and had good intentions, his discharge was overruled.

EXAMPLE: An employee usually ate at his work station, but on a day when he had a headache, he told his group leader he was going to lie down in the rest room and asked the leader to come and get him in 15 or 20 minutes. After about 15 minutes, a foreman discovered him, and he was fired for sleeping on the job with intent to deceive.

In light of all the circumstances, an arbiter decided the employee should be reinstated with back pay. Since he told the group leader where he was going, he obviously wasn't trying to hide anything. Moreover, he was entitled to a break and hadn't been away from the job more than the permissible length of time. Finally, his machine was not in operation when he left it so there was no risk of damage to the company's products. (Kawneer Co., 30 LA 1002)

On the other hand: Where the circumstances showed that a worker might have remained asleep throughout the rest of his shift, an umpire upheld the disciplinary action.

EXAMPLE: Employees in the packing department at one company were allowed two break periods each shift. The breaks were taken without immediate supervision, and the company and union had agreed that employees were on the "honor system." When a foreman caught two employees lying down and asleep during a break, they were fired.

An umpire okayed the discharges. The employees, he pointed out, had deliberately placed themselves in a position conducive to sleep. If this sort of conduct were allowed, he commented, the entire department, in the absence of supervision, might go to sleep during a break and remain asleep indefinitely. (Phillips Chemical Co., 22 LA 498)

Proof of Sleeping on Job

Can a worker be disciplined for sleeping on the job merely on the basis of impressions someone gets by observing him from a distance? Most arbiters agree that there must be convincing evidence that the worker was asleep.

EXAMPLE: A worker had begun his assignment of holding the brake of an overhead crane during a grinding operation when a foreman and several other people walked up. Seeing the worker's head nodding and his eyes shut, the group concluded he was sleeping. Although the worker's foreman arrived 10 minutes after the grinding began and found the worker awake, the company dished out a two-week suspension. T h e worker admitted he had been drowsy, but he said his eyes were shut only because they were smarting from the oil and brake fluid in the crane cab. The union contended that from the 25- or 30-foot distance from which the worker was observed, nobody could tell whether he was asleep.

The arbiter felt that the worker couldn't have fallen completely asleep in the 10 minutes. Finding discipline unjustified, he said the witnesses only assumed the worker was asleep, since they weren't close enough to be sure. (John Deere Ottumwa Works, 27 LA 572)

There is little question concerning an employer's right to discipline employees for striking in violation of a no-strike contract. The issue submitted to arbitration usually is whether the company was arbitrary or discriminatory in selecting the employees to be disciplined.

Arbitrators generally have held that an employer cannot single out individual strikers for discipline unless their actual leadership is proven. (28 LA 121, 27 LA 321, 24 LA 761)

Less proof of guilt is required in the case of union officials because of the feeling that it is a graver offense for them to participate in unauthorized stoppages. (25 LA 774, 25 LA 663, 24 LA 421) The view often has been expressed that officers have the duty not only to refrain from violating a no-strike pledge themselves but to make a determined effort to prevent others from violating it. (18 LA 919, 13 LA 294, 6 LA 617)

GUIDELINES

Wildcat Strikers

Technically, every participant in a breach-of-contract strike is subject to discipline. As a practical matter, however, management usually finds it neither advantageous nor possible to punish all participants alike. A more suitable course usually is to single out the ringleaders or the union officers for discipline.

Attempts to discipline union stewards or officers more heavily than rank-and-file employees may raise the question of whether this amounts to discrimination—the application of unequal penalties for like offenses. Arbitrators almost universally hold that stewards' leadership, or even mere participation, in a wildcat strike is *not* the same offense but a much more serious one than that of the ordinary employee. Thus, one arbitrator explained:

"Joining other employees in a strike that violates a contract and aiding and abetting afterwards by picketing may be e x p e c t e d of the ordinary member of the union and is not ground for singling him out for penalty. Likewise, as to the failure to take active steps to end an unauthorized strike. But a different principle is applicable to officers and committeemen of the union. Union office carries with it responsibilities and obligations both to the company and to the union." (4 LA 744)

After a genuine effort to prevent an unlawful strike or stoppage, a union officer cannot be penalized more than other employees for participating in it, according to one school of thought. (11 LA 675) But others have held that the union officer's mere participation in a strike is a more serious offense than the participation of rank-and-file employees and may warrant more severe discipline. (14 LA 987)

Selective Discipline

Failure of an employer to discipline

or discharge every employee who participates in a breach-of-contract strike makes it difficult for a union to explain the company's selective discipline to its members. Yet, the company often does not have sufficient proof or finds itself in the position where, if it were to discipline all those involved, it might seriously interfere with production and punish itself as well as those of its employees who were innocent of having any part in the illegal work stoppage.

Under the circumstances, arbitrators conclude, it is inevitable that some of the guilty "get away with it," hopefully having learned a lesson from their "lucky break." Management, however, must exercise reasonable, nondiscriminatory standards in selecting those to be disciplined such as all of those employees who it could prove had a substantial role in making the walkout effective as distinguished from the mere "followers." (49 LA 333, 50 LA 491)

Misconduct During Legal Strikes

Even if a strike is lawful, strikers may be disciplined for acts of violence, vandalism, and obstruction. This punishment frequently takes the form of a refusal to reinstate the alleged culprits at the conclusion of the strike. Such action may be tested under the usual "just cause" for discharge standard in the contract or as a result of a strike settlement agreement, under which the parties agreed to let an a r b i t r a t o r determine whether the strikers' misconduct warranted discharge.

Arbitrators generally accept the principle that management may discipline strikers for picket-line misconduct. One umpire observed:

"Picket line violence by an employee may render him unfit for further employment by the a n t a g o n i s m s it arouses and the attitude which it expresses toward management, toward other workers or toward plant and equipment." (11 LA 1138)

The main problem for management is proving the identity of the culprits and the extent of their misconduct. One arbitrator applied these criteria in weighing the strength of management's case:

● How satisfactory is the evidence?

● What was the extent of participation? In any mob situation, the degree of the individual's involvement is important.

● What was the nature of the violence? Shouting and shoving are different from striking a person, for example.

● Was the violence provoked?

● Was the violence premeditated or undertaken on the spur of the moment?

● What will be the impact of the punishment on the employee? Discharge is a more severe penalty for an older employee, for example.

● Was the disciplinary action discriminatory in that others weren't given similar discipline for similar misconduct? (11 LA 1138)

━━━━━━━━━━━━━━━━━━━━━**POLICY GUIDE**━━━━━━━━━━━━━━━━━━━━━

The preceding chapters set forth the general principles in handling the major forms of employee misconduct. Other, less frequent, problems are discussed below.

━━━━━━━━━━━━━━━━ **GUIDELINES** ━━━━━━━━━━━━━━━━

Violation of No-Smoking Rule

Arbitrators agree that a company has every right to set up a rule prohibiting smoking in order to protect its property and employees' lives against fire hazard and to comply with legal requirements. However, where management has permitted violations of a no-smoking rule to go unpunished over a long period of time, most arbitrators hold that the sudden firing of a worker for smoking is not justified. These umpires feel that if a company decides to enforce the rule strictly it must make it clear to all hands. Until such announcement is made, workers may not be summarily discharged for breaking the rule, especially if the company knows that it was being broken for some time. (Douglas Aircraft Co., Inc., 1 LA 350; Baltic Metal Products Co., 8 LA 782)

Violation of No-Firearms Rule

An employer's no-firearms rule was upheld by an arbitrator who found that it did not violate the idea of reasonableness and necessity in carrying on the employer's trucking business. Some customers or employees might well be bothered or disturbed by a gun-toting employee, the arbitrator noted. He added, however, that a different result might obtain if an employee disclosed a special need for carrying a weapon. (50 LA 115)

Loan Sharking

At least one arbitrator has the opinion that the practice of loan-sharking is so undesirable that the offender can be fired without warning, even though there is no plant rule against it.

EXAMPLE: An employee with many years' service with a company decided to run a loan business on the side. Over a period of a year and a half he lent varying amounts of cash to fellow workers for vacations and other needs at a high rate of interest. Questioned by management officials he admitted that he netted 10 to 15 percent a week.

When the company fired the employee for violating a rule against "shameful and indecent conduct," the union protested. It didn't condone the employee's activities, but it pointed out that the company hadn't warned the employee before discharging him.

The arbiter thought the company was justified in firing the employee regardless of whether the company rule actually applied to such a situation. Moreover, he decided that it was unnecessary to give a warning in such a case. The evils of loan-sharking are too well known, and its adverse effect on employees too obvious to require that the usual disciplinary procedures be followed, he said. (Glenn L. Martin Co., 27 LA 768)

Political Activity on Company Property

In the absence of a definite written rule against it, can a worker be fired for carrying on political activity on company property? At least one arbiter has held that discharge was too severe for this kind of offense where most employees did not know that such activity was prohibited. (Four Wheel Drive Auto Co., 4 LA 170)

Firearms

A truck driver who was involved in

an accident was found to be carrying a loaded gun. The arbiter decided that discharge was not for just cause, as the company rule against gun-toting was never made clear to the workers or enforced. (American Synthetic Rubber Corp., 46 LA 1161; see also Philco Corp., 43 LA 568)

Failure To Report Accident

A trucking company was justified in firing a driver for failing to report an accident involving the truck he was driving, an arbiter ruled. Under causes for immediate discharge, the contract listed "failure to report an accident which the employee would normally be aware of." The evidence established beyond a reasonable doubt that this condition was fulfilled. (Maislin Bros. Transport, Ltd., 46 LA 527)

SUBVERSIVE ACTIVITY

Communism as Cause for Discharge

Can a worker be discharged if it is proved that he is, or has been accused of being, a member of the Communist Party? Some arbitrators have ruled that, if reports of an employee's Communist activities cause dissension and unrest in a plant, or result in bad publicity, the company has the right to fire the worker in the interests of business efficiency. These umpires agree that management should be free to take whatever action is necessary to protect its reputation. One upheld the discharge of a worker who was publicly accused of being a Communist, even though the charge was not proven.

On being fired, an employee took up the matter as a grievance under the contract. The union argued that it was unfair to fire a worker merely because charges were aired in a newspaper that he was a Communist; but the arbitrator held that this was not the issue. The issue was whether a company was obliged to keep a worker whose presence caused dissension and resentment in the plant.

"The rights of freedom of thought and of speech are valuable rights," the arbitrator held, "but no company

is under a duty to protect those rights at the sacrifice of its existence." If the charges were false, the arbitrator noted, the worker could go to court and collect damages. If true, the results were caused by the employee's voluntary actions, of whose consequences he should have been aware. (Jackson Industries, Inc., 9 LA 753)

However: Some arbitrators believe that an employer's right to discharge employees either for proven membership in the Communist Party or for mere suspected Communism should be more limited. One of these umpires ruled against the discharge of a worker based only on the company's belief that he was a Communist. He added that the power to judge whether persons are loyal to the United States rests solely with the federal government. (Consolidated Western Steel Corp., 13 LA 721)

Refusal to Testify on Communist Activities

If an employee refuses to answer questions about Communist activities asked by a congressional or other public investigating committee, can he be discharged? Arbitrators generally agree that it is justifiable to discharge a worker for this reason if the refusal tends to injure the company's reputation or to disrupt employee relations. (Burt Mfg. Co., 21 LA 532)

Another test arbiters use to decide whether discharge is justified in such cases is the sensitiveness of the job of the person refusing to testify. An arbitration panel approved the discharge of a newspaper rewrite man who invoked the Fifth Amendment when called to testify before a Senate subcommittee regarding past membership in the Communist Party. Because a rewrite man could do much harm by influencing the presentation of the news, the board said, his position was truly sensitive. The worker's refusal to testify raised doubts as to his connection with Communism, so his discharge was for good cause, the panel ruled. (N.Y. Mirror Div., Hearst Corp., 27 LA 548; See also Bethlehem Steel Co., 24 LA 852)

However: Some arbitrators have held that the refusal to testify about Communist activities is not ground for discharge. One found no proof that workers in nonsensitive jobs hurt the business merely because they refused to testify. (RCA Communications, Inc., 29 LA 567; see also J. H. Day Co., Inc., 22 LA 751; Westinghouse Electric Corp., 35 LA 315)

Distributing Communist Literature

Can a worker be discharged for distributing Communist literature on company property? If a lesser penalty ordinarily is imposed for literature distribution without permission, an arbitrator may hold that discharge is improper. (Spokane-Idaho Mining Co., 9 LA 749)

Discharge for KKK Activities

Threats of violence, boycott, and a wildcat strike justified the discharge of a publicly avowed Ku Klux Klan leader in order to avoid turning the employer's buses into "a battleground in the civil rights movement," an arbiter decided. He reasoned that the worker's conduct went beyond mere belief when he began preaching racial hatred and religious intolerance, and that this breached the worker's duty to foster friendly relations with the public. (Baltimore Transit Co., 47 LA 62)

Poor Work

In administering a disciplinary program, it frequently may be necessary to distinguish between carelessness or neglect of duty on the one hand and incompetence or faulty judgment on the other.

▶ Carelessness generally is regarded as willful misconduct and frequently results in reprimand, suspension, and the other standard forms of discipline.

▶ Incompetence, however, may stem from misunderstanding, lack of knowledge, or over-all or momentary inability to meet the requirements of the job. This may require retraining, transfer, demotion, or termination—remedies that are more corrective than punitive. If an employee is clearly incompetent, warnings and suspensions are pointless.

Many of the reversals of management decisions in this area have resulted from the company's not taking into account this distinction between carelessness, which is actually akin to misconduct, and incompetence, which is not within the employee's power to control—at least not without the help of retraining or reassignment.

Disability is treated much the same as incompetence. As a general rule, employees who become disabled should be discharged only as a last resort. Before taking such drastic action, the company should make an effort to transfer them to lighter work, most arbitrators hold. If this isn't possible, management should place them on layoff if it appears that the disability may not be permanent.

Incompetence

Incompetence, unlike carelessness, generally shouldn't be treated as a disciplinary problem, since the usual remedies of warnings and suspensions clearly are inappropriate and unproductive where the employee is in truth incompetent in the job he holds. If the employee is to be retained, the proper course of action might better be retraining, transfer, or demotion. (See the "Introduction" to this section on the distinction between incompetence and carelessness.)

While management clearly has the right to discharge a worker who is incompetent and has shown himself unable to meet reasonable standards of efficiency, discharge may seem harsh, particularly in large establishments where some job presumably could be found that would more nearly meet his abilities. It also is to the company's advantage in terms of expense and morale to retain the employee in a suitable job.

Where management resorts to the drastic remedy of discharge, arbitrators look for these elements in order to uphold the action:

▶ The charge of incompetency must be properly substantiated.

▶ The employee must have been given adequate warning and an opportunity to improve.

▶ The treatment of the employee must have been fair and nondiscriminatory.

_____ **GUIDELINES** _____

New Production Standards

Arbitrators agree in theory that management has the right to tighten work standards and require better performance, even if this is a break from a past practice of laxness. But to bring about such a reversal of past practice, management may have to do more than merely exhort employees to do better. Discipline of employees who continue to produce at the old standards may not be upheld if the new standards haven't been clearly defined and communicated to the employees. (8 LA 282, 12 LA 527)

Moreover, the production standard that is set must be reasonable. One arbitrator refused to uphold a discharge where no employee had been able to meet the standard for any extended period of time (40 LA 866).

Even where productivity standards are reasonable, d i s c h a r g e probably will be set aside if:

● The employee has not been specifically warned that his performance is inadequate.

● Other employees with equally poor records are not treated the same way.

● The employee shows substantial improvement after being warned.

● The poor work is due to inability, and there is work available that the employee can do.

EXAMPLE: An employee who had been fired as a shirt-presser was hired back as a towel-folder, a simpler job. Later, management persuaded her to take the shirt-presser job again contrary to her wishes and despite her protest that she couldn't meet the quota. Subsequently, she was warned to increase her output, and when this didn't work, she was fired.

In setting aside the discharge, the arbitrator said that when management virtually forced her to take the shirt-presser job the second time, it set a new production standard for her —her best effort. Therefore, it couldn't fire her for failing to meet the regular production standard. He did not require, however, that she be put back on the shirt-presser job. (Lanier Uniform Rental Service, 39 LA 130)

EXAMPLE: By a v e r a g i n g production records of all inspectors over a given period, a company established a standard of about nine orders per hour for the inspection job. An employee who was promoted to an inspector's job was returned to her old job when she was unable, after 10 weeks on the job, to do better than about 7.9 orders per hour.

An arbitrator ordered her put back on the inspector's job. Application of the standard in this case was unreasonable in that it was based on an average of the work of all inspectors and was applied to a new and inexperienced inspector. But defects also were found in the way the standard was set. An averaging standard is fraught with statistical distortion,

the arbiter said, unless controls are instituted, statistics are achieved, and the final production standard is properly weighted with the control statistics. (Magnetics, Inc. 51 LA 1280)

Veteran Workers

Arbitrators are particularly likely to consider discharge too harsh a penalty when applied to a long-time employee who is found incompetent in a new job. In this situation, most arbitrators feel that the employer should return the employee to his former job or transfer him to other work. (26 LA 682, 8 LA 861, 6 LA 593)

Where a demotion or transfer was not possible, one arbitrator decided that the employee should be placed on layoff subject to recall if a job for which he was qualified opened up. (10 LA 807) Discharge decisions have been upheld, however, where the employee refused a chance to return to his old job or to transfer to other work. (26 LA 598, 20 LA 551)

Arbitrators also are reluctant to uphold the dismissal of veteran workers from their old jobs, where it appears that the worker's problem stems from his "slowing down" due to age and that other work might be found for him.

EXAMPLE: A woman who had worked as a toll operator for a telephone company for 26 years was dismissed for continued errors after special training in an effort to bring her work up to snuff.

Though the rehabilitation efforts hadn't been fully successful, management had acted too precipitately in firing her, an arbitrator said. The company didn't have to take her back in her old job, he held, but it surely had work at an equivalent or lower grade that she was capable of performing.

Incompetence, u n l i k e deliberate failure to perform, is one of the least serious in the spectrum of disciplinary offenses, the arbitrator said. It doesn't justify summary banishment to the industrial ash heap of veteran workers who have literally "burnt themselves out" on the job. (Hawaiian Telephone Co., 44 LA 218)

EXAMPLE: A spray painter with 16 years' seniority was discharged for increasingly "carelessness." The discharge was set aside by an arbitrator who found that the employee had been a competent and conscientious employee in the past but had become increasingly unable to keep pace due to medical problems associated with advancing age. The fact that an employee has slowed down, the arbitrator said, doesn't justify capping off his career with a discharge for "carelessness," which carries with it connotations of wilful and wanton misconduct or a don't-care outlook.

He suggested that the parties should be able to devise sufficient flexibility in the assignment of job classifications for older employees to enable them to be shifted about so their physical powers match the requirements of the job. (Fawn Engineering Corp., 54 LA 839)

Probationary Periods

The right of management to discharge an employee for incompetence during a probationary period is unquestioned; that is what a probationary period is for. (40 LA 656)

But if an employee survives his probationary period, arbitrators generally will veto attempts by management to dismiss the employee as incompetent shortly after the trial period is up. If the employee had enough ability to survive the probationary period, a short disciplinary layoff or a warning is the proper penalty for subsequent indications of poor work, it is suggested. (5 LA 306, 10 LA 48, 49 LA 264)

On the other hand, survival of a probationary period is no guarantee of employment ever after. One arbitrator commented:

"The probation clause with regard to discharge simply means that after the probationary period the company shall be *responsible* for any discharge; that is to say, it may occasion a grievance . . . and must defend its acts on the basis of other parts of the contract." (12 LA 495)

Computing probationary period—In

the absence of contract language defining the probationary period, arbitrators tend to hold that it is measured in working, not calendar, days. (48 LA 143, 43 LA 773, 44 LA 301)

Inadequate Equipment or Training

One of the most common grounds for discharges for incompetence is that management has not given the employee proper equipment or adequate training. One arbitrator commented:

"I do not question the right of the company to discipline, discharge, and transfer to another job an employee who is unable to do efficient work. . . . I think, however, that as a prerequisite to taking such action, the company is under a duty to have its machinery and equipment in reasonably good condition so that the employees have a fair chance." (20 LA 854)

Thus, discharges have been set aside in these situations:

● Bad working conditions were present, which the arbitrator felt might have affected the discharged worker more than others. "Phlegmatic people are able to take things in their stride, while those of a nervous disposition may be very much upset," he observed. (20 LA 854)

● A combination of poor equipment and frequent transfers prevented the employee from ever getting really settled in a job. (8 LA 285)

Proof of Incompetence: Sales Records

Arbiters may be hesitant in approving discharges for inefficiency based on sales records. Unlike the output of most production workers, the work records of a salesman are subject to several factors beyond his control. These include different areas and customers, c o m p e t i t i o n, product changes, and prevailing business climate. Umpires agree that these other factors must be considered before using a poor sales record to justify a discharge. Where a company failed to show that a decline in ice cream sales was the driver-salesman's own fault, for instance, an umpire overruled his discharge. (Russell Creamery Co., 21 LA 293)

Carelessness

While management probably should not have a flat rule of "one serious error and you're out," it doesn't have to wait until the building is blown up or all materials are ruined before resorting to discharge of a careless worker. The decision in each case should be based on a careful consideration of the act and related factors. One arbitrator suggested that these points should be considered:

▶ The possibility of the act's recurrence.

▶ The attitude of the employee—his desire and ability to learn from the mistake.

▶ The actual and potential injury involved.

▶ The influence of the discipline on other employees.

▶ The effect of the mistake on the parties with whom the company deals, such as customers or the government.

▶ The employee's length of service. (37 LA 953)

GUIDELINES

Gross Negligence

To sustain a discharge for carelessness, management usually must be prepared to prove that the employee was guilty of gross negligence—that is, an almost willful disregard of what is being done and an almost complete inattentiveness to the job with the opportunity to foresee the likely consequences.

EXAMPLE: A machinist with a prior blemish-free record of 4½ years' employment made an error that cost the company $1,500 and, except for a fortuitous circumstance, could have caused a loss of several thousands of dollars in materials and an even greater amount for failing to complete the company's contract on time. In management's book, the mistake amounted to gross negligence— an offense serious enough to warrant immediate dismissal.

An arbitrator disagreed. The mistake, he noted, did not involve willfulness or recklessness or a wanton disregard for life, health, or property. It amounted to a good-faith oversight on a simple step in a complicated process.

Such a mistake is likely to happen to any person on any job, the umpire observed. And while serious, he said, it normally doesn't warrant discharge for a first offense. Considering the employee's past record, his honesty in reporting the mistake, and his tenure and sense of responsibility, the umpire felt that a two-week suspension would have been appropriate. (Ingalls Shipbuilding Corp., 37 LA 953)

Group Responsibility

It is sometimes difficult to say with absolute certainty just who is responsible for damage to company property through negligence. Arbiters, however, generally will require conclusive proof that an employee was at fault before they will uphold discipline against him.

In a case where $7,500 in damages resulted from the failure to perform an operation that usually was performed by one of two employees, an arbitrator overruled the company's suspension of both men. He came out strongly against holding an entire crew responsible for performing a task that management had not specifically assigned to any one individual. Such a practice would carry discipline to the extreme, he said, by permitting discipline of the group whenever individual responsibility could not be pinpointed. Responsibility for assigning duties and responsibilities rests with supervision, he noted. (44 LA 376)

Errors of Commission & Omission

A distinction sometimes is made between carelessness or negligence in the performance of a task and negligent failure to perform. In the latter instance, it has been held, an individual is at fault only if he was under a positive and affirmative duty to act.

For example, in the previously mentioned case where $7,500 in damages resulted from the failure to perform an assignment that usually was done by one of two employees, the arbitrator noted that one of them should have done the job, but it had not been made clear which one of them had the duty to act. (44 LA 376)

Accident-Prone Worker

Management has the right to discharge an employee who is "accident prone," an arbitrator has said, if it can show that the employee meets the definition of one who has "a greater number of accidents than would be expected of the average individual under the same conditions" or who has "personality traits that predispose to accident." But in the case before him, the arbitrator found that the worker was only prone to filing

insurance claims in instances in which other workers would have been satisfied with merely receiving first-aid treatment. In this situation, a warning against exaggerating accident reports would have been the proper approach, he suggested. (52 LA 325)

Another arbitrator has argued that industrial discipline, particularly the supreme penalty of discharge, should not be based on the notion that an employee is "accident prone." An employee may unluckily be involved in a series of accidents for which he is completely blameless, he observed. On the other hand, a person may act recklessly, and yet escape accidents.

The blameless, but unlucky, employee who has accidents shouldn't be disciplined, this arbitrator said, while the reckless, but accident-free, employee deserves discipline. Thus, the test is not whether the employee was involved in accidents, but whether he has been so careless or inefficient as to justify the conclusion that he is not a safe and competent employee. The reckless employee may be fired for a series of offenses, he reasoned, even though the last one, standing alone, wouldn't merit discharge. (38 LA 1109)

Arbitrators also are reluctant to disturb disciplinary penalties in accident cases if it means the return of an employee who may be dangerous to himself and others and where the legal and financial interests of the company are potentially at stake. Thus, one arbitrator observed, discharges generally have been upheld where such factors as the following were clearly present:

● Numerous accidents and/or poor past records (30 LA 213, 8 LA 837, 24 LA 48).

● Special factors such as transportation of dangerous loads (48 LA 953).

● Gross negligence or willful or wanton conduct.

On the other hand, the penalty of discharge has been set aside and reinstatement ordered (usually without back pay) under these circumstances:

- Negligence not conclusively shown (21 LA 457).
- No danger to the public (21 LA 457).
- Ordinary negligence (46 LA 1161, 30 LA 830)
- Special conditions, such as bad weather (36 LA 537). (Kaiser Sand & Gravel, 50 LA 571)

Payment for Carelessness

Can a worker be justly required to make good any loss caused by his own carelessness? Generally arbitrators have upheld a company's right to make and enforce rules requiring workers to pay for equipment or materials they lose or damage.

Under a contract permitting the company to c h a r g e a reasonable amount for protective clothing lost by workers, an umpire okayed the company's charging a worker for the third protective coat he had lost within a year. Even if the coat had been stolen from the worker's locker-room basket, the a r b i t e r found, it would have been due to his own carelessness. The company had not charged him for the first two replacements and it did not have to keep giving him the benefit of the doubt, the umpire ruled. (Bethlehem Steel Co., 28 LA 780)

Repeated Carelessness

If a worker is guilty of repeated acts of carelessness, none of which is sufficient, standing alone, to justify discharge, can he be fired on the basis of his whole record of careless acts? Generally arbitrators uphold management's right to discharge a worker who has a record of chronic carelessness over a period of time.

Where the umpire found that a company had been patient with a worker and had given him several warnings about his carelessness before discharging him, the discharge was approved. The incidents resulting from his poor work and the fact that

he ignored the warnings proved to the umpire that the worker was careless and inattentive to his job. (International Shoe Co., 32 LA 485)

Cause of Carelessness

According to some a w a r d s, it doesn't seem to matter much what caused a worker's carelessness. One arbiter decided that, where an employee had been given repeated warnings, discharge was justified even though his errors may have stemmed from pressing personal problems.

EXAMPLE: Over a period of six months, a worker with four years' seniority committed a series of costly production errors. His lapses, he maintained, were due to his bereavement at the passing of his parents within a short period prior to the onset of his poor performance. Nevertheless, the company fired him.

The umpire ruled that the errors established the worker's incompetence, whatever may have been the reasons underlying them, and this was the only factor management had to take into account. Since the worker had been r e p e a t e d l y and clearly warned and had failed to improve, the umpire concluded the discharge was for good cause. Whether the worker's personal troubles were to be given weight, and if so how much, were decisions for management to make, he added. (Table Products Co., 23 LA 217)

Failure to Follow Proper Procedure

Can a worker be disciplined for taking short cuts and ignoring precautions in performing his job? Ordinarily, if workers have been given clear instructions to do their job a certain way, arbitrators would probably permit their discipline when they fail to follow proper procedures. But where the company had not objected to a worker's taking short cuts, one arbiter nixed a suspension imposed on him for doing his job wrong.

EXAMPLE: On a construction project it was customary for the operating engineer loading dirt on a truck to signal the driver when the loading was completed. A driver who was stopped by a state trooper because his truck was overloaded was given a week's disciplinary layoff for negligence and insubordination. The company said that checking the load was the driver's responsibility, while the union maintained the driver merely got the go-ahead from the operating engineer. The driver remained in the truck, the union pointed out, and only the operating engineer was in a position to see how much dirt was in the box and to know how heavy it was. But the company insisted the proper procedure was for the driver to get out of the truck.

The arbitrator turned thumbs down on the penalty. The employee, he found, handled the job in the usual way; maybe management didn't think this was the right way, but over a period of time it had failed to object. The umpire concluded the company had no right to sit back and enjoy the benefits on a time-saving practice and then lower the boom the first time something went wrong. (Ken-Wal Construction Co., 30 LA 242)

Disability

In most cases involving physical disability, management's right to terminate, transfer, or lay off depends on whether it has good reason to believe the employee can't perform satisfactorily or without undue hazard to himself and his fellow workers. This in turn usually depends on an evaluation of medical evidence and work requirements and conditions. You should be prepared to support a decision in this area with substantial medical and other evidence.

The mere fact of disability may not be sufficient, especially if it has been of long standing. Witness these rulings—

▶ An arbitrator reinstated an employee who was "industrially blind," it appearing that he had made an amazing adjustment to his infirmity and had worked for years without mishap. (40 LA 799)

▶ Another arbitrator refused to permit a company to discharge an obese employee with high blood pressure and only one good eye, even though it previously had paid a $33,000 damage award to the family of an employee who had suffered a heart attack on the job. Although the discharge was on the company doctor's recommendation, the umpire found the employee was not a serious industrial risk. (41 LA 278)

▶ At least one arbitrator has held that it is up to the employee to decide whether to continue working with a bad heart, where there is little danger to others. (39 LA 918)

▶ An arbitrator told a company it "did the right thing in the wrong way" when it fired an obviously disabled employee from a hazardous job. It should have made use of a layoff procedure that would have allowed him to remain on the seniority roster until a job opened up that he could do. (40 LA 1266)

GUIDELINES

Medical Evidence

The issue in disability cases frequently centers on conflicting medical views as to the employee's condition and his ability to do the job. The general view seems to be that a company is entitled to rely on the opinions of its own doctors, as long as it gives the employee an opportunity to overcome those views before a final decision is reached. (20 LA 480)

Where there are differences between a company doctor's conclusion and the conclusions of an employee's doctor, an effort should be made to reconcile the difference by, for example, having the company doctor discuss the matter with the employee's doctor. (22 LA 138)

Where conflict persist, however, most consideration is given to the physician who has done the most extensive examination or who is more qualified in the treatment of the injury in question. (50 LA 1155)

Raised Physical Requirements

Can an employer stiffen the physical requirements for various jobs and then discharge employees who fail to meet them? Unless there is a definite change in the nature or conditions of a job, a worker may not be discharged for failing to meet physical requirements which are higher than those he met when he was hired for the job, according to most arbiters.

One company, suspecting that poor eyesight on the part of some employees was causing a lot of defective work, set up a new vision-testing program. In some cases, the visual requirements for jobs were raised. Several workers couldn't pass the new tests for their jobs and were discharged.

The arbitrator decided that the discharges weren't for good cause under the contract. He ruled that the workers could retain their jobs as long as they continued to meet the standards in effect at the time they were hired. He noted that in no case were the job requirements changed so as to make higher standards necessary. (Connecticut Telephone & Electric Corp., 22 LA 632)

NOTE: The arbitrator suggested, however, that there was nothing to prevent the company from applying higher visual standards to future placements.

Discharge of Potential WC Claimant

Can a worker be discharged on the ground that his medical history indicates he is likely to become disabled in the future and make the company liable for workmen's compensation? A discharge for such a reason probably would not be upheld.

EXAMPLE: A truck driver stopped working after five years because of pains in his back and drew benefits under a contractual health and welfare plan. The pains, it was found, resulted from a congenital malformation of his lower spine. After a period of treatment, he applied for reinstatement, but the company turned him down. It claimed it had no obligation to risk the possibility of future absenteeism and claims for workmen's compensation.

An umpire held that the risk to the company was outweighed by the worker's interest in his job, which he had performed competently over a period of years. There was no certainty, he pointed out, that the worker would have further trouble with his back. Even if he did, his condition wouldn't pose an immediate hazard either to himself or to other employees, the arbiter commented. Finally, he noted, the worker's doctor had stated that he could safely return to truck driving. (Bethlehem Steel Co., 29 LA 476)

Insurance Costs

In some instances, a company's insurance company may object to the continued employment of a disabled employee or may threaten to raise its premiums substantially if the employee is retained. These cases frequently involve the employment of truck drivers with handicaps.

Presented with the question of whether insurability at normal rates was an implied condition of a truck driver's continued employment, an arbitrator held that it was such a condition. He said that an employer has the right to expect that it will not be exposed to unreasonable risk or expense in the employment relationship. But he also said that management was under a continuing obligation to give the disabled employee any available work that did not involve an insurance problem. (44 LA 1274)

At least one other arbiter has indicated that management is not obligated to pay substantially more for insurance to accommodate a handicapped employee. (37 LA 629)

But another arbitrator disagreed, however, ruling that the insurance carrier shouldn't be permitted to dictate which employees should be fired and for what reasons. This would make the negotiated restrictions on discipline v i r t u a l l y meaningless, he said. (45 LA 217)

Obesity

Where marked obesity is accompanied by high blood p r e s s u r e or other attendant physical conditions that affect an employee's physical fitness for work, arbitrators have upheld management's denial of that work. (37 LA 456, 43 LA 61) One arbitrator held that a company properly denied promotion to a more strenuous job to a senior employee who was 5' 9" tall, weighed 296 pounds, and had a blood pressure of 180/120. (37 LA 1048)

But where the overweight condition hasn't interfered with an employee's work in the past, an employer may not say "You're too fat for me." Thus, an employee with 22 years of service was ordered reinstated, despite her obesity and high blood pressure, where her condition hadn't affected her job performance. (46 LA 719)

Another arbitrator held that a company improperly denied reinstatement to two women on the ground that their obesity was deleterious to their health. The company's concern for their health should not be converted into "an essentially paternalistic attempt to regulate an employee's personal life," he said. A like disqualification, he noted, could be levied against cigarette smokers on the theory that smoking may result in short windedness that could impair employee efficiency.

But the arbiter upheld the company in refusing to reinstate one of the women who suffered from nervousness, hypertension, and dizzy spells, as well as obesity. (48 LA 2)

Mental Illness

Although recognizing a company's natural hesitancy about reemploying a person who has a mental illness that may be of recurrent nature, arbitrators have refused to uphold discharges where there was medical evidence that the employee had recovered to the extent that his return to work would not involve an undue risk to him or to others. Management may not assume that such a risk exists from the bare fact than an employee has been treated for mental illness. (28 LA 333, 26 LA 295)

In cases involving immoral or socially reprehensible conduct resulting from mental illness, arbitrators may direct reinstatement on evidence that the illness has been cured. But these awards have been based in part on the assuances that the employee's fellow workers have no objection to his reinstatement. (24 LA 229, 22 LA 1, 15 LA 42)

Epileptics

In several cases involving the employment of epileptics, arbitrators have ruled against discharge merely because of the existence of the disability if there was no clear evidence of a safety hazard. (12 LA 9, 15 LA 903, 20 LA 266, 38 LA 829)

But a discharge was upheld where the employee had several seizures at work which resulted in injury to him, and the employee himself conceded that medication was not successful in his case in controlling the seizures. (40 LA 18)

A company was upheld by an arbiter in refusing to let an employee who had suffered epileptic seizures return to his former job, even though medical evidence indicated his condition was under control.

The employee had been a lineman for a utility company when he began having seizures. After lengthy treatment, he was cleared by his physician to return to his former job. The company doctor, however, believed he would still be a "hazard", so he was kept in the lower-rated job.

While conceding that medical evidence showed the employee was physically able to perform lineman's work the arbiter upheld the company's decision not to put the employee back on a job that involved unusual hazards. (Gulf States Utilities Co., 45 LA 1252)

Calculating Seniority

IN BRIEF

An employee's relative seniority status in the company usually depends on three basic considerations—when seniority begins to accumulate, the effect of changes in work assignments on seniority, and the effect of interruptions in employment on seniority.

These factors are discussed, with examples of their application, in this section.

GUIDELINES

STARTING DATE FOR SENIORITY

In the absence of language to the contrary, most arbitrators hold that seniority begins to accumulate from date of hiring rather than from the later date the contract went into effect. Problems may arise, however, where formerly separate operations are merged or new businesses are acquired.

Original Hiring Date

Seniority normally is regarded as beginning with the date of hire, not the date on which seniority rights were won.

EXAMPLE: Vacation rights, based on seniority, were established to take effect on May 1, 1963. Employees' length of service for vacation purposes must be computed from the date of employment by the company, an arbitrator held, rather than from May 1, 1963. (National Printing Co., 43 LA 768)

Change of Ownership

To what extent do seniority rights survive a change in ownership? If a new owner simply takes over from the former owner, the employees usually will retain their seniority rights based on their original dates of hire. But a more difficult situation is created where the change in ownership is accompanied by a merger of the newly acquired company with an existing unit of employees.

Some arbiters feel that it would be unfair to the new owner's other employees if those in the newly acquired operation carried their seniority rights intact during a merger of operations. Other arbiters are equally insistent that it would be unfair to strip the workers at the newly acquired facility of seniority rights they've earned over the years. Some arbitrators have tried to dovetail seniority rights in the interest of fair play for both groups of workers.

EXAMPLE: Going by the letter of the sales contract, under which he agreed to assume the labor obligations of the seller, the buyer honored all accrued seniority rights of the seller's work force. But the union that represented the buyer's own work force argued that equity dictated an arrangement whereby the seller's workers would retain, at most, one half their accrued seniority.

On employee benefits, the arbiter decided, the purchase agreement obligated the buyer to honor full seniority. But on competitive status, he added, a full-seniority transfer would work an unfair advantage on the buyer's own workers. To balance these considerations, the arbiter fashioned this formula:

● The seller's workers retain full benefit seniority, governing such matters as pensions and vacations.

● Those who transfer with two or more years' seniority retain one-half their accrued competitive-status seniority, governing such matters as layoffs and promotions.

● Those who transfer with less seniority go to the bottom of the merged competitive - status seniority list. (Country Belle Cooperative Farmers, 48 LA 600)

Seniority in Plant Merger

When a company merges two plants having separate seniority lists, on what basis should a single new seniority list be established? Should length of service govern, or should the workers' relative positions on the separate lists be the determining factor? One arbitrator decided these two factors should have equal weight.

The umpire reasoned that going by length of service alone would be unfair to workers in the plant where length of service was relatively low; for instance, a five-year man in that plant might drop from a near-top position on the old seniority list to a middle position on the combined list, while a five-year man in the other plant might climb from a near-bottom position to a middle one. By the same token, dovetailing the two lists according to workers' relative positions on the separate lists would be unfair to those in the plant where length of service was relatively high.

The umpire's solution was to set up two numerical lists—one based on length of service, the other on position on the separate seniority lists. Then he figured what each worker's average position was on the two lists, and this determined the worker's position on the combined seniority list. (Moore Business Forms, Inc., 24 LA 793)

Another arbiter decided that the most equitable method for determining seniority was to make a pool of the combined jobs resulting from a pool of the combined jobs resulting from a merger, with each group getting a proportionate share of it. In the case at hand, the transferred work accounted for 41.3 percent of the surviving jobs, or 70 percent of what the transferred workers had contributed before the merger. Thus, the arbiter credited the transferred workers with seven-tenths of their seniority at the midpoint date of the transfers. (Sonotone Corp., 42 LA 359)

Under a multi-employer agreement that confined seniority rights to the worker's "plant," an arbiter gave seniority preference to workers in relation to the types of operations they formerly performed at two merged plants. Those whose work was similar at both plants should be assigned from both seniority lists in the proportion that such workers at each plant bore to the total number of workers at both plants, he directed. (Superior Products Co., 42 LA 517.)

Seniority of Employees Hired Same Day

Most arbitrators are of the opinion that employees hired on the same day should have equal seniority. In one case a union urged that where employees had been hired on the same day, seniority should have been computed according to the order of their physical examination. The arbiter ruled that to compute seniority in units of less than one day was contrary to established practice. (Standard Oil Co. of Ind., 3 LA 758)

Tossing a coin may be the only way of resolving a dispute involving two workers with equal seniority, and this is exactly what one arbiter told the parties to do. The contract fixed seniority "from the date of issuance of the union card." Two women were transferred into the unit on the same day and were issued union cards on the same day. Since both women enjoyed the same seniority rights, the arbiter arrived at the coin toss as the most equitable method for deciding which one would be laid off. (McCall Corp., 49 LA 183)

However: In one case where two employees came to work on the same day, one arbitrator resolved the seniority question this way: Since one employee came to work on the first shift and the other on the second shift, the arbitrator ruled that the first employee had the greater seniority. He added that if both employees had started work on the same shift, the next best answer would have been to refer to their respective "clock-in" times. (Robertshaw-Fulton Controls Co., 22 LA 273)

Long-Delayed Challenge of Seniority Listing

Arbitrators differ as to how long an employee retains the right to challenge his standing on the seniority list. Many contracts limit the period during which an employee may challenge his seniority standing. If there is no such restriction, though, one arbitrator has said that an employee has a right to complain about the continuation of an error in the list at any time.

EXAMPLE: A Company gave a man credit for too much seniority in his department, and the error went unchallenged for nine years. Then another employee filed a grievance asking that the error be corrected, thus moving him up a notch on the seniority list. The company rejected his request on the basis of a contract provision stating that grievances must be filed within 30 days of the occurence of the events involved.

The umpire said that the time limit didn't apply in this situation. If it was a contract violation to give a man extra seniority credit in the past, he reasoned, it was a violation to continue giving him the extra credit. Thus any employee who was adversely affected by the error had the right to demand that it be corrected, he said.

The umpire ruled, however, that correction of the seniority list didn't give the employer any claim to wages he had lost as a result of the incorrect listing over the nine-year period and that the preference given to the other employee in the matters of promotion, demotion, and layoffs was beyond challenge. (Bethlehem Steel Co., 23 LA 538)

On the other hand: One umpire had held that if a posted seniority has gone unquestioned for a long period of time, errors cannot be corrected even though there is no "statute of limitations" in the contract. (Creamery Package Mfg. Co., 31 LA 917)

Worker's Right to Challenge Seniority of Others

Does a contract which permits a worker to file a girevance if his seniority date is listed incorrectly allow him to challenge the seniority dates of other employees?

Such a clause doens't bar an employee from filing a grievance over the seniority date of another employee, one arbitrator has ruled, where employees have the right to file grievances over the interpretation and application of the contract. If a contract describes the method of computing seniority, the arbitrator stated, the incorrect listing of a seniority date is a contract violation which any employee can protest. (Republic Steel Corp., 18 LA 907)

Responsibility for a Seniority-List Error

When a company prepares a seniority roster and gives the union a copy which is to be considered final and binding on both parties, who is responsible if the list is in error?

According to one arbiter, the union wasn't jointly responsible for such an error. The rule that the list was final and binding applied only to a correct list, he ruled. Since the company had the sole responsibility for preparing the list, it also had the sole responsibility for any errors. Bethlehem Fabricators, Inc., 41 LA 6)

UNITS FOR SENORITY

Seniority units are defined by the collective agreement, either specifically or by interpretation. A seniority unit may be company-wide, multi-company, or departmental. Or it may be used upon the bargaining unit, or upon an occupational group or classification, or upon a combination of these groups.

Moreover, seniority rights may be acquired in one unit and exercised in another. For example, seniority may be based on service in the company, but its exercise may be limited to the employee's particular department. Similarly, seniority rights may be used upon different units for different aspects of the employment relations. For instance, departmental seniority may prevail for layoff and recalls, while company-wide seniority determines vacation and pension rights.

Where Unit Isn't Specified

If the seniority unit isn't clearly specified, arbitrators are inclined to assume that company-wide seniority was intended, particularly if this accords with operational efficiency.

EXAMPLE: A contract specified that "accepted rules of seniority" shall apply to layoff and that acquisition of seniority would begin on the first day of employment, regardless of classification. Company-wide seniority was held to govern. If, as urged by the union, classification seniority were to apply, the employer would lose the flexibility afforded by the contract, due to the seasonal nature of the work and the varied skills of the employees. (Great Lakes Homes, Inc., 44 LA 737)

CHANGES IN WORK ASSIGNMENTS

Where seniority is not on a company-wide or bargaining-unit basis, provision must be made for employees who transfer from one seniority unit to another. Under the most restrictive approach, the employee loses his seniority in his old job, starts from scratch in his new one. More often, however, the employee retains or even accumulates seniority in his old job—at least for a long enough period to afford protection in case he doesn't work out in the new job. A third approach permits the employee to carry seniority previously acquired over to the new job.

In the absence of contract clauses specifying the seniority rights of employees who are promoted to supervisory positions, arbitrators are divided on the seniority status of such employees when they later are demoted and returned to the bargaining unit. Some arbitrators have held that supervisors continue to accumulate seniority after promotion unless the contract specifically state otherwise (43 LA 228, 34 LA 285, 31 LA 137, 25 LA 595). Other arbitrators, however, have ruled that seniority is strictly a contractual right and may not be accumulated after promotion (32 LA 892, 31 LA 859, 31 LA 200). Still others have held that an employee forfeits all his seniority when promoted because he in effect has voluntarily resigned from the unit (27 LA 30, 26 LA 898, 40 LA 388).

There is more apparent agreement among arbitrators that supervisors who have never been in the unit are entitled to no seniority credit or demotion (41 LA 583, 33 LA 150, 32 LA 274, 29 LA 828).

INTERRUPTION IN EMPLOYMENT

Layoffs & Leaves—Seniority generally is retained or accumulated, at least to some extent, where absence is due to illness, layoff, or other leave of absence. But does an employee retain his seniority where he takes a job with another employer? On arbitrator ruled that other employment during a leave of absence does not terminate seniority in the absence of a clause forbidding the taking of outside work (Goodyear Tire & Rubber Co., 5 LA 234) Another arbitrator ruled, however, that an employee may not accumulate seniority simultaneously with two employers and that an employee forfeited his employee status during a layoff by working for another company. (Fairchild Engine & Airplane Corp., 3 LA 873)

Military Leave—Seniority always accumulates during leave for military service, since this is required by the law governing reemployment rights of veterans. (See 209:475.)

A union contract that went further than the legal requirement and gave seniority credit for time in military service prior to employment with the company was upheld by the U.S. Supreme Court. The Court rejected the contention that such a grant of seniority credit was an abuse of the union's duty of fair representation. (Ford Motor Co. v. Huffman, 31 LRRM 2548)

Effect of Unauthorized Absence on Seniority

If an employee has a good reason for being absent, most arbitrators will protect his accumulated seniority even though his absence is unauthorized—unless, of course, the contract specifically provides for forfeiture.

EXAMPLE: An employee was absent for one week without permission at Christmas time. On his return the company claimed it was rehiring the employee so that his seniority would date from the day of rehire.

The union argued that the company could deprive an employee of his seniority only for absence without good cause. It claimed the employee's reason for being absent—to buy a home for his mother—was a good one, and the company should have granted leave when requested.

The arbitrator agreed with the company that granting or denial of leave was a management prerogative which could not be questioned unless company action was unreasonable or discriminatory to the individual involved. However, in this case the arbitrator ruled that since the absence was for good cause there should be no break in the employee's seniority. (Pittsburgh Metallurgical Co., Inc., 12 LA 95)

Loss of Superseniority

When leaving office, does a union official have the right to retain a job from which he normally would have been bumped during his term of office if the contract had not allowed him superseniority? At least one arbitrator has held that a union official's superseniority and the rights it obtained for him end the moment he leaves office. There was no reason, the arbiter held, why benefits and privileges that a union official acquires by virtue of his super-seniority should continue after he's out of office. (Rockwell Spring & Axle Co., Wisconsin Axle Div., 25 LA 174)

PROBATIONARY & TEMPORARY EMPLOYEES

Termination of Probationary Status

Where an employee is serving a probationary period and that period is defined as a certain number of working days, one arbiter has said, he achieves status as a regular employee the moment he clocks out on the last day of his trial period.

EXAMPLE: Under the provisions of one company's contract, all new employees had to serve a 30-day probationary period before they could become regular employees and begin to accrue seniority. During that period the company could fire an employee without being subject to the contract's "just cause" restriction. One employee clocked out on his thirtieth day of work and received a telegram that evening notifying him that he was discharged for being unsuited for the job. The union insisted that the employee had become a regular

employee at the time he left work and was therefore covered by the "just cause" provision of the contract. The umpire agreed, noting that since seniority began to accrue at the conclusion of the probationary period, full status as an employee was also achieved at that time. (Lyon, Inc., 24 La 353)

Time Not counted in Computing Probationary Period

In determining when a new employee completes his probationary period and thus acquires seniority status, should time lost from work because of illness or other reasons be counted as probation time? Similarly, should a rehired probationer get credit for his earlier term of employment in figuring when his probationary period ends?

Seemingly small variations in contract language may make all the difference in determining the answer to this question. Thus, where the contract stated that an employee would be considered on probation "for the first month of his employment," an umpire held that an employee who worked nearly a month, was discharged, then was rehired 17 days later and worked another three weeks had completed her probationary period. The purpose of a probationary period, he reasoned, is to give the company a chance to make sure an employee is satisfactory. In this case, since the periods of employment were separated by only 17 days, the umpire figured the company had had a chance to judge the employee's suitability. (Kreisler Industrial, 27 LA 134)

Where the contract defined the probationary period in terms of "continuous employment," on the other hand, an arbiter said the company could require a rehired probationer to serve a complete new probationary period. (Armstrong Cork Co., 23 LA 366) Similarly, where the agreement said an employee would be on probation until he'd "performed work" on 30 days within any three-month period, an umpire held that days on which an employee had been sent home because of bad weather could be discounted in figuring his probationary period. It might have been different, the umpire noted, if the agreement had stated the probationary period in terms of time employed. (Bethlehem Steel Co., 27 LA 300)

Seniority of Transferred Probationer

The fact that a worker was transferred out of the bargaining unit during his probationary period didn't change his seniority date, according to one arbitrator. He based his award on the fact that the probation clause of the contract did not bar the accumulation of seniority during time spent outside the bargaining unit. Seniority, the arbitrator concluded, is a vested right that can not be set aside except in accordance with specific contract language. (Muskegon Piston Ring Co., 29 LA 220)

Order of Layoff

*IN BRIEF*_____

Broadly speaking, layoff procedures fall into three categories—(1) layoffs are based solely on seniority; (2) seniority determines the order of layoff, assuming the senior employees can do the available work; and (3) seniority governs only if ability or other factors are equal. Applying procedures in the first category usually poses no serious problem; but procedures in the other two categories are fruitful sources of grievances.

Among other problems discussed in this section are those relating to the exceptions made to seniority rules and those presented by layoffs for brief periods of time.

_____GUIDELINES_____

SENIORITY V. ABILITY

Contract Requiring Equal Ability

If a contract states that seniority shall govern in layoff where ability is "equal," an arbitrator is likely to hold that this means "relatively or substantially equal," not "exactly equal." Ability, umpires reason, cannot be measured precisely.

In one case an arbitrator ruled that an employer violated the contract by retaining a junior mechanic and laying off a senior one on the ground that he was not equal in skill and ability because he had never worked on certain machines that the junior man had. The arbiter stated that, as a general rule, employees within the same classification should be deemed to have relatively equal ability and skill for layoff purposes, especially when their duties are the same. In view of this, he ruled, the senior employee should have been the one retained. (Poloron Products of Pa., 23 LA 789)

Management's Right to Determine Ability

Under contracts making seniority govern in layoffs when ability is equal, most arbitrators believe that it is up to management to determine employees' ability. They say that a union can question a company's judgment, but it has the burden of proving that management was either wrong, discriminatory, or capricious in its decision. (Merrill-Stevens Dry Dock & Repair Co., 6 LA 838; Combustion Engineering Co., 9 LA 515; Bethlehem Steel Co., 10 LA 284)

However: Some arbitrators have placed the burden of proof on the employer. They have held that management must give definite evidence that a junior employee clearly and demonstrably has greater ability in order to retain him in preference to a more senior worker. (Flexonics Corp., 24 LA 869)

Further: A company decided to lay off a senior man with a low efficiency rating, based on a report which compared the relative efficiency of workers in a department. Because this was the first instance of the use of tests, the arbiter held that they were improper. They could be used in the future, however, provided (1) the ratings conform with rules that are the

90

norm for such procedures and (2) the workers are told about management's intentions. (McEvoy Co., 42 LA 41)

Factors in Measuring Qualifications

When contracts make seniority controlling in layoffs if qualifications are relatively equal, what factors should be taken into account in determining employees' qualifications? Arbitrators' awards suggest these guides:

(1) Where a contract said seniority would govern if "ability to perform the work" was relatively equal, the only thing that should be measured was the ability to perform the particular job at stake. (Bethlehem Steel Co., 24 LA 820)

(2) Where a contract said seniority would govern provided ability and skill were relatively equal, a junior worker could be retained on a job in preference to a senior worker who required a much greater amount of supervision in performing the job. (Copco Steel & Engineering Co., 12 LA 6)

Use of Merit-Rating Plan

Under a contract making seniority controlling in layoffs only if ability and skill are approximately equal, can a merit-rating plan be used in determining ability and skill? At least one arbitrator permitted an employer to base ability measurements on a unilateral merit-rating plan. He ruled that the plan could be used because it included factors properly related to measurement of ability and skill, and there was no evidence that the factors were rated incorrectly. (Merrill-Stevens Dry Dock & Repair Co., 17 LA 516)

On the other hand: Where a merit-rating plan utilized such factors as cooperation, safety habits, personal habits, and attitude toward superiors, another umpire ruled that the company could not use it to determine workers relative ability for purposes of layoff. Since these factors were not the same as ability to perform a job, he reasoned, the plan was an unfair measure of ability. (Western Automatic Machine Screw Co., 9 LA 606)

EXCEPTIONS TO SENIORITY IN LAYOFFS

Exceptions often are made to the strict application of seniority in layoffs. The most common exceptions are:

▶ Superseniority granted to union stewards and other representatives to assure that workers remaining on the job during a layoff will continue to have union representation.

▶ Superseniority rights accorded to management to permit it to select key employees for retention during a layoff without regard to the usual seniority rules. Management-designated employees—sometimes equal in number to union representatives with superseniority—may be exempted from the operation of seniority. Employees with special skills who cannot be spared without impairing efficiency also may be exempted.

▶ The lack of any seniority rights for probationary employees, permitting management to designate individual probationers for layoff without regard to their hiring dates.

Superseniority to Union Representatives

Under a union contract giving top seniority on a plant-wide basis to the chairman of the union's shop committee, must management retain him when there is no work available for him and the company has retained only a few bargaining unit employees?

Many arbitrators say that under such an all-inclusive clause the union representative must be kept on the job as long as even one bargaining unit employee is still working.

In one case arising under such a clause, the arbitrator held that a shop chairman clearly had top seniority rights in the entire shop under all circumstances. He said that the superseniority given union representatives under collective agreement is not related to their functions as productive workers but stems from their special status in administering the agreement. (Freed Radio Corp., 9 LA 55)

However: A company was allowed to reduce the workweek of union officers who held superseniority. The arbitrator found that the employer merely was staggering his work schedule to spread available jobs among the work force, which did not constitute a layoff despite the reduced hours. (Wilcox Crittenden Co., 43 LA 1046)

When Representatives Are Unable to Do the Work

Under the contract that gives top departmental seniority to shop stewards and also, in another article, provides that seniority applies in layoffs if employees are able to do required work, do shop stewards have the right to be retained even if they can't do the work? Most arbitrators have held that union representatives must be kept on regardless of their ability so long as other employees are still working in their departments. The purpose of a superseniority clause, they have noted, is to protect union representation during reductions in force. If stewards were laid off before

other employees, the clause would be nullified and the purpose would be defeated, these umpires have observed. (Luders Marine Construction Co., 2 LA 622)

On the other hand: Other arbitrators have decided that all sections of a contract article must be read together to determine the intent of the parties. So where a contract within the same article provides for superseniority for shop stewards and then limits the application of seniority by the ability factor, it is all right to lay off shop stewards who cannot perform required work. (Roberts-Gordon Appliance Corp., 8 LA 1030; see also United States Time Corp., 23 LA 379)

Rights of Alternate Union Officers

According to one umpire, superseniority for union stewards does not extend to their alternates. The arbiter decided one company had a right to lay off an alternate union committeeman on the ground that the benefits attached to the position rather than the worker, and alternates weren't covered by the superseniority clause. There was nothing wrong with the company's extending the benefits to alternates if it wished, he said, but the union did not have the right to insist upon such extension. (Kidde Manufacturing Co., 40 LA 328)

Superseniority No Guarantee of Particular Job

Under a contract giving stewards top seniority in the area in which they serve, is a steward entitled to retain his particular job during a force reduction?

Many arbitrators have held that a clause of this type simply gives a steward preferred seniority in the area which he serves—a division, a department or the plant. It doesn't give him the right to remain in his own job. (Deere & Co., 18 LA 780; National Malleable & Steel Castings Co., 13 LA 628; Clark Grave Vault Co., 17 LA 291)

Superseniority for Employee with No Regular Seniority

Under a contract that permitted an employer to grant superseniority to a certain number of employees of its own choosing, one arbitrator ruled that an employee who had no regular seniority was not disqualified for such superseniority.

EXAMPLE: One contract provided that an employee acquired seniority after he had worked 30 days. It also allowed the company to retain on its "working force" a certain number of employees "without regard to their seniority." When management laid off one man with seniority while keeping another who had not yet worked 30 days, the union protested; superseniority, it argued, could not be given to a worker who had no seniority at all.

The umpire, though, sided with the company. The employee, he pointed out, was a member of the work force even though he hadn't worked 30 days. In the umpire's opinion the phrase, "without regard to their seniority" meant that seniority was not a factor at all. (Bethlehem Steel Co., 28 LA 808)

Worker with Security Clearance

Can seniority rules be deviated from in order to retain a junior worker with security clearance where government-contract work requires such clearance? One umpire held that a company could not do this in a case where it was responsible for the fact that only the junior worker had been cleared.

The company had full knowledge of its contractual obligations, he said, and could have avoided the problem if it had obtained clearance for the senior worker instead of the junior one. The only way the company could have got around its "self-imposed predicament," the umpire suggested, would have been to lay off somebody

who had not yet achieved seniority status. Then it could have assigned the senior worker to that job, at his regular wage rate, until his security clearance came through. (Webcor, Inc., 32 LA 490)

Layoff Order for Probationers

Under most contracts, probationers must be held laid off before employees with seniority are dropped. Within this framework, arbitrators usually have said that probationers do not have to be laid off in any specific order. In cases where unions have questioned management's procedure in laying off such employees, the arbitrators have held that it need not have been according to length of service because the new employees had acquired no seniority. (Goodyear Clearwater Mills, 6 LA 760; Pee Dee Textile Co., Inc., 14 LA 963)

Layoff of Probationary Apprentices

Under a special apprenticeship agreement, one arbitrator has taken the position that an apprentice is immune to ordinary reductions in force even if he is still on probation. He reasoned that it would frustrate the purpose of apprenticeship to make any apprentice subject to layoff by seniority in the absence of such a requirement in the agreement. (California Metal Trades Assn., 27 LA 105)

Layoff of Handicapped Employee

Under a contract giving handicapped employees transfer rights regardless of seniority, do they have any special protection against layoff? One arbitrator ruled that once a handicapped worker had exercised his special privilege of transferring without regard to seniority, he had no further special protection. Unless the contract specifically provides otherwise, the umpire said, handicapped employees must be treated just like other employees during a layoff. (John Deere & Co., 22 LA 383)

TEMPORARY v. INDEFINITE LAYOFFS

For temporary or emergency layoffs, management often is allowed more leeway in selecting employees than in the case of indefinite layoffs.

In the absence of contract clauses making layoff rules inapplicable to temporary layoffs, some arbitrators have held that ordinary layoff procedures must be followed even where the lack of work lasted only a few hours (21 LA 400, 30 LA 441) or one or two days. (5 LA 24, 7 LA 308) The more common view, however, is that the frequently cumbersome seniority rules needn't be followed in the case of a brief temporary layoff. (4 LA 533, 12 LA 763, 41 LA 970, 43 LA 1092)

In the case of layoffs caused by emergency breakdowns or other conditions beyond the control of the employer, arbitrators generally have upheld disregard of seniority rules applicable in the case of ordinary layoffs. Examples include (1) a three-day layoff due to an acute gas shortage (8 LA 807); (2) a temporary shutdown caused by a breakdown in equipment (31 LA 93); and (3) an eight-day layoff due to heavy snowfall. (8 LA 506)

But where it wasn't shown that application of seniority rules would cause a hardship, an arbitrator ruled that seniority should have been followed during an emergency layoff. He found nothing in the contract to authorize the company's unilaterally established rule that layoffs did not include periods of less than three days. (40 LA 1115)

Temporary Layoffs for Taking Inventory

Does layoff for the purpose of taking inventory have to follow seniority provisions? Arbitrators have ruled both ways on this question. Some have said that seniority must be applied to any period of slack work, no matter what the reason.

EXAMPLE: A company closed down its plant for two days to take inventory. Certain production employees were called in to assist but the selections were not all made in accordance with seniority. The contract was silent on the exact point but did provide that seniority would govern in case of layoffs.

The question here was whether the shutdown constituted a layoff subject to seniority. The arbitrator ruled that the shutdown actually "constituted a slack work period resulting in layoffs of employees within the meaning of the agreement." Therefore seniority had to be considered, and the company erred in laying off men with more seniority than some of the employees put to work to take inventory. (Warren City Mfg. Co., 7 LA 202)

On the other hand: In another case an arbitrator held that a shutdown for inventory purposes was only a temporary cessation of operations and not really a layoff. Therefore, he said, management could select any people it wanted to help take inventory, and the remainder of the working force could be laid off without regard to seniority. (Caterpillar Tractor Co., 7 LA 555)

Layoff Notice & Pay

Various problems may arise when a company agrees to give either advance notice of layoff or pay in lieu of notice, but most center around two main issues. These are (1) whether management is excused from both notice and pay under particular circumstances, and (2) the form of the notice and to whom it should be given.

Some contracts provide for payment of a separation allowance to employees who are laid off or who lose their jobs for other reasons. Problems in this area also are taken up in this section.

GUIDELINES

If a contract requires advance notice of layoffs, arbitrators generally hold that a layoff notice must be clear and specific and directed to the individual attention of the employees affected. Thus, one arbitrator ruled that a notice requirement wasn't met by an employer's repeatedly telling a union at their regular joint meetings that there was a possibility of a layoff. (Phillip's Waste Oil Pick-Up & Road Oiling Service, Inc., 24 LA 136)

Similarly, a general notice to the union of an impending layoff without identifying those to be laid off doesn't satisfy a requirement of written notice in advance of a layoff. The purpose of an advance notice requirement is to give employees a chance to look for other work, so the employer is required to list those employees to be affected. (Donaldson Co., 21 LA 254)

Exceptions for emergencies—Many contracts require notice in advance of layoff except in emergencies. What is considered an emergency? Such occurrences as machine breakdowns, fire, and inclement weather generally are recognized as circumstances beyond management's control. Other situations which have been looked upon by arbitrators as emergencies outside of management's control and therefore excusing the failure to provide advance notice include (1) a strike affecting supplies, (2) an unforeseen materials shortage, (3) snowstorms and (4) unforeseen business or financial crisis. (5 LA 295, 12 LA 726, 49 LA 1140, 50 LA 290)

If a contract doesn't provide for exceptions to a layoff notice requirement, is management still bound to give notice or pay except in emergencies? Arbitrators have ruled both ways on this. Some have held that in the absence of a written exception in the contract, employers must meet notice requirements even in emergencies. (18 LA 227, 29 LA 706) But other arbitrators have taken the view that a clause requiring notice applies only to situations where management reasonably can given notice—and management is not obligated for pay in lieu of notice when an emergency prevents it from giving notice. (14 LA 134)

Receipt of Notice Required

Under a contract stating that an employee "shall receive" advance notice of a layoff, one arbitrator has ruled that merely "sending" a notice was not enough to relieve the employer of reporting-pay liability.

EXAMPLE: A company sent telegrams to employees who were being laid off. One employee didn't get the word, although he was at home at the time it should have been delivered. He reported for work as usual the next day. The company denied his claim for reporting pay, saying that its obligation was met by sending a correctly addressed telegram.

The word "receive," the arbiter pointed out, means that more than the sending of a message is necessary. The contract, he said, recognized this, for it used "shall be notified" instead of "shall receive notice" in another provision. Although the employee had a telephone, no attempt was made to reach him by this means. So, the umpire figured, all reasonable efforts were not made, and the employee was entitled to pay. (Douglas & Lomason Co., 28 LA 406)

Computing Notice Period

When a contract requires advance notice a certain length of time prior to the layoff, can nonworking days be counted as days of notice? At least one arbitrator has ruled that they can not. He noted that one purpose of advance layoff notice is to allow the union time to try to find other employment for the laid-off workers. This purpose, he said, would be defeated if non-working days could be counted in the notice period. (Hoke, Inc., 3 LA 750)

Layoff Shorter Than Notice Period

Some contracts provide for notice a specified length of time in advance of layoff or pay for the same period in lieu of notice. Are workers entitled to pay for the full notice period when they're laid off, without notice, for a shorter period of time? A state arbitration board held that employees laid off without advance notice were entitled to pay for the full period, even though they were laid off for a shorter time.

EXAMPLE: A contract said that workers wouldn't be laid off without a week's notice or a week's pay in lieu of notice. The workers were given no advance notice when they were laid off for two days. The union claimed the company owed them a week's pay. But the company claimed it hadn't been possible to give advance notice.

The arbitration board conceded that application of the contract provision seemed harsh since the layoff lasted only two days, but it pointed out that it wouldn't have seemed so if the layoff had lasted longer. The company's obligation under the contract was clear and unqualified, the board ruled; therefore one week's pay was due each of the workers. (General Baking Co., 28 LA 621)

On the other hand: The fact that a contract provides for two weeks' notice of layoff or pay in lieu thereof does not necessarily mean that employees not given two weeks' notice must be granted a full two weeks' pay, according to one arbiter.

EXAMPLE: A contract provided for two weeks' notice of layoff or pay in lieu of notice for employees with six months' service. The company made a general layoff with only a few days' prior notice. Some employees lost less than two weeks' work, but the union claimed the full two weeks' pay in lieu of notice in addition to their regular earnings for any work done within the period.

An umpire ruled that the most reasonable interpretation of the provision was that employees were entitled to "pay in lieu thereof" only for layoffs from work which fell within the two weeks after notice was given. In other words, he said, they could expect to receive only their regular pay for the two weeks following the layoff notice. This included pay for both time worked and layoff time. (Phillip's Waste Oil Pick-Up & Road Oiling Service, Inc., et al., 24 LA 136)

Where Notice Is 'Impossible'

A company that had agreed to give three days' advance notice of layoffs, "except where such notice is impossible," violated the contract when employees were laid off without any advance notice due to lack of work. The arbiter ruled since the word "impossible" was not explained, it should be given its ordinary definition and only an emergency of major proportions would release the company from its obligation of giving notice. Decline or even cessation of orders does not qualify as such an emergency. (Mobil Chemical Co., 50 LA 80)

Notice of Layoff Caused by Wildcat Strike or Slowdown

When a layoff is made necessary by an unauthorized and unexpected work stoppage by employees in other departments of the plant, most arbitrators excuse employers from giving layoff notice or pay. One ruled that to require it under these circumstances would be completely unreasonable. (International Harvester Co., 9 LA 784)

Similarly: A slowdown has been held to be a situation that relieved an employer of the notice requirements. Under a contract that required advance notice of layoff except in emergencies, one arbitrator held that there was an emergency within the meaning of the contract when a company had to lay off several workers on short notice because of a slowdown in one department. The umpire said the employer was justified and did not have to give the workers layoff pay since the layoff was neither planned nor desired by the company. (Lone Star Steel Co., 28 LA 465)

Under similar contract terms, another employer was upheld for laying off workers due to a local union strike against his suppliers, since he was not given prior notice. (Burgermeister Brewing Corp., 44 LA 1028)

Bumping & Transfer to Avoid Layoff

IN BRIEF

Seniority rights lose much of their meaning if senior workers do not have a right when faced with layoff to claim jobs held by their juniors. At the same time, companies often oppose bumping on the ground that it impairs efficiency. Accordingly, bumping questions give rise to many grievances.

Even where the right to bump is expressly spelled out in a contract, knotty problems may arise. For example, may a worker bump only in his own department, or anywhere in the plant? May he displace any worker with less seniority, or only the least senior worker? May he claim a higher-rated job if he is qualified for it? Has he a right to a trial period to prove he can do the work?

In general, arbiters have held that bumping rights are implied by a contract providing for the application of seniority when the work force is being reduced. They have further ruled that, in the absence of express contract language to the contrary, a worker may displace *any* worker down the ladder who has less seniority, not merely the *least* senior man.

GUIDELINES

Plant-Wide Seniority Implies Bumping

If a contract provides for a plant-wide seniority system to be applied in layoffs, most arbitrators agree that bumping rights are implicit, even though they are not specifically mentioned. Such an interpretation, they say, means that a worker whose job is discontinued may displace a junior worker in an equal or lower classification provided he can perform the junior worker's job. (Loew's, Inc., 8 LA 816; Darin & Armstrong, 13 LA 843; National Gypsum Co., 14 LA 938)

However: Not all arbitrators will conclude that bumping rights exist when not mentioned in the contract. At least one has ruled that no such rights exist unless stated in clear and unambiguous terms in the agreement. (Norwalk Co., 3 LA 535)

Bumping Rights Under Plant-Wide & Departmental Seniority

When a contract provides for both plant-wide and departmental seniority, is an employee facing layoff permitted to bump to any job in the plant held by a junior worker? Under such a provision, whether bumping rights are expressed or implied, many arbitrators have ruled that departmental seniority should be applied first so that the senior worker would bump to a lower job in his own department. Plant-wide seniority, they say, should apply only when there are no jobs remaining within his department. (Pennsylvania Salt Mfg. Co., 3 LA 205; General Electric Co., 30 LA 472; Standard Oil Co., 38 LA 939)

Bumping Limited to Choice of Classification

Under a contract permitting an employee, during a layoff, to bump a man with less seniority in any department if he had the ability to do the work, one arbitrator ruled that the senior worker's choice was limited to picking a classification. Management had the right to decide which job within the classification he could fill, the umpire ruled. (Fulton-Sylphon Co., 2 LA 116)

However: Under a similar provision, another arbitrator held that a worker could choose the job he liked best within a classification because of nonwage factors.

EXAMPLE: Under one contract, an employee slated for layoff could displace a man with less seniority in any department, provided he had the ability to do the job. An employee whose shift was discontinued bumped to a work crew on another shift. He requested one job on the crew but was given another. Both positions were within the same job classification and paid the same wage rate, and the company argued it had a right to decide which one the employee should have.

An umpire, though, said the company was wrong. The fact that the two jobs carried the same rate didn't mean there was nothing to choose between them, he said; nonwage factors made one seem more desirable to the employee. Moreover, the umpire found that past practice had been to post particular jobs on the crew for bidding. Hence he concluded that the employee should be given the job he wanted. (Dayton Steel Foundry Co., 29 LA 191)

Bumping Limited to Particular Job

Under a contract providing that an employee subject to layoff was entitled to bump the employee with the least seniority in his occupational group, one arbitrator held that a worker was limited to bumping into only one job—that held by the least senior worker in the same job grouping. Since she was not able to do that particular job, the company was justified in laying her off, the umpire

ruled, even though workers with less seniority were kept working. He said that the contract clearly would not permit her to bump into just any job held by a worker with less seniority. (Ford Motor Co., 1 LA 462)

Further: A laid-off worker wasn't entitled to select the particular job on which to exercise her bumping rights where the contract referred to ability to do "required" work and willingness to accept the "work proffered." The arbiter said that the element of choice was in the hands of the company rather than the worker. (United Screw & Bolt Corp., 42 LA 669)

However: Under a contract simply making seniority the governing factor in layoff, but not mentioning bumping rights, another arbiter decided that a worker facing layoff could bump *any* junior man in an equal or lower classification. He was not limited to bumping only the *most* junior worker, the umpire said. If that was the intent of the parties, they should have said so in the contract, he reasoned. (Warren Petroleum Corp., 26 LA 532)

Ability as a Factor

Where a contract allows bumping if the senior employee is capable of performing the job of a junior employee, who is to decide on the ability of the senior employee? Most arbitrators hold that management has the right to determine ability. The union can challenge management's decision through the grievance procedure but has the burden of proving that management's judgment was either wrong, arbitrary, or capricious. (American Air Filter Co., Inc., 6 LA 786; U.S. Slicing Machine Co., 22 LA 53; San Francisco Newspapers Publishers Assn., 41 LA 148)

Need for Break-in Period

To qualify for retention during layoff, senior employees must be able to perform the necessary jobs after a minimum break-in period and are not entitled to any extended instruction or training, according to many arbitrators. (7 LA 526, 11 LA 667, 23 LA

584) Some go even further and hold that the senior employee, in order to exercise his bumping rights, must possess the ability to perform the job in question without benefit of any training or trial period. (44 LA 694, 44 LA 24)

Efficiency as a Factor

Under a contract requiring a senior worker to be able to do another worker's job efficiently in order to bump him, can it be assumed that the senior employee is not qualified just because he has never done the job at that company? One arbitrator has ruled that such an assumption is not justified. He suggested that an employer, in judging an employee's ability to do the work efficiently, is obligated to take into consideration his entire work record, including jobs he had at other firms.

EXAMPLE: During a force reduction at one company, a milling machine operator was not permitted to bump a junior man who operated an engine lathe. The contract said employees would be given preference in layoff in accordance with their length of service, "subject to their ability to perfom the work in question, it being understood that efficiency is a necessary requisite." Since the employee had never operated the lathe, the company argued, he couldn't do the job efficiently. The union, though, pointed out that the employee had had 12 years' experience at his trade and had operated engine lathes at other companies.

An umpire sided with the union. Under the contract, he said, the company could not deny the employee the job unless it could prove he couldn't do it efficiently. This it had failed to do, the arbiter noted, even though checking on the employee's performance at the other firms where he claimed he'd run a lathe would have been a simple matter. (Cobak Tool & Mfg. Co., 30 LA 279)

Right to Second Bump

If an employee fails to qualify on the first job he bumps into, does he have the right to try out on another job held by a junior employee? Arbitrators are generally agreed that no second bump need be allowed when the contract is silent on the matter.

EXAMPLE: An employee slated for layoff was given the choice of bumping into a job held by a junior employee, as required under the contract. She chose a job she had never before performed; after a week's trial she was informed that she lacked the ability to do the job satisfactorily and was then laid off. The union protested, saying that she had not been given time enough to become familiar with the new job and that, even if her disqualification was proper, she should have been offered an opportunity to bump into another job rather than being laid off.

The umpire ruled that the layoff was proper. He said the employee had been given a reasonable opportunity to demonstrate her ability in the job and that she was not entitled to bump into another job, since the contract didn't provide for repeated bumping. The arbitrator decided that the employee herself was largely responsible for her poor selection of a job to bump into, since she had purposely passed up a job she knew she was capable of doing. (U. S. Slicing Machine Co., 22 LA 53; see also West Virginia Pulp & Paper Co., 12 LA 391)

Right to Bump Upward

Can an employee about to be laid off bump a junior worker in a higher-rated job classification? Arbitrators have ruled both ways on this question. In the absence of contract restrictions, some arbitrators have said that a senior worker may bump upward into a higher-rated job as long as he has the necessary experience and skill to perform it. (International Harvester Co., 21 LA 214; Aetna Paper Co., 29 LA 439)

Another arbitrator decided that, where the contract stated that both ability and seniority were determining factors in bumping, "present rather than potential" ability was called for.

Where the senior worker had the required ability, junior workers—including those in higher-rated jobs—had to be laid off first during a reduction in the work force. (Greater Louisville Industries, 44 LA 694)

On the other hand: Other arbiters have decided that bumping upward amounts to promotion. When a contract neither permits nor prohibits upward bumping but makes the promotion clause separate from the layoff provision, layoff is no occasion for promoting employees to higher-paying jobs, these umpires have ruled. (International Harvester Co., 15 LA 891; Poloron Products of Pa., Inc., 23 LA 789; U.S. Rubber Co., 25 LA 417)

Similarly: Ambiguity in the bumping procedures or contrary past practice also can limit the right of senior workers to bump. When a worker sought to bump into the top mill crew job, the company refused to promote him. Historically, it contended, workers never had been permitted to bump into top jobs that they actually hadn't performed. According to the arbiter, established past practice and failure of the contract to provide a training period for bumping supported the company's right to turn down workers who it determines are unqualified. (Empire-Reeves Steel Corp., 44 LA 653)

Right to Bump at Will

Can employees use their accumulated seniority to bump whenever they wish into jobs occupied by employees with less seniority? Most arbitrators hold they can not. They limit bumping rights to a situation where an employee is moved out of his job as in a layoff.

EXAMPLE: An employee bid on the creeler job and was awarded it on the basis of his seniority and qualifications. A year later because of advancing age he attempted to exercise his seniority to bump or "roll" into the oiling job. The company allowed this and the oiler was discharged when he was unable to handle any of the available jobs offered him.

The employee protested the discharge, claiming that the bumping right did not apply to such a situation. The contract provided that in layoffs the last one in would be the first out.

The arbitrator agreed that "This necessarily implies that a senior employee can 'roll' a junior employee when the former's job is abolished." But the arbitrator limited that right solely to such a situation. He ruled that advancing age was not reason enough to permit an employee on his own initiative to pick out a job held by a junior employee and bump him. The arbitrator pointed out that "the company could not operate efficiently if an employee was free to 'roll' a junior employee at any time he desires to do so." (Anchor Rome Mills, Inc., 9 LA 595)

However: Under a contract stating that employees with seniority could bump into more desirable jobs, another arbitrator ruled that they could do so any time they desired. He said if the parties had meant to limit bumping rights only to situations when vacancies occurred, they should have said so in the contract. (Continental Oil Co., 8 LA 171)

Responsibility for Initiating Bumping

Who is responsible for seeing to it that the bumping provisions of a contract are carried out—the employer, or the employee and the union? Does the company have to start the bumping machinery in a layoff or should the senior worker put in a claim for the job to which he is entitled? When the contract did not specifically spell out the procedure, some arbitrators held that it was up to employees to claim their rights.

EXAMPLE: One employee, a crane follower, was laid off for five months, when he was recalled as a punch helper. A week later, he bid for and was awarded a job as a rivet heater being held by a junior employee. He also put in a claim for back pay to the time of his layoff, claiming he should have replaced the junior rivet heater at that time.

The arbitrator agreed with the company that the employee had some obligation to be diligent in asserting his rights, either by himself or through his steward. If he didn't do so, he shouldn't be permitted to collect back pay from the company, for that would mean that the company was paying twice for the work—once to the man laid off, and once to the man who kept the job. (General American Transportation Corp., 15 LA 672)

Right to Refuse Downgrading

When a contract is silent on the matter, can an employee elect to be laid off rather than downgraded during a reduction in force, or can the employer discharge him if he refuses to accept a lower-rated job? According to one arbitrator, in the absence of contract language requiring employees to take available work or be discharged, they have the right to choose layoff.

EXAMPLE: Two employees' jobs were eliminated during a reduction in force, and they were offered lower-rated jobs on the basis of their seniority. They refused to take the jobs and were discharged. The company said the discharges were for just cause since the men had refused the only work available to them.

The arbitrator, however, decided that the right of senior employees to bump into or to take lower jobs was not the same as a requirement that they take such jobs. In the absence of clear contract language requiring them to take available work or be discharged, the umpire concluded that they were free to request layoffs and subsequent rehire in line with their seniority. He ordered the company to change the separation status of the employees from discharge to layoff. (Caterpillar Tractor Co., 23 LA 313).

Moreover, employees may continue to elect layoff rather than demotion, despite the introduction of a supplemental unemployment benefit plan, an arbitrator held, where this right of election had existed in the past. (United Engineering & Foundry Co., 47 LA 164)

Worksharing

During a period when work is in short supply, a reduction in the workweek may seem like a good idea to the company. The union, however, may see things differently. Particularly in situations where the contract provides supplemental unemployment benefits, the union is likely to favor layoff for the few, normal working hours for the many.

There seems to be pretty general agreement among arbiters that if a contract (1) says nothing about worksharing and (2) requires that seniority be followed in cutting the work force, a company may not shorten the workweek in preference to making layoffs. If management could telescope the workweek at its pleasure, they reason, seniority rights wouldn't mean much.

GUIDELINES

Management's Right to Shorten Work-week

If the contract contains no specific provisions relating to worksharing, is the employer free to cut the workweek in order to spread available work among the largest number of employees? The answer to this question depends on the interpretations placed on other types of contract clauses. If the agreement states that seniority must be followed in cutting the work force, an arbitrator is likely to hold that management may not shorten the workweek in preference to making layoffs.

EXAMPLE: One company, relying on a clause recognizing its right to "curtail production," chopped a day off the regular workweek for all employees. An umpire decided the workweek reduction was a contract violation. The agreement, he noted, stated that force reductions were to be made in order of seniority. If management could cut the workweek to four days, it could make further reductions, he pointed out, and seniority wouldn't mean much. (Kennecott Copper Co., 32 LA 244; see also International Harvester Co., 24 LA 311; Morris Machine Works, 40 LA 456)

On the other hand: Clauses stating that the regular workweek shall consist of so many hours and so many days generally have been held not to prevent management from cutting the workweek instead of laying employees off.

EXAMPLE: One employer reduced the normal workweek from 40 to 35 hours by scheduling five seven-hour days when business slowed down. The union argued that this was a violation of a contract provision stating that the regular workday would be eight hours and the regular workweek five days. The arbitrator disagreed, saying that this provision didn't establish a guaranteed eight-hour day, five day week but was merely a statement of the normal operating schedule for purposes of figuring overtime. He said that nothing in the contract prohibited the employer from shortening the regular workweek. (Wausau Iron Works, 22 LA 473; see also Geuder, Paeschke & Frey Co., 12 LA 1163)

Layoff Before Worksharing

Many arbitrators believe that it is only fair that regular employees or those with seniority should be kept on a regular workweek as long as possible. Therefore, they agree that probationary or short-service employees should be laid off before the workweek is reduced. (Western Automatic Machine Screw Co., 12 LA 38)

The point at which layoffs should stop and cutting hours should begin may be found in the specific language of the contract. One agreement stated that when it became necessary to make layoffs involving employees with two or more years of service, operations would be reduced to a single shift or to a 32-hour week before further layoffs were made. An arbiter held that this clearly required the company to lay off all workers with less than two years' service before reducing the workweek to 32 hours. (Aetna Ball & Roller Bearing Co., 22 LA 453)

However: Where the contract didn't provide the answer, one umpire said that employees should be laid off until the work group was reduced to a "reasonable minimum." When it reached the point where a further reduction in the work force would have impaired the standard of quality set for the group, then the company could reduce the workweek, he said. (Bloom-Ease, Inc., 12 LA 941)

Worksharing Before Layoff

A contract may call for a reduction in working hours before any layoffs can be made. One agreement required a reduction in the workweek to 32 hours before employees were laid off. The company claimed it could make layoffs to eliminate the night shift instead of reducing hours as long as the volume of work didn't drop enough to justify instituting a 32-hour week. An arbitrator ruled that the company could not lay off workers as long as there was enough work

to keep everybody working for 32 hours or more per week. (Babcock Printing Press Corp., 10 LA 397)

Another employer could not discharge permanent employees for lack of work, but had to reduce hours of individual employees in order to comply with the contract which stated that "all work of any classification in any shop shall be equally distributed among the employees of that classification without discrimination." The arbiter reasoned that the provision was intended to apply to decreases in available work, as overtime distribution was dealt within a separate provision. The entire structural thrust of the contract, he concluded, was toward the work-sharing principle, and it would take explicit contract language to justify other conclusions. (Wilshire Mfg. Jewelers, 49 LA 1079)

In another case the employer had the right to reduce hours of all employees, including union officers, in a department for lack of work. The contract granted union officers super-seniority in layoffs, but also stated that a "reduction in hours of work or a staggering of work schedules of employees is not a layoff requiring the application of" seniority. Although the slips given employees when their hours were reduced stated that employees were being "laid off", the slips also contained the dates upon which employees were scheduled to return to work. Since the other facts indicated that the employer's action constituted staggering of work schedules, with sharing of available work among all employees, according to the arbiter, this was not a "layoff" as defined in the contract. (Wilcox Crittenden Co., 43 LA 1046)

Group Affected by Worksharing

Can hours be cut for one group of workers while other groups are still operating on a full schedule? Where a contract with a provision for worksharing specifies that the shorter workweek shall apply to a single classification or department, or to the whole plant, an arbitrator will undoubtedly require strict adherence to the contract language.

EXAMPLE: One contract stated that when work slowed down in any department, hours should be reduced to 32 a week for 30 days before any layoffs were made. The company reduced the workweek for one class of employees within a department, but not for others. The arbitrator said this action was a violation of the contract because all classes of employees within the department should have been put on a shorter week. Employees whose hours were cut were awarded pay for the time they lost. (Mueller Brass Co., 3 LA 271)

IN BRIEF

Since nearly all contracts provide that rehiring shall be done in the reverse order of layoff, many rehiring problems are automatically eliminated when the order of layoff is determined. Disputes frequently arise however, over such questions as the company's right to give physical examinations on recall, whether a worker can continue on layoff rather than accept an undesirable job, and the company's obligations with respect to recall notices.

On the matter of physical exams, umpires usually have held that management does have the right to require workers to take them upon returning from an extended layoff. They also have said, though, that a company may not set higher physical standards for returning employees than for those already at work.

GUIDELINES

Seniority v. Ability in Recall

Under a contract which contained a seniority clause but was silent on applying seniority to recall, one arbitrator ruled that a senior employee should be recalled if able to perform the required work. Management should not bypass a senior worker able to handle the work just because a junior worker could do a better job, even though the contract didn't outline the recall procedure, the arbiter said. (Laher Battery Production Corp., 11 LA 41)

Ability, Skill & Efficiency as Factors in Recall

Under a contract making seniority govern in recall where ability, skill, and efficiency were equal, one arbitrator ruled that senior workers did not have to be given a break-in period to become proficient on jobs where junior workers had already proved themselves the most efficient through past performance. The umpire upheld the recall of the junior workers in preference to the seniors.

EXAMPLE: A contract provided that in recall after layoff, seniority would govern if ability, skill, and efficiency were equal. When two junior employees were recalled to their jobs, the union protested that there still were five employees on layoff who had more seniority and were qualified to do the work; two of these five should have been recalled, the union argued.

An arbitrator upheld the company. While the five senior employees might have done the work proficiently after a break-in period, he found that *at the time of recall* the junior employees were the most efficient on the jobs in question. Since the contract made seniority controlling only where efficiency already was equal and made no provision for a training period, the umpire concluded that recall of the junior employees was proper. (Curtis Companies, Inc., 29 LA 50)

Measuring Ability in Recall

When seniority governs in recall where skill and ability are equal, what sort of yardsticks can be used in measuring employees' ability? Is a foreman's opinion that a junior worker has greater ability enough to justify his being recalled before a senior man? Many arbitrators have said that the mere belief of a foreman is not enough to establish greater ability on the part of a junior worker. They agree that, while foremen's opinions should be considered, they can not stand alone. (Copco Steel & Engineering Co., 12 LA 6)

Physical Exams on Rehiring

Can laid-off employees be required to take a physical examination upon return to work? Arbiters generally agree that, in the absence of a specific contract ban on the practice, management may require employees returning to work from extended layoffs, strikes or leaves of absence to have new physical examinations. (Ford Motor Co., 8 LA 1015; Goodyear Clearwater Mills, 11 LA 364; Connecticut Telephone & Electric Corp., 22 LA 632)

However: Management should follow a consistent practice in the use of medical exams. When a company bypassed a senior worker because of his past medical record, an arbitrator said it was acting improperly. It should have based his recall on present medical information, as it did with other workers. (National Lead Co., 42 LA 176)

Physical Standards on Rehiring

Most umpires have ruled that a company may not set higher physical standards for workers returning from layoff than are applied to workers still on the job.

EXAMPLE: An employee about to be recalled from layoff was found by the company doctor to have blood pressure higher than that permissible for new employees, although within the range allowed for persons already employed by the company. Accordingly, the employee was denied recall.

An arbitrator ruled that the employee was entitled to recall, pointing out that the contract contained no provision for denial of recall rights to a laid-off employee whose physical condition would have been acceptable if he were still working for the company. (Allegheny Ludlum Steel Corp., 25 LA 214)

Further: A company had no right to refuse to reinstate a laid-off electrician on the basis of a doctor's report, according to another arbitrator. Although the company admitted that it gave recalled workers "more tolerant treatment" in medical exams of new hires, the arbiter found that this worker was given the same examination as that given new employees. Further, the refusal to reinstate the worker was based on the possibility of future recurrence of back trouble, not on his present condition. Therefore, the company was ordered to rehire the worker. (Weatherhead Co., 42 LA 513)

However: In one situation, even though a worker's physical condition was the same at the time of recall as it was upon layoff, an arbitrator held that the company could refuse to put him back to work to protect his health.

EXAMPLE: A 300-pound man with a heart murmur was denied recall because the company medic said it would endanger his health to work. An arbitrator upheld the company's action. The fact that the man worked until he was laid off was no sign he wasn't endangering his health all that time, the umpire said; it merely indicated the company didn't know about his condition. When it found out, it had every right to refuse to recall him in order to protect his health, the umpire concluded. (Potter Press, 26 LA 514)

Worker with Superseniority

If a worker is elected to union office while on layoff and thus acquires superseniority, is he entitled to immediate recall? One arbitrator has held that management need not recall the worker in such a case until there is a job opening he can qualify for. The

purpose of superseniority, he remarked, is to insure continuity in the
administration of the contract, not to
make jobs for union representatives.
(Queen City Industries, 33 LA 794)

Refusal to Accept Lower-Rated or Different Job

Can employees refuse to accept a
recall notice to a lower-rated job
without jeopardizing their seniority
rights? If there is nothing in the
contract to the contrary, most arbitrators hold that employees can refuse notices to lower-rated jobs without loss of seniority. (Service Conveyor Co., 9 LA 134)

Similarly: It has been held that
employees do not have to accept recall to perform a job different from
that held prior to layoff under a contract allowing workers to choose between layoff and transfer.

EXAMPLE: An employee was laid
off when his department closed for
vacations and maintenance. During
his layoff he refused an offer of a job
in another department, saying he preferred to wait for recall to his own
department. When his department re-
opened, however, e m p l o y e e s with
shorter service were recalled ahead of
him. The company said that he had
waived his right to recall by refusing the other job.

The arbitrator decided that, since
the contract permitted employees to
take a layoff instead of a transfer
to another department, an employee
could refuse an offer of a job in a
different department without losing
his right to be recalled to his own
department in line with his seniority.
(International Harvester Co., 22 LA
773)

Recall to Lower-Rated Job

When a laid-off worker does accept
recall to a lower-rated job, at what
rate should he be paid? One arbitrator ruled that recall to a lower-
rated job is the same as a transfer,
and accordingly is governed by contract provisions relating to transferred employees.

EXAMPLE: A company's contract
provided that an employee transferred
to a lower-rated job would continue
to receive his former rate for 15 consecutive working days. A worker recalled from layoff to a lower-rated job
received his old rate for only five
days, whereupon he claimed that he
was entitled to the old rate for 10
additional days.

The union, pointing to a contract
provision that a recalled employee
must accept the job offered or lose
seniority, argued that since the
worker didn't have the option of refusing the lower-rated job he had in
effect been transferred by the company. The company based its case
on a past practice of not treating
recalls to lower paying jobs as transfers.

The arbitrator ruled in favor of the
union. The word "transfer" as used
in labor agreements, he pointed out,
means a shift or change from one
job to another. The worker in this
case clearly moved from one job to
another; no one claimed that such a
move wouldn't have constituted a
transfer if the worker hadn't been
laid off, the arbitrator noted. In his
opinion the layoff didn't change the
picture. (National Can Corp., 25 LA
177)

However: Another umpire, while
upholding the right of employees to
refuse recall to a lower-rated job, did
not agree that acceptance of a lower-
rated job when recalled is the same
as a transfer. (Service Conveyor Co.,
9 LA 134)

Recall After Strike

When a contract provides for observance of seniority in layoff and
recall, do recalls after a strike have
to be made according to seniority?
According to one arbitrator, layoff
and recall provisions in a labor agreement do not apply to recall after a
strike.

EXAMPLE: A plant's production
and maintenance employees went out
on strike for 12 days. As soon as the

employees agreed to come back to work the company drew up a schedule for resuming operations and notified employees when to report.

The union claimed that the recalls were not made strictly according to seniority as provided for in the contract. The company argued that the contract was not applicable to this situation. It pointed out that operations had to be started up bit by bit and that not all employees could be rehired together.

The arbitrator ruled that the contract "was obviously not drafted to deal with a situation like this one. This situation did not involve any layoffs and hence did not involve rehiring after layoff." Therefore the arbitrator ruled for the company that production could be resumed bit by bit and that employees could be called without regard to strict seniority rules. (Swift & Co., 8 LA 295)

Refusal to Recall Senior Employee with Poor Record

Can a laid-off senior employee be refused recall as a form of disciplinary action for such an offense as poor attendance? If a contract requires that employees be recalled to work in line with their seniority, one arbitrator has ruled, such other factors as a poor attendance record do not justify a denial of the employee's right to be recalled.

EXAMPLE: While the high-seniority employee at one company was on layoff, a temporary job came up and was filled with a man holding lower seniority. Management supported its action on the ground that, among other things, the employee had a record of several unexcused absences in the past.

In rejecting the company's justification of its refusal to recall the employee, the umpire decided that the employee's absenteeism was an extraneous issue. The company should not have considered the employee's attendance record in considering his recall, said the arbiter, because this was something that should have been disposed of at the time the absences occurred. Such an offense, he said, should not be made the basis for denial of job opportunities for the indefinite f u t u r e. (Cleveland-Cliffs Iron Co., 24 LA 599)

Failure to Send Proper Recall Notice

What constitutes proper notice of recall from layoff? If the contract specifically requires that laid-off workers be notified of recall by a certain means, most arbitrators say that method must be used without exception. If the company does not give the proper notice, these umpires say, it may not take away the workers' seniority and re-employment rights.

EXAMPLE: One company's contract required that laid-off employees be recalled by registered letter and that they report within five days after receiving notice. Instead of sending registered letters, however, the firm sent the union steward a request that he tell employees to come to the plant for rehiring. One employee who was not notified by the steward and who did not report within the five-day period was permanently laid off.

The arbitrator decided that the employee had not been notified of recall in the manner prescribed by the contract, that is, by registered letter; nor had she been contacted in any other way by the company. Accordingly, the umpire ordered her reinstated with full seniority and back pay starting with the fifth day after she should have been notified. (Ohmer Corp., 13 LA 364)

Failure to Receive Recall Notice

When is an employee's failure to receive notice a valid excuse for not reporting? One arbiter said that a worker was entitled to back pay and full seniority when his failure to receive recall notice was not his fault, even though the company had met its notice requirements.

EXAMPLE: One company complied with the contractual requirement that employees be notified of recall either by letter or telegram by mailing a notice to the apartment house where an employee lived. Through some slip of the post office, the notice was sent to the wrong apartment and the employee failed to report on time. The employee lost his seniority for failing to report on time after the recall. The arbitrator found that while the company had met its obligation, the employee failed to receive the notice through no fault of his own. Under these circumstances, the umpire decided, the employee had not been properly notified of recall and was, therefore, entitled to back pay and full seniority. (Levinson Steel Co., 23 LA 135)

However: If it appears that a worker has intentionally avoided receiving a recall notice or ignored it and its requirements, arbitrators are likely to uphold a company refusal to rehire him. (20 LA 238)

Rehiring Employee Who Has Lost Seniority

When a contract gives preference in hiring to former employees, one arbitrator has said, the same employment standards can not be used in judging them as are used for other job applicants. He held that former workers should be given the inside track when their qualifications are as good or better than those of other applicants.

EXAMPLE: One agreement stated that "preference will be given in employment to those former employees who lost their seniority as a result of layoff and who apply for employment." When one woman in this category applied for employment, she was rejected on the ground that she didn't meet the company's employment standards. The company later gave two reasons for the rejection: (1) the employee's personnel record had been marked "do not rehire" at the time

she lost her seniority and (2) a check with her former supervisor at the time she applied for employment showed he still didn't want her back

An arbiter said the firm didn't give the employee preference in accordance with the contract. Instead, she was disqualified on the basis of absolute standards. The preference clause the umpire explained, didn't give ex-employees an absolute right to available jobs, but it did give them the inside track where they were as good or better than other candidates. Here the company didn't attempt to compare the employee with other people applying for jobs at the same time Management, the umpire decided, had to give the worker proper consideration the next time a job opening occurred. (Libby, McNeill & Libby, 30 LA 309)

Recalling Women

Women who had been laid off in a job classification customarily filled only by women weren't entitled to be recalled to fill temporary vacancies in these jobs, according to the arbiter, when men were available to do the work. While past practice favored the females, this was wiped out by the contract which (1) specified that it controlled to the exclusion of past practice and (2) provided recall rights only where permanent, not temporary, openings were created. (Oxford Paper Co., 44 LA 630)

Another employer was not forced to recall workers from layoff in order of seniority where recalling senior women first would have violated the state's protective law. The employer recalled men first to handle "heavy" jobs, which was in keeping with the state law fixing a 25-pound ceiling on weights that could be lifted by women. (General Fireproofing Co., 48 LA 819)

Paid Sick Leave

Most workers are covered by contracts that provide some protection against wage loss due to sickness. This may take the form of sickness and accident insurance or paid sick leave. Some contracts provide for both, such as where paid sick leave covers the waiting period before sickness and accident insurance takes effect.

Most companies also permit unpaid sick leave for workers who aren't covered by paid sick leave or by insurance plans or who have exhausted their paid leave or insurance benefits.

GUIDELINES

Arbiters generally view sick leave as an earned right. This means that an employer can't establish conditions for eligibility other than those prescribed by the contract or past practice. Thus it has been held that—

A company couldn't withhold sick leave pay until employees returned to work. (Malester Operating Corp., 20 LA 534)

An employer couldn't require an employee who'd been absent for six weeks to submit to a physical exam where the contract specifically stated that examinations would be required of employees absent for 10 days or more. (Buckeye Forging Co., 42 LA 1151)

A company couldn't deny sick pay to an employee just because he didn't file a claim for it until five months after his illness. (Republic Oil Refining Co., 16 LA 607)

When strikes or other unusual circumstances occur, questions may arise as to the continued eligibility of employees already on sick leave when work interruptions take place. One arbitrator vetoed a company's denial of sick pay to an employee who was on leave when her union called a strike. The company, he said, had gone too far in assuming that the employee would have refused to work if she had been well. (Outboard Marine & Mfg. Co., 11 LA 467) On the other hand, another umpire ruled that an employee wasn't entitled to sick pay when most employees were off duty because of a strike by another union. The arbitrator reasoned that the purpose of a sick-pay provision is to pay a worker not because he's sick but because his illness prevents him from working. If no work is available, he's not entitled to sick pay. (Trans World Airlines, 41 LA 312)

The latter reasoning normally applies to layoff situations. Employees usually arent entitled to sick pay for periods when, in the usual course of events, they would have been on layoff. (International Harvester Co., 23 LA 459) Conversely, if the seniority of an employee on sick leave when layoffs occur is such that he would be eligible to bump a junior employee and remain on the job, he must be transferred on paper, rather than put on layoff status. (Hatfield Wire & Cable Co., 17 LA 548)

Receipt of workmens compensation may pose some problems under sick-pay provisions. If the clause doesnt specifically call for the deduction of workmen's compensation from sick pay, an arbiter may award full or supplemental sick pay to an employee who also is receiving workmen's compensation. (Republic Oil Refining Co., 16 LA 607; Heil Packing Co., 27 LA 90) At least one arbitrator, however, rejected an employee's claim to sick pay in addition to workmen's compensation on the ground that nothing in the contract indicated the parties intended to have any sort of supplemental arrangement. To order the company to make such payments would have the effect of amending the contract, he said. (Babcock & Wilcox Co., 22 LA 456)

Can management demand that an employee waive his right to workmen's compensation as a condition of reinstatement after sick leave? Arbitrators have expressed opposite views on this subject. One umpire, for example, in ordering the reinstatement of an employee who had a hernia, decided that the company could require him to sign a waiver of all compensation claims that might stem from his condition. (Consolidated Vultee Aircraft Corp., 10 LA 1950; see also Allen Mfg. Co., 25 LA 216) Another view is that waivers can't be required if such a requirement is in effect a contract modification. (Royal McBee Corp., 23 LA 591)

Effect of Used Sick Leave on Credits under New Plan

Can sick leave already taken be counted against the credits workers have coming to them under a new sick leave plan? If there is no restriction in a new plan, it is usually considered prospective in nature, without any retroactive effect, and arbitrators will hold that employees start with a clean slate.

EXAMPLE: A company adopted a plan which provided for paid disability leave for a specified number of days during any 12-month period. Under this plan, the company said, benefits paid to employees in the 12-month period preceding the effective date could be deducted from the total for which they qualified under the new plan. The firm maintained that the 12-month period referred to in the contract didn't necessarily mean the period starting with the effective date of the new plan, since the plan merely continued and modified a plan already in existence.

The arbitrator, however, ruled that in the absence of any definition of "12-month period," the usual interpretation that a newly adopted plan is prospective must apply. The new plan, he said, couldn't work retroactively by charging previously paid benefits against workers' credits. (Timken-Detroit Axle Co., 21 LA 196)

However: Usually *service* acquired with an employer before a sick leave plan goes into effect can be counted towards eligibility. One umpire noted that it is general practice to base sick leave eligibility on total service, not just on service acquired after a plan becomes effective. (Holga Metal Production Co., 19 LA 501)

Effect of Break in Service on Eligibility

Under a contract basing sick-leave rights on length of service, what happens to a worker's credits already built up if he is laid off? Generally, if the contract provides for retention of seniority during layoff, it is held that sick-leave rights also are retained. But in at least one situation where an arbitrator found no clause that preserved continuity of service during layoff, he decided that workers had no right to sick-leave credits acquired before being laid off. (O'Brien-Suburban Press, Inc., 18 LA 721)

Sick Pay During Temporary Shutdown

When a company closed down because of a hurricane, it refused to grant sick or injury pay to those workers who had been out on such leave at that time. It asserted that they had no right to benefits on a day on which they wouldn't have been able to work even if they were well. The arbiter, however, held that they were entitled to the pay since the primary cause of their unemployment continued to be their illness or injury. Neither injury nor sick benefits were geared to work done by able-bodied workers; if this were the case, he reasoned, then those on leave could claim extra pay if able-bodied employees worked overtime. (Eastern Air Lines, Inc., 41 LA 801)

Disabiilty v. Sick Leave Pay

One umpire held that a company had no right to deduct disability payments from sick leave pay when past practice had been to grant the full amount of both benefits. He found nothing wrong with a worker's receiving benefits in excess of his regular wages. Sick leave pay was a negotiated benefit to which the worker had a right, the arbiter said, and he paid his share for the disability benefits. (Mohawk Airlines, Inc., 39 LA 45)

Disability Layoff & Sick Pay

According to one arbitrator, the fact that a worker was given a disability layoff and may have been entitled to further workmen's compensation benefits didn't mean he also had a right to sick pay.

EXAMPLE: A lineman employed by a utility company requested a transfer to lighter work after pain from an electric shock he had received three years previously began to bother him. After having the employee examined, the company placed him on an indefinite layoff for medical disability reasons. The laid-off employee then claimed the full amount of sick pay provided by the contract.

The umpire ruled, however, that the former employee had no right to any sick pay because he wasn't sick at the time he was laid off; and he was laid off because of an occupational disability, not for an injury or illness. Proof of incapacity caused by the occupational disability, said the umpire, didn't amount to proof that the employee was sick at the time he left the company. There may have been equities calling for workmen's compensation or other adjustments, the arbitrator explained, but they didn't alter the fact that the sick-leave provisions of the contract couldn't be stretched to cover a case where there was no actual illness. (Southern Indiana Gas & Electric Co., 14 LA 167)

Falsifying Sick Leave Claims

Where there is evidence that a worker falsified his claim of illness, an arbitrator would probably uphold discipline of him unless the sick-leave policy or plan itself specifies how abuses are to be handled.

EXAMPLE: An arbitrator upheld a two and one-half week suspension of an employee who reported in sick and was discovered the next day operating a tractor on his farm. Although the employee had been ill the day before and was still suffering from his ailment, the arbitrator found he wasn't too sick to work, since operation of the tractor was considerably more strenuous than his duties as a television engineer. (Station KMTV, 39 LA 324)

But discipline was overturned by an arbitrator in another case where an employee admitted that he had performed outside "remunerative work" while drawing benefits under a sickness and accident plan. The plan itself specified that the penalty for engaging in such work, where not detrimental to a speedy recovery, was forfeiture of benefits, not discharge, the arbiter noted. (Corn Products Co., 44 LA 127)

Similarly, an arbitrator held that a company was not justified in discharging an employee who falsified his time card to claim sick leave improperly. The contract's sick leave provisions said the company could reduce or eliminate sick leave privileges if abuses were found, the arbitrator noted. So management should have invoked these remedies instead of resorting to discharge. (Central Illinois Public Service Co., 44 LA 133)

Sick Pay for Overtime

Where a contract defined a "normal work day" as eight hours, one arbitrator held that a worker regularly scheduled for a longer than normal work day could not collect sick pay for the overtime he was used to working.

The clause involved called for one day of sick leave after a year's service, two days after two years, and so on.

The parties split over whether a "day" under the clause was the man's usual work day or the normal day as defined by the contract. The arbitrator reasoned that the parties had some definite notion of the price tag when they negotiated the sick-leave clause. So he thought it likely that they were thinking in terms of a normal day. Thus, he held. the worker was entitled to sick pay for just the regular eight hours, not for the overtime. (Bell Aircraft Corp., 26 LA 558)

Sick Pay During Vacations

When a worker became ill just before his scheduled vacation, the company charged his absence to extended vacation pay. The arbitrator said that this was not proper. He held that problems arising from absenteeism because of illness occur whether or not employees are scheduled for vacations, so that circumstance should not affect the employer's responsibility to pay for sick leave. (U.S. Steel Corp., 44 LA 615)

Payment of both disability and vacation benefits was not required by this arbiter, despite the company's history of having done so. The contract "precluded payment of disability benefits if wages were received." The arbiter said that a past practice couldn't modify the application of clear contract language. (Westinghouse Electric Corp., 45 LA 131)

Job Rights after Absence for Illness

Can a worker returning from sick leave bump a man hired to replace him? Under contracts with seniority provisions, most arbitrators uphold the right of an employee returning from sick leave to exercise his seniority to get his former job back. When a senior worker returned from approved sick leave, an arbitrator ruled that the company had to take him back even though it had hired a replacement on his job. The umpire reasoned that the returning worker's job had not been eliminated, so he was entitled to the same protection as he would have received had he not been on leave. Therefore, he was entitled to displace the junior worker and get his job back, the umpire concluded. (Everett Dyers & Cleaners, 11 LA 546)

Even under a contract that had no provision for sick leave but did have a seniority clause, an arbitration board decided that a worker who had been absent because of illness was entitled to his job under the contract. The company refused to take him back but the board found no evidence that he had quit or had been discharged. On this basis, the board said that he should still be considered an employee, even though the company had hired a replacement. The board reasoned that when the absent worker returned to work, the company had one too many employees. Therefore, the arbiters ruled, the layoff provisions of the contract should apply and whichever of these two workers had the most seniority should get the job. (Don Lee Broadcasting System, 1 LA 571)

However: Under a contract stating that a worker on sick leave would be returned, if qualified, to his old job or one like it, an umpire ruled that a man who was unable to do his old job was not entitled to just any job he could do. The employee was a lineman for an electric company and was recovering from tuberculosis. His own doctor said he could work in any job that didn't involve climbing or heavy lifting. The company decided this ruled out lineman work and similar jobs and so refused to rehire him. The arbitrator upheld the company, stating that the contract did not require the employer to give the man any job he could perform. He also noted that reinstatement under this contract depended on the worker's being qualified. (Southern California Edison Co., 26 LA 827)

Effect of Leave on Eligibility for Automatic Increase

Should time spent on sick leave be counted in fixing the date on which an employee becomes eligible for an automatic increase? In the absence of a contract provision on the matter, some arbitrators have ruled that workers do not have to be given credit for time spent on sick leave in determining their eligibility for length-of-service raises. They have observed that automatic wage increases are designed to reward workers for increased proficiency that comes from continued experience on the job. Job proficiency cannot be gained on sick leave, they have noted. (Bell Aircraft Corp., 17 LA 230; Hanovia Chemical & Mfg. Co., 18 LA 847)

DOCTORS' OPINIONS

While management may have the right to require a doctor's statement as proof of illness, arbiters disagree as to whether such certificates may be required in all instances. One arbitrator held that it was unreasonable for a company to require a doctor's certificate in all cases of sick leave since such a rule imposed a hardship on many in order to punish a few who abused their sick-leave privileges. (General Baking Co., 40 LA 387) Another arbitrator held just the opposite, deciding that a rule requiring a doctor's certificate for each day of sick leave taken was reasonable. (Federal Services, Inc., 41 LA 1063) Still another umpire decided that an employee's refusal to submit a doctor's certificate, even though his illness was genuine, relieved the company of its obligation to pay him for his leave. (Philips Petroleum Co., 45 LA 857)

Whether a company can require an employee returning from sick leave to get a medical clearance is another issue on which arbiters are divided. One umpire, for emample, held that an employee returning from a long illness didn't have to obtain a medical release from his doctor since the contract said nothing about such a release. (Inspiration Consolidated Copper Co., 7 LA 86; see also Magnavox Co., 28 LA 554) Another umpire concluded that a company could require employees absent for more than three days to submit to examinations by the company doctor. (Reserve Mining Co., 29 LA 367)

Where Doctors' Opinions Conflict

When the company's physician is of the opinion that a worker is unsuited for his former job but other doctors hold a contrary view, can a company refuse to reinstate a worker? In one case, finding a preponderance of the medical evidence in the worker's favor, the arbiter ordered the worker's reinstatement.

EXAMPLE: When a worker—a conductor on the plant railroad—sought to return to work after a six-month absence caused by a heart condition, the company barred him on the basis of an examination by the plant physician. Though his personal doctor reported that he had fully recovered, a third physician noted that a job requiring less strain would be better The worker then was examined by the state hospital's work evaluation unit whose findings were favorable. Still he was unable to get his old job back.

The arbiter said the case for reinstatement was supported by the largely positive evidence, especially the findings of the work evaluation unit But since he believed the company was motivated by concern for the employee's welfare, he denied back pay for the period prior to the work unit's findings. (U.S. Steel Corp., 38 LA 395)

Most all companies have a policy of granting employees leaves of absence without pay where it is necessary for personal reasons. At least in the case of leave for illness, many companies feel that they have nothing to lose by such a policy—if the employee is a good worker and will have to be absent anyway, it is better to make some provision for getting him back on the payroll in regular fashion than take the chance of losing a valuable employee forever.

Usually, however, management wants to reserve the right to decide each case of personal leave on its own merits. For this reason it will phrase its leave policy in very general terms: "Leave will be granted for good cause," or "Management will approve a reasonable request for leave." The theory here is that management holds the reins and can grant or deny a leave request at will.

But this is not always the case. Employees have long memories, and if leave is granted in one case and denied in another, a feeling that management is being unfair may spring up and spread to other employees. In other words, if a company grants a certain type of leave—maternity leave, for example—in a few cases, it has, in effect, established a *policy* of granting this type of leave and, except for unusual circumstances, will have to continue to do so for morale purposes. (Leave rights based solely on past practice will also be enforced by arbitrators, in most cases.)

Except as restricted by the contract, a company has the right to grant or deny leaves of absence for personal reasons at its discretion. Unless management acts in an arbitrary or unreasonable manner in passing on a request for leave, an arbitrator is unlikely to disturb its decision.

More than two fifths of contracts specifically make provisions for unpaid leave of absence for sickness, and most companies probably would grant such leave for a limited period of time even if not required to do so by contract. The rights of workers upon returning from sick leave, rather than the granting of the leave, are the subject of the awards discussed in this section.

Also taken up are questions relating to maternity leave, funeral leave and leave for jury duty.

GUIDELINES

What Is Good Cause for Leave?

Although admitting that management has the right to grant or deny leaves of absence under most contracts, arbitrators insist that companies apply this right reasonably and w i t h o u t discrimination. Sometimes they upset a company's judgment as to whether the reason for leave was good cause.

EXAMPLE: In one case a contract specified that leaves of absence "shall be granted for reasons acceptable to company and union." It also stated that seniority could be broken for three days' absence without good cause. A worker requested leave during the Christmas holidays for the purpose of securing a home for his mother. When the company disapproved his leave, he took off anyway. Upon his return to work he was considered a new employee by the company and thus lost his seniority rights.

The arbiter recognized the company's right to grant or deny leaves of absence. However, he believed that here management had been unreasonable. Since the worker had asked for leave for a good cause, the umpire ruled, he was entitled to reinstatement with full seniority. (Pittsburgh Metallurgical Co., Inc., 12 LA 95)

On the other hand: Where a union failed to show the company had discriminated against a worker in denying her leave to attend a religious function, an arbitration board held that the company's judgment could not be questioned. (Union Oil Co., 3 LA 108)

A company does have the right to inquire into the general nature of a worker's absence for "personal reasons." When one worker was absent in order to see another man's wife, his two-day suspension was upheld despite the claim of absence for "personal reasons." (Fairbanks Morse Co., 47 LA 224)

Falsifying Reasons for Leave

Where there is evidence that a worker falsified his reasons for wanting leave, an arbitrator would probably uphold the company's right to discipline him.

EXAMPLE: An employee requesting leave presented to his foreman a telegram stating that his mother was seriously ill in another city. His foreman told him to see the general foreman at the end of the shift. The employee worked out his shift without protesting the delay and received permission to take a leave of absence. Furthermore, he told the foreman that he definitely would be back to work on a certain date. The foreman became suspicious of the employee's nonchalance about the delay and his willingness to set a date for his return, so the company hired an investigator, who discovered that the employee's mother wasn't seriously ill and that the employee actually was taking time off to attend a convention which was being held in the city where his mother lived. The employee was discharged upon his return.

At the arbitration hearing, the employee admitted that he knew his mother wasn't seriously ill but simply old and w o r r i e d about her son. Although he did attend the convention from time to time, he insisted the primary purpose of the trip was to see his mother.

The arbitrator decided the employee had, in any event, misrepresented the reason for the leave. The employee should have explained that his mother simply wanted to see him instead of saying she was ill. The discharge was upheld. (International Harvester Co., 14 LA 980)

Seniority Protection During Indefinite Leave

If a company grants a worker leave of absence and then reinstates him without loss of seniority, can the union object that this is unfair to other workers and require management to reinstate the man as a new employee?

A company may think it has a right to be generous with an employee in any way it pleases, without interference from the union. But this right may depend on how the contract is worked. In one case, where the contract contained *no* leave clause, but did contain a seniority clause, an arbitrator held that the union could prevent management from giving an employee seniority credit while on leave.

EXAMPLE: An employee desired to work his farm and requested an indefinite leave of absence. The company granted his request. Over a period of a year the employee returned to work only for a few scattered days. At the end of the year the company put the man back on full time when he requested it. The union complained that the employee should be treated as a new employee within the meaning of the c o n t r a c t. The company answered that the employee had been on an indefinite leave of absence and was merely returning from his leave. While there was no leave provision in the contract, the seniority clause provided for the accumulation of s e n i o r i t y while on sick leave or layoff.

The award held that the employee should be rehired as a new employee.

The arbiter reasoned that if there was no limit placed on the length of leaves, a company could defeat the seniority clause by granting leaves up to two or three years in duration. He stated that the seniority clause had to be given a reasonable interpretation in order to carry out its meaning. He concluded that the clause governing seniority could not be read so as to protect the employee's seniority. (National Gypsum Co., 2 LA 566)

Promotion Rights During Leave

If a contract bases promotion on seniority, is a senior worker who is on leave when a vacancy comes up entitled to a chance at the promotion after he returns? Some arbitrators feel that, unless the contract specifically waives seniority rights during leave, management is required to reopen the bids after the return of a senior worker.

EXAMPLE: An employee was on a leave of absence when a higher-paid job for which she was qualified was given to another employee who was her junior in point of seniority. The employee contended that her seniority had accumulated during her absence and that she was entitled to the promotion when she returned. The company based its refusal on the wording of the layoff clause reading: "In case of a layoff, if the employee next in line for return to work is not available, he then forfeits his right to the job."

When the case went to arbitration, the employee who had been absent was ordered promoted to the higher job. The arbiter stated that since there had been no question raised as to the employee's ability or physical fitness, he could not hold otherwise. He refused to apply the "layoff" clause to a situation where the employee was on an authorized leave instead of being laid off. He concluded that the "leave" clause provided for the retention and accumulation of s e n i o r i t y during leave, and the "seniority" clause stated that seniority was the controlling factor in promotions; therefore, as the employee had seniority, she should be promoted. (Curtiss-Wright Corp., 9 LA 77)

MATERNITY LEAVE

Union's Right To Be Consulted on Abandoning Practice

Even though a contract was silent on granting maternity leave, one arbitrator upheld the union's right to be consulted by the company before such a leave policy was dropped. The company had started granting maternity leave unilaterally, but it had become a long-established, important, and known practice and, the umpire said, a condition of employment. For this reason, he ruled that the union must be consulted concerning the elimination of the policy. (Northland Greyhound Lines, Inc., 23 LA 277)

On the other hand: A company was justified in refusing maternity leave to a woman by virtue of its past practice of never having done so. For 15 years this policy had gone unchallenged by the union, as no complaint had been registered. When a protest finally was lodged, the arbiter ruled that it came too late. (Chattanooga Box & Lumber Co., 44 LA 373)

Maternity Leave Under General Leave Clause

Do employees have a right to maternity leave under a contract providing merely for leaves of absence? One umpire recognized that a contract clause of this kind left to the company the right to grant or deny leaves. He concluded that there was nothing in the agreement qualifying that right. Noting that there is a distinction between sickness and pregnancy, the arbiter held that this company could grant sick leave without being compelled to grant maternity leave. (American Stove Co., 8 LA 779)

On the other hand: Where a company had granted maternity leave on several occasions in the past, another arbiter held that it had to continue to do so. This situation, too, was covered by a general leave of absence clause. The arbitrator said, however, that management must administer the clause fairly and justly in the interests of all the employees and of the company. (Gen. Electric Mfg. Co., Inc., 11 LA 684)

Maternity Leave for Illegitimate Pregnancy

Can an unmarried woman employee demand rights under a company's maternity leave policy? When this situation arose in one plant, management

dismissed the worker instead of granting her leave. However, an arbitration board ordered the company to reinstate her and grant her leave. There was no association between her conduct and her job, the board held. (Crane Co., 12 LA 592; see also Allied Supermarkets, Inc., 41 LA 713)

Maternity Leave and EEOC

It should be noted that most of the decisions reported in this section that uphold a denial of maternity leave benefits were handed down prior to the rulings by the Equal Employment Opportunity Commission on maternity leave.

Interpreting the ban on sex discrimination in Title VII of the Civil Rights Act, EEOC has ruled that a "leave of absence should be granted for pregnancy whether or not it is granted for illness." (EEOC Decision YAU-9-026, July 10, 1968, 2 FEP Case 294)

But some arbitrators have emphasized that the "up to three days" language should not be construed as a guarantee of three days' funeral leave. Thus, one arbitrator refused to allow paid leave for the day after the funeral, which was spent in assisting relatives in their travel plans. This did not qualify as time spent either in attending or arranging for the funeral, the arbitrator held. (Trane Co., 53 LA 1108)

Similarly, another arbitrator indicated that as a general rule the company should not have to pay for time after the funeral. (Warner & Swasey Co., 47 LA 438)

PAID FUNERAL LEAVE

Definition of Family

In one case the problem of deciding which provisions should be included in a contract was submitted to an arbitration board during negotiations. The arbitrators decided that the contract should include a provision in an employee's immediate family. The board defined "immediate family" as he worker's father, mother, sister, rother, wife, husband, son, daughter, ather - in - law, or mother - in - law. West Penn Power Co., 11 LA 166)

In another case where a contract tated that a worker would receive aid leave in the event of the death of is "father, mother, wife, husband, hild, brother, or sister" an arbitrator eld that the provision covered the eath of a worker's stepfather. The ompany objected that the deceased vas not the worker's legal father. Iowever, the umpire pointed out that ie had acted as her father and was o regarded by the community. Therefore, he ruled, the worker deserved he pay. (Sylvania Electric Products, nc., 26 LA 108; see also Hercules Powler Co., 40 LA 1230)

But another arbitrator ruled against a stepfather's qualifying as "immedite family." (Wyman Gordon Co., 51 A 289)

Length of Funeral Leave

The usual provision is for "up to hree days" funeral leave. Arbitrators enerally agree that funeral leave is iot intended solely for allowing travel ime to attend out-of-town funerals, ut that it also can serve the addiional purpose of enabling the emloyee to assist with funeral arangements. Under this view, arbitraors are inclined to permit employes to have the choice of which three lays to take off. Those who are atending out-of-town funerals probbly will take the day before, the day of, and the day after the funeral. Those who don't need the travel time night take the three days ending with he funeral. At least one arbitrator who subscribed to this school of thought on funeral leave nevertheless thought that the employee should iot have the option of taking the fuieral day and the two days after the funeral, since this would not accord with either of the purposes of the three-day funeral leave. (Champaign-Urbana Courier, 53 LA 490)

Time and Scope of Funeral Leave

Is a worker whose vacation is interrupted by a funeral entitled to be paid for funeral leave? Several arbiters have held that this is a subject that should be decided by negotiation rather than by arbitration.

EXAMPLE: One worker took his two-week vacation to honeymoon. His mother died after the wedding, so he canceled his plans and attended to the details of the funeral and Buddhist mourning services that followed. The company granted a two-day unpaid extension of his vacation, but denied funeral-leave pay.

The language of the funeral-leave clause tied benefits to loss of working time, the arbiter said, and since the worker suffered no such loss, he was not entitled to funeral-leave pay. (Maui Pineapple Co., Ltd., 46 LA 849)

EXAMPLE: Night-shift w o r k e r s were entitled to the same funeral leave provisions as day-shift workers. The contract did not make any distinction between different types of workers, the arbiter held, so the company could not arbitrarily introduce different treatment of night- and day-shift workers. (Lehigh Portland Cement Co., 47 LA 840)

Proof of Attendance

An employer need not extend funeral-leave pay until proof of attendance has been submitted. When a company discovered that a worker had not been to a funeral as claimed, it refused to grant him any pay. The umpire disallowed the union's claim of "automatic" payment for funeral leave, and said that the company had the right to establish a procedure for determining whether workers met the contract requirement of funeral attendance. (Borg-Warner Corp., 47 LA 691)

JURY DUTY PAY

Computing Supplemental Jury Duty Pay

What is the basis for figuring supplemental jury duty pay? One umpire has held that such pay should be computed on the basis of the hours a worker would have worked rather than on the contractual minimum workday.

EXAMPLE: A contract required the company to pay the difference between a "full day's pay" and the amount a worker received for each day he served on a jury. When a worker was paid the difference between his jury-duty rate and the six-hour daily contractual guarantee, he complained that he ordinarily worked more than six hours a day and so should be paid more.

Both the contract language and its interpretation in the past led the arbiter to decide that the parties' intent was to prevent workers from losing pay while serving on juries. He therefore computed the pay on the basis of the hours the employee's replacement worked, minus the time the replacement spent on other jobs, plus overtime pay for the overtime hours of work the jurist actually would have performed, less the $6 daily jury-duty rate. (American Bakeries Co., 40 LA 1195)

Jury Pay for Shift Workers

Under a contract providing pay for working time lost because of jury duty, is management required to pay workers on late shifts who can't work because of daytime jury duty? One arbitrator has ruled that a late-shift worker is entitled to pay for time lost.

EXAMPLE: A contract called for payment of the difference between regular earnings and jury pay when it was necessary for an employee to be away from this work because of jury duty. An employee on the night shift demanded pay when he took off from work for three days because he had to be in court by 9:00 a.m. and his shift didn't end until 8:00. The company maintained it didn't have to pay the employee for time lost because the jury duty occurred outside his regular workday.

An umpire decided, however, that the employee was entitled to pay under the contract. He lived 11 miles from the plant, and the court was 35 miles from his home. Under the circumstances, the arbiter concluded that it was necessary for the employee to be away from his work if he was to arrive at court on time and in proper condition to fulfill his obligation as a juror. (Ozark Smelting & Mining Co., 27 LA 189)

Moreover: An employee was held entitled to jury-duty pay under one contract even though he could have worked his regular shift while on jury duty.

The company had agreed to pay the difference between an employee's wage loss and the amount he received for jury duty. It turned down one employee's claim because he was on the second shift—from 4 p.m. to 12:30 a.m. It figured he could have worked while serving on the jury if he'd wanted to and it also pointed out that the employee hadn't proved he'd done more than report to the courthouse each morning.

The umpire reasoned that the purpose of jury pay is to assure employees' willing acceptance of jury service by doing away with the money loss they would otherwise sustain. Requiring a man to work his regular shift after doing his civic duty, said the umpire, would defeat that purpose. (Greenleaf Mfg. Co., 32 LA 1)

Computing Overtime Pay & Jury Duty

Arbitrators are split on whether jury duty should be counted as "time worked" in computing overtime in a week in which an employee spends one or more days on jury duty and other days on the job for a combined total of more than 40 hours. Several arbitrators have held that jury duty does not count as time worked and that therefore employees are not entitled to overtime premiums when their combined hours on the job and on jury duty exceed 40 per week. (52 LA 357, 52 LA 575)

But others hold that this in effect penalizes the employee for serving on the jury and that a more equitable policy would be to count jury duty as time worked in computing overtime. (55 LA 510)

Leave for Union Business

Leave to discharge official union duties may take one of two forms: (1) short-time leaves for delegates to conventions, etc., and (2) long-term leaves for officials who are elected or appointed to full-time union offices for a designated period of time. Questions that may arise when leave for union business is considered include:

▶ Should there be a limit on the number of employees allowed to be on leave for this purpose at any one time?

▶ What is the maximum duration of the leave—90 days, six months, one year, or longer?

▶ Is the leave permitted for any union purpose? For example, is political action on behalf of the union covered?

▶ Does management have the right to require the union to explain the purpose of the leave before it is granted?

▶ What procedures should be followed when employees return from union leave? Is advance notice required? How much time is allowed?

▶ Does management have the right to deny union leave for certain reasons, such as during its busy season?

▶ Does seniority accumulate while an employee is on union leave?

▶ Should a distinction be made between business for the local union and business for the international?

This section describes how arbitrators have attempted to answer some of these questions when the contact is unclear.

GUIDELINES

Frequent Short Absences Not Allowed

Even under a contract permitting leave of absence for union business most arbitrators agree that union officials do not have the right to leave their job at frequent intervals to attend to union affairs. These umpires uphold management's right to insist that union officials tend to this job regularly or demand that they take extended leave if their frequent absences interfere with production. Some arbiters hold that a company can discipline union officials for leaving their jobs too often.

EXAMPLE: When one union representative left his work place to post union notices after the company had refused him permission, he was suspended. The union claimed that the company could not discipline him because he was on leave for union business. The arbitrator upheld the company's action on the ground that the union leave clause did not allow a union representative to leave his job for frequent short periods of time to transact union business in the shop. He said the clause was clearly intended to permit absences for more extended periods outside the plant. Thus, he ruled, the worker was properly disciplined. (Ampco Metal, Inc., 3 LA 374)

However: U n d e r similar circumstances one arbitration board, while agreeing that a company could take some disciplinary action when a union representative frequently left his job, held that the penalty could not be too severe. He said that discharge was too drastic. (Brown & Sharpe Mfg. Co., 1 LA 423)

Unlimited Union Leave Permitted

When a contract placed no limit on the length of leave for holding union office, one arbiter held that the company had no right to terminate such leave.

EXAMPLE: A worker received a leave of absence to take the position of full-time staff representative with the international union. After two years, the company notified him that it was cancelling his leave and expected him to report back to work. When he didn't, he was fired. Management claimed that it was unreasonable to expect it to grant union leave for eternity, when seniority and pension rights were accruing all the time.

Whether this was equitable or not was beside the point, the arbiter said. The contract stated that union leaves "shall be available" in reasonable number. The parties' failure to place any time limitation on union leave clearly indicated to the arbiter that no such limitation was intended. (Blaw-Knox Co., 41 LA 739)

On the other hand: A local official should not be allowed to devote too much company time to union business. Although the contract granted the worker paid time off for union business, it wasn't "carte blanche permission to spend as much company time as he pleased on union business," the arbiter held. He further said that having full-time union officials on the company payroll could smack of unlawful domination of the union by management. (Pratt & Letchworth, 48 LA 1345)

Area of Union Business

Can "union business" be interpreted as applying only to local union affairs? Under a contract providing for leave to be granted for union business, arbitrators are likely to rule that a company may not limit this privilege to business involving just the local union. One arbitration board reasoned that there are many cases where a worker would be called upon to perform work for an international of which the local union was a member. It said that the union business may in no way involve the local union. Thus, the board ruled, the meaning of "union" in the leave provision could not be restricted to the local union. (Robertshaw-Fulton Controls Co., 11 LA 1074)

Content of Union Business

Few contracts specifically cover all instances that may be considered "union business" in the leave provisions. Distinguishing between what is and what is not "union business" is further complicated by the varied nature of union activities.

At least one arbitrator ruled that serving on a political action committee was not "union business" under a contract which permitted leave for the purpose of transacting union business or representing the national union. He said that the company rightly denied a worker's request for leave to serve on a union political action committee. He decided that the contract was intended to provide leave for the purpose of taking care of business for the union in its role of bargaining agent and to represent the national union in the traditional ways. (Anchor Duck Mill, 5 LA 428)

However: Where a contract's part-time leave provisions allowed reasonable time for elected union representatives to attend conventions or conferences of the union, an arbiter held that a man should be granted leave to attend to legislative affairs. The umpire said that conferences might well include a meeting between union representatives and members of the state legislature. (Le Roi Mfg. Co., 8 LA 350)

Organizational Work

Can a worker claim union business leave to engage in organizational work for the union at another company? Under a contract granting leave to a union officer "to perform his duties as an executive officer of the union," an arbiter ruled that an officer was entitled to time off for proper union activities which the officer was required and authorized to do. Applying this test, the umpire held that organizational work authorized by union members was a proper occasion for leave. The fact that the company disapproved of the organizing was irrelevant in the umpire's view. (Telex, Inc., 35 LA 873)

Picketing as Union Business

One arbitrator has ruled that a union-business leave clause does not give a large number of employees in a plant the right to leave in order to picket at the place of business of another company. He reasoned that if the union could, by merely submitting a written request, create mass absenteeism it would hamper the general operation of the plant and thus defeat the right of management to direct its affairs and working forces. He further stated that the "leave" clause had not been intended to apply to late reporting or temporarily absent employees but had been intended to refer to those on extended periods of absence. (Chrysler Corp., 11 LA 732)

When Union Refuses To State Nature of Union Business

Is a union obligated to give a reason for a request for leave for union business? Where a contract specified that leave would be granted to permit workers to engage in labor activities, one arbitrator ruled that the company had the right to ask the union the purpose of any leave it requested. In order for the company to determine whether the leave was for bona fide labor activity, it would have to know the nature of the union business, he reasoned. If the union refused to give the reason, then the company was not obligated to grant the leave, the umpire decided. (Carter Carburetor Corp., 11 LA 569)

However: Another umpire held that an employer may not inquire into the nature or location or the business to be performed. Doing so, he reasoned, would amount to prying into the internal affairs of the union.

The umpire listed three questions which management reasonably may ask a worker requesting leave—(1) whether the worker holds a union office that entitles him to leave, (2) whether the leave is to be used for official duty, and (3) how much time off is required. (Telex, Inc., 35 LA 873)

Leave for Rival Union Business

Leave to work for a union other than the contracting union is not permitted under a "union activity" clause, one umpire ruled, although it may be permissible to grant such leave requested under some other clause in the contract.

EXAMPLE: A clause in the contract provided for leave of absence to local union representatives "chosen by the union" and to employees "elected to a full-time position with the union." Another clause provided for leave of absence for "good and sufficient reasons." An employee was granted leave to attend to his duties as an officer of a rival union. Upon his return to duty, the contracting union claimed that the employee had lost his seniority rights as his leave was unauthorized under the contract terms. The company contended that the employee was on authorized leave under both the "leave for union activity" clause and the "leave for good and sufficient reasons" clause.

In his decision the arbiter was critical of the company's action in permitting leave to work for a rival union. The arbiter felt that the company's action had violated the spirit of the contract as to what were "good and sufficient reasons." However, because it had not violated the *letter* of the contract, he upheld the company's granting of the leave.

In its attempted application of the "leave for union activity" clause, the company was held in error. The arbiter stated: "Beyond any conceivable doubt, these two sections were included in the contract solely for the benefit of members of the contracting union . . . when acting for the union." (Swift & Co., 6 LA 422)

Discipline for Taking Unauthorized Leave

One arbiter has ruled that where a worker in good faith requests leave and, in the face of a rejection by management, takes leave anyway, he is not subject to discipline. Union business leave, the umpire reasoned, is for the benefit of the union and not of the individual worker. To say that a worker is personally liable if he mistakenly goes on leave, he added, would be like saying that a supervisor is personally liable if he mistakenly discharges or suspends a worker. The company's recourse in such cases, according to the umpire, is to file a grievance against the union to test whether a good-faith absence comes within the scope of the union-business-leave clause. If it is found not, a worker taking leave under similar circumstances thereafter would be subject to discipline, the umpire said.

On the other hand, the umpire held, if a worker acts dishonestly or in bad faith in claiming the leave privilege, he is subject to discipline. (Telex, Inc., 35 LA 873)

Effect of Leave on Automatic Increase

Is a worker who takes time off to accept a full-time union job entitled to automatic increases he would have received if he had not taken leave? One arbitrator held that a worker was entitled to such increases where

the contract provided for reinstatement without loss of seniority following union leave. (Spartan Aircraft Co., 28 LA 859)

Time Spent Handling Grievances

While an employer may challenge, in specific cases, the amount of time claimed by union officials for grievance activity, he may not unilaterally set a limit on such time. When the number of hours spent on grievance settlement increases greatly, the employer limited the amount of time allowed, excusing his failure to negotiate the matter on the ground that it was a reasonable measure designed merely to return to the previous practice. The arbiter dismissed this as contrary to the contractual obligation to pay for all time reasonably and actually required for handling matters under the contract. (Goss Co., 44 LA 824)

Is an arbitration hearing part of the paid grievance time allowed union officials? It depends on the time and circumstances of the hearing and the individual contract.

EXAMPLE: The contract required the company to pay "for all time spent during working hours investigating and adjusting grievances and complaints." A number of stewards attended arbitration hearings and gave testimony regarding various grievances. Their requests for pay for time spent at the proceedings were turned down by the company. The company said that the stewards were necessary participants in grievance adjustment, but not in arbitration hearings. The argument was upheld, and the stewards were not paid, as the time did not qualify for payment under the terms of the contract. (Consolidated Industries, Inc., 43 LA 331)

For years, the chief steward walked through the plant at the start of each work day to permit the workers to make known any grievance they might have. Although it had not objected before, the company began refusing to pay for these visits unless the chief steward first requested and received permission to do so. The contract gave the steward the right to reasonable time off to investigate grievances "upon notice and approval" by management.

According to the arbiter, the practice followed by the steward for years without objection from the company was the same as notice to and approval by the company and was not subject to unilateral change by the company. (American Saint Gobain Corp., 46 LA 920)

Arbitration is merely the last step of the grievance procedure and, as such, is governed by the grievance language of the contract. Thus, the contract clause granting time off for grievance investigations entitled the local union president to accompany an industrial engineer on a union-requested time study, the arbiter decided, despite management's objection. (Hupp Corp., 48 LA 524)

Arranging Leave

In setting its policy on leave of absence, management really has two separate and distinct problems: (1) Short-term absences, usually due to illness, or other unavoidable failure to report for work; and (2) longer absences, which employees can plan for in advance, and which may be granted for any one of a dozen different reasons.

For short-term leaves, most companies merely require that the employee *notify* the company that he is going to be absent. This notice must come in within a specified time, usually the first day or the first morning of the absence. Disciplinary penalties are specified for failure to make proper notification. (This subject is discussed in more detail in the chapter on *Discipline for Absenteeism.*)

For long absences, or short-term leaves which are *not* unavoidable, companies usually require advance notice and *approval* from the proper management official before the leave is taken.

Like many other company policies, formal requirements for leaves of absence are often allowed to lie neglected in the rule book. If a company has followed a lax policy in arranging and granting leaves, an arbitrator is not likely to be too sympathetic if management suddenly decides that an employee should be discharged because he was a bit too informal about his leave-taking.

GUIDELINES

Oral or Written Grant for Leave of Absence

Companies often require that authorization for leave of absence be put in writing. Despite this requirement, management sometimes grants oral leaves of absence. In such instances the question arises as to whether the employee was on an authorized leave.

An arbitrator is likely to decide that management has given up the right to discipline an employee by giving oral permission to be absent.

EXAMPLE: An employee was absent on an extended leave after obtaining oral permission from management for a leave of absence. The employee, upon returning to work, was notified by the company that he had lost his seniority rights, because the leave authorization had not been put in writing. A contract provision stated "Management agrees that leave shall be in writing and a copy thereof sent to the union."

The arbiter held that the leave was authorized and that the employee did not lose his seniority rights. He reasoned that the provision concerning a written leave was for the protection of the company. The company, in this case, had given up its privilege to require a written leave when it granted oral permission to the employee. The company, therefore, could not use its own action, in not putting the leave in writing as an excuse to deny the employee his seniority rights. (Gem Electric Mfg. Co., Inc., 11 LA 684)

Moreover: The fact that a contract provides that employees who request a leave of absence for a period of more than six days must make application in writing does not preclude finding that an employee who orally requested time off for one day was on "leave of absence."

EXAMPLE: An employee, the fourteenth member of a work crew, requested time off to visit a friend. Under the contract, the company agreed to guarantee 13 men on the crew and to replace the fourteenth if he was on leave. The union, on the other hand, agreed to absorb the work of the fourteenth member if his absence was due to sickness, accident, or absenteeism. Both parties agreed the absence was excused, but the company referred to it as an excused "absence," and the union as "leave."

The umpire, in holding for the union, ruled that the contract implied that a leave of absence for a period of less than six days would not be reduced to writing. There is a clear difference, he said, between "absenteeism" and being off duty with prior permission. (Emge Packing Co., 15 LA 603)

Oral Discussion with Management

If management wants to make sure that leaves will be granted only after formal authorization, it should make this requirement fairly specific in its contract or personnel policy. Otherwise, an employee may claim that he was "granted" leave of absence when the company intended no such thing.

EXAMPLE: An employee contracted tuberculosis and was told by his doctor to take a long rest. The personnel director told him not to worry and that everything would turn out okay. The employee considered the statement a grant of a leave of absence and was gone for over a year. When he returned, he discovered he had been discharged.

The arbiter ordered payment of half the wages the employee would have earned from the date he applied for reinstatement until the date of the award. He reasoned that the company's interest in the health of its employees, and its liberal policy in respect to leaves of absence for illness, strongly suggested that the employee had been granted a leave of absence. The words of the personnel director, he says, when considered in the light of all circumstances, must be construed as an oral grant of leave "or a sufficient equivalent." (Morey Machinery Co., Inc., 9 LA 570)

"Reasonable Notice" for Leave of Absence

Several questions may arise when the term "reasonable notice" is used in a contract provision on leaves. Who determines what is "reasonable" and what is not "reasonable"? What length of time can be considered "reasonable"?

Unless the agreement says otherwise, the union probably can demand an equal voice in answering such questions.

EXAMPLE: A contract provided that "reasonable notice" should be given to the proper company official before an employee could leave his job. The company, without consulting the union, posted a rule stating: "reasonable notice is deemed to be 48 hours . . ." An employee requested permission for immediate absence for a few hours and left his place of employment when the request was denied. When the company disciplined the employee, the union contended that he was on legitimate leave and should not have been disciplined.

The umpire's ruling was not based upon the "reasonable notice" issue but he did discuss it. He indicated that the company had no right to set a specific period of time without first obtaining the union's consent. When the "reasonable notice" clause was inserted in the contract, he said, it became a proper subject for bargaining and management could not unilaterally fix its meaning by posting a company rule. (Ampco Metal Inc., 3 LA 374)

Notice to Company to Return to Work

Contract clauses covering leave sometimes provide for notice to the company when an employee intends to return to duty. Unless the contract terms are very specific, confusion may arise as to the proper timing of the notice.

In such an instance one arbiter held that an employee had a "reasonable" time to submit his request for rehire.

EXAMPLE: A union official was absent for several years on an authorized leave of absence for union business. Upon discharge from his union duties he waited 12 days before submitting a request for rehire to the company. The company refused on the ground that he had not given notice, as was required by contract, immediately after his release from union duties. The company also argued that the "Increasing forces after layoff" provisions in the contract required an employee to report for work within five days after he was recalled from a layoff. The union argued that the "Leave for Union Activity" clause merely required the employee to notify the company one week before he was ready to go back to work.

The employee was ordered reinstated with seniority and back pay. The arbiter held that the "Increasing forces after layoff" clause had no application in fixing the period of time required for giving notice at five days. He stated that a careful examination of the leave clause failed to reveal any requirement as to a fixed period of time for giving the rehire notice and, therefore, that a "reasonable" period should be allowed. The arbiter concluded that 12 days

was not too long a period of time in this instance. (Armour & Co., 10 LA 140)

Reinstatement after Leave of Absence

If any employee requests reinstatement after an extended authorized leave of absence, how much time has management to reinstate the employee?

In the absence of specific policy to cover the situation, an arbiter held in one instance that the company had a "reasonable" time but that waiting two weeks was "unreasonable."

EXAMPLE: An employee who was absent for six months on authorized leave requested that he be reinstated. Management delayed two weeks before he was put back to work. In answer to the employee's claim for two weeks' salary, the company stated that it was entitled to at least several weeks' notice before placing the employee, since the nature of its operations required that much time to plan work and set up schedules.

It seemed to the arbiter that it would be unfair to require the company to put the employee back to work on the same day he decided to return to work. Since the employee had been absent for six months, the company should have been allowed a reasonable opportunity to find out where he could best be used. Because of the nature of the operation, the arbiter concluded that the company should have found out in one week where best to place the employee. (Crawford Clothes, Inc., 12 LA 1104)

In another case, an employee who had been injured on-the-job was held by an arbiter to be entitled to her former position even though she had been out for more than a year, since she had obtained a medical certificate approving her return. She had been told by the employer that she could return to her job when such a condition was fulfilled. The arbiter ruled that the contract provision permitting leave of absence for one year only was not applicable since it was not intended to apply to forced absence for on-the-job injury. The employee had neither requested nor received formal leave of absence, and the employer in describing conditions for the reinstatement had not mentioned time limits. The employee was capable of performing her work since she had obtained two medical releases for work without restriction. (Textile, Inc., 48 LA 509)

Extension of Leave

If a company requires employees on leave to renew the leave at definite periods, can it discharge an employee who does not get his request in before the expiration of the leave period?

When an employee is late with his request for renewal, management would seem to be within its rights in considering the worker no longer an employee of the company.

EXAMPLE: An employee requested an extension of his leave of absence two days after his original leave had expired. The contract required that such leave be renewed each six months. Another provision of the contract stated that an employee was deemed to have quit, with subsequent loss of seniority, if he failed to report for work for three consecutive working days and had not been granted leave of absence. The union argued that the seniority protection clause applied in this case as the employee had been absent only two days beyond the termination of his leave. The company took the position that the renewal had not been requested within the six-month time-limit; and therefore the employee had not complied with the contract.

The arbitrator, in ruling for the company, reasoned that the only logical construction that could be placed upon the six-month renewal qualification was that the request for renewal of leave must be made before the expiration of the original period. He also stated that the three-day seniority protection clause, for actively employed workers absent without leave, had no application to absentees overdue from leave of absence. (Campbell Wyant & Cannon Foundry Co., 1 LA 254)

Cancelling Leave after It Is Granted

If management has the sole right to grant or deny leaves of absence, can it also cancel leaves which have been authorized?

Undoubtedly the right to deny leave extends also to the cancellation of leave already granted. This probably should be handled, however, by notifying the employee and giving him a chance to return to work, not by changing his status from "on leave" to "quit."

EXAMPLE: An employee on the day shift was told the company was moving her to the night shift in order to avoid laying her off. For personal reasons she could not work nights. She orally requested a leave of absence, which was granted. While she was on leave, the company marked her record "quit." The employee entered a claim .for vacation pay and the company answered that she was a "quit" and was not entitled to payment.

A majority of the arbitration board decided that the company had the right to deny the employee the leave. The board said, however, that the denial should have been made at the time the request was made. The majority pointed out that it was entirely possible that the employee, given the choice of her job or the night shift, might have changed her decision. The board held that the company's action in changing from approval to disapproval without notifying the employee was unfair. (Anchor Rome Mills, Inc., 9 LA 497)

IN BRIEF

More than a third of contracts require the company to post job vacancies so that workers may bid on them; almost all such contracts are in manufacturing industries. Ordinarily, workers in the department or occupation where the openings occur get first crack at them; only then may workers elsewhere in the unit apply.

This section shows how arbitrators have settled disputes over which jobs should be posted, how posting should be carried out, and which workers are entitled to bid on posted jobs.

GUIDELINES

WHICH JOBS MUST BE POSTED?

Newly Created Jobs

When a contract provides that job vacancies shall be posted, the company should post all vacancies, including newly created jobs. Arbitrators have ruled that the term "job vacancy" refers to any and all openings, including new positions.

In one case, management filled a newly created job with someone from the outside. The union protested on the basis of a contract clause stating that "job vacancy in each department shall be posted for a minimum of 48 hours." The company replied t h a t this wasn't a job vacancy, but a new job. The umpire, however, ruled that any job opening is a "vacancy" at the instant the company decides there is a need for the job to be manned. Any other holding, he said, would undermine the posting and job-filling sections of the contract. (Borden Co., 34 LA 658)

Temporary Vacancies

Do the posting and bidding requirements of a contract have to be applied to temporary vacancies? Some arbitrators hold that such vacancies

do not have to be posted or filled in accordance with seniority. They reason that to apply these requirements to every brief vacancy would be a handicap and a detriment to the efficient management of the business. (Wilson & Co., Inc., 5 LA 695; Pennsylvania Transformer Co., 29 LA 589)

However: At least one arbitrator believes that there is a limit to what can be considered a temporary vacancy. He said that a vacancy expected to last for at least one year during a leave of absence should be posted and filled by the senior qualified bidder. (McLouth Steel Corp., 11 LA 805)

Job Originally Filled "Temporarily"

When it becomes apparent that the person who left a job temporarily will not return, does the worker who replaced him temporarily have to be removed and the job posted for bidding as a "permanent" vacancy? At least one arbitrator has said that if an employee promoted temporarily remains in the new job for a considerable period of time, his promotion becomes permanent, and the company is no longer obligated to post the job. (Bethlehem Steel Co., 16 LA 478)

On the other hand: In a situation when it became clear that a temporary summer job would turn into a permanent one, an umpire held, a company had to post the job for bidding in line with seniority. He said that the company violated the agreement by awarding the job on a permanent basis to the worker who had been filling it temporarily.

EXAMPLE: The parties had worked out a system whereby temporary jobs were created to permit all workers to take their vacations during the summer. These jobs lasted only a couple of months or so, and they were posted and filled in accordance with seniority by workers in lower classifications. At the end of the vacation season these workers returned to their regular jobs. (Phillips Petroleum Co., 29 LA 833)

Job Posting v. Transfer

Under a contract with requirements for posting vacancies, one arbitration board ruled that an employer could not transfer a worker facing layoff to fill a vacancy instead of posting the job for bidding.

EXAMPLE: An employee at one company was scheduled to be laid off within two days when an opening occurred in another department. Instead of posting the job and allowing employees to bid on the vacancy, the firm filled it with the employee facing layoff. When an employee with higher seniority complained that he had not been allowed a crack at the job, the company justified its action by saying that the contract was broad enough in intent and language to allow it to anticipate layoffs and retain employees. The company argued that it had an obligation to maintain the workforce and to give employees the highest-paid available jobs.

A board of arbitration ruled, however, that the company couldn't suspend its obligation to follow the posting clause. The company's personnel

situation at the time didn't make any difference, the board decided. Interested employees had to be allowed to apply for the job on the basis of their seniority and ability; and besides, said the board, there was a time lag before the actual layoff was due which should have been used as a posting period. The company was ordered to reopen the job to competitive bidding. (Shell Oil Co., 24 LA 748)

POSTING REQUIREMENTS

Information Required on Job Notice

When a contract requires notices to be posted for all vacancies, the notice need contain only reasonable identification of the vacant job, according to one arbitrator. He ruled that the posting does not have to give details, such as the degree of skill required, that may be determined upon inquiry. (John Deere Tractor Co., 3 LA 742)

However: Under a similar provision where the practice had been to name specific jobs in posting vacancies, one arbitrator decided that the company could not suddenly change to listing merely classifications of vacancies. He said the practice of posting specific job openings by name had to be continued. (Lion Oil Co., 25 LA 549)

Notices Should Be Posted Uniformly Throughout Plant

Even though a contract did not require posting of vacancies, a company whose practice was to post jobs in *some* departments had to post them in *all* departments, an umpire ruled. Failure to post job openings in certain departments, he said, unfairly prevented workers there from exercising their seniority rights. (National Malleable & Steel Castings Co., 4 LA 175)

WHO MAY BID?

Bidding in Same Classification

Under the promotion provisions of a contract, can a worker bid for a job in the same classification as his own? Arbitrators have generally held that, in the absence of a specific definition in the contract, "promotion" means a movement to a higher classification, not a lateral movement to a job which the employee thinks is more desirable. (U.S. Steel Corp., 21 LA 707; Blaw Knox Co., 23 LA 159; Continental Paper Co., 24 LA 723; Bethlehem Steel Co., 30 LA 550)

However: At least one arbiter has held that promotion should be construed to include improvement in working conditions as well as increases in pay. He found nothing in a contract that restricted the term "promotion' to advancement in classification. He said such an interpretation did not interfere with management's rights or with efficiency. (Medart Co., 18 LA 701)

Bidding Downward

Can a worker bid for a job in a classification lower than his own? Under a contract providing for vacancies to be filled by promotion within a department or if not filled in that manner, to be posted for plant-wide bidding, an arbitrator held that an employee could not bid down into a lower classification. He said that taking a lower-rated job was a demotion even if it provided better chances for advancement or steadier work. The bidding provision, he ruled, allowed employees to bid only for jobs at higher pay. (Superior Paper Products, 26 LA 849)

When a senior worker requested to fill a temporary vacancy in a job rated below his own, the company has the right to refuse him. The arbitrator said that the worker couldn't assert seniority rights to downward transfer unless a local practice to that effect existed, which he found was not the case. (Bethlehem Steel Co., 44 LA 457)

In a similar decision, the arbiter held that the contract contained no language permitting downward bidding. Therefore he disallowed the worker's use of seniority to get a lower job. (Pittsburgh Plate Glass Co., 44 LA 7)

On the other hand: Other umpires have come to the conclusion that senior qualified bidders have a right to a job, even though it is in a lower classification. In one case, even though the bidding clause made some reference to promotions, the arbiter decided it didn't restrict movement to promotions alone. (Southern Bakeries Co., 41 LA 329; see also Kilgore, Inc., 26 LA 789; Indiana Chair Co., 34 LA 856; Yardley Plastics Co., 40 LA 1305)

In another case, under a contract stating "seniority shall govern" in transfers and promotions, the arbitrator ruled that an employer couldn't reject a bidder solely because he wanted a downward transfer. According to the arbiter, the test of whether an employer improperly denied downward transfer was whether the denial was arbitrary or discriminatory. (Max Factor & Co., 45 LA 918)

Bidding Rights of Supervisor

Can a supervisor bid for a job that opens up in a bargaining unit? Where a contract permitted an employee to continue to accumulate seniority for a year after transfer out of the bargaining unit, an arbiter ruled that a supervisor who was once in the unit could bid for a job in the unit. Since the supervisor still had seniority, the umpire held that he had the same bidding rights as other employees. (Owens-Corning Fiberglas Corp., 28 LA 578)

However: In a case where a supervisor was not, and never had been, a member of the bargaining unit, an arbitrator said he had no right to bid on a posted job. Although the bidding clause referred to "employees," the umpire decided it clearly referred to members of the bargaining unit. Since supervisors weren't members of the unit, they couldn't accumulate seniority under the contract, and thus had no right to bid. (Boardman Co., 41 LA 215)

Right to Trial Period

A senior worker correctly contended that he had a right to a trial period on a higher job, according to the arbiter. The contract stated that qualifications for promotion were "with normal supervision, the factors necessary for the satisfactory performance of the work for which the employee is being considered." The worker wasn't entitled to a training period on the job; however, he was entitled to a chance to show that he had the ability necessary to fill the job without more than normal instruction. (John Deere Chemical Co., 42 LA 443)

On the other hand: An arbiter decided that a senior worker didn't have a right to a trial period on the job, but she did have the right to apply for the vacancy. The company improperly filled a job without first notifying the steward of the opening, so the arbiter ruled that the promotion was invalid and ordered the company to fill it in the proper manner, which included consideration of the senior worker's application. (Ivers & Pond Piano Co., 42 LA 88)

IN BRIEF

Although seniority is made a factor in promotion in more than two thirds of contracts, it is usually not so important a factor as in layoff. Ability to do the job commonly is taken into account, and frequently it is the dominant factor.

POINTERS—

▶ Arbitrators usually let management's judgment stand in the selection of workers for promotion, unless it can be shown that the company ignored the terms of the contract or acted in an arbitrary manner.

▶ In making promotions to supervisory positions, the company normally has a free hand.

▶ If no present employee is qualified to perform a vacant job, the company ordinarily has the right to hire on the outside.

GUIDELINES

Seniority To Break Ties

Where seniority is a determining factor only when ability is relatively equal, arbitrators have held that management has the burden of proving, when challenged, that it determined ability correctly, not merely that it did not act in an arbitrary, capricious, or discriminatory fashion. It must be shown that the selection was "reasonable," as well as free from arbitrariness, favoritism or bias (44 LA 283, 42 LA 1093)

One arbitrator ruled that the employer's burden of proof extended to showing that (1) the standards for comparison of job bidders' qualifications were established in good faith, (2) the standards were not patently inadequate, (3) the standards were applied fairly and impartially, and (4) a decision favoring a junior employee was not clearly unreasonable. (Atlas Powder Co., 30 LA 674)

Management, arbitrators have held, has the right to judge, weigh, and determine the necessary qualifications

of the respective applicants so long as the methods used are fair and non-discriminatory (25 LA 748). The qualifications compared must relate directly to the requirements of the job in question. (21 LA 565)

Experience has a definite place in determining comparative fitness, ability, and qualifications. And the experience factor need not be limited to prior experience of the job in question. Arbitrators have upheld giving preference to a junior employee where the experience of the junior employee is more closely related to the work involved than the experience of the senior employee. (21 LA 565, 30 LA 237, 50 LA 283)

Under a contract making seniority controlling in promotion where ability to perform the work and physical fitness are relatively equal, one arbitrator said that proved ability, not potential ability, was the test for selection. Even if potential ability is about the same between two bidders, he held, management can promote the junior man if he alone can step in and take over the job immediately.

EXAMPLE: Two jobs opened up in a plant and the company posted notices of the vacancies in accordance with its general policy. The company made promotions on the basis of (a) ability to perform work, (b) physical fitness, and (c) seniority where the first two factors were equal. The company assigned two junior employees to fill the vacancy of weighman, truck sales, bypassing several applicants having greater seniority.

The arbitrator ruled for the company. He pointed out that under the ability clause the company had the right to select the junior employee with demonstrated ability, as proved by experience on the job, rather than one who had never actually performed the job and had never demonstrated the particular skills which the job called for. (Pittsburgh Limestone Corp., 6 LA 648; De Kalb-Ogle Telephone Co. 50 LA 445)

Under a contract requiring that a vacancy be filled by the employee with most seniority where skill and ability are equal, the employer was not justified in promoting an employee with less seniority, even though he had experience in the other departments. The arbiter reasoned that this experience was fully balanced by the senior bidder's higher educational accomplishments. (Lockheed-Georgia Co., 49 LA 603)

Seniority & Aptitude as Factors

Under a contract making seniority and aptitude factors in promotion, an umpire held that a company could not refuse a senior employee a promotion on the ground that he was not able to perform the job at the time. Choosing a junior man for the promotion was not justified even if he was the only one able to perform the job, the umpire said. There was no reason to think the senior men could not have learned it. "Aptitude," the arbiter said, means the potential to learn a job, and the bidder with highest

seniority should have been given a trial period to determine whether he had the aptitude. (Vulcan Mold & Iron Co., 29 LA 743)

Seniority & Ability as Factors

If a contract requires that both seniority and individual ability be taken into account in making promotions, arbitrators usually will not substitute their own judgment of employees' ability for management's. Most of them seem to try to strike a balance between management's right to judge ability and workers' seniority rights. Generally they uphold the company's judgment unless it is found to be discriminatory, arbitrary or erroneous. They rule that it is the union's responsibility to prove that management's judgment was faulty.

EXAMPLE: One arbitrator upheld the company's choosing of a junior applicant due to his superior overall job experience. The contract did not indicate the order of importance of the three factors—seniority, ability, and previous experience — in job assignment, thus he overruled the union's contention that these criteria are in descending order of importance. (Reliance Universal, Inc., 50 LA 397)

However: Where it is shown that two workers have relatively equal ability to handle a job, the senior man should not be passed over merely because a supervisor has an *impression* that the junior worker is better qualified, according to one arbitration panel. (Shell Oil Co., 4 LA 13)

Seniority as Crucial Factor

Where primary emphasis is put on seniority in determining promotion rights, arbitrators have held that a better qualified employee may not be given precedence over a senior employee capable of doing the work. To pass over a senior employee, an employer must be able to show that the employee is not capable of doing the job. If seniority is controlling, the company can't ignore seniority and promote the "most qualified" or "best qualified" (41 LA 353, 25 LA 631, 30 LA 460).

EXAMPLE: An employer was not allowed to promote a Grade C electrician to a Grade B vacancy for which a Senior Grade B man was available, despite the employer's contention that the senior man took an unreasonably long time to perform some of his tasks and sometimes wasted his time.

The arbitrator said that the senior employee was reasonably capable of performing the higher-rated work, even though he was deficient in some of the qualifications that would make him an employee of the highest caliber. (American Monorail Co., 21 LA 589)

Definition of "Ability"

Arbiters differ on the problem of what factors can be taken into consideration in determining "ability" to do a job. Thus, one umpire has expressed the view that management must confine its determination to whether the worker is capable of handling the job at hand; how he gets along with other people, his attendance record, and other considerations don't count. (McQuay-Norris Mfg. Co., 1 LA 305)

Some arbiters, though, are inclined to give management more latitude. One upheld the company's rejection of a union steward for promotion. The contract gave management a free hand in judging the ability and qualifications of workers; as long as it honestly believed another man could do the job better, the umpire ruled, its judgment couldn't be upset. Taking note of quarrels between the steward and management representatives, the arbiter saw no evidence of anti-union discrimination since the quarrels had no direct connection with union business. (Norwich Pharmacal Co., 30 LA 740)

Probationer v. Seniority Worker

Even where seniority was only a secondary factor, one arbitrator ruled that management could not promote a probationer who had better qualifications. The contract stated that in selecting workers for promotion, three factors would be considered—seniority, qualifications and ability, and physical flitness: Where the last two factors were relatively equal, seniority would govern.

The company had no authority to promote the probationary worker, the umpire said, even though he was the best qualified of the bidding employees. The reason was that he had no seniority, and in the umpire's opinion the agreement required that a man possess all three promotion elements in some degree to be considered for promotion. As long as workers with seniority had bid for the job, the arbiter concluded, the probationer was not eligible. (Borden Chemical Co., 32 LA 697)

Selection for Training Leading to Promotion

If a contract provides that promotion will be based on seniority where ability is equal, can management choose a junior employee for special training leading to a promotion? One umpire ruled that without a clear understanding with the union beforehand, a company had to follow seniority in selecting workers for training that would lead to promotion.

EXAMPLE: A company decided to give special training in inspection procedures. Although it admitted that the ability of two candidates for the training was equal, the junior employee of the two was picked. After completing the course, she was assigned to a newly created higher-rated job. When the senior employee protested, the company consulted with the union and agreed to give the senior employee the special training. However, after finishing the course she was denied the disputed job on the ground that its requirements had changed in the interim.

The arbitrator maintained that in this case the company was under an obligation to show the union at the outset that it genuinely needed flexibility in developing the new job and was not trying to bypass seniority rules. Since management failed to do this and let the matter drift, the umpire ordered the company to pay the senior employee the earnings she lost by not being selected initially for the special training. (Purolator Products, Inc., 25 LA 60)

In another case, an arbitrator held that requiring a high school education or its equivalent was a reasonable requirement for promotional training, but that a 30-year age cutoff for bidders was too low. The educational requirement was sustained because it related to the need for mathematical ability on the job. Because the contract referred to age 65 as retirement age, the arbiter said that workers completing the training course could have enough years of useful work left to repay the employer's investment, even if the workers were older than 30. (Ball Bros. Co., 46 LA 1153)

Potential for Supervisory Job

In filling a job within the bargaining unit, one arbiter held, the company couldn't promote a junior worker over a senior one on the ground that it was looking for future supervisors. Since the union could not control the company's choice of foreman, the umpire reasoned, the company could not put into the contract the requirements of the skills and potentialities of prospective foremen. This would amount to measuring bargaining-unit members by nonunit standards at promotion time. (Ross-Meehan Foundries, 40 LA 321)

Promotion of Union Steward

Can an otherwise qualified union representative be denied promotion on the ground that the time he spends on union affairs during working hours limits his ability to do the job? Unless past practice has been to restrict the promotion of union officials engaged in their duties during the working day, a company can't deny promotion to an employee who is otherwise qualified on the basis of his seniority and ability, one arbitration board said.

EXAMPLE: Two employees at a company were promoted to leadman jobs ahead of a union steward who had more seniority and more than enough ability to do the work. The company justified its action in bypassing the steward by saying that although he was qualified for the job in every respect, he spent too much time on union business to be able to do the leadman's job satisfactorily.

A board of arbitration decided that only the presence of an established past practice limiting the promotion of union representatives could justify the bypassing of the union steward. They found no such past practice at the company and accordingly decided that the steward should have received the promotion. (Douglas Aircraft Co., Inc., 23 LA 786)

Similarly: When a worker who had shown her ability to perform a job was denied the position because she could not devote full time to it due to her union duties, an arbiter said the company had unfairly discriminated against the union. He further said that if workers "find that their union positions are handicaps in obtaining preferred job assignments, it will become practically impossible for the union to attract the leadership it needs to carry on its work." (American Lava Corp., 42 LA 117)

Compulsory Promotion

Must an employee accept a promotion to a vacancy for which he is eligible against his own wishes? Under one contract stating that a promotion shall be given to the senior eligible employee in the department, an arbitrator held that all this required was that the company offer the vacant job to the senior employee. He was not obligated to accept it, and if he turned it down, the umpire ruled, it should have been offered to the next senior qualified worker. (Electro Metallurgical Co., 20 LA 281)

However: Another arbitrator decided that if the right to waive a promotion isn't spelled out in the contract, management normally has the right to make promotions regardless of employee desires. This is true, he noted, provided the employees' job security and seniority aren't jeopardized. (Gisholt Machine Co., 23 LA 105)

PROMOTION TO SUPERVISORY POSITION

Management's Right to Select Supervisors

Most arbitrators agree that management has the exclusive right to select its supervisors without union interference. They limit the application of contract clauses dealing with promotion to those jobs covered by the union contract or that fall within the bargaining unit. And they specifically point out that since supervisory positions are not within the bargaining unit management has the sole and exclusive right to fill them as it sees fit. (New York & Brooklyn Casket Co., 2 LA 517; Pennsylvania Greyhound Lines, Inc., 6 LA 16)

Retention of Duties after Promotion to Supervisor

Is an employer permitted to have a worker who is made a supervisor perform the same work he did while in the bargaining unit? One arbitrator ruled that since a worker's duties while in the unit were largely supervisory in nature, an employer could assign him the same work after he became a supervisor. Because his duties were largely supervisory, the umpire found no merit in the union's argument that work was being taken from the bargaining unit. He said that the union should have objected earlier when the worker was assigned the duties while still in the bargaining unit, not when he became a supervisor. (Chrysler Corp., 23 LA 247)

PROMOTION VS. NEW HIRE

Passing Over Qualified Bidder

Unless the contract shows an intent to give employees preference over outsiders, one umpire has held that management is not required to promote from within.

EXAMPLE: One union filed a protest when management hired an outsider to fill a designing job. A draftsman already working for the company wanted the job, and the union claimed he had the necessary ability. Since the contract stated that promotions were to be based on seniority and ability, the union argued, the inside man was entitled to be promoted.

There was some disagreement as to the adequacy of the draftsman's qualifications, but the umpire said this aspect of the case was irrelevant in any event. The important thing, he held, was that the contract placed no restriction on outside hiring. All it did was outline the procedure to be followed if the company decided to fill a job through promotion. If the parties had intended to give present employees preference over outsiders, the umpire concluded, they should have said so in the agreement. (Chrysler Corp., 32 LA 988)

However: Where a contract requires consideration of unit employees on the basis of seniority and qualifications, an employer could not hire outside where several unit bidders were qualified to fill a vacancy. The arbiter reasoned that the posting provision would be meaningless if the employer could hire from the outside or promote from within as it pleased, rejecting qualified unit applicants. (The Burdick Corp., 49 LA 69)

Hiring from Outside When Bidders Lack Ability

If a contract requires the company to fill vacancies on the basis of seniority, assuming capacity to perform the work, can a worker be hired from the outside to fill a job? Most arbitrators rule that under such a provision an employer can hire from the outside to fill a vacancy when no present employee is capable of performing the job.

EXAMPLE: To fill a vacancy on a maintenance job a company posted notice of the vacancy for bids. Of the twelve employees that bid, eleven agreed that they lacked the qualifications for the job; the twelfth was noncommittal and failed to press his claim. Under these conditions the company hired a new employee to fill the vacancy. The union opposed this action arguing that one of the bidders should have been given a trial period on the job.

The company replied that it had always been its policy to bring in men from the bottom and train them and then up-grade them to top skills rather than bring new men in at the top. But in this case, the company pointed out, there was no one available to upgrade who would be able to handle the job and in such an exceptional case it was necessary to resort to outside hiring.

The arbitration board ruled that "the circumstances warranted the company, in this case, from all the evidence, in departing from its usual and commendable procedure of upgrading and giving full opportunity to men within its own plant." The board found that since the bidders were not qualified for the job the company was justified in filling the job by new hire. (Atlantic Foundry Co., 8 LA 807; Bethlehem Steel Co., 31 LA 267; American Bosch Arma Corp., 40 LA 403)

Hiring Outside Applicant with More Training

Under a contract requiring that promotions be based on length of service, training, and efficiency, one arbiter ruled that previous training could not be a requirement for promotion to an apprentice. He said that a company could not hire a new man in preference to a senior employee merely because the senior worker had not graduated from a vocational school.

EXAMPLE: One company selected an outside applicant for an apprenticeship instead of promoting an employee to it. After deciding that the apprenticeship itself was a training program, an arbitrator awarded the vacancy to the untrained employee instead of to the outsider who had completed a vocational training program. To deny an employee the opportunity to enter the apprenticeship program, the arbitrator said, would nullify the purpose of the program. According to the umpire, the selection of an apprentice should be made on the basis of length of service and efficiency, without regard to the training factor. The company, he said, couldn't have both an apprenticeship program and a requirement that applicants have prior training. (Hershey Estates, 23 LA 101)

How Ability Is Measured

If a contract bases promotion on merit or ability as well as seniority, arbitrators generally have ruled that management has considerable freedom in deciding how it will measure "ability." (Seniority takes a back seat to ability in nearly three tenths of contracts.) Any tests that are used should be objective, however, and the results must not be applied in an arbitrary or capricious manner. Furthermore, the union may have solid ground for complaint if a worker whose job performance is good is refused a promotion on the basis of a test.

Where there has been doubt as to a senior worker's ability to do the job in question, arbitrators often have held that a trial period on the job is the best way to settle the matter.

Any test used to screen applicants for a job should be designed to measure qualities that have been shown to be related to performance on that job. For example, a test designed to measure mathematical aptitude shouldn't be used on applicants for a clerk-typist job that requires little or no work with figures. The use of tests that aren't validated for job-relatedness not only is wasteful; it may be regarded as a violation of the fair employment practice laws if the result is to screen out minority-group members who lack the education or background needed to pass the tests.

GUIDELINES

Written Test as a Measure of Ability

Whether or not an arbitrator approves the use of a written test to determine workers' ability in making promotions seems to depend largely on the weight the contract gives to seniority in filling vacancies.

If a contract makes seniority the governing factor when fitness and ability are equal, many arbitrators allow the company to require employees bidding for promotions to take written tests. Under this kind of clause the company has to measure the relative or comparative ability of candidates for a job, and an objective written test is a fair way to do this, these arbiters hold. (M. A. Hanna Co., 25 LA 480)

A frequently expressed view is that an employer may use tests to assist in deciding whether an applicant meets the job requirements but that the test results may not be relied on to the exclusion of other considerations. (29 LA 262, 29 LA 29)

EXAMPLE: An employer could use two aptitude tests in judging an employee's qualification for a job, even though the tests were never used in the past and the contract did not expressly permit them. The employer promised that the tests would not be used to pass or fail an applicant, but only as additional criteria in judging an employee's qualification; and despite the employer's decision regarding the applicant, he would have the right to redress under the grievance procedure. (Union Carbon Co., 49 LA 465; See also Scott Paper Co., 47 LA 552)

One umpire said an employer could use such a test provided it was fairly applied and management did not use minute differences in scores to deny promotion to senior workers. (Stauffer Chemical Co., Inc., 8 LA 278; see also Westinghouse Electric Corp., 41 LA 902; Containers, Inc., 49 LA 589)

On the other hand: If a contract states that all vacancies shall be filled by the senior applicant provided he has the ability and physical fitness to perform the job, an arbiter may rule against the use of a test. One arbiter held that this kind of clause did not permit the company to promote a worker because he was better qualified for the job than workers with more seniority. He said that since the senior worker had to be given the job if he could do the work satisfactorily, the company could not base promotion on the results of a written test. (Marquette Cement Mfg. Co., 25 LA 127; see also American Meter Co., 41 LA 856)

Arbiters generally uphold management's right to use tests that have been specifically designed to determine an employee's ability to perform a certain job. However, they also hold that aptitude tests, not directly related to the work in question, properly should be used by management only in the selection of new employees, in counseling employees, or in other general uses. But such general tests should not be used as a standard for denying a senior employee a promotion. (31 LA 1002, 41 LA 1025, 34 LA 16, 43 LA 1184, 52 LA 633)

In a ruling against the use of a general aptitude test for promotions, one arbitrator said that "men were denied promotions not for lack of ability to perform the work but for lack of ability to pass written tests having little or no relationship to the jobs sought." It is quite conceivable, he said, that the company's best bricklayer could not pass a written test on bricklaying. He gave these ground rules:

● If a job doesn't require the ability to read and write, no written test whatever may be given.

● If a job requires ability to read and to copy words and figures, a written test must be limited to testing ability to read and copy words and figures.

● If it requires simple arithmetic, the test must be only of simple arithmetic. (34 LA 37)

Note: While arbitrators may be more inclined to permit the use of general aptitude tests for new hires, EEOC looks with equal disfavor on the use of such tests for hiring and for promotions In either case, EEOC has said (with Supreme Court approval) use of the test may be justified only if it can be shown that success on the test is correlated statistically with success on the job.

Oral Exam To Determine Qualifications

In a situation where the contract does not specify any method to be used to determine employees' qualifications for promotion, one arbitrator has said that a company has the right to use any method it sees fit, including oral examinations. But the test should be related to the skill and knowledge required for the job and otherwise not be unfair or unreasonable.

EXAMPLE: A contract required the company to consider for promotion only those employees "who are deemed qualified to do the work." When a job opening occurred in the top classification in one department, one employee in the department was given an oral test by the foreman to determine whether he was qualified for the job He failed to pass the exam and was denied the job. The union took the matter up as a grievance, arguing that the test was unfair because there was no prescribed standard exam and no written job description on which the test could be based.

The arbitrator upheld the company's action. Since the contract did not specify a particular method for determining whether a worker was qualified for promotion, he said that it was okay to use an oral exam. Furthermore, he found that the test was a fair one, partly because all workers then in the job had previously passed the same test. (Hammarlund Mfg. Co., Inc., 19 LA 653)

Merit Rating & Efficiency Rating as Measures of Ability

Some arbitrators have upheld management's right to use the results of a formal merit rating plan in selecting employees for promotion. Under a contract requiring the promotion of the senior worker where ability was relatively equal, one arbitrator said that one company's merit-rating plan was an acceptable method of measuring relative ability. (Acme Steel Co., 9 LA 432)

Aptitude Test as Prerequisite to Trial Period

Is a company justified in requiring bidders for better jobs to pass aptitude tests before being given a tryout on the job? Where training workers for better jobs is an expensive process, arbitrators are likely to uphold the use of tests to screen out applicants who can't show the aptitude that would warrant the expense of a tryout, even though as senior employees, they would have first bid for the jobs. But the tests should be objective and should measure, as far as possible, the aptitude for the jobs involved. (United Rayon Mills, 14 LA 241)

On the other hand: Where a contract specifically provided for a trial period, an arbiter ruled that the company had no right to turn down the senior bidder for a job simply because she had failed a mathematical test. (National Seal Co., 29 LA 29)

In another case, the employer was held to have violated the contract when it promoted a junior employee to a new position of electrical trainee on the ground that he was the only applicant who passed a written test showing extent of electrical knowledge. The arbiter ruled that the test used was not a fair measure of ability to perform the job since the position was created to give employees a chance to develop electrical skills. (Vulcan Materials Co., 49 LA 577; see also U.S. Steel Corp., 49 LA 1160)

Trial Period To Test Ability

When is a senior worker entitled to a chance to prove himself on a job for which he is bidding? Arbitrators' awards suggest that a trial period may be in order, in appropriate circumstances, under two common types of promotion clauses.

The first is a provision that makes seniority determining in promotions if the senior bidder is able to perform the work. Under one contract providing that seniority should govern in promotions if the senior worker "has the competency for the job," an umpire held that a senior worker should have been given a breaking-in period to prove he was able to do the job. The company had passed over the senior man and promoted a more competent junior worker who was able to do the job without a breaking-in period because of his past experience. This was immaterial, the umpire said. He pointed out that the contract required the company to promote the most senior applicant who was competent, not the most competent applicant. Thus, the senior worker should be given a trial period to prove whether he could perform the job, the arbiter ruled. (Beaunit Mills, Inc., 15 LA 667)

The second type of promotion clause is one which makes seniority controlling where ability is relatively equal. When a company has no objective measure of relative ability under such a provision, some arbitrators say that a trial period is the best way to clear up any doubts about the ability of the senior bidder.

In one case, when a hoist-operation

job opened up, the supervisor gave it
to a worker in preference to an older
man with more seniority. His reason
was that he felt the latter worker was
too old to handle the job. An arbitrator pointed out that this worker was
strong and rugged and his supervisor's
doubt as to his ability did not justify
bypassing him for promotion. Since
the supervisor's decision was based on
such a weak assumption, the arbiter
said the worker should be given a
chance to prove his ability on the job.
He concluded that although a trial
was not necessary in all cases it should
not be denied where there was a reasonable doubt of ability and where it
would cause no serious inconvenience.
(Ford Motor Co., 2 LA 374)

Trial Period v. Training Period

If a contract provides a trial period
for promoted workers and m a k e s
seniority a factor in promotion, must
management give the senior applicant
for a job a trial period even though
he is not qualified for the job?

According to one arbiter, there's a
big difference between a *trial* period
and a *training* period. A trial period
must be granted only after a worker
has been selected for promotion, he
said, and this rules out those who do
not have the necessary qualifications.

EXAMPLE: Besides granting a 12-
day trial period to employees who
were promoted to higher-rated jobs,
one contract said that seniority would
be the determining factor in promotion, "all circumstances being reasonably equal." When the company bypassed the senior bidder for a job
requiring some s p e c i a l preparation
and experience, the union lodged a
complaint. It conceded the junior man
was qualified and that the senior man
wasn't, but it argued that the latter
should have been given an opportunity
to prove he could handle the job.

The umpire disagreed. The contract
did not entitle the senior bidder to a
period of on-the-job training, he said.
Management was essentially correct in
arguing that the trial period became
available only after an employee had

been selected for promotion. However, the arbiter warned, management
must be prepared to justify the denial
of a trial period to a senior bidder.
(Colonial Baking Co., 34 LA 356; see
also Purex Corp., 39 LA 336)

Length of Trial Period

How long a p e r i o d of training
should an employee be allowed to show
that he can perform a higher-rated
job? To a large extent, the answer to
this question depends on the job to
which the employee is being promoted.
In one case, an arbitrator held that
five weeks was not long enough to
provide an adequate measure of an
employee's ability as a crane operator
and awarded him an additional two
weeks. (Lukens Steel Co., 18 LA 41)
In another case, an umpire ruled
that three months was a reasonable
period in which to determine whether
an admittedly qualified employee had
the proper temperament for the higher-rated job of floor inspector. (Seeger
Refrigerator Co., 16 LA 525)

Moreover: It has been held that if a
trial period for promoted employees
is established, it should be well defined
and applied equally to all employees.
(Consolidated Water Co., 23 LA 427)

Past Performance as Measure of Abil-
ity

Arbiters' decisions suggest that a
worker's record of on-the-job performance should be regarded as a key
indicator of ability. Under one contract
providing for job transfers based on
seniority where knowledge, training,
and ability were substantially equal,
an arbitrator held that a supervisor's
preference could not overrule evidence
of a senior worker's on-the-job ability.
When two workers bid for a maintenance mechanic job, the junior man
was promoted on the basis of the supervisor's judgment of knowledge,
training, and ability. The umpire
found that the senior worker had performed the job satisfactorily in the
past and this was more objective evidence of ability than the supervisor's
opinion. On the ground that their work
experience showed that the two men

were relatively equal in skill, knowledge, and ability, the umpire concluded that the senior man should be promoted. (Plymouth Cordage Co., 27 LA 816)

By the same token: Failure to make the grade during a previous trial on a job is enough evidence that a worker is not capable of handling the job, according to one arbiter. In such an event, he said, a worker is not entitled to a second trial period. (Republic Steel Corp., 3 LA 761)

Lack of Interest as Measure of Ability

Can a senior worker be bypassed for promotion because he shows lack of interest in his work? At least one arbitrator has ruled that "lack of interest" cannot be considered in measuring ability, particularly where it seems to be temporary and not consistent with the employee's usual attitude.

EXAMPLE: A contract required that the senior employee be given preference in promotions where abilities were equal. In filling the job of "Job Foreman," the company bypassed a senior employee on the ground that he showed a "lack of interest" in his work. The union filed a grievance arguing that since the abilities of the two men were equal the senior employee should have gotten the job.

The arbitrator agreed with the union contention. He ruled "that interest in work or lack of interest in work is a matter of incentive to exercise ability or capacity and is not one of the norms for measuring ability." The arbitrator then went on to point out that this lack of interest in the present case was a temporary condition apparently contrary to the worker's customary attitude so far as could be determined from his total job history. Therefore, since abilities were equal, the arbitrator held that the senior employee should have been given the promotion. (Ford Motor Co., 7 LA 324)

Union contracts infrequently provide special procedures applicable to the general subject of permanent transfer. As a rule the procedures governing promotion apply similarly to most types of transfers. Special transfer rights, however, sometimes are accorded to handicapped or aged workers. For example, special transfer rights are provided for handicapped workers (sometimes defined so as to include aged workers) in nearly three tenths of contracts.

Temporary transfers present a different situation. In the absence of specific contract language, arbitrators usually have upheld the right of management to assign workers to new and different tasks on a temporary basis, provided such transfers do not. violate seniority or other contractual rights. An important consideration in such cases often is whether the agreement contains a management clause recognizing the company's right to direct the work force.

(For cases dealing with transfer to avoid layoff, see p. 95:171.)

GUIDELINES

PERMANENT TRANSFER

Unit Attrition by Transfer

Seniority need not prevent the transfer of a worker whose job performance is not satisfactory while retaining more able junior workers in the same classification. This was done as part of a general movement to streamline a telephone company's desk unit. Because the general policy was aimed at upgrading the unit's performance level, the arbiter felt the company was justified in considering ability as well as seniority. (Southwestern Bell, 45 LA 229)

Transfer to Job Employee Can't Handle

Assuming management has an unrestricted right to transfer employees within occupational groups, can an employee complain if he is transferred to a job he cannot perform and then discharged for lack of qualifications?

Arbitrators generally agree that where management is given the right to transfer personnel it must be exercised reasonably. One arbitrator, for example, felt that transferring an employee to a job at which she had no prior experience and which she lacked the physical ability to do was unreasonable; the employee, he said, should not have been fired for failure to qualify for the job after a short trial period. (Curtiss-Wright Corp., 11 LA 139)

Transfer for Health Reasons

Can a worker be transferred against his wishes for the purpose of protecting his health? In the absence of a specific contract restriction on transfers of this nature, it is likely that an arbitrator would uphold management's right to make such transfers where it is apparent that they are made in good faith are **not** for discriminatory purposes, and are supported by reasonable medical findings.

EXAMPLE: A company transferred to a lighter (and lower-paying) job an employee who had undergone two operations. It did so on the advice of its plant physician, who said the employee could not safely handle his regularly heavy work. The employee wanted his regular job, however, and produced a note from his own physician saying he could return to work.

The arbitrator held the transfer was proper. He declared that "management had an obligation to avoid exposing employees to undue hazards to their health or safety and that this obligation created a right, under the management-rights clause, to transfer an employee if his presence in a given occupation created an undue hazard for himself or others.'"

The arbitrator considered it important that no discriminatory purpose was apparent in this case, that there was no question of bad faith, and finally, that the recommendation of transfer was made by the plant physician, who was more familiar with the types of work involved than the employee's personal doctor. (International Shoe Co., 14 LA 253)

Worker Bumped by Returning Veteran

What are the job rights of a worker who is transferred after the veteran he replaced returns to work? In the absence of a specific contract provision on the subject, one arbitrator decided that an employee transferred to make room for a returning veteran has the same rights as an employee on layoff.

EXAMPLE: When a veteran returned to his old job, the man who had been hired to replace him was transferred to a lower-paying job in another department. Another employee was given the first vacancy that occurred in the veteran's department on the basis of his plant-wide seniority. The union filed a griev-

ance, arguing that the transferred employee had first crack at the job in his old department because of his greater departmental seniority.

The arbitrator noted that the contract was silent on the subject of replacements for men in the military service. Under the draft law, however, a company is simply required to reinstate a returning veteran, the arbitrator pointed out; it can do as it pleases about his replacement. In the arbitrator's view, a company had an option of either continuing operations with a larger-than-normal work force or laying off the replacement. If it took the second alternative, the layoff would be no different from another, the arbitrator said. Since the contract in this case specified that departmental seniority would govern layoff and recall, the arbitrator concluded that veteran's replacement was entitled to the job in his old department just as he would have been had he been laid off. (Mead Corp., 22 LA 292)

Plant Transfer Rights and Obligations

An auto manufacturer wasn't bound to transfer workers from plants where certain models were discontinued to plants which still assembled those models. Because the same type of work was done at both plants, the arbiter did not feel that the "operations" had been transferred; so the company was not obligated by the contract to transfer the workers. (Chrysler Corp., 43 LA 349)

When a warehouse was permanently shut down, the parent company was not made to absorb the displaced workers. The arbiter found that the contract did not include the warehouse workers as part of the "company." Thus, the contract's seniority clause, for job-transfer purposes, excluded the warehouse workers. (Marsh Wall Products, 45 LA 551)

Transfer When Union Business Interrupts Work

If a union official is frequently

called from his job to tend to union business, can he be transferred to a job where his absences would not interfere with production? One arbitrator has said that such a transfer is not discriminatory in itself.

EXAMPLE: A union officer employed as a dispatch clerk was needed on her job regularly because she determined work schedules for other workers. When union business required her to keep interrupting her production work, the company ordered her to trade jobs with another woman. In the new position her pay and working conditions were the same as in the clerk's job. The union protested that the transfer violated a contract clause prohibiting discrimination against union members.

The umpire said that the employer had not violated the non-discrimination clause since the woman's new pay and working conditions were the same as before. He also reasoned that the new job permitted her to carry out her union business. (Oliver Corp., 15 LA 65)

Limitation on Transfer of Union Officials

Is a provision that shop stewards may not be transferred without their consent limited only to transfers outside the bargaining unit? One arbitrator said that such a provision could not be given such a narrow interpretation. When the chief shop steward at one company was transferred first to the second shift and later to the third shift, the union protested that the company violated the clause prohibiting transfers of stewards without their consent. The company claimed that the clause referred only to transfers outside the bargaining unit. Upholding the union, the umpire found that a movement from one shift to another was a transfer within the general meaning of the word. (Midland Rubber Corp., 18 LA 590)

On the other hand, a company was not required to transfer a worker from the second shift to the first shift just because he was elected chief steward. Although the contract implied that the chief steward should be on the first shift, it did not say that he must work the first shift or that the company must transfer his work from one shift to another. The company allowed the chief steward to have unlimited access to the plant, which was all that was required of it. (Chrysler Corp., 42 LA 1018)

As for shifting departments, a worker's right to serve as shop steward in his "home" department wasn't limited by the employer's right to transfer him elsewhere. Thus, a company was forced to recognize a welder as steward for his home department despite the fact that he had been transferred to another department. Since the company's power to assign could have eliminated a desirable union candidate, this right should not be construed to narrow the privilege of selection. Likewise, the right of selection doesn't bind the company to transfer a worker back to his home department, for the purpose of representation, without prior negotiation. (New York Shipbuilding Corp., 44 LA 924)

Union officials holding superseniority may not be transferred from the units they represent. Superseniority is designed to provide continuity of representation for the units in which the officials are elected, to allow the officials to police the contract in their departments, and to make them readily available to unit members and supervision. (New York Shipbuilding Corp., 43 LA 741)

Shift Transfers

If a contract is silent on the matter, do workers have a right to choose their shifts on the basis of their seniority? Most arbitrators feel that, in the absence of a specific contract provision permitting it, workers may not exercise their seniority to transfer to a shift of their choice. One union claimed that senior workers could bump juniors on more desirable shifts. It argued that seniority should be applied to shift transfers as well as governing layoffs, recalls, and demotions under the contract. The arbitrator, however, decided nothing in the contract gave senior workers the right to displace juniors on other shifts. (Kuhlman Electric Co., 19 LA 199)

Lateral Transfers

Seniority entitled a qualified worker to a lateral transfer, regardless of relative ability. So long as the man had the basic ability to perform the job, he was entitled to it over a newly hired man. The fact that he was "efficient" or "badly needed" on his present job should not stand in the way of his transfer.

EXAMPLE: A turret lathe operator requested a transfer to a new tape-controlled tracer lathe, where the operator's job carried the same rating but offered greater opportunity for promotion. In rejecting the transfer request, the company said the worker was "one of our most efficient operators on assignments that require the full capabilities of trained operators." Under the contract, seniority, skill, and ability were made the determining factors in passing on transfer request.

The contract didn't mention "efficiency" as one of the factors to be considered, the arbiter noted. An able employee shouldn't be penalized for his ability by denying his seniority rights. (Steel Products Engineering Co., 47 LA 952)

Further, lateral transfers should not be denied simply because the job does not pay more than the previous one. If it offers a better chance for advancement, it should be considered a "promotion" and follow normal contractual procedures for promotion and lateral transfers. (Picker X-Ray Corp., 42 LA 179)

TEMPORARY TRANSFERS

Temporary v. Permanent Transfer

Since management usually retains an unrestricted right to make temporary transfers to fill short-term gaps in the work force, arbitrators frequently are asked to pass on the distinction between "temporary" o "permanent" transfer where the con tract contains no definitions. The di viding line often is set at a week o two. (36 LA 767, 23 LA 581)

Where contracts specify the time limit on temporary transfers, a com mon maximum is 30 days.

Worker's Right to Refuse Temporary Transfer

When a contract does not spell i out, do workers have a right to re fuse temporary transfers to othe jobs? Where the assignment was t lower-rated work, an arbitrator or dered a worker reinstated because management went too far in termi nating his employment for refusal t accept a transfer. (Great Atlanti & Pacific Tea Co., 1 LA 63; see als Moore Enameling & Mfg. Co., 7 L 459)

However: Another arbitrator ha ruled that an employee must accep a temporary transfer unless the con tract specifically spells out his righ to refuse it. (Phillips Oil Co., 18 L 798)

In a related group of cases, arbi trators have upheld employee refus als to accept transfers regarded a "unreasonable." For example, a employer was held to have acted un reasonably in asking some glaziers t do temporary work as painters. (LA 782)

Temporary Transfer to Higher-Rated Job

Is a worker transferred temporarily to a higher-rated job entitled to the regular pay for that job? If the pay practices for temporary transfers are spelled out in the contract, there is no problem. But at least one arbiter has held that, even when the contract is silent on the matter, management is obligated to pay the rate for a higher job to a man who temporarily fills the job. He reasoned that it is inherent in a classification system that an employee should receive the higher rate if he performs a job in a higher classification. (Tide Water Oil Co., 17 LA 829)

In-Grade Transfer to Temporary Job

In the absence of contract provisions and any established past practice, can a temporary job be assigned to a worker from another classification rather than to one in the same grade? Reasoning that a case has to be decided on the basis of logic and equity where no other guides are available, one arbitration board ruled that a man in a helper classification has more right to a temporary helper's job than an employee from another classification. They said that fairness dictated that the company give the helper the job since losing it meant a loss of pay. As long as the company failed to show that there was an unreasonable administrative burden involved, the arbiters ruled, the job should have gone to the helper. (National Carbon Co., 23 LA 263)

Voluntary Transfer to Lower-Paying Job

At what wage rate must a worker be paid who is given a choice of taking work on a lower-paying job to avoid layoff or for some other reason? Most companies make clear that where an employee is required (for company convenience) to take a lower-paying job, he receives his regular rate for the period; but where he voluntarily accepts a lower-paying job, as in a force reduction, he receives the rate of that job. Most arbitrators have upheld this practice, even where no clear distinction was made between voluntary and required transfers. (General Chemical Co., 1 LA 546; Telex Products Co., 2 LA 119)

On the other hand: Under a contract stating that employees would continue to receive their regular rate of pay when they were required to fill the place of another employee at a lower-rated job, one arbiter has held that workers must be paid their own regular rate for any lower-rated job to which they are temporarily transferred. He ruled that the contract required this whether the transfer was compulsory or voluntary. (U.S. Pipe & Foundry Co., 5 LA 492)

A company had the right to force a senior worker to return to his regular job after he temporarily had been allowed to take a lower-rated job to avoid being laid off. When the work force returned to normal, the arbiter held, the job merely was reinstated; only new jobs required posting. And nothing in the contract prohibited the company from requiring the senior worker to take the higher-rated job. (Warner & Swasey Co., 43 LA 1011)

IN BRIEF

Even though a vacation policy is spelled out in detail in the contract, numerous questions may arise when it comes to determining the rights of individual workers. The most common disputes relate to workers who are not actively at work during the vacation season (for example, employees on layoff) and those whose employment is terminated for one reason or another before vacation time rolls around.

Another source of controversy involves what effect absences have on vacation eligibility. The types of absences that may be held to break vacation eligibility include—

► Layoffs for slack work.

► Time lost during a strike.

► Time lost after a strike, before return to work.

► Time lost because of illness.

► Time lost because of occupational injury.

► Leaves of absence for union business.

► Leaves of absence for personal reasons.

► Leaves of absence for "civic" or military reasons.

► Chronic absenteeism.

GUIDELINES

EFFECT OF LAYOFF

If an employee has met all the regular requirements for a vacation, there is little doubt that he is entitled to vacation pay if he is laid off before the vacation season rolls around. The usual practice is to treat vacation rights, once earned, as a vested benefit.

Thus, one employer's contract stated that an employee would be entitled to a paid vacation provided he had a specified amount of service and was "in the employ" of the company on April 15. An arbitrator said the employer was wrong in denying vacation pay to employees who were laid off before April 15 after meeting all the other requirements for a paid vacation. (27 LA 1)

It may be a different story, however, if the contract says employees must be "on the payroll" as of a certain date. Some, though not all, arbitrators have held that when an employee is laid off he ceases to be on the payroll for vacation purposes. (23 LA 298 and 15 LA 13, but see 14 LA 1017 and 13 LA 880)

While a laid-off employee generally is entitled to previously earned vacation-pay rights, it does not follow that the time he spends on layoff will be credited towards meeting the service or work requirements for future vacations. The general rule is that vacation pay "is associated with work and does not accrue during periods of unemployment or layoff unless . . . the agreement so provides expressly or by necessary implication." (34 LA 170)

Definition of "Service" & "Employment"

Many contracts base vacation eligibility on a certain amount of "service." Management's reasoning often is that "service" means actual work, and that therefore, layoff time should not be counted in figuring vacation eligibility. On the other hand, workers will argue that their "service" hasn't been broken while on layoff because "service" is synonymous with "seniority." This latter view has been upheld in arbitration.

EXAMPLE: Under a contract requiring a certain number of "years' service" for vacation eligibility, the company maintained that "service" meant being on the job. Hence, it argued that a three-week layoff period should be deducted in calculating "service," with the effect that a laid-off worker wouldn't be eligible for a vacation until a year and three weeks had passed. The union's position was that "years of service" was the same as seniority.

The arbiter noted that the contract made seniority dependent on "length of continuous service," and that in this connection "service" never was considered broken by layoffs. Therefore, the union's position was upheld as "the one ordinarily adopted," since the agreement failed to set forth specific work requirements for vacation eligibility. (St. Louis Smelting & Refining Co., 8 LA 219)

Likewise: When a contract bases vacation eligibility on "employment," some umpires hold, this too is the same as seniority. If a laid-off worker has a right to recall on a seniority basis, then his employment is not generally thought to be ended by layoff, one arbiter noted. Thus, he reasoned, laid-off workers who fulfilled the conditions that qualified them for recall were entitled to have their layoff periods counted as employment in determining vacation credits. (Hanchett Mfg. Co., 28 LA 235)

EFFECT OF STRIKE

A strike may raise several questions regarding vacation eligibility—

▶ Are employees who fail to return to work at the end of the strike still entitled to claim vacation benefits?

▶ Does time spent out on strike count the same as working time in determining service requirements for vacation eligiblity?

Since vacation benefits usually are considered an earned right, those who quit during a strike generally are entitled to claim their vacation pay if they have otherwise met the eligibility requirements. Vacation benefits may be denied, however, if strikers who terminate fail to meet notice requirements for resignation.

Where vacation eligibility is tied to "continuous service," arbiters generally rule that time spent on strike should not be counted in computing continuous service. (42 LA 929, 48 LA 213, 47 LA 319, 47 LA 1164) One arbiter, however, ruled that taking part in a strike, even though it was in violation of contract, wasn't in itself cause to deprive employees of vacation credits. In the umpire's view, the strikers would have forfeited vacation credits if management (1) had fired them before the vacation credits accrued or (2) had notified them that their return to work would be conditioned on a waiver of vacation credits. (6 LA 238)

Strike v. Lockout

Where a contract provided vacations for workers in "continuous service" for a specified period of time, the arbiter held that the time employees spent on strike could not be counted in computing "continuous service" but the time they were locked out could be counted. He reasoned that the lockout was voluntary on the part of the company and prevented workers from accruing the "continuous service" required for vacation eligibility. The strike, however, didn't come within the exceptions to the vacation provisions, so it must be considered as a break in service. (Denver Upholstered Furniture Mfrs., 42 LA 929)

Strike as "Excused Absence"

On arbiter held that time spent by the employees on strike did not constitute "excused absence" within the meaning of a contract provision. The strike was "legal" in that it violated no law, but the arbiter doubted that it was "excused" by the employer, and further, such an interpretation would require the employer to "subsidize the strike." (Motor Car Dealers Assn. of Kansas City, Mo., 49 LA 55)

EFFECT OF ABSENCES

Some contracts deal with the effect of absences on vacation eligibility by fixing a cut-off point of a designated number of absences after which the right to vacation benefits is affected. For example, it might be specified that "an employee's vacation pay will be prorated, if during the vacation-eligibility year, he was absent for more than 60 days regardless of the reasons for the absences.

In the absence of such a provision arbitrators tend to adopt a cut-off rule of their own under which they may ignore absences of relatively brief duration but may disallow or prorate vacation pay where lengthy absences are involved.

Special rules apply where an absence is caused by an employee's entering the military service or meeting military training obligations. Such absences generally must be counted as time worked (see p. 22:525).

Absences for Illness, Injury

Do employees who are absent because of illness or other disability lose their right to vacation pay? Unless the contract specifically says so, workers should not be denied their vacation rights because of absences for illness or injury, according to most arbitrators.

Even where a worker's absenteeism was partly his own fault because of excessive drinking, an umpire held that he was entitled to vacation pay since there was proof that he also could not work because of an injury. (Chicago & Harrisburg Coal Co., 2 LA 57)

However: Where a contract provided that "time lost for illness" would not affect vacation pay, an arbiter ruled that an "injury," even though occurring on-the-job, was not "illness" for purposes of computing these benefits. (Modecraft Co., 44 LA 1045)

Leaves of Absence

Generally, where there is no controlling contract provision, arbiters uphold the company's right to deny vacation benefits to workers who have been on leave of fairly long duration.

Absence for Union Business

Does time spent on union business count as time worked for purposes of vacation eligibility? In some cases, umpires ruled that it didn't.

EXAMPLE: Under the contract, eligibility for vacation benefits hinged on a work requirement of 1,400 hours in a vacation year. The local's president was 64 hours shy of the requirement. The union pointed out that up to 340 hours of leave could be credited toward satisfying the vacation work requirement; and absence for union activity was leave time under the contract. Since the officer had spent more than 64 hours on union affairs, it added, he had a right to vacation benefits. The company replied that elsewhere in the agreement a distinction was made between "excused union activity" and "authorized leave of absence." Hence it denied the president had been on leave. The arbiter upheld the company's position, saying that if union activity had been meant to be a leave of absence there would have been no reason for making the distinction cited. (American Air Filter Co., Inc., 39 LA 942)

Similarly: where a contract's vacation clause required employees to have been "continuously in the service of the company" as of the eligibility date, an umpire upheld the company's refusal to grant vacation to a worker who had been on union business leave for six months. The arbiter

reasoned that "continuously in the service" meant "continuously available to the employer," which the man on leave was not. (Chamberlain Co. of America, 8 LA 755)

Similarly: Another arbitrator upheld a company policy of paying vacation pay *only* after workers returned from leave of absence. He said that it would be unfair to the company to require payment of a benefit when there was no certainty that employees intended to return to work. (Beaunit Mills, Inc., 22 LA 670)

Maternity Leave

How does maternity leave affect a worker's vacation rights? At one plant where the vacation clause called for a year's "continuous employment," those who took an enforced six-month pregnancy leave forfeited their eligibility for that year, an arbiter ruled. Workers on maternity leave weren't "continuously employed in the company's plant" during the year, and in this sense were "laid off." The union had argued that pregnancy was not an "illness" or a "layoff" which would interrupt a worker's continuous service for vacation purposes. The sense of the vacation provision, he found, is that benefits are a reward for actual continuous employment. (Clean Coverall Supply Co., 47 LA 272)

EFFECT OF TERMINATION

The current tendency to treat vacation pay as an earned right generally means that an employee who has met all of the eligibility requirements for a paid vacation is entitled to claim his vacaton pay if he is terminated prior to taking his vacation.

But what if he has met all of the eligibility requirements except a requirement that he be on the payroll as of a certain date? After an extensive review of prior court and arbitration decisions, an arbitrator concluded that the principle was well settled in industry generally that employment on the specified date is not a condition of eligibility for vacation pay and therefore that termination prior to that date does not disqualify the individual for the vacation pay that he is otherwise entitled to. (49 LA 837)

This principle is followed fairly closely in cases where the termination is involuntary, such as in the case of a shutdown or disability retirement. Exceptions may be made, however, where the termination is voluntary such as a quit or a voluntary retirement. In such cases, the employer's past practice may be decisive.

Effect of Discharge

In the absence of specific language of disqualification, arbitrators generally hold that an employee who otherwise meets the requirements for vacation pay is not disqualified by virtue of his being discharged before he takes his vacation.

An employee discharged for chronic absenteeism was ruled eligible for vacation pay where the contract didn't cover the situation. The arbitrator decided that to permit the disqualification would amount to an amendment of the contract. (Weaver Mfg. Co., 19 LA 325)

Discharge for cause was held by another umpire not to disqualify a worker under a contract that did not specifically bar payments under such a condition. (General Foods Corp., 18 LA 910)

An employee discharged for negligence was not held disqualified for terminal vacation pay under a contract that specified only that resignations or discharges for rule infractions would relieve the company of its obligation to make vacation payments. (Byerlite Corp., 12 LA 641)

At least one state court has ruled that employees discharged for striking in violation of a no-strike clause were entitled to vacation pay earned prior to the strike. (Pattenge v. Wagner Iron Works—Wis CircCt, MilwaukeeCy (1956), 38 LRRM 2615)

Effect of Permanent Shutdown

Are employees entitled to vacation pay when they are terminated because of plant shutdown? Arbitrators have generally held that previously acquired vacation credits are earned or additional wages payable even if a permanent plant closing takes place before the vacation actually becomes due. (Mays Landing Power Co., 12 LA 860; Premier Worsted Mill, 13 LA 804)

Some umpires have held that workers idled because of a shutdown were entitled to vacation pay, even though the agreement expired before the eligibility date. In one such instance the arbiter noted that the employees had been laid off when the plant was closed and the contract stated that a man was not terminated until he had been on layoff for two years. Thus, he said, the workers were still in the company's employ and their earned rights survived the contract's expiration. (Botany Mills, Inc., 27 LA 1)

In another case an umpire held that workers who lost their jobs in a plant shutdown had pro rata vacation pay coming to them because they were terminated through no fault of their own. The fact that the contract had expired before the vacation eligibility date was immaterial, he said. (Brookford Mills, 28 LA 838)

Death of Worker before Vacation

When a worker dies before receiving the vacation that is due him, are his survivors entitled to the vacation pay? Where no set rule has been developed on this problem, arbitrators seem to consider what other circumstances do or do not break a worker's vacation eligibility.

Even where a contract disqualified employees who quit, retired, or were discharged from receiving vacation pay, an arbiter held that "death" was not an implied exemption as maintained by the company. In awarding accrued vacation benefits to the survivors, the arbiter stated that to hold "death" as a disqualification would be to alter the contract. (Pittsburgh Steel Co., 43 LA 860)

Similarly: Where the contract required an employee to work at least

1,000 hours in one year in order to be eligible for a vacation the next year, and also provided that "if an employee shall have earned a vacation but dies before such vacatior. has been taken, the vacation pay shall be paid to his widow," an umpire ruled that the widow was entitled to that pay, even though the worker died in December of the year before he was to take the vacation. The umpire rejected the company's argument that no pay was due the widow because vacation pay went only to those still on the payroll as of January 1. Nothing in the contract specified that, he said, and the employee had worked his 1,000 hours. (Clinton Corn Processing Co., 41 LA 513)

Death before Eligibility Date

One company was required to pay pro-rated vacation pay to the estates of two employees who died in March and April of a vacation-eligibility year that ended on June 30. (Burnham Corp., 46 LA 1129) Similarly, a company was required to pay vacation pay to the widows of two employees who had performed no work in the year in which their vacations would have been taken. The contracts, he noted, destroy vacation eligibility only upon quit, disccharge or retirement. He held that it would be improper to modify the contract to add "death." (Pittsburgh Steel Co. 43 LA 860)

On the other hand: Where a contract provided for vacation rights to be forfeited if employment was terminated prior to January 1 of the vacation year, the arbiter upheld the company which had consistently denied benefits to survivors of workers who died before January 1. The arbiter maintained that giving the language its normal meaning, death must obviously be held to terminate the employment relationship. (Bethlehem Steel Corp., 47 LA 258)

Vacation Rights of Retirees

Whether vacation pay is due employees who retire voluntarily prior to the vacation season often depends upon past practice and the wording of the contract, and particularly upon whether the contract fixes a specified date for determining vacation eligibility.

EXAMPLE: A contract's vacation pay eligibility requirements were (1) being on the payroll on January 1. (2) having at least one year continuous service as of January 1, and (3) having worked for the company in 26 of the 52 weeks immediately proceding January 1. An employee who met requirements (2) and (3) but who retired prior to January 1 sought vacation pay.

In upholding the company's denial of vacation pay, the arbitrator said the company was entitled to enforce the requirement of being on the payroll as of January 1 in this case, even though it might not be be entitled to do so in cases of involuntary terminations, such as those due to shutdowns or disability retirements. (Rex Chainbelt, Inc., 49 LA 646)

EXAMPLE: But in a case where the contract did not have a vacation eligibility date an arbitrator directed the payment of vacation pay in one year to an employee who had retired the prior year. The employee prior to his retirement had met the dual contract requirements of having worked at least 800 hours in the current vacation year and of having at least six months service as of the prior calendar years. (B & T Metals Co., 50 LA 205)

Vacation scheduling involves a balancing of the employer's interest in scheduling vacations at such time as best meets the needs of the business with the employee's interest in taking his vacation at the time most desirable for him. One arbitrator elaborated some general guidelines that may be followed in striking this balance:

"Absent specific contract language, it is generally understood in industrial relations that a vacation is an earned equity and is generally to be taken in terms of the employee's preference, subject to the exigencies of the company's production and maintenance requirements. Where the contract is silent on the specific policy or procedure to be followed, it must be assumed that the employee will request his vacation at a time suitable to his own preferences and that his preference will be honored to the degree that company requirements will permit. However, where the contract is silent, it must also be assumed that managerial discretion is greater than in those cases where contract language puts the burden on management to show need for the employee to take his vacation at a particular time, or not to take vacation at a particular time." (29 LA 459)

Arbitrator's Vacation Formula

Faced with the problem of how workers' desire to choose the time for their own vacations can be reconciled with management's need to maintain efficient operations, one arbitrator came up with a formula. It was based on a contract providing that vacations would be granted at times most convenient to workers with consideration given to maintaining production—

(1) Management establishes a quota system indicating the weeks available for vacations and the number of employees needed to work those weeks. By December 1 it must publish a vacation schedule for the following calendar year based on this quota system.

(2) Employees must indicate four vacation choices by December 10. They may split their vacations, but the minimum period is one week.

(3) Since vacation priority is based on seniority, a list is set up by assigning varying numbers of points to the various seniority groups. The company must post the list by December 15. If an employee has to settle for his second or third vacation choice, his priority points are doubled or tripled the next year.

(4) The company must publish a vacation replacement list showing whether it plans to hire replacements or will rely on overtime by present employees to maintain production.

(5) A vacation grievance committee is set up to resolve employees' com-

plaints on schedules and replacements. (Mansfield Tire & Rubber Co., 32 LA 762)

Vacations During Slack Periods

Many companies have a practice of scheduling vacations each year during an annual plant shutdown. In the absence of such a practice, however, management may run into trouble if it tries to require employees to take their vacations during periods of layoff due to lack of work, particularly where the layoff is for an indefinite period.

The late Harry Shulman, as umpire under the contract between Ford Motor Company and the Auto Workers, held that management could not require employees to take their vacations during a period of indefinite layoff where to do so would destroy the substantive features of a vacation. He explained:

"A vacation is a period of rest between periods of work. A layoff is a period of anxiety and hardship between periods of work. The tremendous difference lies in the assurance of the vacationer that he will return to work at the end of his vacation and the equal assurance of the employee on layoff that he does not know when he will return to work." (3 LA 829)

Even where a shutdown for lack of work is for a definite period, arbiters have overruled attempts to require employees to take their vacations during that period. Usually such decisions arise in cases where management previously promised to give some consideration to employee preferences in scheduling their vacations. The reasoning is that those workers who don't choose to take their vacations during the shutdown are deprived of their opportunity to state their preferences by the unilateral scheduling of vacations during the shutdown. (31 LA 462, 32 LA 776, 42 LA 1321, 48 LA 1018)

However: It sometimes has been held that management may schedule vacations during a brief, temporary layoff or shutdown. One arbiter allowed a company to do this because he found nothing in the contract to prevent it. Although the agreement did give senior workers preference in picking vacation dates, the umpire said this right was subject to considerations of operating efficiency. He held that under its right to manage the business, the company could schedule vacations as it saw fit so long as it was not discriminatory and did not violate the contract. (Aro, Inc., 30 LA 225)

Vacation During Sick Leave

If an employee is out on paid sick leave when his regular vacation period arrives, is he entitled to another vacation period at a later date? Sick leave and vacation leave are entirely different privileges, according to an arbitration board, so the employer should re-schedule the vacation period of an employee who is on sick leave during his regularly scheduled vacation. (Derby Gas & Electric Co., 21 LA 745; see also 25 LA 94)

Where an employee was on sick leave when his scheduled vacation came up and his vacation couldn't be rescheduled, an arbitrator held that he was entitled to vacation pay in addition to sick pay. (Tenneco Oil Co., 54 LA 862)

Shutdown vs. Individual Vacation Periods

If a company has scheduled vacations on a staggered basis for several years, it can't all of a sudden require workers to take their vacations during a shutdown, according to some arbitrators. Even if the contract requires management's approval of the times workers ask for, the company's past practice and industry practice carry much weight in referees' decisions.

EXAMPLE: A contract said each employee must schedule his vacation in advance at a time acceptable to the company.

When the company had to shut down for two months due to a lack of orders, it claimed authority to require all workers to take their vacations at that time. However, the arbiter overruled the company's action, reasoning that those workers who didn't choose to take their vacations during the shutdown were deprived of their opportunity to specify what times they wanted. Moreover, the right given the company to allot vacation periods in order to insure "orderly operation of the plant" may allow management to spread out vacations to avoid too many replacements at one time, but "orderly" isn't synonymous with "economical" or "efficient," the arbiter said. (Koppers Company, Inc., 42 LA 1321)

EXAMPLE: One arbiter found that a company wasn't free to join the trend toward plant shutdowns for vacation, as the contract bound the employer to "endeavor to comply" with vacation requests While acknowledging the gradual changes in factory conditions, such as increased vacation tenure and a larger work force, the arbiter still maintained that in planning a shutdown, the employer was "in fact endeavoring not to comply with requests." (Welch Grape Juice Co., 48 LA 1018)

On the other hand: In the absence of contract language or binding past practice, management has the inherent right to fix employee's vacation time, an arbiter ruled. The company decided it no longer could afford the disruptions that accompany individual vacation scheduling, and it unilaterally designated the week of July 4th for a plant-wide vacation shutdown. The arbiter overruled union objections based on past practice, finding that the union had never participated in past disagreements over vacation schedules. (Vogt Mfg. Corp., 44 LA 488)

Caution: A company that unilaterally changes its past practices on vacation scheduling runs the risk of being charged under the Taft Act with violating its duty to bargain with the union over changes in working conditions.

Workers' Desires vs. Efficient Operations

Under a contract that allows workers to choose the vacation periods they want subject to requirements of the business, the company must have real and valid reasons for denying them the period they ask for.

When one company turned down a worker's request for a specific vacation period because it overlapped with that requested by another worker, an umpire ruled against this action. Although the contract provided that the "needs of the business must be considered in scheduling vacations," the arbiter found that both workers' being gone at the same time would not necessarily conflict with efficient operations. To turn down a request for a given vacation time, the umpire said, management should show that a vacation at that time would adversely affect production, safety, or general employee relations. (Tin Processing Corp., 15 LA 568)

However: In another case, establishment of a "one man, one week" vacation rule, under which only one employee in a department could be on leave at any given time, was upheld by another arbiter as a proper exercise of management's right to insure the orderly operation of its plants. (U.S. Steel Corp., 46 LA 887)

Where a contract gave the employer the right to schedule vacations throughout the year, an arbitrator upheld management's right to allot vacations to eligible employees over the full year on an equal basis, thereby eliminating the "summer bulge" of vacations. (Laclede Steel Co., 54 LA 506)

But an arbiter ruled that management could not make a blanket denial of all vacation requests for a certain week, even though the contract made workers' requests for vacations subject to operational requirements. The company had announced in advance that no vacations would be given during Christmas week. In the umpire's view, the company violated the vacation clause requiring it to make every effort to meet the desires of employees in scheduling vacations. Also, it had failed to show that absolutely nobody could be spared, the arbiter noted. (Bethlehem Steel Co., 30 LA 899)

However: Another umpire ruled that management could refuse to schedule vacations during months when peak business was expected, even though that business didn't materialize. The contract said management would fix vacations according to the workers' wishes "in so far as practical" and "in accordance with the needs of the business." In the arbiter's view, this gave the company the sole right to limit vacation-time selection, as long as heavy business forecasts were reasonable. (Westinghouse Electric Corp., 40 LA 972)

In a case where it had been a practice for two years to commence vacations on a Monday, an umpire held that the company could continue this practice. The contract gave the employer the right to schedule vacations in the interest of plant efficiency. The union wanted each worker's vacation to start after his regular days off. But the umpire said that, by starting vacations on Monday, the company was justifiably exercising its right to increase efficiency and avoid costly premium payments. (Sinclair Refining Co., 12 LA 193)

Vacation—Workers v. Foremen

Where a contract gave workers their choice of vacation dates in seniority order, the company was obligated to give workers vacation preference over foremen where the two conflicted, as long as there was no operational problem, the arbiter stated. Since nothing indicated that management assigned the vacation weeks to foremen on the basis of anticipated production needs, he concluded that foremen had to take second choice. (Air Reduction Chemical & Carbide Co., 42 LA 1192)

Adoption of an extended vacation plan didn't give a company the right to abandon a past practice of allowing workers and foremen to work out the schedule, one arbiter decided. Although the company may set the total number of workers who may be on vacation at one time, it may not determine when particular workers shall be off. Rather, it is bound by past practice and must permit foremen and workers to work this out among themselves, subject only to the limits of plant manpower needs. (Reynolds Metals Co., 43 LA 1150)

Extended Vacations in Basic Steel

In a grievance against a company's refusal to grant a worker his preferred vacation period, an arbiter provided several observations and principles for the scheduling of extended vacations in the steel industry:

Observations: Subject to the company's right "to insure orderly operation of the plants," extended vacations should be granted "at times most desired by employees." To implement this plan, a procedural agreement was adopted permitting the company to establish plant and unit quotas and allowing workers to select vacation periods within these quotas in order of seniority.

Principles: (1) The employer isn't bound to continue quotas used in a prior year. (2) He is bound to honor vacation selections on the basis of seniority within separate lines of progression. (3) He may continue to schedule vacations by calendar quarter, since this had permitted most workers to receive time off during preferred summer quarters. (4) Exceptions should be made in special cases of hardship, where granting of worker's request wouldn't interfere with production. (Armco Steel Corp., 45 LA 120)

Further: Another arbiter asserted that the company may not give workers entitled to regular vacations priority over extended vacationers. The company may require a worker to take his vacation during a period other than the one he requested, only when its decision is related to the

need to maintain orderly plant operation. (Pittsburgh Steel Co., 42 LA
1002)

Work During Vacation

Under a contract allowing management to *request* employees to work
during their vacations, at least one
arbitrator has held that this gives the
employer the right to *compel* employees to skip their vacation.

EXAMPLE: At the end of the first
week after a return to work from a
strike the company issued vacation
checks to all employees instead of
scheduling free time. The contract
specified that: "Under unusual circumstances, the management may request certain or all of the employees
to work during their vacation but in
such event the employees will be paid
their regular pay in addition to their
regular earnings."

The union contended that under
this clause, management might only
request, not compel, employees to
work during their vacations. It argued
that "request" would require the employee's *approval.*

The arbiter ruled otherwise, stating
that the obvious intent of the contract was to give management the
right to require work under unusual
circumstances. Furthermore, it was
held that the definition of "unusual
circumstances" must be left largely
up to the employer. The arbiter found
no abuse of that discretion. (Maxwell
Bros., Inc., 5 LA 449)

Vacation Pay

IN BRIEF

While contracts usually specify the manner in which vacation pay is to be computed, disputes over vacation pay frequently must be settled by impartial arbitrators. For example, should an incentive worker's vacation pay be figured on the basis of his average earnings or his base rate? If a man has received a wage increase during the year, how should his vacation pay be computed? What happens to vacation pay if the plant is on a short workweek when vacations are taken?

How arbiters have answered these and other questions relating to vacation pay is discussed in this section.

Inclusion of Incentive Pay

Should a worker's incentive payments be included in vacation allowances paid him? Incentive bonuses usually are considered by workers as a part of their earnings. Thus, if vacation payments are based on "current hourly earnings" arbiters most likely would hold that incentive pay must be included.

EXAMPLE: A company agreed that: "The rate of vacation pay per week shall be the same as the current hourly earnings for a full scheduled workweek as worked the previous two months prior to June 1st."

In spite of this language, which had appeared in various contracts, the company contended that vacations were payable on the basis of "base rate." It argued that the "base rate" had been used in the past, and that the wage-incentive payments at the plant never entered into calculations or discussions regarding vacations.

The arbiter ruled against the company, using this line of reasoning: The terms, "base rate" and "current hourly earnings" have well established and quite different meanings. The first refers to a minimum rate, the second to actual earnings of an employee. There was no reason here for ruling that the two terms were identical. Therefore, vacation pay should "be calculated on the basis of 'hourly earnings' to include incentive bonuses over and above base rate and on the basis of the workweek 'as worked' by the several employees entitled to vacation pay." (Schneider Metal Mfg. Co., 4 LA 100)

Under a contract basing employees' vacation pay on "gross earnings" of the preceding year, a lump sum paid to employees to "buy out" an old incentive plan in favor of a new one must be included in computing employees' vacation pay. The arbiter ruled that the written contract must prevail and that the ordinary meaning of "gross earnings" encompasses payment. (Johnson & Johnson, 49 LA 841)

Inclusion of Overtime Earnings

Under a contract which excludes overtime earnings from vacation pay, does this mean all earnings during overtime hours or merely the premium rate for the overtime? One umpire held that it was clear that a company was not obligated to base vacation pay on any earnings over 40 hours. (Webster Tobacco Co., Inc., 5 LA 164)

Furthermore: Even if a contract is silent on whether overtime premiums should be included in figuring vacation pay, chances are that an arbitrator will not require the company to include them. Under one such agreement that based vacation pay on average hourly earnings, defining such earnings to include regular day rates, incentive rates, and shift premiums, an umpire ruled that overtime pay did not have to be included since it was not specifically mentioned in the definition. (Kensington Steel Co., 17 LA 662)

Inclusion of Shift Premiums

Should shift differentials be included in vacation pay which is based on "regular rate"? At least one arbitration board has given an affirmative answer to this where the employees worked regularly on second or third shifts. (Hans Rees' Sons, Inc., 10 LA 705)

On the other hand: It has been held that where shift premiums have not been included for a period of years, this past practice should prevail. (Bell Aircraft Corp., 9 LA 65)

Inclusion of Holiday Pay

Under a contract that bases vacation pay on "straight-time earnings," should holiday pay be considered part of earnings? While management may feel that employees can hardly have "earnings" while they are off work because of a holiday, at least one arbitrator has required holiday pay included, under such a vacation clause.

He held that the parties agreed in effect to treat employees eligible for holiday pay as though they had come in and worked on the holiday. He declared that:

". . . Holiday pay cannot fairly be said to be similar to a shift bonus, overtime bonus, or a Christmas bonus. On the contrary, holiday pay more closely resembles vacation pay since both are paid at straight time rates rather than bonus rates."

It was concluded that holiday pay should be included in figuring "earnings." (Master Weavers Institute, 11 LA 745)

Inclusion of Vacation Pay

Under a contract providing vacation pay equal to a specified percentage of earnings for "hours worked" during the preceding year, must vacation allowances paid in that year be included in figuring total earnings? According to one arbitrator, such allowances needn't be included in computing

earnings unless it can be affirmatively shown that the parties intended them to be. Standing alone, he said, the words "hours worked" can refer only to hours actually worked during the year. (John Deere Spreader Works of Deere & Co., 20 LA 670)

However: Another arbiter ruled that the company violated the contract which stated that "employee's gross earnings for the 52 weeks prior to January 1 of the vacation year shall be the basis for computing vacation pay" by excluding the prior year's vacation pay. Even though the employer has been computing vacation pay in the same way for ten years, the method was incorrect and constituted a continuing violation of the contract. (Huffman Mfg. Co., 49 LA 357)

Inclusion of Other Pay

Most other forms of pay for authorized leave time usually are included by arbitrators in vacation pay computations. Thus, one arbitrator held that vacation, holiday, bereavement, and jury duty pay must be included in computing an employee's average straight time earnings for the previous year for the purpose of computing vacation pay.

After an extensive review of prior decisions, the arbitrator concluded:

"The almost consistent trend of arbitral authority is that all monetary benefits paid to an employee pursuant to the provisions of a collective bargaining agreement and incidental to his employment relationship are to be treated as earnings and included in the employeee's earnings for the purpose of vacation pay. Any exceptions from the generally accepted meaning of the phrase 'straight time earnings' should be expressly set forth by specific contract language." (Ridge Machine Co., 53 LA 394)

Where Employee Works at Two Rates

If a contract bases vacation pay on the employee's "regular rate," what is his regular rate if he has worked on two or more jobs paying different rates throughout the year? Arbitrators have interpreted such provisions in several ways.

Where a man had been permanently transferred to a lower-rated job, an umpire held that he was properly given vacation pay at that lower rate under a clause which based vacation pay on the rate of the worker's regular job. The contract defined "regular job" to mean that to which an employee is regularly assigned or the job he is working on immediately prior to his vacation, whichever is higher. The umpire said that the lower-rated job was his regular job since he had been permanently assigned to it a week before his vacation. (Olin-Mathieson Chemical Corp., 24 LA 116)

Where a man was working at a job only temporarily, however, or where his work required him to shift frequently from one job to another, some umpires have held that he should be paid vacation benefits at the rate he received the majority of his time during the preceding year. (Hiram Walker & Sons, Inc., 5 LA 186)

Effect of General Wage Increase

When a new contract is negotiated which increases pay rates, should the old or new and higher rates be used in figuring vacation pay?

Unions may insist that rates *in effect at the time the vacation is taken* should be the basis for computing vacation pay, while management will argue that the vacation has been *earned* at the old rate.

Here again, where the contract is unclear, arbitrators tend to be guided by the employer's past practice. After reviewing prior awards, one arbitrator concluded:

"Thus, in all cases that have come to the attention of the arbitrator here, the unanimous view has been that where the contract language is not clear, the long established past practice must be followed." (Sweden Freezer, Inc., 43 LA 471)

Where there is no past practice, an arbitrator may conclude that the parties must have intended that the rate prevailing at the time of vacation is the one that should be used.

EXAMPLE: A company and union negotiated a new contract during May. This new agreement granted substantial wage increases, effective June 15. The company distributed vacation pay on June 27, using old rates although it recognized the new vacation benefits as to length of service, overtime, etc. Its position was that pay rates in

effect when the vacations were earned were the ones to be applied.

An arbitrator disagreed. He declared that when the parties drew up their new contract it was far more likely that they were thinking of the vacations just ahead of them than of the next year's vacations. Furthermore, the new rates were to be effective for two years, and if the parties had meant to use a different rate for vacation purposes, they would have said so, according to the arbiter. It was concluded that the rate prevailing at the time of the vacations should be used. (Lynch Corp., 9 LA 115)

Compromise systems of pay also have been worked out by arbitrators faced with the question of whether old or new rates should govern.

EXAMPLE: A company and union signed a new contract in April retroactive to March 31, which provided for a wage i n c r e a s e and a completely new vacation plan. Many employees. would have received less vacation under the new plan, so the parties agreed that the year's vacations would be figured under the old contract. There was no discussion, however, as to rates of pay for vacation time, so the question was submitted to arbitration: Should the old or new rate be applied in figuring vacation pay.

An arbitration board held that it was the responsibility of both parties to bring up the matter of applicable pay rates and to secure an agreement on the matter. Since neither party met this responsibility, it was concluded that it would be fair "for the parties to . . . share equally the benefits and penalties of their failure by fixing the rates at a point half way between those originally sought by the union and those sought by the company." (Crosley Motors, Inc., 8 LA 1024)

Effect of Retroactive Increase

When a wage increase is agreed to after vacations have been taken, and the increase is made retroactive to a date preceding the vacation, should the extra pay be included in the vacation pay? At least one arbitrator has said it should:

"As a general rule, when a wage increase is made retroactive, it applies to all hours for which employees have been paid during the retroactive period. That rule is applicable whether such hours are those of holidays, vacations or hours of work. . . ." (Pioneer Alloy Products Co., Inc., 5 LA 458)

Effect of Annual Improvement Increase

Must an annual-improvement factor be added to a worker's vacation pay if the increase goes into effect while he is on vacation? In the absence of any contract provision on the subject, one arbitrator ruled that such an increase must be incorporated in pay for any part of a vacation which falls after the effective date of the increase. (Ford Motor Co., 17 LA 512)

Effect of Strike

Can time spent on a strike be excluded in computing vacation pay?

The answer usually turns on the past practice of the parties or upon the wording of the contract. Where a contract based vacation pay on "time worked," an arbitrator held that management had a right to deduct strike time. (Modecraft Co., 38 LA 1236)

But where the contract was silent, an arbitrator was persuaded by a past practice of allowing full vacation pay in strike situations. (Mobil Oil Co., 42 LA 102)

Past practice worked to managements' favor in a case where the company, in figuring out weekly vacation pay, followed the practice of dividing the employees' earnings in the past year by 52 weeks. In view of this practice, the arbitrator saw nothing wrong in using the 52-week divisor in a year when the employees had lost six weeks' earnings due to a strike. (Blaw-Knox Co., 47 LA 1164)

Effect of WC Payments

An employee who received 15 weeks' pay for working and 30 weeks' pay from workmen's compensation during one year is not entitled to vacation pay for that year according to one arbiter. The contract provided that an employee has a right to vacation pay if he has worked for the employer for one year, and received 40 "paychecks" within the year. Considering the union's unsuccessful attempt to include reference to WC checks, the arbiter maintained that "paycheck" meant a check for work done. (Ohse Meat Products, Inc., 48 LA 978)

Further: Employees were not entitled to have included in computation of their vacation pay time they were absent from work because of injuries received on the job, for which they were compensated under state workmen's compensation law. (Modecraft Co., 44 LA 1045)

Quit Before Eligibility Date

Where a contract stated that employees must have a certain period of service and must have worked a certain number of days "prior to August 1 of the vacation year," to be eligible for vacation pay, the arbiter ruled that those who fulfilled the requirements but left the job before August 1, were entitled to vacation pay. It is a generally recognized principle in industry that under this type of vacation clause employment on a specific date is not a condition of eligibility for vacation pay. (Telescope Folding Furniture Co., 49 LA 837)

Effect of Plant Shutdown

Employees who were terminated as a result of an employer's voluntary shutdown of the plant are entitled to pro rata vacation pay for the time worked prior to the shutdown, an arbiter ruled, even though the contract required a minimum number of hours worked as eligibility. He reasoned that vacations are additional wages and no longer considered merely periods of rest. Therefore, vacation benefits already earned under the unexpired contract cannot be completely annulled by the shutdown. (National Plumbing Fixture Corp., 49 LA 421; see also 51 LA 400)

VACATION PAY BASED ON "WORKWEEK"

Actual vs. Normal Workweek

Some contracts spell out what a "normal" workweek is, and then in the vacation clause they base vacation pay on the "workweek." If, under such a contract, a plant has actually been operating on a schedule longer or shorter than the normal workweek, which period should be used in computing vacation pay—the actual or the normal week? Decisions have gone both ways in solving this problem. It has been held that the workweek as defined in the contract is the one to be used, even when management has been basing vacation pay on the actual workweek in the past. (Dunkirk Radiator Corp., 1 LA 249)

On the other hand: At least one arbitrator has held that the number of hours actually being worked by employees was the proper base for vacation pay. The contract in this case based vacation pay on the "scheduled workweek in the previous calendar year" and also defined the "normal" workweek as 40 hours long. Reasoning that "scheduled" refers to a time established in advance and consistently adhered to, the umpire decided that vacation pay should be based on the six-day week actually worked since the employees usually expected to work on Saturdays unless otherwise notified. He found that 65 percent of the time they did not receive such notice. For this reason he ruled that the six-day week was the "scheduled" workweek. (Cemenstone Co., 9 LA 41)

Individual vs. Plant Workweek

Where different employees work a different number of hours per week, another common problem in computing vacation pay arises—whether the workweek of each employee or the standard workweek for the whole plant should be used. Several arbitrators have held that the plant's workweek is the one to be used to avoid confusion.

For instance, under a contract basing vacation pay on the "weekly hours worked by the company in a majority of the workweeks of the vacation year," the union contended that the weekly average of actual hours worked by all employees should be used in computing vacation pay. An arbiter upheld the company's view that the number of hours scheduled for the whole plant should be the base. He reasoned that the word "company" in the clause refers to a whole and not isolated parts of the operation. The union's position, he said, would cause much confusion and destroy the meaning of established work schedules. (G. C. Hussey & Co., 5 LA 446)

Similarly: In another case an arbitration board decided that the exclusion of overtime payments from vacation pay pointed "to a definite workweek in the plant as a whole." (International Harvester Co., 9 LA 35)

Effect of Changes in Workweek

Where the length of the workweek has varied from time to time during the vacation year, which period should be used in figuring vacation pay? One arbitrator has held that the workweek in effect at the time the vacation is taken is the proper one. (General Controls Co., 12 LA 852)

However: Under a contract that specified 48 hours as the base for figuring vacation pay, an umpire held that the company could not reduce vacation benefits to 40 hours' pay just because the workweek had been reduced to 40 hours. (Kempsmith Machine Co., 5 LA 520)

Eligibility for Holiday Pay

IN BRIEF

Although some contracts grant holiday pay to all workers without restriction, more than three-fourths of contracts specify that certain eligibility requirements must be fulfilled. These may be attendance requirements (by far the most common being work on the day before and the day after the holiday) or service requirements (for example, three months with the company). The former are much more common than the latter.

POINTERS—

▶ It's generally recognized that the purpose of requiring work on the days surrounding a holiday is to prevent "holiday stretching." So umpires often have awarded holiday pay to workers who failed to meet work requirements through no fault of their own.

▶ Laid-off workers continue to be "employees" of the company. So if a contract grants holiday pay without restriction, chances are that a laid-off worker is entitled to it—particularly if the layoff is brief.

▶ If a contract designates certain days as paid holidays and does not limit pay to cases in which the holidays fall on scheduled days of work, an umpire is likely to hold that holidays falling on nonwork days must be paid for.

WORK REQUIREMENTS

Incomplete Day's Work

If workers must work both the day before and the day following a holiday in order to qualify for holiday pay, do they have to put in *full days*? What if workers are absent *part* of one of the qualifying days? It is generally recognized that the real purpose of such a provision is to prevent stretching of holidays. Going on this assumption, most arbitrators hold that workers who take time off for good reason on the day before or after the holiday have fulfilled their requirements under this kind of holiday clause.

One arbiter made the distinction between "stretching" a holiday and "arranging the necessary adjustments to make the holiday available." Thus, he said that a worker who left work a half hour early the day before a holiday so he could catch a train was eligible for holiday pay. (John Deere Tractor Co., 9 LA 21). Where a man was 36 minutes late to work on the day before a holiday, he was held to be qualified for holiday pay because he had worked *on* the scheduled working day as required by the contract. (Lake City Malleable, Inc., 25 LA 753).

On the other hand: It has been held that partial absences are to be considered as depriving an employee of holiday eligibility under a before-and-after-work requirement. One umpire held that workers who received permission to leave early on the day before or after Christmas Day were not entitled to holiday pay under a strict interpretation of the requirement. He based his decision on the fact that the parties had discussed the clause at great length and agreed upon it in order to avoid disputes over excused absences. (American Bemberg & North American Rayon Corp., 10 LA 384).

Definition of "Working Day"

Is a "working day" the day which actually precedes or follows a holiday, regardless of whether an employee was scheduled to work on that day, or is it the first day preceding or following a holiday on which an employee is told to come in and work? An arbitrator would probably hold that "working day" was the first day on which management expected work from an employee.

EXAMPLE: A contract obligated any employee "to work his full shift on both the working day before and the working day after the holiday."

A holiday fell on Thursday. An employee worked the preceding Wednesday, and was told not to work on the day following the holiday, Friday. She was scheduled to work on Monday, but didn't report.

The employee contended that Friday should be considered the "working day after the holiday." Management argued that "working day" meant a day on which an employee was actually scheduled to work, and that Monday should be considered the "working day."

The arbiter sustained the company. He held that ordinarily "working day" referred to a day on which an employee was expected to work. He noted also that minor variation from schedules were the rule. In other words, there was no evidence that the instructions to some employees not to work on the Friday following the Thursday holiday were connected with the occurrence of the holiday. (American Thread Co., 10 LA 250).

Eligibility Days Not in Holiday Week

Under a holiday clause requiring work on the day before and day after the holiday, do these eligibility days have to be in the same week as the holiday? In many instances arbiters have held that they do not.

EXAMPLE: A company promised to pay holiday pay "provided such holiday falls or is celebrated within the regularly scheduled workweek, and provided further that such employee works the workday previous to and the workday following such holiday."

A holiday fell on a Thursday and the plant was closed for the rest of that week. An employee was denied pay for the holiday because he was absent the next Monday.

An arbitration board majority upheld the company's position that the days preceding and following a holiday on which work was required did not have to fall in the same workweek as the holiday. The opinion stated that:

"It is likely that the union will discover upon investigation, that in nearly all cases where a clause such as this is in a contract, it is applied so that the "workday" before or after the holiday may be in a workweek other than that in which the holiday occurs." (Veeder-Root, Inc., 11 LA 33; see also Link-Belt Co., 12 LA 886; Whitehead Metal Products Co., Inc., 14 LA 766)

Saturday as a "Work" Day

If Saturday is a scheduled work day, can workers who fail to report for overtime on Saturday he denied pay for a Monday holiday which follows? In answering this question, arbiters look at the exact wording of the agreement.

Thus, under a contract that required employees to work the regularly scheduled work day before and after the holiday to be eligible for holiday pay, workers were held entitled to pay, for a Monday holiday, even though they failed to report for work scheduled for the preceding Saturday. The arbiter found that the contract defined a regular week's work as consisting of 40 hours, Monday through Friday, inclusive. In view of this, he said, Saturday could not be considered a regularly scheduled work day. (Hinde & Dauch Paper Co., 22 LA 505)

However: At another plant workers failing to report for Saturday work were held ineligible for holiday pay for the following Monday because the contract did not limit the hours em-

ployees could be required to work. The
arbiter decided they had not met the
contract's requirement of working on
the last scheduled work day, even
though it was overtime. (Great Lakes
Spring Corp., 12 LA 779)

In order to count Saturday as a
scheduled work day, when it is overtime work that is involved, an arbiter
has ruled that the company must
have the right to force such overtime
work. In this case, where the contract
spoke of normal Monday-through-
Friday workweek and of "requests" to
work on Saturday or Sunday, Saturday was not allowed to be counted
as the last "scheduled" work day before a Monday holiday. (Amron Corp.,
47 LA 582)

Where an employer had the right to
require Saturday overtime work, however, an arbitrator held that employees who failed to report for such work
prior to a Monday holiday thereby
failed to meet the requirement that
they work the last scheduled work
day prior to the holiday. (Sargent-
Welch Scientific Co., 54 LA 923)

Failure to Work Scheduled Holiday

Many contracts state that holiday
pay is not required for workers who
fail to report on holidays when work
is scheduled. In spite of such apparently clear contract language,
many problems have come up when
workers have claimed their holiday
pay, even though they did not work.
In such cases arbitrators give considerable weight to the method used
in informing employees that work
had been scheduled as well as to past
practice.

In one instance an umpire ruled
that it was enough for a company to
post notices a week beforehand that
work was scheduled for the following
Monday, a holiday. Since many workers on vacation called in to find out
if work was scheduled for the holiday,
the arbiter decided that others on
vacation had no valid claim to holiday pay on the ground that they had
not received sufficient notice. (Bethlehem Steel Co., 22 LA 781)

At another plant it was held that
workers who failed to show up for
scheduled work on Christmas day
were properly denied holiday pay.

The fact that the foremen asked
them whether they planned to work
on the holiday didn't mean that they
had a choice of working or not the
umpire said. (Bethlehem Steel Co.,
25 LA 680)

Also workers who refused to report
for holiday work after an emergency
call-in lost their right to holiday pay,
under a provision making ineligible
those who were requested or scheduled to work and failed to do so. An
umpire held that this did not require
advance requests or scheduling for
holiday work as contended by the
union. (Firestone Tire & Rubber Co.,
29 LA 469)

However: Although one arbiter
recognized a company's right to make
changes in the work schedule, he
ruled that one day's notice to report
for work on a holiday was not
enough. Thus, in spite of the contract provision denying holiday pay
to those failing to report for work
on a holiday when scheduled, the
umpire concluded that the absent
workers were entitled to holiday pay.
(Bethlehem Steel Co., 23 LA 271)

Holiday Pay After Termination

When terminated workers receive
accumulated vacation pay, they also
may be entitled to pay for holidays
falling within the period covered by
the vacation allowances, according to
one arbitrator.

EXAMPLE: Some employees who
were terminated in May and June
received from one to three weeks'
accumulated vacation pay. The union
contended that certain of them
should have received additional pay
for Memorial Day and the Fourth of
July since these holidays fell during
the weeks covered by their vacation
pay. In rejecting this claim, the company relied on two contract provisions—one stating that an employee
had to work his scheduled work days
before and after a holiday to qualify
for pay and another saying that a
laid-off employee would get holiday
pay only if the layoff occurred in the
holiday week.

An umpire found neither clause
controlling. He reasoned that the purpose of the work requirements was to

prevent holiday stretching; and that, although the layoffs didn't take place during the holiday weeks, the company by granting vacation pay deferred the effective dates of the layoffs beyond the holiday weeks. Hence he concluded that the applicable clause was one granting holiday pay in addition to vacation pay for a holiday falling during an employee's vacation. (Continental-Emsco Co., 31 LA 449)

EFFECT OF SHUTDOWN

Permanent Shutdown

Are employees eligible for holidays which come after a plant closes down permanently? Although arbitrators have ruled both ways on the problem, their decisions seem to turn on whether individual workers are otherwise eligible for the holiday pay rather than the facts surrounding the shutdown itself.

Where one plant shut down on New Year's Eve, an umpire held that employees were not eligible for pay for New Year's Day because they had not worked the following day as required by the contract. (Calif. Metal Trades Assn., 11 LA 788)

Temporary Shutdown

Most arbitrators have ruled that workers fulfill their work requirements for pay for a holiday falling during a temporary shutdown if they work the last scheduled working day before it and the first scheduled working day after it. Such a ruling is usually based on the assumption that a plant's closing down is something which workers cannot control.

In one case an umpire pointed out to the company that the contract required work on the *working days* before and after a holiday rather than the *day* before and after the holiday. Since the workers had worked December 30 and had been told not to report again until January 5 the arbiter held that these were the working days. So, he concluded, the workers were entitled to pay for New Year's Day. (Aerolite Electronic Hardware Corp., 10 LA 215)

On the other hand: It has been held that a month-long shutdown does deprive workers of holiday pay under a before-and-after work requirement, whereas a brief shutdown of only three days does not have this effect. (Vulcan Detinning Co., 4 LA 483). Also workers were properly denied pay for a holiday falling during a shutdown where the contract specified that holidays must fall within a scheduled workweek. An umpire ruled that no scheduled workweek was in effect. (Sefton Fibre Can Co., 12 LA 101)

Involuntary Shutdown

When a company was shut down because of a strike by another union, an arbiter decided that the workers were not entitled to pay for the holiday that fell during the shutdown. Certain of the assumptions underlying a labor contract precluded the holiday-pay claim, he said, and primary among these was that the company must be operating and able to provide employment opportunities. Since the company had to suspend publication involuntarily through no fault of its own, the umpire concluded that a liberal reading of the contract would raise an obligation never expected or intended by the parties. (Publishers' Assn. of New York City, 40 LA 140)

EFFECT OF LAYOFF

In Absence of Eligibility Requirements

When a contract contains no specific eligibility requirements, are employees on layoff entitled to holiday pay? A common argument for awarding them pay is that companies might lay off their employees for the express purpose of avoiding holiday payments if laid-off workers were held ineligible. Some arbitrators have held that those on just a temporary layoff do not lose their rights to holiday pay.

One ruled that the equities of a situation required that workers laid off because of a machine breakdown should be paid holiday pay since the breakdown was not their fault. (Thompson Mahogany Co., 5 LA 397) Another umpire found that, in a somewhat seasonal industry where layoffs were fairly regular, workers would suffer a serious inequity if they lost holiday pay just because of a lay-off when they had worked through-out most of the contract year. (Otto Guggenheim & Co., Inc., 11 LA 1130)

In keeping with the strict language of the contract, an arbiter required that an employer abandon a past practice of 14 years. The only require-ment for holiday pay was that the "employee actually works during the payroll week in which the holiday falls." A separate clause said that a worker would lose his standing as an "employee" if he was laid off for 12 consecutive months. When seven workers, who had been laid off for a little over nine months were recalled the day after Labor Day, they quali-fied for holiday pay under the terms of the contract. The employer's prac-tice of not granting holiday pay if re-turn followed the holiday was ruled improper. (Anaconda Aluminum Co., 48 LA 219)

On the other hand: It has been held that if the layoff is bona fide, workers should be denied holiday pay. One arbitrator noted that, if holiday pay were granted, laid-off workers who had secured jobs somewhere else would get holiday pay from two com-panies. (Tenney Engineering Co., 10 LA 307)

Before & After Holiday Work Re-quirement

Are laid-off employees considered as having met a requirement for work-ing on the days preceding and follow-ing the holiday?

One arbitrator ruled that the par-ties must have intended that workers on layoff should receive holiday pay even though they did not work on the days before and after the holiday. His reasoning was that there would have been no reason to write a con-tract clause requiring employees to have earned some wages within the 30 days before the holiday if the par-ties had meant to exclude laid-off employees from holiday-pay eligiblity. (Thomas L. Leedom Co., 21 LA 740)

However: It has also been held that laid-off workers are not exempt from work requirements. One arbitrator reasoned that if he ruled otherwise, workers laid off for a whole year could claim pay for all six holidays pro-vided by the contract. This, he said,

would conflict with the fundamenta purpose of the work requirement, tha is, to cut down the monetary cost tc the company. (Chrome-Rite Co., 1: LA 691)

Laid-Off Workers as Employees

Under a contract which grants holi-day pay to employees without any qualification, are laid-off workers en-titled to it? Most arbiters have hel< that being on layoff does not deprive a person of his employee status. Thus it follows that as long as he is ar employee he is entitled to his holida) benefits under such a contract. One umpire observed that it is generall) accepted that workers temporaril) laid off do not cease to be employee: of a company unless they secure regu lar employment elsewhere. He note< further that the work of one compan) was seasonal and so the plant wa usually shut down over Christma and New Year's. Therefore, he hel< that the provision for holiday pay for these two days would be meaningles if pay were not awarded for holiday falling during the shutdown. (Grin nell Lithographic Co., Inc., 10 LA 887

Employees on the Payroll

If the holiday-pay clause of a con-tract applies only to those workers on the payroll, are laid-off employees considered on the payroll? Generall) arbiters hold that laid-off workers are not technically on the payroll and thus are not entitled to the bene-fits of that status.

In trying to define "on the payroll" one arbitrator found help in anothe section of a contract. The sick-leave clause specified that workers were on the active payroll if not laid off. S< he reasoned that persons who were laid off were not on the payroll and therefore not entitled to holiday pay (Armour & Co., 9 LA 338)

Similarly, under another holida) clause with an on-the-payroll require-ment an umpire ruled that laid-of workers did not go on the payrol until they went back to work. (The Flintkote Co., 26 LA 526)

Workers on Disciplinary Layoff

Can workers who fail to meet the work requirements because of discipli-nary layoff be denied holiday pay'

In most cases arbitrators hold this practice to be justifiable.

In one situation an arbiter concluded that if the parties had meant to provide holiday-pay eligibility for workers on disciplinary layoff, the contract would have said so. He based his decision on the fact that other sections of the contract specifically mentioned "disciplinary layoffs" as being covered. (McInerney Spring & Wire Co., 11 LA 1195; see also Ford Motor Co., 11 LA 1181)

However: At least one arbitrator has held that the company was wrong in denying holiday pay to an employee who was on a two-day disciplinary layoff on the days immediately preceding and following the holiday. The arbitrator pointed out that the purpose of requiring an employee to work the days before and after a holiday is to discourage him from stretching the holiday on his own volition. But in this case the employee wasn't absent by his own choice. Since he had been ordered not to report for work, the arbitrator said he couldn't be held responsible for missing the days which the contract required for eligibility. Accordingly, the company was ordered to pay him for the holiday. (Inland Steel Co., 20 LA 323)

EFFECT OF STRIKE

Workday Before Strike

Even where employees failed to work the full workday before a strike due to a breach-of-contract walkout, arbitrators have held the employees entitled to holiday pay, absent a showing that the strike was a result of a premeditated plan and that the part-day's work was intended only as token compliance with the holiday-pay eligibility requirements. (20 LA 649, 16 LA 317)

On the other hand, other arbitrators have held that employees who, because of a work stoppage, work only part of the day before or after a holiday do not qualify for holiday pay. (35 LA 117, 11 LA 462, 40 LA 673)

Absence of Agreement

Holiday pay normally does not accrue during a strike if there is no collective bargaining agreement in effect when the strike occurs. This principle has been applied to strikes that take place after the expiration of a contract, to lawful strikes under a wage reopener, and to unauthorized strikes during the contract term. (24 LA 561, 30 LA 671, 33 LA 681, 36 LA 1276, 37 LA 3, 43 LA 539)

As one arbitrator explained:

"When an employee has chosen to detach himself temporarily from the contract effects by a strike or stoppage running through a holiday, he has surrendered the holiday benefit just as surely as he surrenders pay on any other day of such a stoppage. The surrender is certainly not lessened by the fact that the stoppage is an unauthorized one during the life of the agreement and barred by its terms." (Hellenic Lines, Ltd., 38 LA 339)

But one arbiter allowed holiday pay for New Year's Eve Day where a legal strike beginning on the day after a contract expired made it impossible to work the "next scheduled workday." (A. O. Smith Corp., 51 LA 1309)

Retroactive Agreements

A special problem arises when strike-settlement agreement is made retroactive to the starting date of the strike. Does this mean that the strikers should be paid for holidays occurring during the strike?

In one case, a claim for holiday pay was denied on the grounds that (1) the new contract required work on scheduled work days before and after the holiday, (2) the plant was operating during the strike and work was available on the pre- and post-holiday work days, and (3) the strikers had failed to meet the eligibility requirement by working on those days. (Alside, Inc., 42 LA 75)

No Work Requirement

If employees are out on strike at the time a holiday comes up, does that make them ineligible for holiday pay? Sometimes, if there was no work requirement for holiday-pay eligibility, it has been held that workers on strike were entitled to pay for holidays falling during the strike. (Royle & Pilkington Co., Inc., 18 LA 451)

Refusal to Cross Picket Lines

Can workers who are absent because they refuse to cross picket lines be denied holiday pay on the ground that they don't meet work requirements? Generally arbitrators have held that holiday pay does not have to be paid in such cases even if the contract gives workers the right to respect picket lines. One arbiter with this view said that it is one thing for an employer to agree that employees may respect picket lines, but it is something else again to approve their absence when they do. (Schlage Lock Co., 30 LA 105; see also Stockton Automotive Assn., 25 LA 687; Kansas Bakery Employers' Labor Council, 54 LA 754)

Strike by Another Union

When a company was shut down because of a strike by another union, an arbiter decided that the workers were not entitled to pay for the holiday that fell during the shutdown. Certain of the assumptions underlying a labor contract precluded the holiday-pay claim, he said, and primary among these was that the company must be operating and able to p r o v i d e employment opportunities. Since the company had to suspend publication involuntarily, through no fault of its own, the umpire concluded that a literal reading of the contract would raise an obligation never expected or intended by the parties. (Publishers' Assn. of New York City, 40 LA 140)

EFFECT OF VACATIONS

When Vacation Includes Holiday

When a scheduled vacation period includes a holiday, are workers still entitled to pay for the holiday? Several arbitrators have held that eligible workers have the right to pay for a holiday even though it does fall within a vacation period.

Thus, in one situation where a plan shut down for vacations beginning July 3, an arbitrator ruled that the employees were justified in their claim for pay for the Fourth. The company argued that, even though the contract said July 4 was a holiday, it should not have to give employees vacation pay and holiday pay

for the same day. But the umpire said that, once the workers had qualified for paid vacation and paid holidays, the right to these earnings could not be cut off by the company's timing of the vacation period. (Koler Cigar Co., 8 LA 143)

In a similar instance an arbiter held that workers should be paid for holidays falling within their vacations even if they chose the time of their vacations themselves. He said this was not shifting any loss to the company, but only requiring it to pay the worker as much if he chose a vacation in which there is a holiday as he would have received if he chose one without a holiday. (Tioga Mills, Inc., 10 LA 371)

Late Return from Vacation Including Holiday

When a worker returned from vacation a day late, was he entitled to pay for a holiday that fell during the vacation period? One arbiter held that he was, since the eligibility tests for vacations and holidays were separate.

In this case, the contract provided for an extra day's pay when a holiday fell during a vacation period, and also stated that workers must work the day before and after a holiday to be eligible for holiday pay. The company argued that the worker didn't meet the work test for holiday-pay eligibility since he didn't show up the day after his vacation.

The worker did qualify, the arbiter decided, since the holiday-during-vacation clause had to be entirely separate from the work-test clause. Otherwise, he reasoned, the contract could be interpreted to require workers to show up for work on the days "immediately" preceding and following a holiday, even though they were on vacation. (Streitmann Supreme Bakery of Cincinnati, 41 LA 621)

EFFECT OF ABSENCE

Absence for Illness

Are workers who are out sick entitled to holiday pay? Arbiters' reasoning leads them to different conclusions on this question, depending upon the wording of the contract in question.

One contract stated that workers would not lose straight-time pay because of holidays. So an umpire denied pay for New Year's Day to a worker who was absent for illness from December 29 to January 5. He reasoned that the sick employee did not lose pay because of the holiday since he wouldn't have worked if the day had not been a holiday. (General Mills, Inc., 10 LA 53)

Also, where a contract provided for both paid sick leave and paid holidays, an arbiter held that a worker who was receiving sick pay for Christmas and New Year's Day could not get holiday pay for those days, too. The umpire reasoned that if the parties had meant to duplicate sick pay and holiday pay for the same days, they would have clearly stated it in the agreement. He noted further that this had never been done in the past. (Standard Oil Co. (Indiana), 26 LA 206)

However: Where a contract clearly waived a day-before-and-after work requirement for holiday pay in the case of sickness, an arbitrator said, it meant that workers out sick were entitled to holiday pay, no matter when their illness began. (Bakers' Negotiating Committee, 24 LA 694)

Absence for Union Business

If workers don't meet holiday eligibility requirements because they are absent on union business, are they entitled to holiday pay? In one case an umpire answered "Yes" to this question. The holiday clause required employees to work on the day preceding and following a holiday in order to be eligible for holiday pay. The arbiter based his decision on a contract provision stating that time lost in conducting union business would be counted in figuring service and attendance records. (International Harvester Co., 11 LA 1166)

Involuntary Absences

Is a worker entitled to holiday pay if his failure to meet work requirements was due to circumstances beyond his control? Some arbitrators have ruled in favor of the employees in such cases. This problem came up under one contract which required employees to work the scheduled days before and after a holiday to be eligible for holiday pay, except in the case of "justified absence." On the last scheduled workday before the Fourth of July, some employees could not get to work because of a bus strike.

Arguing that their absence was not justified, the company denied them holiday pay. But an umpire held they were entitled to it. Noting that the purpose of a work requirement in a holiday clause is to prevent holiday stretching, he concluded that these workers were absent because of the bus strike and not because of a desire to lengthen their holiday. (Bemis Bros. Bag Co., 25 LA 429; see also National Rejectors, 28 LA 390)

On the other hand: At least one arbitrator has ruled that a company was justified in sticking to the letter of its contract which contained before-and-after work requirements with exceptions for illness or layoff only. So he decided that workers who were absent the day before a holiday because of a bad snowstorm could not draw holiday pay. (Steinway & Sons, 7 LA 289)

HOLIDAYS FALLING ON NON-WORK DAYS

Saturday Holidays

Holiday clauses which simply designate certain days as paid holidays invite the question: When those listed holidays fall on Saturday what happens to workers' eligibility? Are they still entitled to pay for the holidays, or have they lost their rights?

In finding an answer to this as well as other eligibility problems, many arbitrators view a provision for paid holidays as a negotiated wage increase. Pay for a certain number of holidays is often considered to be part of the employee's annual compensation. Thus in the absence of clear contract language prohibiting it, it is frequently held that, no matter what day a holiday falls on, workers should be paid for it. In one case where the holiday clause was ambiguous, an arbitrator reasoned that if he denied employees pay for holidays falling on Saturday, he would be adding a proviso to the contract which was not intended. (Carson Electric Co., 24 LA 667) Furthermore, where a contract stated that Saturday was a regular four-hour working day, one umpire held that employees were entitled to a full eight-hour's holiday pay when a holiday fell on Saturday. (Safeway Stores, Inc., 7 LA 599)

On the other hand: Many arbitrators back up management's viewpoint that the purpose of a paid holiday clause is to protect workers from loss of pay caused by holiday falling during the regular workweek. They reason, then, that if workers are not ordinarily scheduled to work on a day when a holiday occurs, they can not draw holiday pay under an unrestricted holiday clause. Thus it has been held that a Saturday holiday should not be paid for when a contract merely lists paid unworked holidays without going into the matter of the days the holidays fall on. (Standard Grocery Co., 7 LA 745) Also where it had been the past practice not to grant pay for Saturday holidays, arbitrators have ruled that employers did not have to begin to do so all of a sudden under an ambiguous holiday clause. (M. E. Stern & Co., Inc., 11 LA 635; G. W. Carnrick Co., 8 LA 335)

Saturday as Scheduled Work Day

If a contract limits holiday pay to those holidays which fall on a scheduled work day, and a holiday falls on Saturday, do employees rate the pay for it if they have been working overtime on Saturdays? In several instances arbitrators have denied pay for Saturday holidays under this kind of requirement.

EXAMPLE: Under a contract granting pay for a holiday "falling on the employee's scheduled work day," a union demanded pay for New Year's Day, which fell on Saturday. Until some time in November the plant had

been on continuous operations, with employees working a five-day week and sometimes being called in for overtime. From November on, however, business fell off, and employees worked no more than five days a week, Monday through Friday.

The union contended that since management had scheduled work for some employees on some Saturdays during eleven-twelfths of the year, it should pay all employees for the Saturday New Year's holiday.

In ruling against the union, the arbitrator stressed the contractual requirement that the holiday must fall on "the employee's scheduled work day." He concluded that "New Year's Day not having been a scheduled work day for any of the employees, none of them under the provisions of the agreement are entitled to pay for that day." (Minnesota Mining & Mfg. Co., 12 LA 165)

On the other hand: It has been held that the requirement that a holiday fall on a "scheduled" day did not deprive an employee of Saturday holiday pay. (Kraft Foods Co., 12 LA 43)

Definition of "Without Deduction from Pay"

Under a contract which grants holidays without deduction from pay, are employees entitled to pay for Saturday holidays? At least one arbiter in one situation reasoned that since employees lost nothing by being off on Saturday, they had no right to extra pay for the holiday. He noted that the contract did not contain the usual phrases "paid holiday" or "holidays with pay." But it did provide specifically for an extra day's pay when a holiday fell during a vacation. Thus, he decided that if it had been the mutual intent of the parties to provide for general holiday with pay, the contract should have said so. (Standard Brands, Inc., 7 LA 663)

Pay for Holiday Work

*IN BRIEF*_____

Nearly all contracts that take up the subject of holidays specify premium pay for holiday work. (In about a third of the contracts failing to provide such pay, holiday work is prohibited.) The premium pay may be expressed as holiday pay plus pay for hours worked, or simply as pay at a given rate for hours worked.

It is the latter type of clause that gives rise to most of the disputes over pay for holiday work. The question is whether a worker is entitled to the premium rate only, or to the premium rate plus what he would have received had he not worked. The answer to this question must be based on careful reading of the contract.

After reviewing prior rulings, one arbitrator said that a holiday provision that calls for (a) straight-time pay for holidays, and (b) doubletime for work on a holiday has been interpreted to call for triple-time only where:

▶ It is provided that the premium time for work on a holiday shall be given "over and above straight holiday pay" (26 LA 573); or

▶ There has been an established practice of awarding holiday pay in addition to the premium pay provided for actual holiday work (16 LA 1951); or

▶ The provision for holiday pay fails to contain the limiting words "when not worked" (26 LA 491).

On the other hand, this arbitrator continued, where a contract is silent on the question of whether holiday pay as such should be awarded in addition to premium pay for working on a holiday, two reasons prevail for denying it:

1. If triple pay is contemplated, it should be expressly provided for in the contract inasmuch as it is not usual in industry practice. (22 LA 564)

2. An award of holiday pay in addition to premium pay for the work performed on a holiday would permit two provisos of the contract to apply to the same hours. (25 LA 432, 39 LA 1262)

From this review of prior awards, the arbitrator concluded that triple time for holiday work was not required under the contract before him. (Southern Standard Bag Corp., 47 LA 27)

Failure to Meet Work Requirements

Even though workers at one plant failed to meet the work requirements for pay for an unworked holiday, an umpire ruled that they were entitled to premium pay for work on a holiday as provided by the contract.

EXAMPLE: One provision of a contract said that a worker would receive pay for certain holidays not worked, provided he worked his full schedule on the workdays before and after the holiday. Another provision stated that a worker who was required to work on a holiday would be paid double time for all hours worked. Two workers who didn't work on the days preceding and following a holiday but who did work on the holiday were paid only straight time for their holiday work. The company claimed that this was proper, since they hadn't met the requirements applying to unworked holidays.

The umpire disagreed. He said that the two provisions, while appearing in the same section of the contract, were independent of each other and had different purposes; one was intended to penalize the company for scheduling holiday work, the other to discourage the practice of stretching holidays.

So, he concluded, a worker was entitled to double time for holiday work even if he didn't meet the eligibility requirements for pay for an unworked holiday. (Alpha Cellulose Corp., 27 LA 798)

Work on Holiday, Which Also Is Premium-Pay Day

When an employee works on a holiday, which also happens to be a premium pay day (such as the sixth or seventh day of work), complicated questions are likely to arise. The principal problem seems to be whether pyramiding (paying overtime rates on overtime rates) should be required. Several arbitrators have held that employees are entitled to two overtime rates.

EXAMPLE: Certain e m p l o y e e s worked on a Saturday holiday, after having worked the regular workweek of Monday through Friday. They were paid time and one-half for the Satur-

day holiday worked, and claimed they should have received triple time. They contended they were entitled to time and one-half for having worked more than 40 hours a week plus time and one-half for having worked on a holiday.

The contract provided that (1) time and one-half would be paid for work after eight hours a day or 40 hours a week; (2) "no overtime shall be paid on overtime"; and (3) when certain holidays, including the one involved here, were worked, "time and one-half additional shall be paid."

An arbitration board ruled that the provision prohibiting pyramiding of overtime was applicable only to daily and weekly overtime work, and that the word "additional," in the holiday pay clause meant "additional to such other pay as would be received on the day involved." Therefore, it was concluded that employees were entitled to triple time—time and one-half for hours worked over 40 in the week and time and one-half for holiday work. (L. A. Jewish Community Council, 11 LA 869)

On the other hand: Arbitrators have ruled against pyramiding of premium pay for weekly overtime on top of premium pay for a worked holiday.

EXAMPLE: A contract provided time and one-half pay for Saturday work, straight-time pay for certain unworked holidays, and double time for work done on holidays. The parties also had agreed that a holiday falling on a Saturday would not be paid for if it were not worked. The union requested triple-time pay for any Saturday holiday on which work was performed. It argued that work on a Saturday holiday should be paid for at the premium rates for both the Saturday (an overtime day) and the holiday.

The arbitrator ruled that:

"The parties have agreed on double time as the appropriate premium for holiday work. But there is no necessity that this means double the overtime rate when the periods coincide. The purposes of overtime and holiday pay are separate. For work on Saturday the parties have agreed on a rate of time and one-half.

"If the Saturday should coincide with a holiday the higher premium for holiday work will prevail. The arbitrator is not convinced that the premium should be pyramided. It is a reasonable provision that holiday work shall be paid for at double time, but that this be uniformly applied as double the straight-time rate." (Heating & Air Conditioning Contractors, 11 LA 816)

Daily Overtime on Holiday

What rate should be paid an employee for overtime hours on a holiday? Under a contract providing double time for holiday work and time and a half for more than eight hours work in one day, one arbitrator allowed employees to collect pay at triple time since the contract did not expressly prohibit pyramiding of premiums.

On the basis of the same reasoning, the arbiter also held that time and one-half the double time rate was in order for work on a sixth day (after 40 hours' work) when the sixth day also was a holiday. (Phelps Dodge Refining Corp., 9 LA 474)

Holiday Rate for Incentive Workers

Under a contract providing double time for hours worked on a holiday, incentive workers were entitled to twice their full earnings, according to one arbitrator. The company thought that it only had to pay workers their full straight-time earnings plus a premium of eight times the base rate. It argued that this had

been the practice for eight years without protest from the union. But the umpire said that past practice is immaterial where it is clearly in conflict with the plain language of the contract. The agreement said that workers would "receive double time for hours worked on any of the designated legal holidays." Clearly, the umpire ruled, this meant the incentive base rate plus incentive earnings plus shift premium, all multiplied by two. (Ford Motor Co., 27 LA 142)

When Does Holiday Begin?

Premium pay was meant to apply to all time worked during the "calendar day" definition of Thanksgiving, according to one arbiter. The night shift did not end until 1 a.m. Thanksgiving morning, but the company refused to pay doube time as the workers demanded. It argued that since the contract was silent as to whether holiday premium pay was based on the work day or calendar day, its past practice of paying straight time only when a regular shift overlapped a calendar holiday was controlling. According to the arbiter, Thanksgiving Day is not a technical term with special meaning in labor-relations parlance; therefore, its normal meaning of midnight to midnight was binding, and the workers were entitled to double pay for the hour worked on the holiday. In addition, the "past practice" had not been used often enough to render it binding. (Grand Rapids Die Casting Co., 44 LA 954)

*IN BRIEF*_____

Disputes rarely arise between management and the union over the amount of benefits due workers under a health and welfare plan. This is spelled out in careful detail in the policies issued by the insurer and, therefore, is out of the parties' hands. In some instances, however, where the union contract was more liberal than the insurance policy purchased by the company, arbitrators have held that the contract was controlling.

In the absence of specific contract language, the eligibility for coverage of employees who are absent from work because of layoff or for other reasons may be a source of disagreement. The employees' seniority status under the basic contract and the company's past practice often are the determining factors in such cases.

Coordination of Benefits

Insurance companies in their agreements with employers often insert a "coordination of benefits" c l a u s e which has the effect of prohibiting a family's recovery of double benefits in cases where husband and wife work for separate employers who provided separate hospitalization coverage for each. Arbitrators are split over the effect of such clauses on the employer's obligations under his union contract.

One school of thought is that the possibility of double coverage is one of the benefits under the union contract and that it therefore may not be terminated unilaterally by the employer without the union's consent. (52 LA 557, 54 LA 583)

Other arbiters, however, take the position that the intent of the parties in negotiating for insurance benefits was not to permit an employee to make a profit out of the group insurance plan. They therefore find no objection to coordination of benefits. (47 LA 1142, 49 LA 833, 54 LA 335)

Coverage of Absent Employees

Does an employer have to keep up the payments for health and welfare benefits for employees who are absent from work because of layoff, sickness or leave of absence? Depending upon the wording of the contract and the company's past practice in each case, arbitrators have reached different conclusions on this problem.

In one situation where a contract required the company to pay 75 percent of the cost of hospitalization and surgical insurance for all employees, an arbiter ruled that the company had to keep up its share of the premiums for workers on indefinite layoff. He noted that the contract provided for the retention of seniority rights for two years after layoff. So these workers were still employees, he decided. For this reason he held that the company had to make insurance payments for the laid-off workers for at least two years afterward. (National Lead Co., 30 LA 333)

In a similar manner, one arbiter held that management couldn't terminate the insurance coverage of a worker on a two-year disability leave. Noting that since the worker had retained her seniority and that her name was on the latest seniority roster, he decided that she was still an employee within the meaning of the contract, so the company had to pay the premiums. (Dayton Economy Drug Co., 40 LA 1182)

Another umpire ordered a company in a similar situation to keep up insurance payments for sick and injured workers for the duration of its contract. He based his decision on the company's practice under the previous contributory plan, which was to go on paying its share of the premiums for workers on extended absence as long as they paid their part. (Dayton Steel Foundry Co., 28 LA 595)

However: In some cases companies have not been required to make premium payments to health and welfare plans for absent workers. One arbiter, for example, allowed a company to continue to make payments into a group insurance fund only for persons on the payroll at the time the payments became due because it had done this for eight years without protest from the union. (Crown Upholstering Co., 20 LA 422)

Retroactive Coverage of Health Plan

Suppose some employees are out sick when a new health insurance plan goes into effect. Can they claim benefits under the plan? At least one arbitrator has decided that although persons out sick may be employees as far as other benefits are concerned, they aren't covered employees for health insurance purposes until they return to work.

EXAMPLE: Several employees who were out on sick leave when a health insurance plan went into effect put in claims for health benefits, saying that under NLRB rulings they were "employees," and that the plan covered "employees in the bargaining unit." The umpire rejected their claims on two counts. First, he said that since the plan limited the coverage with respect to laid-off employees, it was logical to make a similar distinction for those on sick leave. Second, he pointed out that insurance is by its nature prospective and designed to protect employees against future contingencies. He ruled, therefore, that employees couldn't be covered until they returned to active status in the company. (Schlitz Brewing Co., 23 LA 126)

Eligibility of Strikers

Are employees who are out on strike, or who haven't been recalled after a strike, eligible for health and welfare benefits? At least one arbitrator and a state court have come to the conclusion that a striker is still an "employee" and therefore eligible for benefits.

EXAMPLE: During contract negotiations, the union at one company went out on strike. As part of the settlement of the dispute, the company agreed to reinstate all the strikers as they were needed. One of the strikers died before he was recalled for work, and the company refused to pay death benefits under the life insurance policy in effect "for all employees covered by this agreement," because the employee hadn't been working at the time of his death.

The arbitrator said the company had to pay the benefits because it would have treated the employee as a continuing, rather than new, employee if he had returned to work before his death, which he had been willing and waiting to do. (Sidney Blumenthal & Co., Inc., 12 LA 715)

EXAMPLE: About three months after a union went on strike, one of the strikers was injured as the result of an accident that had no connection with the strike. Because of this injury, the employee was hospitalized and didn't fully recover until a month after the rest of the strikers had returned to work. The company turned down his claim for disability benefits under the insurance plan in effect for its employees on the ground that he was not an "active" employee at the time of the injury.

A state court ruled that the claimant had not lost his status as an employee by going out on strike, so he was entitled to benefits since the employer hadn't notified employees that their insurance coverage would be cut off during the strike. The court found that the company had discontinued premium payments for employees on strike, so it ruled the employer, rather than the insurance carrier, liable for the benefits payments. (Tedesco v. Turner & Seymour Mfg. Co.—Conn CtComPls, Litchfield Cty (1954), 35 LRRM 2691)

EXAMPLE: When employees went on strike, the e m p l o y e r cancelled the hospitalization program without notifying the union or its members of his action. He contended that the strike had terminated the contract and that the cancellation of the insurance was a legitimate countertactic. The arbiter held that the union's exercise of its right to strike did not destroy the contract relationship, so the employer had no right to cancel the insurance. Therefore, the employer was held liable for the claims of two men who were hospitalized during the strike. (National Seating Co., 45 LA 476)

However: In another case, cancellation of sickness and accident insurance during a strike was in keeping with the terms of the contract. Several workers suffered disabilities before the parties reached a settlement which again extended the coverage. These workers claimed benefits, but were not awarded them by the arbiter. He said that to do so would be to back-date the coverage to the period of the strike, which would be contrary to the terms of the contract. (E.J. Lavino & Co., 43 LA 213)

Discrepancy Between Contract & Insurance Policy

When an employer-union contract conflicts with the terms of the insurance policy covering the employees, which one takes precedence? Arbitrators generally have held that an employer must live up to the agreement made with the union. In the case of a discrepancy, therefore, the company usually is held liable for benefits which the insurance carrier won't pay but which employees are entitled to under the union agreement.

EXAMPLE: An employee at one company was laid off because of illness and drew sick benefits for a period of 13 weeks. He did not return to work, and died more than a year after his absence started. His family claimed benefits provided by the contract and the insurance policy at the time of the employee's sickness layoff. However, the insurance policy for the employee had expired. The family, backed by the employee's union, maintained that the employee had been on a layoff status for the entire period of his illness and therefore had been covered by the union contract and its insurance clause for the same period. The company insisted that the employee's layoff had ended when his 13 week's sick benefits ended and that liability under the insurance clause had stopped there.

The Connecticut Board of Mediation & Arbitration, however, went along with the employee's family and the union and ruled that the employee was in the same position as a laid-off employee. Hence the company had to pay the claim, even though the carrier was no longer liable. The Board pointed out that the contract provided for seniority accumulation during a continuous layoff period of up to two years. Furthermore, they said that the contract provided insurance for "the employees and their dependents," but did not mention the status of employees on layoff or leave of absence. Since there was no distinction in the contract between active and laid-off employees with respect to benefits, the Board ruled that the company should have kept up the insurance and, since it didn't do this, must pay the insurance benefit. (Jenkins Brothers, 22 LA 364)

EXAMPLE: An employee at one company lost four weeks' work because of illness. When she applied for the $10-a-week sick benefit specified by the union contract, the insurance carrier rejected her claim on the ground that she had been treated by a chiropractor rather than by a physician or osteopath as required by the insurance policy.

An umpire ordered the company to pay the sick benefits. The employee clearly was entitled to them, he pointed out, since the contract granted them after three months' service and didn't call for a doctor's certificate or other proof of illness. (Crown Cotton Mills, 32 LA 3)

On the other hand: In one case where the union agreement was ambiguous, the umpire used insurance-plan standards as a guide to whether or not the employer was liable for benefit payments.

EXAMPLE: The contract with the union said simply that employees would be paid $2 for calls at a doctor's office and $3 for calls at home or a hospital. Since there were no other restrictions written into the agreement, the union said that payments to employees under the medical plan had to be made for all doctors' visits, while the company argued that benefits were payable only when employees were totally disabled and absent from work.

The arbitrator upheld the employer's point of view. Since the contract didn't describe eligibility rules, he said, it didn't settle the matter. Therefore, he decided the union was bound by the standard eligibility provisions of comparable insurance plans, and they paid benefits only if employees were unable to work. Also, the background of negotiations showed that the union had suggested a plan at a cost of 40 cents a month per employee. At this figure, the arbitrator noted, it wasn't possible to provide the comprehensive coverage which the union claimed was required by the contract. (Weaver Mfg. Co., 15 LA 471)

Coverage of Dependent-Worker

Where there are separate hospitalization plans for bargaining-unit workers and nonunit workers, which plan applies to the wife of a worker in the unit if she was a worker outside the unit? In one such situation, an arbitrator held that a dependent wife's previous status as an employee didn't bar her husband's claim to dependant benefits.

EXAMPLE: A company had a hospitalization plan for office workers with somewhat smaller benefits than the plan covering the bargaining unit. Company policy stated that employees who were also dependents of employees couldn't have double coverage.

While one bargaining-unit worker's wife was employed in the office, she became pregnant. Five months later she quit. When she delivered her child, the company paid her hospitalization benefits under the office plan. Her husband claimed the higher benefits for her as his dependent under the bargaining-unit plan. But the company argued that, because she was an employee at the time she became pregnant, she couldn't be insured as a dependent. Even if she could, it claimed, maternity coverage required a nine-month waiting period in either case, and it hadn't been that long since she quit and became covered as a dependent.

The umpire said the nine months should be figured starting with the date the husband's insurance became effective, not the date the dependent became covered. In addition, the arbiter threw out the company's argument that the woman was an employee when her pregnancy began. Her status as her husband's dependent when she went to the hospital was what counted, he said. (Minnesota Mining & Mfg. Co., 32 LA 843)

Medicare For Dependents

An employer wasn't permitted to deduct Medicare benefits received by dependents from the minimum benefits specified in his collective bargaining contract, an arbitrator held, even though a rider to the insurance company's master policy provided for such deductions. The rider, which went into effect when Medicare became effective, was issued after the effective date of the prior agreement, the arbitrator noted, and the union objected strenuously to it at the time. There was no indication that the subject was discussed in negotiation of the current contract or that the union agreed to the deductions. (Indiana General Corp., 52 LA 45)

Who Pays for Insurance Rate Increase?

If the insurance carrier raises its rates on a contributory health and welfare plan, who is responsible for paying the increase—the employer or the employees? There is no problem, of course, if the agreement states that both the company and the employees pay a specified percentage of the cost. Then the parties would share equally the burden of any increase. But where a contract said that employees would pay a certain dollars - and - cents amount, with the employer paying the difference, one arbitrator required the company to pay the increase. He ruled that by agreeing to pay the difference, the company had assumed the risk of a possible change in rates. (Goodman Mfg. Co., 15 LA 489)

However: In a case where the company paid a flat dollar amount and workers picked up the balance plus any increase, one arbitrator held that management had to pick up any increase for retirees. The contract stated that the "above mentioned" plan applied to retired people, but didn't fix any limit on the company's contribution for them. Since the contract required management to provide medical coverage for retirees, and in fact the company already was paying more than the contract specified for their insurance, the umpire said management had to pick up the increases, too. (National Lead Co., 38 LA 772; see also Stokely-Van Camp, Inc., 54 LA 472)

Furthermore; Even though workers were supposed to pay the full cost of the premium for dependents, management couldn't pass on an increase to them, another arbiter held. Dependents' coverage was a negotiated benefit offered to the workers at a monthly price of $1.95. Since the contract bound the company to maintain existing benefits "for the duration of the agreement," it had to pay the premium boost, he said; any change in the amount of the workers' contribution would have to be negotiated. (Goshen Rubber Co., 38 LA 1231)

Who Gets Insurance Dividends?

If a negotiated insurance plan says that costs are to be split equally between the company and its employees, dividends from the insurance company should be divided 50-50, one arbitrator has held.

EXAMPLE: One union negotiated a package deal that included increased hospital and medical benefits; the cost of these benefits was to be shared equally by the company and the workers. After the plan had been in effect for a while, the company received some dividends from the insurance carrier; it pocketed half of these and applied the other half against future employee contributions. The union protested, arguing that the dividends represented deferred wages and therefore belonged entirely to the workers.

The umpire, though, said the company did right. The insurance agreement, he pointed out, did not provide for a fixed contribution by the company; it stated that costs were to be shared equally. Insurance dividends are an element of these costs, so it is fitting to divide them equally, he con-cluded. (Philip Carey Mfg. Co., 27 LA 651)

However: Where the company paid a flat cents-per-hour per employee toward the cost of insurance, another umpire said the workers were entitled to the full amount of an insurance rebate. The company's contribution of 5½ cents was payable whether the rates went up or down, he emphasized. Since the company hadn't made any overpayments, the umpire held, the entire rebate should go to the workers. (Perkins Machine & Gear Co., 41 LA 435)

Regular Employees

According to an arbitrator, 20 years' practice established a longer-than-normal waiting period for purposes of life insurance coverage. While employees were considered "regular" for most purposes after the expiration of their probationary period, it had been the custom to wait six months before issuing life insurance to workers. The workers were aware of this practice, so the claim for a worker who had died after working only four months was disallowed. (Clinton Paper Co., 48 LA 702)

Another employer tried to treat workers who w o r k e d less than 30 hours a week as "not regular employees" for purposes of welfare-fund coverage. The arbitrator said that this was improper; that any employee whose h o u r s systematically were scheduled in advance was a regular employee. (Veterans Linen Supply Co., 46 LA 741)

Arbitrability of Insurance

Disputes under an insurance plan are generally not proper subjects for arbitration when the insurance is separate from the contract. Settlements of disputes of that nature are generally held to be topics for negotiation. (Mobil Oil Co., 43 LA 1287) Where the insurance plan has been mentioned in the collective agreement and figured in the parties' contract settlement, however, arbitration becomes the method for settlement of grievances. (Torrington Mfg. Co., 45 LA 1176)

It is generally recognized that a company retains all of its usual rights that it has not given up in bargaining. This does not necessarily mean though, that a company can do anything its contract does not expressly forbid. The Taft Act prevents it from taking certain actions, and arbitrators may find *implied* limitations on a company's rights in its bargaining agreement.

POINTERS—

▶ If a company brought up a subject in negotiations but failed to get its demands written into the contract, it may have lost its right to take unilateral action in that area.

▶ Management generally is conceded to have the right to make technological improvements, even if some workers are adversely affected, unless its contract says otherwise.

▶ Similarly, a company normally has the right to eliminate a job it no longer considers necessary. The union will be watchful, though, to make sure the duties of the job aren't in fact transferred to other workers.

▶ Even in the absence of a contract clause forbidding supervisors to do bargaining unit work, umpires sometimes have held that they could not do such work if people in the bargaining unit would be adversely affected.

Rights Retained When Not Limited by Contract

Most arbitrators agree that management retains all its rights that are not given up in the contract. This is so even if the agreement does not list all the rights that have been retained by management or has no management-rights clause at all. (Illinois Bell Telephone Co., 15 LA 274; National Dairy Products Corp., 41 LA 506)

On the other hand: The fact that a company retains all rights not given up through specific contract provisions doesn't mean it has a free hand to take any action it wants in the name of management rights. It is well established that a company's decisions made under a management-rights clause are subject to arbitration just like any other disputes over the interpretation or application of the agreement. (McInerey Spring & Wire Co., 9 LA 91)

Rights Surrendered by Negotiating

By asking the union's advice on a certain matter, management may lose its right to assert exclusive control over the subject, according to many arbitrators. In making awards, they attempt to find the intent of the parties at the time of the discussion. A company may intend only to obtain the union's views on a subject, but if it has actually become a matter of collective bargaining and an agreement is made, arbiters insist that the employer live up to such agreement.

Thus, one employer association couldn't reduce the number of electricians on a ship to five after having agreed with the union that eight would be employed, even though there was no specific contract provision for this. The arbiter said that an employer could not submit a managerial function to collective bargaining, reach an agreement on it, and then repudiate the agreement. (Pacific American Shipowners Assn., 10 LA 736)

Furthermore: If a company brings up a matter in negotiations and fails to reach agreement with the union on it, management may lose the right to take action on the matter, even though it would otherwise be able to do so under the management rights clause.

EXAMPLE: During contract negotiations a company demanded a clause making overtime work compulsory, but the union refused to agree to one. The company signed the contract without it. Later, when some workers were suspended for refusing to work Saturdays, the company claimed it had a right to require overtime work because the agreement was silent on the point. But the umpire decided that since the matter had been brought up in negotiations and no agreement was reached, the company had lost its absolute right to require employees to work overtime. (Sylvania Electric Products, Inc., 24 LA 199)

TECHNOLOGICAL CHANGE
Introduction of New Machines

Employers generally claim the absolute right to install new and improved machinery. When it seems likely that it would result in rate changes or a cut in the number in the work force, the union may challenge management's right to make the change. But usually arbiters have held that a union cannot block technological improvement unless there are specific contract restrictions on the matter.

Where one contract specifically allowed a company to install new machines, an arbiter ordered the workers to run them to their full capacity in good faith, even though it meant the piece rates would have to be lowered. The umpire stated that there was sound economic justification for upholding management's right to introduce technical improvements. To rule for the union, he said, would lead toward economic stagnation. (Associated Shoe Industries of Southeastern Mass., Inc., 10 LA 535)

Transfer of Work Because of Mechanization

When work is mechanized, does management have the right to assign it to employees outside the bargaining unit? Awards suggest that it depends on how much change takes place in the way the work is performed. If a union can show that the workers in the unit are capable of continuing the work after the new machines are installed, then its gripe against transferring the work is likely to be upheld.

EXAMPLE: Employees in the bottling department of a brewing company had performed a manual testing operation on beer cans for seven or eight years; then the firm purchased a machine that could prepare the cans for testing more efficiently. It proposed turning the operation over to its machinists, who were in another bargaining unit.

The umpire found that installing the machine wouldn't really change the nature of the testing operation but would simply allow it to be done faster. Accordingly, he concluded that the proposed transfer would violate two sections of the union contract—the recognition clause, which gave the union jurisdiction over the customary work of the bargaining unit; and the job security clause, which reserved jobs in the bottling department for employees on the seniority list there.

All the signs were that the bottlers would be able to operate the machine satisfactorily, the umpire noted. If they couldn't after a fair trial, he added, the company could then give the work to the machinists. (Hamm Brewing Co., 28 LA 46)

On the other hand: If a company can show that the nature of the work has changed so that the workers who were assigned to it can no longer handle it efficiently, an umpire will no doubt uphold a decision to transfer it.

EXAMPLE: Timekeepers c l a i m e d

that their seniority rights were violated when the company installed automatic data processing equipment that eliminated some of the duties formerly performed by the timekeepers. In rejecting the timekeepers' beef, an arbitrator said that the company had the right to mechanize its work procedures by utilizing data processing equipment. Moreover, he noted, the eliminated duties were not performed by any workers within or outside the bargaining unit, but by a machine. (Bethlehem Steel Co., 35 LA 72; see also Van Norman Machine Co., 28 LA 791)

Further: A union's recognition clause did not guarantee that bargaining unit work would continue unchanged indefinitely, according to the arbiter; hence he didn't bar transfer of unit work to another department. When a publisher installed a computer in the subscription department, there was no longer any need for an addressograph operator. The arbiter held that the recognition clause extended to departments, not to types of work. Thus the union could not claim jurisdiction over a new system introduced into another department. (McCall Corp., 44 LA 201)

ASSIGNING WORK
Work Not Covered by Job Descriptions

According to one arbitrator, management's freedom to assign work is not restricted by job descriptions unless the contract expressly says so. The purpose of job descriptions, he said, is to describe duties for classification purposes; they seldom list all job requirements. Unless the contract says otherwise, he added, management is free to change duties and assignments; workers must perform assigned tasks, saving their protests for the regular grievance channels. (Pittsburgh Steel Co., 34 LA 598; see also Vare Corp., 53 LA 1130)

When a new contract dropped the status-quo provisions that had prevented unilateral changes in work assignments, management was no longer bound by a past practice of only assigning one job at a time to mold makers, according to another arbitrator. His ruling was that past practice under a prior contract isn't binding

unless the language giving rise to that practice is continued in the current contract. Therefore, he concluded, dual work assignments could be made unilaterally by management. (Overmyer Co., 43 LA 1006)

Eliminating Job

Does a contract clause giving management the right to assign work forces permit the company unilaterally to eliminate a job? A number of arbitrators have held that management can eliminate or combine jobs in the interest of efficiency or economy, so long as its action is not arbitrary and is not prohibited by the contract. In a plant where a change in operations made a helper's duties unnecessary, one umpire said that to uphold the union's claim to keep the job would be featherbedding. He found nothing in the contract that prevented the company from doing away with the job. (Union Starch & Refining Co., 15 LA 783)

Likewise, where a company had revived an old job solely to make work for a demoted foreman, an arbiter held that the company could eliminate the job when he retired. (U.S. Steel Corp., 23 LA 561) Still another umpire held that, even though there was no management-rights clause in a company's contract, it could eliminate jobs in order to meet operational demands. (Potter Brumfield, Inc., 29 LA 324)

A company wasn't required to fill a vacancy created by normal retirement where need for the job had ceased. The company's argument that it could adjust its work force to meet plant needs, and that it was merely discontinuing the job until such time as it might again be needed was upheld by the arbiter. (Sinclair Refining Co., 43 LA 1276)

However: A contract may have other clauses that restrict a company's decision to do away with a job under the management-rights clause. Thus, where a contract gave the company the right to assign work forces, but also prohibited changes in job classifications except where a new job was created or changes made in the production process, one arbiter wouldn't permit the company to wipe out a mouldman-leader's job which had not changed in content. (Bethlehem Steel Co., 17 LA 295)

Eliminating Classifications

If there is no longer any work required in a job classification, can an employer do away with it? Awards apparently depend upon the wording in individual contracts. One umpire held that a company was prohibited from divvying up the duties of the welder-inspector classification and abolishing it without getting the union's approval because its contract specifically said that job descriptions and classifications would remain unchanged unless both parties agreed to change them. (Lone Star Steel Co., 26 LA 160) Even where there was no specific restriction but where the contract established rates of pay for several classifications, an umpire ruled that the company could not eliminate a classification by itself. He said that the combining and elimination of classifications was a subject for negotiation between the parties. (Kansas Grain Co., 29 LA 242)

Although a "bargaining unit work" clause didn't freeze work, a company was not allowed to abolish a unit job only to reassign its duties as a non-unit job. The company said that, since the jobs were clerical, they shouldn't be considered part of the unit; however, the arbiter found no evidence in the contract that the parties had intended to limit the bargaining unit to actual production work. (Gisholt Machine Co., 44 LA 840)

On the other hand: Several arbitrators believe that in the absence of contract restrictions, management has the right to eliminate a classification by transferring its duties to others. One decided that a company didn't violate the seniority provisions of the contract by laying off men in one classification and assigning their duties to workers with less seniority. Seniority rights don't guarantee that a job will remain in existence or that its content won't be changed, he reasoned. (Axelson Mfg. Co., 30 LA 444; see also Alton Box Board Co., 54 LA 365)

Combining Jobs

If the work on a certain job is reduced through technological changes, can the worker be required to take on duties belonging to another classification? In one case an arbitrator found nothing in the agreement to prevent combining jobs in this way. But, he warned, such combinations could not be used to fill vacancies.

EXAMPLE: Because of technological changes, a time clerk and a die setter didn't have enough work to occupy them full time. To keep them busy, the company had them spend part of their time on work in other classifications. The union argued that this violated the seniority provisions of the contract; if more people were needed in these other classifications, it said, the regular procedure for filling vacancies should have been followed.

An umpire found nothing in the contract forbidding out-of-classification assignments. On the other hand, he said, the company couldn't use this device to fill vacancies. To determine whether any vacancy existed, the umpire applied this rule: If either the time clerk or the die setter spent more than 50 percent of his time on work in some other classification, he filled a vacancy in that classification. Since neither employee did so, the company acted within its rights. (Fletcher-Enamel Co., 27 LA 466; see also Martin-Marietta Corp., 53 LA 33)

Another arbiter found nothing wrong with the action of an employer who combined the duties of three jobs into one classification and offered to negotiate with the union over a wage rate for the new job. He said that the job-protection clause primarily was aimed at maintaining the pay scale, not at preventing all change in classifications. (Sewanee Silica Co., 47 LA 282)

Moving Jobs Between Shifts

Where there was no specific contract ban on it, at least one arbitrator ruled that a company could move a vacant job from one shift to another in the interest of efficiency.

EXAMPLE: When a day-shift cleaning job opened up at one company, management posted it as a night-shift job. It figured the cleaning work could be done better when regular employees were out of the way. It assured the union that it wasn't going to transfer any of the day-shift cleaners but would simply move jobs to the night jobs to the night shift as vacancies occurred. The union nevertheless contended that the job should have been posted as a day-shift vacancy.

An umpire noted that the posting provision of the contract was of the ordinary type, requiring the posting of new jobs and vacancies. In his view, nothing in the clause limited the company's choice of the shift to which a particular job was assigned. The union's claim that upholding the company's action would pave the way for a wholesale transfer of jobs to the night shift didn't impress the arbiter; the existence of night-shift premiums was an effective deterrent, he remarked. (White Motor Co., 29 LA 153)

WORK BY SUPERVISORS

Absence of Contract Ban on Work by Supervisors

Does management have the right to assign production work to supervisors if the contract doesn't specifically say they can't do the work usually performed by members of the bargaining unit? Under these circumstances arbitrators permit employers to assign production work to supervisors only so long as the rights of bargaining-unit employees aren't violated.

For example, one arbitrator said that although a company had the right to assign certain work to supervisors, it could not exercise this right if it would deprive employees in the unit of their right to work when sufficient work was available. (Bethlehem Steel Co., 14 LA 159; see also Fafnir Bearing Co., 39 LA 530)

Also, under a contract where the job of gang-boss was made a part of the promotion sequence, a company was not allowed to assign this job to supervisors outside the unit because it violated the seniority provisions. (West Virginia Pulp & Paper Co., 12 LA 1074)

Another arbiter similarly held that a company could not assign duties of shipping checker to a foreman without the union's consent because the transfer meant changing the job's content, which had been set by the agreement. (Kraft Foods Corp., 10 LA 254)

However: One umpire said that under its contract management was allowed to transfer supervisors to bargaining-unit jobs during slack seasons. The contract said that the company could retain as many as 30 employees regardless of their seniority if, in the sole judgment of the company, their special training, experience, or ability was needed. Although the union argued that this clause applied to technical workers only, the arbiter said it extended to supervisors. Since the company was "sole judge" of who needed to be retained, it has the right to make 30 transfers of nonunit workers to bargaining-unit jobs, he decided. The only limit on management, he added, was that it couldn't act in bad faith in selecting the men for transfer or use the clause to subvert the union. (Jefferson City Cabinet Co., 35 LA 117)

Work by Supervisors During Emergency

Contract bans on supervisors' performance of bargaining-unit work often contain an exception permitting such work in an "emergency." Arbitrators generally take a narrow reading of such exceptions and require firm evidence of a true emergency.

Thus, sending a supervisor to an airport to pick up a cylinder was held not be to be an "emergency." (Masonite Corp., 53 LA 965) Nor were "emergencies" found in the use of supervisors to make withdrawals and requisitions for employee (Masonite Corp., 53 LA 965) or in the performance by supervisors of Sunday washroom work caused by a temporary breakdown at another plant. (F. W. Means & Co., 54 LA 874)

Application of "De Minimis" Principle

Arbitrators may decide to overlook a technical violation of a ban supervisors performing bargaining unit work, where the violation was so minor as to warrant application of the "de minimis principle," which calls for ignoring inconsequential violations.

Thus, no substantive violation was found in a supervisor's distribution of hand tools to pipefitters while the counterman was off duty (Stauffer Chemical Co., 53 LA 706) or in a supervisor's dusting and sweeping an office where there was no indication that any employee was adversely affected. (Ideal Cement Co., 52 LA 9)

Effect of Other Clauses

Even under contracts which do not clearly forbid supervisors to do bargaining-unit work, some arbitrators have found the parties' intent in other clauses. In one such situation a working foreman was advanced to assistant superintendent but kept doing production work. The union complained that this violated a clause limiting the number of supervisors to three. But an umpire held that this must have been meant to limit only the number of working supervisors because a company's right to employ any number of nonworking supervisors is not ordinarily restricted. The company had not exceeded this limit, so the umpire ruled that the superintendent could continue doing production work. (Mt. Carmel Public Utility Co., 16 LA 59)

Under another contract lacking a definite ban on production work by supervisors, an arbiter found help from a clause stating that no employee would be temporarily transferred to a job in another department where the worker regularly handling the job was on layoff. This, the arbiter said, prevented the company from letting a foreman do a job ordinarily done by a bargaining-unit man who was laid off. (Sayles Biltmore Bleacheries, Inc., 26 LA 585)

Effect of Past Practice

When faced with ambiguous contracts some arbitrators have answered questions of work by supervisors by looking at the company's past practice.

One umpire, noting that a contract definition of bargaining-unit work was ambiguous, focused on the way in which the definition had been applied. Over a period of three years, he noted, management had on every occasion withdrawn supervisors from assignments which the union claimed were

bargaining-unit work. Since management itself had given this consistent interpretation to the contract terminology, the arbiter found it binding, despite the fact that the union had tried unsuccessfully to negotiate a specific ban on supervisors' doing production work. (Los Angeles Drug Co., 29 LA 38)

However: One arbiter wouldn't let a company continue assigning supervisors to bargaining-unit work merely because it had done so for several years without the union's forcing arbitration of the issue. (Great Lakes Pipe Line Co., 27 LA 748)

Monitoring of Automated Machinery

Can management, after installing automatic equipment to operate its machines, assign supervisors to monitor the equipment and eliminate the job of machine operator? Even where the contract contained a prohibition on the performance by supervisors of "work normally performed" by bargaining-unit workers, an arbitrator ruled that this was permissible. The machine operator's duties had been taken over by mechanical devices rather than by supervision, he reasoned. Control - room monitoring, he stated, is closer to the normal duties of supervisors than to the work done by bargaining-unit workers.

At the same time, the umpire held that it would be improper for supervisors to operate the machines manually or to do physical work in cleaning, repairing, or adjusting them. (Goodyear Tire & Rubber Co., 35 LA 917)

Work by Supervisors to Test Standards

Under a contract containing a general ban on the performance of production work by supervisors, one arbitrator ruled that management violated the agreement when it assigned supervisors to such work, outside regular hours, to prove that production standards were fair. However, in view of a clause stating that supervisors could do production work for the purpose of instructing workers, he said the assignment in question would have been proper if the workers who regularly performed the work had been called in to observe the demonstration. (National Lead Co. of Ohio, 34 LA 235)

Effect of Strike

A ban on assigning supervisors to bargaining-unit work does not apply during a strike, in the opinion of one arbitrator. Such a ban is designed to protect the job rights of union members on duty or available for work, he said. It has no application when the members refuse to work, he reasoned, since in such a case they are not *displaced* by supervisors. (Texas Gas Corp., 36 LA 1141)

Ban Applied to Other Nonunit Workers

At least one arbiter has decided that a contract clause forbidding supervisors to do bargaining unit work applied to other workers outside the unit as well.

EXAMPLE: At one company, requisitions for materials on night and week-end shifts were too infrequent to justify having a stock clerk on duty. Plant guards, who weren't in the bargaining unit, handled the occasional requisitions on those shifts. The union protested. It would have been okay to have some other bargaining unit member take over stock-clerk duties, the union said, but it was wrong for plant guards to do the work.

The arbitrator agreed. Although having plant guards handle bargaining-unit work wasn't specifically forbidden by the contract, the umpire thought the effect of using them was the same as that of using supervisors; it deprived members of the bargaining unit of work that should have been theirs. Unit members have a vested right in bargaining-unit work, the arbitrator stated, and no worker outside the unit has the right to horn in on it. (Reynolds Metals Co., 26 LA 756)

PRODUCTION STANDARDS

Right to Establish Production Standards

If your contract doesn't provide yardsticks for measuring employee efficiency, can management adopt its own standards? One arbiter says it can, so long as whatever standards it sets are fair and reasonable.

EXAMPLE: One company gave an

employee a warning stating that he was producing only 42 percent of the average of other employees doing comparable work. The union squawked, pointing out that the contract made no reference to production or efficiency standards. Neither side meant for such standards to be used in evaluating performance, it claimed. The company, though, figured its action came within the scope of the management rights clause, under which it retained the right to manage the plant, direct the work force, and suspend and discharge employees for just cause.

An umpire upheld the company. The right to manage the plant and direct the work force would be almost meaningless, in his opinion, if the company couldn't judge efficiency and require a reasonable level to be maintained. If some benchmark was to be used to measure performance, he added, management had to discipline all those individuals whose records compared least favorably with the standard. Failure to apply the standard in an even-handed manner would violate the "just cause" requirement, he commented. (Menasco Mfg. Co., 30 LA 264)

In like manner, another umpire said management could establish production standards where workers previously had set their own standards. Nothing indicated that the parties intended old practices to be continued indefinitely, he noted, and the union had been notified that the establishment was being contemplated. There was no evidence that the new standards were unreasonable, he said, and the company's failure to exercise a right didn't waive that right. Further, the contract allowed management to "establish production and work standards" and to eliminate practices which were inefficient or unreasonable. (Mead Corp., 41 LA 1033)

On the other hand: Where new standards are set for just a single department, one umpire has held, they must not be out of line with the work pace elsewhere in the plant.

EXAMPLE: A company set new piece rates for a newly mechanized department. After the rates had been in effect for a time, the men in the department complained they were making less than they had been and less than employees doing comparable jobs in other departments. The company replied that the standards had been set by accepted methods.

An umpire agreed that the standards were not unreasonable when judged by usual industrial-engineering standards. But he found that they required the men in the department to work faster than in the past and faster than employees in other departments. Holding that the company was obligated to maintain the established relationship between effort and earnings, as well as the existing wage relationships among departments in the plant, the arbiter ordered a 5-percent increase in the rates (Simmons Co., 33 LA 725)

Right to Change Size of Work Crew

If the contract mentions the number of employees to be used in the work crew on a particular job, can the company adjust the size of the crew because of changes in the volume of business or other factors?

Under a contract which stated that "no less than three men shall be employed in a crew . . ." an arbitrator ruled that, regardless of workload, the company couldn't cut the size of the crew for the duration of the contract. (Weston Biscuit Co., Inc., 21 LA 653)

In another case, where the contract banned reduction in existing crew size but permitted negotiations on size in certain situations, an arbitrator held that management couldn't negotiate for a smaller crew. Although the contract didn't expressly confine negotiations to increasing, rather than decreasing crew sizes, the umpire thought it was the parties' intent to maintain the stated minimum manning, at least for the contract term. Nothing barred them from resolving the issue when the new contract negotiations occurred, he added. (Sinclair Oil Corp., 41 LA 878)

When a salt company installed new conveyor equipment, it didn't have the right to eliminate workers engaged in sacking the salt, an arbitrator decided. The contract's wage schedule specified that the crews consist of 11 workers, and, for this reason, the employer was not allowed to reduce the size of the sacking crews, despite the fact that only nine men were needed. (Barton Salt Co., 46 LA 503)

But: Another arbitrator upheld a company's action in reducing the size of a work crew after the work had been mechanized and thus required fewer workers. The contract required a certain crew size "under present conditions." The "present conditions" mentioned in the contract no longer existed, the arbitrator said. (Theo. Hamm Brewing Co., 35 LA 243)

PLANT TRANSFER

Relocation of Operations

What effect does a contract between a company and a union have on management's right to move the entire plant or relocate some of the operations to locations outside the union's jurisdiction?

The U.S. Supreme Court has ruled that a company that moves a plant to a new location may be required to arbitrate the question of employment rights at the new plant even though (1) the new plant is a considerable distance away and (2) the contract has expired. (Carpenters v. Kimball Co.—US SupCt (1965), 57 LRRM 2628)

In one case, an arbiter said management had a right to shut down, buy out a competitor, and transfer operations during contract term. As to its duty to bargain, this meant consulting with the union on its decision to move, he held, not yielding to union opposition to the move. In this case, management refused to give workers any transfer rights, which the union contended violated seniority provisions. However, the umpire decided the workers had no seniority at the other plants, since these were under contracts with other locals. (Sivyer Steel Casting Co., 39 LA 449)

In another case, even though several workers were laid off as a result of subcontracting the work which they had been doing, no violation was found by the arbitrator. The contract did not place any restrictions on this action because it was taken to accomplish great financial savings. (Curtiss-Wright Corp., 43 LA 5)

Remedy for Improper Relocation

Depending on the cirumstances and the wording of the contract, arbitrators have fashioned remedies for the workers affected by plant closing and relocation ranging from severance pay to an order directing the company to reestablish the original plant.

EXAMPLE: A contract between a union and a clothing manufacturer specifically prohibited removal of the plant or the manufacture of garments in any other factory without the consent of the union. After a shutdown that the union was told was temporary, the manufacturer moved his operations to a new plant in another state. The move was accomplished at night and over weekends without the union's knowledge.

Finding that the move violated the contract, an arbitrator directed the manufacturer to discontinue operations in the new plant, reestablish the factory in the state from which he had moved, and pay the union damages of over $200,000 covering wage, vacation, and welfare-fund payments for 300 workers. (Jack Meilman, 34 LA 771; see also Sidelle Fashions, Inc., 36 LA 1364)

EXAMPLE: When one company announced that it was going to move its finishing operations from Danbury, Conn., to Philadelphia, the union charged that this would be a lockout in violation of its contract.

An umpire found that the shift was being made for business reasons. This being so, he said, only an express contract provision could stop the move, since a company's freedom to move isn't limited by the mere existence of a contract. Nevertheless he ruled that management should have discussed the move in advance with the union. Moreover, he said, available jobs should have been offered to those employees willing to go to Philadelphia, and their moving expenses paid. Those who didn't make the move, he decided, were entitled to severance pay plus a share of the pension fund. The company voluntarily offered to pay supplemental unemployment benefits totalling about $45,000 to employees staying in Connecticut, but the umpire figured this wasn't enough. He wasn't sure that he had authority to order payment of severance benefits; but to the extent that he did, he ordered the company to set aside $100,000 for severance pay and moving expenses. (John B. Stetson Co., 28 LA 514)

MISCELLANEOUS PROBLEMS

Regulation of Coffee Breaks

Can management, during the term of a contract, unilaterally establish definite rules regarding coffee breaks to replace a practice of allowing individual workers to select their own coffee-break times? According to one arbitrator, such an action is a legitimate exercise of management's rule-making powers.

EXAMPLE: For years employees at one company had been permitted to take breaks for coffee and other refreshments according to their individual wishes. In time this arrangement reached the point where it was seriously hindering production—an employee might take a break that would stop a production line and when he returned another might knock off, and so on down the line. To remedy this situation, the company made a rule limiting breaks to set periods in the morning and afternoon. The union immediately protested that this amounted to a change in working conditions in violation of its contract.

An arbiter pointed out that the firm's action did not end the practice of allowing breaks but actually gave it official recognition and status. This was not a change in working conditions, he concluded. (Dover Corp., 33 LA 860; see also Metal Specialty Co., 39 LA 1265)

On the other hand: An employer couldn't unilaterally reduce the number of rest periods which had remained the same for five years. According to the arbitrator, such a seasoned practice took on the status of an obligation binding on both parties. It was a working condition set by past practice, and, as such was not subject to unilateral action. (Formica Corp., 44 LA 467)

Installation of Time Clocks

Does management have the right to

install time clocks without first getting the union's go-ahead? Time clocks are a condition of employment over which a company is obligated to bargain, one arbitrator has said. But if the subject of installing them is raised in contract negotiations and the union registers no objection, management may be able to put in time clocks without discussing the matter further with the union.

EXAMPLE: Shortly after signing a union contract, a company started requiring office employees to punch time clocks. The union claimed this step violated a contract clause requiring the company to negotiate with the union on conditions of employment. The company maintained that it merely had exercised a management right. Even if the issue were bargainable, the company argued, the union had waived its right to bargain about installation of time clocks by failing to negotiate on the point when management representatives brought it up in negotiations.

An arbitrator decided that the company did have an obligation to bargain over the time clocks, but he agreed with management that the union had lost out by failing to pursue the matter in negotiations. The union might have ground for complaint, he added, if the time clocks were used in an unfair way. (Motor Wheel Corp., 26 LA 931)

On the other hand: The exact procedures for clocking in and out were within the exclusive authority of management. While manual time clocks had been used in the past, the arbitrator found nothing wrong with the company's introduction of IBM units for clocking in and out. He said that the installation of new equipment was not a condition of employment, and therefore, not a subject for union involvment. (Babcock & Wilcox Co., 45 LA 897)

Change in Pay Periods

Does management have the right to change the frequency of pay periods during the term of a contract without getting the union's consent? It probably does, one arbiter's ruling suggests, if the contract doesn't say when employees are to be paid.

EXAMPLE: When a company decided to pay employees on a bi-weekly basis instead of weekly, the union argued this was a change in past practice that violated its contract. The umpire disagreed. In the first place, he said, the dispute wasn't even arbitrable since the contract said nothing about pay periods and specifically stated that only grievances arising out of the operation or interpretation of the agreement could be arbitrated.

Despite what the agreement said, the umpire noted that he might have ruled on the merits of the case if the parties had had an informal understanding about pay periods. But although the company had had a weekly pay system for years, the union never said anything about it; such "mute acquiescence" didn't establish a binding past practice, the umpire concluded. (Cone Mills Corp., 30 LA 100)

Method of Paying Wages

If workers have always been paid their wages in a certain manner, and the contract is silent on the subject, can the company change the method of payment? Decisions on this have gone both ways, depending on past practice or on the reason for the change.

In one case, the umpire said management couldn't begin mailing checks home after a long practice of passing them out on the job. The question of where workers were to be paid was not wholly one for management decision—the men also had rights as creditors, he said. He noted that in 1946 the contract had been revised to say that "wages shall be paid weekly on company time." That the parties assumed that payment would be made on the job was borne out by management's attempt in 1960 to alter the practice. The union's rejection of management's attempt meant that past practice governed, he concluded. (Manitowoc Shipbuilding, Inc., 39 LA 907)

However: Despite a long practice of paying in cash, another umpire held that management was within its rights in switching from cash to checks for paying wages. The practice had been in effect for 45 years, the union argued, and was as much a fringe benefit as the coffee break, in which the company had agreed not to make unilateral changes during contract term. The arbiter, however, decided that management's intent was to make the payroll process uniform and efficient. Absent evidence that the method of payment is a condition of employment, he added, it couldn't be a benefit protected by past practice. (Diamond Alkali Co., 38 LA 1055)

No consistent pattern has emerged in arbitrator's rulings on whether a company may require workers to retire at a fixed age. All the circumstances of the particular case must be examined—what the basic contract says, what the company's past practice has been, what has happened in past negotiations, and the like.

POINTERS—

▶ There's little doubt that a long-standing policy of retiring workers at a certain age may be continued by a company, despite the existence of a bargaining agreement.

▶ If the union has had an opportunity to bargain on the subject of retirement and has passed it up, the company may be within its rights in putting a policy into effect during the contract term.

▶ It has usually, though not always, been held that a forced retirement does not violate a just-cause discharge provision.

▶ A compulsory retirement policy, to be valid and enforceable during the term of a contract, must have been announced in clear terms to workers and applied consistently.

GUIDELINES

An extensive review of the arbitrators' rulings on compulsory retirement was undertaken by Arbitrator John E. Gorsuch in Cummins Power, Inc., 51 LA 909. Here are some of the points he made:

In the later 1940's and early 1950's there could not be any dispute as to the right of an employer to unilaterally set a mandatory retirement age in the absence of specific contractual restriction. In the middle 1950's, a different theory began to emerge under which if the union didn't acquiesce, but instead object to institution of a compulsory retirement plan, forcible retirement of an otherwise physically able employee would be held to violate the job security provision of a contract.

Since then there has been a split of authority on the employer's right unilaterally to set a mandatory retirement age in the absence of a specific contract restriction. Thus, witness these holdings:

▶ Retirement is a very important condition of employment, and a union has the right to bargain for a condition of employment. (Consolidated Packaging Corp., 51 LA 47)

▶ Discharge, as used in collective bargaining, is not synonomous with termination by retirement, and it is "a well-established principle in arbitration" that in the absence of any contract restriction, the employer has the unilateral right to establish and administer a compulsory retirement policy. (Brown Line Co., 50 LA 597)

▶ Enforced retirement of a physically able and competent employee is a violation of his security and seniority rights, especially where the retirement policy and plan is unilaterally announced and is not spelled out in a jointly-established agreement. (Armour Agricultural Chemical Co., 47 LA 513)

Arbitrator Gorsuch indicated agreement with the latter holding.

RETIREMENT POLICY AS MANAGEMENT RIGHT

Long-Standing Policy

If the company has had a compulsory retirement policy in effect for several years before it ever signs a contract with a union, does it retain the right to follow this policy after the contract goes into effect?

Management is free to continue following any company policies in effect when a union contract is signed, according to one arbitrator, as long as the contract doesn't specifically mention such policies. Furthermore, since management has the prerogative of directing the work force in the interest of plant efficiency, it has the right to require workers to retire at a certain age, the umpire said. (Metals Disintegrating Co., Inc., LA 601; see also General Aniline & Film Corp., 25 LA 50; S. H. Kress & Co., 25 LA 77)

Effect of Negotiations

According to many arbiters, management's right to force workers to retire is strengthened if the union (1) has had an opportunity to negotiate but failed to do so, or (2) brings up the matter in negotiations but fails to get agreement and signs a contract with no mention of the policy.

EXAMPLE: A pension plan providing for automatic retirement at age 65, adopted unilaterally, had been in effect for five years before the union brought a grievance over an employee's forced retirement. An arbitration board said the company could continue to follow its established practice until such time as the policy was restricted through collective bargaining. The board noted that the union had tried unsuccessfully to do this in the most recent bargaining sessions. Generally, the board concluded, employees are entitled only to the rights they have won in the contract. If the right to work beyond age 65 isn't specified in the contract, the arbitrators said, it doesn't exist. (Hercules Powder Co., 23 LA 214)

On the other hand: At least one arbitrator believes that if a union consistently objects to a compulsory retirement policy the company may have no business forcing workers to retire against their wishes. In one case he found that the union not only demanded bargaining when a com-

pulsory retirement plan was set up—
a request that was refused—but had
protested every time the company
threatened to enforce it. The umpire
noted that the agreement set forth
the circumstances under which seniority was lost but didn't mention
forced retirement. Thus, he ruled, the
company had introduced a new reason
for loss of seniority without giving
prior notice to the union and bargaining as required by law. (Trans-
World Airlines, Inc., 31 LA 45)

Contract Specifying "National Retirement Age"

Where either the contract or a pension plan agreed to by the union and
the company expressly provides for
compulsory retirement, arbitrators
find little difficulty in upholding the
company's right to compel a worker
to retire. But where the contract is
silent on the subject and there is no
long-standing policy acquiesced in by
the union, arbitrators generally hold
that management does not have the
right to compel a worker to retire.
In such a case, language specifying
a "normal retirement age" and the
manner in such the parties have
interpreted the language may be important.

EXAMPLE: A contract stated that
"age 65 is considered the normal retirement age." The company retired
an employee against his wishes when
he reached 65, and the union filed
a grievance. In upholding the company's right to retire the employee,
an arbitrator noted that "normal retirement date" was defined in an earlier pension agreement between the
parties as the date beyond which a
worker could not continue working
unless specifically requested to do so
by the company. The only logical interpretation of the present language,
the arbitrator said, was that the parties intended to carry over the same

concept of compulsory retirement that
had existed under the pension plan.
(National Airlines, 35 LA 67)

However: Under a pension plan
which stated that an "employee may
be permitted to remain" at work after
the normal retirement age of 65 until
he reached age 70 provided he was
physically able to do the job and
performed his duties satisfactorily,
and permitted continued work after
age 70 "only upon the request of the
company," an arbitrator said management couldn't force retirement of
a 65-year-old worker who met the
standards. The pension plan was not
originally negotiated, but was written
by the company, the umpire noted.
Thus, if the company had wanted
to make the 65-to-70 privilege exclusively within its control, it could have
stated so in concise language, just as
it did the provision for workers over
age 70, he reasoned. Since this was
not done the arbiter concluded that
the worker must be allowed to remain at work if he fulfilled the qualifications. (Central Soya Co. 41 LA
370)

Discriminatory Retirement Policy

Some retirement plans allow employers to retire workers at different
ages depending on the ability of the
individual. Generally arbitrators have
okayed the use of such flexible retirement policies only as long as they
are administered consistently and
fairly. Thus a policy that allowed
old-age employees to continue working only as long as they continued
on the same job was held to be discriminatory and a violation of the
contract. (Barrett-Cravens Co. 12 LA
522) Another umpire ruled that there
must be substantial proof that an
employee's work is unsatisfactory before he can be forced to retire under
a contract giving the company discretion in retiring employees 65 or
over. (Ford Motor Co., 20 LA 13)

The right of management to subcontract, in the absence of specific contract restriction, has been the subject of countless grievances. In earlier cases, arbitrators generally held that management has the right, if exercised in good faith, to subcontract work to independent contractors.

Most of the later cases, however, have held that management's right to subcontract is not unrestricted. Many of these cases fall into one of these categories.

● Management's right to subcontract must be judged against the recognition, seniority, wage, and other such clauses of the agreement; standards of reasonableness and good faith are applied in determining whether these clauses are violated.

● Management's right to subcontract is recognized, provided it is exercised reasonably and in good faith.

One arbitrator, after examining prior arbitration decisions, found that arbitrators have ruled that management is prohibited from subcontracting (1) unless it acts in good faith; (2) unless it acts in conformity with past practices; (3) unless it acts reasonably; (4) unless the act deprives only a few employees of employment; (5) unless the act was dictated by business requirements; (6) if the act is barred by the recognition clause; (7) if the act is barred by seniority provisions; or (8) if the act violates the spirit of the agreement. (American Sugar Refining Co., 37 LA 334)

Another study of these awards found these general propositions running through many of these cases:

● Most contracting out is not found to present a sufficient threat to the scope of the bargaining unit to warrant invoking the implied limitation on management's right to subcontract.

● Recognizing the union and signing the contract do not establish an agreement that all the jobs then in existence will continue to be performed by members of the bargaining unit.

● The company cannot undermine the union by subcontracting for the sole reason of getting the work done by employees who are being paid lower wage rates.

● The company cannot contract out bargaining-unit work to its non-unit employees.

● Arbitrators are more apt to rule against subcontracting where it involves temporary or irregular work. ("The Arbitration of Disputes over Subcontracting," by Donald A. Crawford, in "Challenges to Arbitration," published by BNA, 1960)

Still another review of the subcontracting cases found that the standards most frequently applied by arbitrators are:

1. *Past practices.* Whether the company has subcontracted work in the past.

2. *Justification.* Whether subcontracting is done for reasons such as economy, maintenance of secondary sources for production, plant security, etc.

3. *Effect on union.* Whether subcontracting is being used as a method of discriminating against the union and substantially prejudicing the status and integrity of the bargaining unit.

4. *Effect on unit employees.* Whether members of the union are discriminated against, displaced, laid off, or deprived of jobs previously available to them, or to lose regular or overtime earnings, by reason of the subcontract.

5. *Type of work involved.* Whether it is work that is normally done by unit employees, or work that is frequently the subject of subcontracting in the particular industry, or work that is of a "marginal" or "incidental" nature.

6. *Availability of properly qualified employees.* Whether the skills possessed by available members of the bargaining unit are sufficient to perform the work.

7. *Availability of equipment and facilities.* Whether necessary equipment and facilities are presently available or can be economically purchased.

8. *Regularity of subcontracting.* Whether the particular work is frequently or only intermittently subcontracted.

9. *Duration of subcontracted work.* Whether the work is subcontracted for a temporary or limited period, or for a permanent or indefinite period.

10. *Unusual circumstances involved.* Whether an emergency, "special" job, strike, or other unusual situation exists necessitating the action.

11. *History of negotiations.* Whether management's right to subcontract has been the subject of contract negotiations. ("How Arbitration Works," by Frank and Edna Elkouri; published by BNA, 1960)

Union Rights

Contract provisions dealing with union representation and other rights typically are among the most carefully drafted parts of the agreement. Visitation, grievance-investigation, and information rights often are spelled out in detail, with the result that arbitration awards in these areas are not very common. More troublesome are clauses dealing with the use of union bulletin boards. Arbitrators usually have interpreted such provisions broadly, holding that any intended restrictions should be written into the contract.

In this area perhaps more than any other, what the contract says is only part of the story. The union also has important grievance-handling and information rights under the Taft Act.

Union's Right to Information

Most arbitrators agree that the union should have any information necessary for the processing of grievances and for making sure that the contract isn't being violated with respect to the company's wage administration practices. One company whose contract specified that it would furnish complete data and figures on the operation of its merit review system refused to disclose the names and department numbers of employees who had received increases. But the arbitrator ruled that the agreement required the employer to give the union such information. (Sperry Gyroscope Co., 18 LA 916)

Where a contract required the company to furnish the union with detailed information pertaining to changes in work assignments, another umpire ruled that this meant it had to supply all the basic time-study data, not just summaries. (Celanese Corp. of America, 27 LA 845)

Still another contract didn't spell out the employer's obligation to furnish the union with specific information, but an umpire said the company must give the union a list of pay rates so that it could bargain effectively on merit increases. (I. Lewis Cigar Mfg. Co., 12 LA 661)

Since a union was entitled to bargain over an employer's proposed amendments to the retirement plan, an arbitrator held, the employer was required to produce for inspection by the union the text of all proposed and existing amendments and all actuarial data concerning all participants. The actuarial data was considered absolutely necessary in order to evaluate the presence or absence of benefits resulting from employees' contributions. (Anti-Defamation League B'Nai B'Rith, 53 LA 1332)

Furthermore: Under an SUB plan providing that the company "will comply with reasonable requests by the union for other statistical information on the operation of the plan," an arbitrator held that the union was entitled to monthly lists of names of recipients and amounts paid. The company's contention that the lists were not "statistical information" placed an unduly narrow restriction on the term, the umpire said. The union had a legitimate reason for wanting the information, he said; it wanted to check for possible errors, since the funding obligation of the company was determined by the average weekly amount paid during the preceding year. (Mack Trucks, Inc., 36 LA 1114)

However: Under a contract that said nothing about seniority lists, one arbiter agreed that the union had a right to seniority information only when it specifically asked for it. (Bethlehem Steel Co., 24 LA 699)

Another union was held to have bargained away its right to be furnished seniority lists where its contract required a grievant to go first to his immediate supervisor, not to the union, and also made seniority disputes subject to the procedure. (Spartan Mills, 27 LA 256)

Contract provisions making payroll data available upon request didn't require a company to furnish such records for uncovering claims during a dispute over seniority in layoffs, an umpire held. The records were to be used only for testing the validity of specific claims, he said. (Santa Clara & Central Calif. Meat Processors' Assn., 36 LA 42)

Rights of Decertified Union

A decertified union still has the right to prosecute a grievance, one arbiter has held. Thus, where a union had processed a grievance but was decertified before the case reached arbitration, the umpire said it had a right to settle the beef. A distinction exists between the collective bargaining function and the processing of a grievance, he noted. Though a decertified union may not bargain for the workers, he said, federal law does not bar it from representing them in arbitration. (Trumbull Asphalt Co., 38 LA 1093)

Posting of Union Notices

Under a contract permitting the union to post notices on bulletin boards with the company's approval, what type of notices can the company disapprove?

Usually the union is free to put up any notice dealing with union business, and the company can't withhold approval unless the material is slanderous or derogatory to the company. Types of union notices against which companies have protested, but which arbitrators have upheld, include a notice stating that the purpose of a forthcoming union meeting was to consider strike action against the company (Fairchild Engine & Airplane Corp., 16 LA 678); a seniority list drawn up by the union after the parties had failed to agree on a seniority list (Lennox Furnace Co., 20 LA 788); and a notice urging union members to register for voting (Warren City Mfg. Co., 7 LA 202).

On the other hand: One arbiter has held that a clause permitting the posting of union "announcements" couldn't be stretched to include organizational material. (General Electric Co., 31 LA 924)

When the union posted a listing of nonmemebrs under the title, "Scabs," it was acting improperly, according to the arbiter. The lists smacked of coercion and embarrassment and created an atmosphere of intimidation to join the union. The underlying purpose was to blacklist employes; an illegitimate recruitment tactic and misuse of information. (Union Carbide Corp., 44 LA 554)

The discharge of an employee for posting unauthorized inflammatory notices pertaining to the employer was upheld by an arbiter where the employee had been given repeated warnings concerning other notices he had posted and had been ordered not to post the notice that led to his discharge. (Beaver Precision Products, Inc., 51 LA 853)

Furthermore: Some arbitrators have interpreted posting clauses calling for company approval of union notices to mean that the employer may refuse to approve a submitted notice for any reason whatsoever. On this theory,

mpires have okayed management's
ction in turning thumbs down on a
otice consisting of a comparison of
ages paid at another of the com-
any's plants and at plants of a com-
etitor (Reynolds Metals Co., 13 LA
78); and an announcement that a
trike at another company with which
ne union had a contract had ended,
)gether with a summary of the pro-
isions of the new agreement at that
ompany. (Danly Specialties, Inc., 13
A 499)

However: Not all arbitrators agree
hat a clause providing for employer
pproval of union notices gives man-
gement a carte blanche to deny post-
ng privileges. These arbitrators gen-
rally require the company to show
just cause" for denying posting
rivileges.

EXAMPLE: An employer refused to
ermit posting of a letter from a
nion international representative on
he ground of its being inflammatory.
n arbitrator held that the refusal
as improper. Although the letter
dmittedly contained some dubious
tatements, its basic purpose was to
void an imminent wildcat strike and
o assure the members that the union
ould fight their grievance through
egal means. (Fruehauf Corp., 54 LA
096)

Union's Right to Investigate Departments Not in Unit

Do union representatives have the
ight to investigate in departments not
overed by the contract? One arbiter
uled that a company had no business
efusing to allow a union representa-
ive to investigate a possible grievance
nvolving a department specifically ex-
luded from the bargaining unit but
lso involving a charge that the de-
artment was doing bargaining unit
vork.

EXAMPLE: By decision of NLRB, engineering department employees were
xcluded from the bargaining unit at
ne company. So, when the union got
vind of a report that people in the
lepartment were doing bargaining
unit work, the chief steward sought to

enter the department to find out
whether the report was true. The company blocked his attempt, saying he
should tell what he knew to the personnel manager. The latter would then
make an investigation and report on
his findings, the company said. One
reason given by the company for its
stand was that some of the work in
the engineering department was classified, and the union representative
didn't have security clearance. It is
also argued that it didn't have to let
union representatives roam around on
"fishing expeditions."

An umpire found no merit in these
contentions. The contract, he pointed
out, permitted the union to file grievances on its own motion; the union
was not limited to processing, grievances that came to it from employees.
So if it got word that the contract
wasn't being kept, it had a right to
make an investigation, regardless of
the source of its information. And the
umpire said the company could not
require such an investigation to be
made through the personnel manager.

As for the company's fears about
security, the umpire saw no problem.
The firm, he said, could assign a "conductor" to accompany the union investigator and make sure no violation of security regulations occurred.
The company's action, he concluded,
amounted to a violation of the recognition clause of the contract. (Libra-
scope, Inc., 30 LA 358)

However: Another arbitrator has
held that where a union can't initiate
grievances, it can't go all over the
plant looking for contract violations.

EXAMPLE: A union suspected that
unit work was being done in a department where none of the workers
belonged to the unit. To investigate
the situation, it requested access to
the site; the company turned it
down. Under the contract, management noted union officers could leave
their work for "the proper handling
of grievances." But that didn't mean
the union could go where there were

no unit members and look for trouble, it said.

The arbitrator agreed that the union had the right to police the contract, but in his opinion the right was limited to cases of already-existing disputes. By the terms of the contract, he noted, only the company and the workers could be parties to grievances. Since the union couldn't bring up beefs on its own hook, it couldn't roam the plant looking for them. (Bendix Aviation Corp., 39 LA 393)

Denial of Access to Plant

Some contracts permit outside union representatives to come into the plant to investigate grievances or for other purposes. Can they be denied such privileges under any circumstances? One umpire said that when union representatives do not behave in a civilized manner while exercising visitation rights, they may be denied access to the plant.

EXAMPLE: A union representative visited the company president in his office to discuss an alleged contract violation by management. During a heated argument the representative suddenly got out of his chair, stepped behind the president's desk, and began to twist his arm and poke him in the chest. He then invited the president outside to settle the matter. Thereafter the company refused to allow the representative to enter the plant.

Although the contract said that the union agents would have access to the plant during working hours to take up complaints and determine whether the contract was being complied with, an umpire ruled that the denial of access was justified. The representative's conduct had no place in labor relations, he said. (Glendale Mfg. Co., 32 LA 223)

However: In a case where management denied the chief steward access to the plant except during his own shift, an arbitrator held that the steward had the privilege of entering the plant at all reasonable times. If he were limited to his own shift, the umpire said, he would be no different from a department steward, and his plant-wide constituency would be ignored. However, the arbitrator cautioned that the chief steward must not abuse his privilege. (Buddy-L Corp., 41, LA 185)

Furthermore: An arbiter said the union had a right to send in its own international staff man to make a time study of new production standards which the union had challenged. The contract permitted the union to bring in "any representative of the union not an employee of the company" for the purpose of investigating grievances and said the company "recognizes that some grievances by their very nature may require investigation on the job," the umpire noted. The union's time-study man wouldn't interfere with work any more than management's own man had, he added, and there was no basis for the company's fear that its secrets would be divulged to its competitors. (Armstrong Cork Co., 41 LA 1053)

Grievances

The grievance-settlement machinery is one of the most vital elements in the union-management relationship. As such it has been the subject of numerous arbitration decisions.

Although the contract gave the employer the right to "discharge employees for any reason whatsoever," the former workers had the right to protest through the grievance machinery. The arbitrator held that since the contract excluded appeal of discharges of probationary workers only, the implication was that all other discharges were subject to appeal. (IBEW Local 441, 46 LA 831

Also, a union president had the right to present a grievance, even though the grievance-arbitration clause mentioned only disputes between "an employee and the company" and the subject of the complaint did not affect the union head as an "employee." The protest was on behalf of a union member and was allowed because, according to the arbitrator, "it would e inappropriate to impose a legalstic restriction on the right of the arties to settle their disputes by use f the grievance machinery." (Ohio ower Co., 45 LA 1039)

Similarly, an arbiter decided that a nion could file a grievance even if he workers involved wanted no part f it. If the union could not file on ts own, there would be no procedure nder which controversies as to interretation or claims of violation could o to arbitration unless some worker ctually affected brought up the latter. (Atlantic Seaboard Corp., 42 A 865)

When a company and a union orally greed to certain changes in the grievnce procedure, it made no difference hat the membership did not formally pprove the changes. An attempt was lade to repudiate the changes when the union elected new officers; however, the arbitrator ruled that if the union were free to invalidate agreements made by its previous officers, the company would be able to invalidate all agreements by merely replacing its representatives. (Gertman Co., 45 LA 30)

Sale of Plant

Where a company was sold and two new companies divided up the business, the union contract should be observed by both new firms, according to the arbiter. The original contract stated that in the event of sale of the entire operation or any part of it, the operation would continue subject to the union contract. Thus, when two mechanics quit and were replaced, the replacements were subject to the old contract. (Lake States Leasing Corp., 46 LA 935)

*IN BRIEF*_____

Nearly all union contracts contain a ban on strike action by th
union during the life of the agreement. Usually there is no doul
whether a strike is taking place; workers leave their jobs, and that
that. On occasion, though, where production suddenly falls off or man
workers call in sick simultaneously, the situation is by no means so clea
cut.

Arbitrators generally have taken the position that any union-inspire
activity that interferes with production, whether or not called a strik
is in fact a strike.

Union Meetings on Company Time as a Strike

Does a union meeting during working hours constitute a strike? Union meetings called during working hours usually result from some company action which employees don't like or are intended to allow employees to reach a decision on some matter, which the union thinks requires fast action. Most arbitrators have held that such meetings amount to strikes.

One declared that a planned mass departure from the workplace that halts productive work and disrupts the company's production schedule is a work stoppage and violates a contract's no-strike clause. (Nathan Mfg. Co., 7 LA 3) An arbitration board threw out one union's argument that a stoppage has to be for an indefinite period of time to be a strike. The board reasoned that a union meeting during working hours is a strike just as certainly as the company's action would be a lockout if it stopped production to hold a directors' meeting. (Atlantic Foundry Co., 8 LA 807; see also Kaiser Steel Corp., 51 LA 1041)

Employee Gathering as Strike

Situations may arise where workers feel they have an urgent request or question that must be taken care of before they start working. They may then gather together and say the won't work until management lister to them. Most arbiters take manage ment's side in this situation and cor sider that when employees gather tc gether informally instead of workin they are in effect striking.

Such was the case where severa brick-mason helpers waited over a ha. hour to see their foreman before start ing work. An umpire ruled that thi was actually a strike. Even though th workers had the right to discuss grievance with the foreman, the ar biter said, it was obviously a violatio of the no-strike clause when so larg a body of men exercising this righ interrupted production to a large ex tent. (Republic Steel Corp., 6 LA 85)

On the other hand: At least one ar biter believes that a gathering of em ployees does not amount to a strik where they are not making any de mands but rather are seeking informa tion concerning a change in thei working arrangements.

EXAMPLE: A company decided t change the departmental organiza tion of its crane operators. Under th old arrangement, crane operators wer all together in one department an were assigned by supervision in tha department to particular cranes i the various departments. Under th new plan, management intended t

ace the crane operators permanently
. the various departments instead of
signing them each day to a depart-
ent. At the beginning of their shift
stead of their time cards crane op-
ators found cards telling them to
 to other locations to punch in.
here was considerable confusion and
ie operators were about an hour late
 starting work. Management main-
ined that the delay in starting con-
ituted a strike violation of the con-
act.

The arbitrator held that manage-
ent itself caused the delay by its
ilure to tell the employees before-
and about their transfer. This was
ot a strike but rather a delay result-
ig from a failure of information,
imparable to delay resulting from a
ower failure, he said. (Ford Motor
o., 10 LA 148)

imultaneous Absences as Strike

If many employees call in individ-
ally to say they can't work because
f illness or some other reason, can
iey be considered on strike? Unless
ie union can show evidence that the
multaneous absences are a coinci-
ence and that each absent worker's
xcuse is legitimate, an arbitrator will
robably consider this to be a strike.

EXAMPLE: Shortly after a union
leeting, a group of 20 employees in
vo departments failed to return to
ork. Each phoned the company to
eport that he was sick. The company
harged that the mass absences were
 strike in violation of the contract
nd discharged the employees.

An arbitrator, asked to d e c i d e
rhether the absences were a strike,
uled that they were. Although testi-
iony was presented to show that sev-
ral of the employees actually were ill,
he excuses of most were not backed
p by evidence. It was this lack of
roof that led the arbitrator to con-
lude that the mass absence was more
han a coincidence and constituted a
trike. (American Cyanamid Co., 15
A 563; see also City School District,
:ity of Elmira, 54 LA 569)

**.efusal to Work Because of Health &
Safety Hazards**

When employees refuse to work because they feel there is danger to their
health or safety, are they engaging in
a strike? Generally refusal to work
under dangerous health or safety conditions is not considered a strike.

On the other hand: One arbiter
did not feel that good-faith belief
that working conditions were a health
hazard was enough reason to justify
a walkout. According to his interpretation of the issue, it must be demonstrated that a hazard actually does
exist. Thus, he denied the request for
holiday pay or sick leave passes for
the workers who left work prior to
quitting time because they felt the
poor ventilation coupled with prevailing high temperatures presented a
health hazard. (Wilcolator Co., 44 LA
847)

Similarly: Where it was found that
workers had refused to work until
management agreed never to operate
under the alleged dangerous conditions in the future, one arbiter held
that they were clearly engaging in an
illegitimate strike. He said that this
was more than just a mere refusal to
incur an undue health hazard. (Ford
Motor Co., 6 LA 799)

Slowdown as Strike

Does a slowdown constitute a strike?
At least one arbitrator has rejected
a union's argument that a strike
means only a walkout of employees
and ruled that a slowdown was a
strike.

The umpire noted that the first
sentence of the clause on strikes stated
that the union would not permit any
sitdown, stay-in or slowdown, and that
the second sentence prohibited strikes,
stoppages, or picketing until all the
contractual bargaining procedures had
been exhausted and negotiations had
been conducted for five days. These
two sentences were held to outlaw
certain kinds of strikes under any
circumstances (sitdowns, stay-ins or
slowdowns) and to require certain conditions (exhausting grievance procedure and negotiations for five days)
before strikes, stoppages, or picketing
could be conducted. The arbiter ruled
that if the union's position were upheld (that "strike" referred only to a

walkout) this would be the result: the union would have the right to oppose discipline resulting from slow-downs, sitdowns, or stay-ins, which were placed under an absolute ban by the contract, and would not have the right to oppose discipline in a walk-out situation where the walkout might have been legitimate (if bargaining and negotiation standards had been met first). Therefore, it was concluded that a slowdown did constitute a "strike" within the meaning of the contract. (Chrysler Corp., 9 LA 789)

Similarly: Under a no-strike pledge covering any slowdown, work stop-page, strike, picketing, boycott or other job action, another arbiter decided that any union action, including a pause at work, that interfered with the employees' duty to do their jobs amounted to a violation of the con-tract. (Restaurant-Hotel Employers' Council of Southern California, 24 LA 429)

However: Not every slowdown in the rate of production need constitute a strike. In deciding that the slowdown of several crews was not a "slowdown" in violation of the contract, an arbi-trator noted that there was no labor dispute involved. In its normal usage a slowdown implies a dispute in which workers intend to get some advantage from their action. While it was true that the crews weren't producing as much as they had previously shown they could, they still were performing at a rate that was considered satis-factory for other workers. He con-cluded that the only fair way to judge effort and production was by the job, not by the individual. (Kelly-Springfield Tire Co., 42 LA 1162)

Production Holdback by Incentive Workers

Suppose employees working on an incentive basis reduce their output below the rate they usually make. Can this be considered a slowdown and thus a violation of a contract ban? Several arbitrators have held that such a drop in the customary produc-tion level does amount to a slowdown.

In one case, where the contract ex-pressly banned strikes and slowdowns, incentive employees, under instruc-tions from their union, dropped the production level to cover only the base rates before bonus earnings. The union argued that this was not a slow-down because production did not drop below base rates. But an arbiter held that this was a slowdown in violation of the contract because the drop in output continued over an extended pe-riod of time. (Pittsburgh Plate Glass Co., 7 LA 438; see also Wallace-Mur-ray Corp., 55 LA 372)

Similarly: Even where a contract did not have a specific ban on slowdown, an umpire ruled that concerted re-fusal of incentive workers to maintain their former high level of production was a slowdown and interfered with management's right to schedule pro-duction. (Aluminum Company of America, 7 LA 442)

Observance of Picket Line

If nothing in the contract specifi-cally gives them the right, can em-ployees observe a picket line set up by fellow employees? Where two or more unions bargain with a company for different groups of employees, mem-bers of one union may be entitled to honor the picket line of the other un-ion, if the picket line is set up as the result of a genuine labor dispute, even though the contract has a no-strike clause.

EXAMPLE: Clerical employees of a waterfront terminal company went on strike to enforce their demands. Longshoremen employed by the com-pany refused to cross the picket line set up by the other union.

The company claimed that their contract with the longshoremen re-quired them to cross the picket line since they had agreed to settle all dis-putes through final arbitration, with-out a strike or lockout.

Asked to rule whether the long-shoremen were required to cross the picket line, one arbitrator ruled that this was the type of legitimate picket line which union members could re-fuse to cross. The contract contained no promise from the union to pass through another union's picket line, he pointed out.

And in view of a union's basic teaching that it cannot be used to break the strike of another union, the company should have known that the longshoremen would not cross such a line. The clerk's picket line was a legitimate one which grew out of a common and typical labor dispute and would be observed by employees belonging to another union or another unit of the same union. (Waterfront Employers' Association of the Pacific Coast, 8 LA 273)

However: A distinction may be drawn between a refusal by individual employees to cross a picket line of a sister union and a directive from their union that they respect the sister union's picket line. In the latter case, the union may be held to have violated its obligations under the no-strike pledge. This converts the situation from a refusal to work by individual employees into a sympathetic strike called by their union, one arbitrator held. (Amalgamated Lace Operative, 54 LA 140)

Struck Work

Can workers refuse to handle struck work? If there is a clear provision in a contract permitting them to handle work going to or coming from a struck plant, of course there is no problem. But in the absence of a hot-goods clause, arbitrators have held that employees cannot refuse to handle struck work. In one case an arbiter ruled this way where the agreement didn't even have a no-strike clause.

EXAMPLE: Communications workers at a cable company refused to forward messages through a company which was on strike during a period when an emergency condition made impossible to transmit the messages over their own company's facilities. They were suspended for refusing to handle the so-called "hot traffic."
The arbiter held that neither the contract nor past practice gave employees the right to refuse to handle the messages bound for a struck company. He noted that the work in question was not part of the ordinary work

flow, but was caused only by a cable break. Allowing employees to refuse to handle the work would amount to adding something to the contract which was not put there by the parties, according to the arbiter. Finally, it was noted that the union should have followed the contractual grievance procedure rather than taking matters in its own hands. The suspensions were upheld. (Commercial Pacific Cable Co., 11 LA 219)

Union Liability

Unions have been held not liable for their members' violation of no-strike agreements where the evidence failed to show union involvement. When craftsmen refused to cross picket lines established by janitors, the company demanded that the unions pay damages. The arbiter held that the refusals were voluntary acts committed by individual members; there was no showing of official involvement. (Booth Newspapers, Inc., 43 LA 785)

On the other hand: A contractor was awarded damages when a union caused work stoppages on three days in connection with a dispute over crew size. The contractor's use of the courts to enjoin the strike was not a repudiation of the grievance clause, according to the arbiter, and damages for actual work lost were granted. (American Pipe and Construction Co., 43 LA 1126)

The responsibility of union stewards to prevent violations of no-strike clauses was emphasized in a later case. Because the grievants had a "very unsophisticated and low grade comprehension of their union duties," they were not held liable for the strike that occurred; however, the arbiter suggested that a joint statement to all stewards outlining their duties under the contract be issued so that there could be no excuse given by any steward in the plant, in the future, that he was unaware of his official responsibility when a violation of the no-strike clause is threatened. (Blue Ridge Textile Co., Inc., 46 LA 763)

IN BRIEF————————————

Management is forbidden by law to discharge or otherwise discrimi nate against workers for exercising their right to strike for better wages or working conditions, or to protest against company unfair labor prac tices. This rule does not hold, however, where the union has waived its right to strike during the term of a contract. In such cases the company may impose whatever penalties are called for by the agreement and even in the absence of a contractual statement of penalties arbitrators often have upheld disciplinary action.

POINTERS—

▶ Stiff penalties against union officials who participated in, or failed to try to prevent, strikes in violation of contract often have been okayed by umpires.

▶ As for rank-and-file workers who take part in a strike in violation of contract, the company ordinarily must treat all alike. If it can prove that certain workers were the ringleaders, though, it probably can mark them for more severe punishment.

Discipline of Union Leaders

May union officials be singled out for discharge or discipline when a strike occurs? In matters of contract observance union officials are sup posed to set good examples for the rank and file to follow. Holding this view, most arbitrators have ruled that, if union officers do not carry out their responsibility of seeing to it that workers live up to a contract's no-strike clause, they can be disciplined. (Cuneo Eastern Press, Inc., 36 LA 214; McConway Storley Corp., 55 LA 31) Many arbiters have okayed the discharge of union leaders who in cited, led, or refused to try to prevent an illegal strike. (Texas Co., 7 LA 735; Ford Instrument Co., 4 LA 403; Seabright Co., Inc., 53 LA 154)

The following cases are examples of instances in which arbitrators have sustained disciplinary actions against union officers:

● Discharge of a union president for failure to take affirmative action to prevent a wildcat strike and to put an end to it as soon as it occurred. (Ford Motor Co., 41 LA 609)

● Discharge of union officers who actively participated in picketing, re fusal to work, and other activities. (General American Transportation Corp., 42 LA 142)

● Discharge of shop steward for making no convincing effort either to prevent the walkout or to secure a return to work after it occurred. (Gold Bond Stamp Co. of Georgia, 49 LA 27)

● Discharge of union president for instigating a one-day walkout, even though he subsequently tried to secure a return to work. (McGraw-Edison Co., 39 LA 76)

● Discharge of union committeemen who probably were the instigators of a walkout but who, in any event, were derelict in their duty as union officers to try to get employees back to work. (Bell Bakeries, 43 LA 608)

● Discharge of union officers for participating in an unauthorized work stoppage, the arbitrator holding that union officers cannot discharge their responsibility by a passive attitude that would allow them to merely be swept along by the tide of rank and file action. (Drake Mfg. Co., 41 LA 732)

One arbitrator has stated the duty of shop stewards in a wildcat strike situation as follows:

"Indeed, a shop steward's duty in the face of an unauthorized work stoppage is well settled. Not only should he make a determined effort to prevent the stoppage before it begins, but upon its development must actively and unequivocally attempt to bring an end of the stoppage at the earliest possible moment. Moreover, he must set an example by either reporting to work himself or by clearly indicating a willingness to work if his employer wishes him to do so. And obviously if he is either requested or directed to work, he must do so. Only in this way can the steward comply with his responsibility to uphold the integrity of the contract and its orderly processes for dispute settlement." (United Parcel Service, Inc., 47 LA 1100)

On the other hand: Arbiters have upset or reduced penalties imposed on union officials where:

(1) There were mitigating circumstances. In one instance an umpire reduced a discharge penalty to a five-month loss of pay because the officers were new and inexperienced in handling strikes and union affairs. (New York Car Wheel Co., 7 LA 183)

(2) The company could not show that union leaders were more to blame than other strikers. In one case the officers had actually ended the strike. (Jones & Laughlin Steel Corp., 29 LA 644). In another, a steward walked off his job on the first day of an illegal work stoppage, but returned the next day and was either on his offdays or stayed away from work for fear of violence during the rest of the strike period. (Union Carbide Corp., 55 LA 1159)

(3) Union officers *did* carry out their responsibilities by urging employees not to strike, even though their efforts failed and the strike proceeded. One arbiter ruled that union officials were not subject to punishment just because the rank and file did not follow their advice. (Armour & Co., 8 LA 758)

Participation by a union official in a wildcat strike wasn't ground for discharge, where he later tried to halt it. The company failed to prove that he promoted the strike; however, his participation was ground for a one-year probation. (Cyclops Corp., 45 LA 560)

When a union president failed to get his men back to work within five minutes, the company placed him on 60-day suspension. The arbiter set this aside because it was not clear whether the president caused the wildcat strike or was simply caught up in it. (Weatherhead Co., 43 LA 442)

Moreover: One umpire has taken the position that union officers d not owe any special allegiance to management by reason of their election to union office. They haev a duty to try to prevent strikes in violation of contract, he said, but the duty is to the union and other union members rather than to the company. So in his view the company cannot single out union officers for more severe punishment than rank-and-file workers who participate in a strike.

The arbiter stressed that he was speaking only of cases in which union officers merely took part in strike action, not cases in which they led or incited strikes. (Pittsburgh Standard Conduit Co., 33 LA 807)

Discipline of Rank-and-Filers for Strike Leadership

As a general rule, arbitrators hold that an employer who is confronted with an illegal wildcat strike is not required to deprive himself of the services of all employees participating in the strike. He may select those for punishment as he deems fit, provided his selection is not capricious. (53 LA 45, 55 LA 1159)

The employer has the right to assign varying penalties, up to and including discharge, on the basis of his evaluation of the degree of seriousness of the conduct of participants in an illegal strike—again, subject to the general principle that his evaluation not be arbitrary or capricious. He also should exercise his right of discipline within a reasonable time limit. (M.S.L. Industries, Inc., 53 LA 75)

The general principle followed in these cases has been stated as follows:

"No agreement provision and no obligation to justice compels the company to discipline in every case of employee misconduct. Inequality of treatment in disciplinary matters does not amount to unjust discrimination if there are rational grounds for distinguishing between those to be disciplined and those not to be disciplined. It is only where the grounds for distinction are irrational, arbitrary, or whimsical that disciplining of some employees and not others may be looked upon as unjust and discriminatory. (Ford Motor Co., 41 LA 609)

One arbiter held that the initiators of a strike bore a heavier responsibility than other strikers. So he allowed the company to give suspensions just to the first ones to walk out. This was not discrimination, he said, but was justified because the company could not have given all 800 workers disciplinary layoffs without shutting down the whole plant. (Goodyear Atomic Corp., 27 LA 321)

Another arbitrator upheld the discharge of nine workers who were involved in a wildcat strike, even though others who had walked off the job were kept on. He reasoned that the nine men weren't discriminated against, since they were the only ones who had also illegally walked out 13 months earlier. (H. O. Canfield Co. 40 LA 1209)

Similarly, one umpire upheld the discharge of 13 out of 39 workers who went on strike in violation of a "no-strike" clause. The company had indicated that the discharged men were instigators or in the forefront of the strike, but presented no evidence on how those who were fired were selected. Even though the discharges seemed arbitrary to the umpire, he pointed out that there was no evidence that the penalties were dealt out to discriminate against union members. Nor was there a provision in the agreement limiting the right of the company to discharge for cause or for just cause, he noted. (L. B. Jones Co., 35 LA 590)

Selective discharge was allowed when the entire work-force staged a wildcat strike. Three top union officers were observed acting as captains and leaders of the picket line, both before and after their discharges. According to the arbiter, "A company that is the victim of an illegal strike cannot be expected to 'cut off its nose to spite its face' by firing all participants." (Charles Mundt Sons, 46 LA 982)

Responsibility for a strike can be a collective matter, as was the case in which 132 workers were discharged for refusing to commence work. The workers were given one hour in which they could begin work, after which the company pulled their time cards. The arbiter found any worker who defied the return-to-work order "an employee responsible" for the strike and subject to discharge. (American Air Filter Co., 47 LA 129)

However: The employer must be able to show some basis for selecting out individual strikers for discipline. One umpire set aside suspensions imposed on five employees accused of being the first to walk out of the plant gate during a wildcat strike, where their identification was based on a supervisor's observation from a window located about 50 yards from the gate from which employees exited in a state of confusion. (W. S. Hodge Foundry, Inc., 55 LA 548)

Another arbiter held that a two-week suspension was too stiff a penalty for some wildcat strikers, even though they probably were guilty of inciting the strike. The umpire reasoned that the workers probably didn't need much encouragement to strike anyhow and found no evidence that the strike wouldn't have occurred even if the instigators had done nothing. (International Minerals & Chemical Corp., 28 LA 121)

Discipline of Strikers Heeding Back-to-Work Order

According to one arbitrator, employees who strike in violation of a contract can be disciplined even though they return to work at the union's request.

EXAMPLE: In a contract the parties agreed that (1) the company had the right to discipline employees for just and proper cause, (2) the union would not engage in any unauthorized work stoppage, and (3) the company would not hold the union liable for damage resulting from an unauthorized work stoppage provided the union immediately instructed its members to return to work. The last clause further provided that the company could take any disciplinary action it considered appropriate in the event employees ignored a back-to-work order.

Employees who walked off the job on one occasion returned to work at the start of their next shift. When the company slapped them with five-day disciplinary layoffs, the union filed a grievance. In its view, the contract permitted the company to discipline strikers only if the union failed to tell them to go back to work and they continued their walkout. In this

case, the union pointed out, it had issued the required instructions, and the men had in fact returned to work.

An umpire wouldn't buy the union's argument. He figured the union was saying that, because the company had the right under the contract to act in one set of circumstances, it necessarily had forfeited the right to act in other circumstances. The arbiter didn't think this was so. Since the contract didn't specifically cover the case at hand, he decided it came under the provision affirming the company's general right to impose discipline. Accordingly he upheld the suspensions. (Bell Aircraft Corp., 30 LA 153)

Damage Awards as Penalty

Arbitrators are increasingly inclined to assess damages against a union that violates a no-strike pledge.

EXAMPLE: While finding that full compensatory damages were not required due to the limited nature of the union's violation and the employer's share of blame for the underlying dispute, an arbitrator allowed damages for breach of the no-strike clause that included (1) out-of-pocket expenses and lost profit on a specific transaction that the employer was unable to complete due to the violation, and (2) a reasonable portion of overhead expenses and general loss of profits arising from the shutdown. The arbitrator refused, however, to allow recovery of attorney's fees sustained in an effort to get an injunction to end the strike. (Mercer, Fraser Co., 54 LA 1125)

EXAMPLE: An arbitration board determined damages allowable to an employer for a breach-of-contract strike amounted to $20,334 for fixed and standby expenses and for demurrage. The board declined to include an award for loss of profits, primarily because of a failure to establish definitely the loss, if any, that had occurred. (Vulcan Mold and Iron Co., 53 LA 875)

EXAMPLE: As a remedy for a strike against a construction company on a

highway project, an umpire allowed
damages including labor costs, rental
value of its own equipment, rental
value of rented equipment, and the
prorated costs of traffic protection.
(Foster Grading Co., 52 LA 197)

EXAMPLE: An arbitration board
decided it had power to award damages for a union's breach-of-contract
strike, even though the contract made
no mention of this remedy. It declined, however, to award damages for
loss of good will, since this was too
speculative. (Oregonian Publishing
Co., 33 LA 575)

Arbiters' Injunction vs. Strikes

In some instances, and particularly
where the parties have a permanent
umpire, the employer may be able to
get a back-to-work order from an
arbitrator similar to a court injunction.

EXAMPLE: A department store was
held entitled to an injunction against
sympathetic picketing by its sales employees during lunch hours and before and after work in support of a
strike by its warehouse employees.
(Macy's New York, 40 LA 954)

EXAMPLE: After finding that the
union's work stoppage violated the
no-strike clause in its contract, an
arbitrator ordered the employees to
return to work and the union to secure
compliance with the no-strike provisions. The order was issued on an ex
parte basis in the absence of the union, since the union had received proper notice and an invitation to appear
and hadn't objected to the employer's
taking the dispute to arbitration on
an ex parte basis. (Pacific Maritime
Assn., 52 LA 1189)

Cancellation of Seniority as Penalty

Even though workers who strike in
violation of a contract can be disciplined, at least one arbitrator thought
that cancellation of seniority was an
improper penalty for such conduct.

EXAMPLE: When employees at one
company staged a wildcat strike, the
company notified all 2,500 strikers
that they were suspended for five days

and would be terminated if they
failed to return to work by a certain
deadline. It later informed the strikers that those who failed to report
before the deadline would be taken
back as new employees.

An umpire held that the company
had the right to fire the strike leaders
but ordered it to reinstate the others
with the seniority they had prior to
the walkout. He didn't think the company really intended to discharge all
the strikers; it had no reason to think
it could find enough replacements.
The contract mentioned suspension
and discharge as disciplinary measures, the arbitrator notes, but said
nothing about loss of seniority. Such
a penalty was inappropriate, he
thought, because seniority is in the
nature of a vested right and affects
the relative standing of all employees. Upholding the penalty, he commented, would lead to continuing dissension between employees who stayed
on the job or returned before the
deadline and the "new hires."

The award called for gradual reinstatement of the strikers, in order of
their seniority, over a nine-month
period. None of the strikers got any
compensation for lost wages, however. (Lone Star Steel Co., 30 LA 519)

Docking for Lost Time During Stoppage

Awards suggest that arbitrators will
allow a company to dock the pay of
employees for time lost during a work
stoppage if certain conditions are
met. These are (1) that there is sure
proof that *all* employees took part in
the work stoppage and (2) that there
was work that could have been done
during the stoppage and none of the
workers did it.

EXAMPLE: A work stoppage occurred in one department of a trailer
company, and management docked
every employee who participated for
the time lost. The union contended
that only those actually responsible
for the stoppage should have had pay
deductions. The union went on to say
that since management couldn't de-

termine exactly which employees caused the stoppage, the deducted pay should be restored to all employees.

The arbiter held that, if innocent employees had been forced to stop working because of others' activities, they should not have been penalized. Here, however, there was work that could have been done, so "it is quite manifest that each employee who stopped did so upon his own responsibility and should suffer any resultant consequences of such action." He concluded, therefore, that the pay deductions were warranted. (Fruehauf Trailer Co., 1 LA 155)

On the other hand: Where an umpire found it impossible on the basis of the evidence to conclude that all the workers in one shop participated in a stoppage, he decided that none of them could be docked. (S. Co., Inc., 10 LA 924)

Although production had been halted by a strike, the company broadcast over the radio the message that it would be operating. As a result, some workers showed up for work, but were later told to go home. Others never showed up, as they had been told not to do so by their supervisors. The arbitrator held that both of these groups of workers were entitled to pay, even though the contract specified no payment for time lost to strikes. He reasoned that their lost time was primarily attributable to the employer's instructions. (U.S. Steel Corp., 45 LA 509)

Partial Strikes

According to one arbiter, workers can be penalized for engaging in an intermittent work stoppage lasting for part or all of a shift even though the contract doesn't contain a no-strike clause.

EXAMPLE: When a company refused to arbitrate grievances over the pay of skilled trades—as it had a right to do under its contract—the union proceeded to hold meetings lasting two hours on each of three shifts. The third time this happened, the company warned that further meetings would lead to disciplinary action. The next day, another series of meetings was held, and the participants were given a one-day suspension. Claiming that the discipline was a contract violation, the skilled tradesmen staged a one-day strike, and management told the union that one-day suspensions would again be imposed unless the union promised there wouldn't be any repeat performances. The union didn't give any such assurance, and the company followed through with the suspensions.

An arbiter upheld the company's actions. Although the contract gave employees the right to engage in a "whole strike," that wasn't the same as a "partial strike," he said. An employee must either work or strike; and he can't set his own working conditions, the umpire held. The union's attitude suggested that more stoppages might occur; under these circumstances, the arbitrator decided the penalties were justified. (General Electric Co., 31 LA 28; see also Philco Corp., 39 LA 629)

Discharge for Slowdown

Can workers be fired for taking part in a slowdown? Arbitrators are likely to hold that discharge is too severe a penalty for this. In one case a group of workers was fired because they had collectively decided not to increase their output when production standards were raised as a result of job changes. But an umpire reduced their penalty to a month's layoff in view of their long seniority and the fact that they did not actually decrease their output. (Armour & Co., 8 LA 1) Similarly, even though another arbiter was convinced that a worker had deliberately pulled a slowdown, he changed his penalty from discharge to a four-week layoff because he had a long record of satisfactory performance. (Reed Roller Bit Co., 29 LA 604)

Discipline of "Silent Partners" in Slowdown

If a slowdown occurs on an incentive operation, can employees be disciplined who are down the line from the bottleneck and therefore don't have primary responsibility for the drop in production? If such employees don't call management's attention to the fact that they're not getting as much material to process, they must be regarded as "silent partners" in the slowdown, one arbitrator has decided; and they're just as much at fault as those who take the initiative in restricting production. (John Deere Harvester Works, 27 LA 744)

Discipline of Union Officers for Slowdown

Disciplinary suspensions were in order for shop committeemen who took part in a slowdown, thus giving it their silent if not active okay, one arbitrator has ruled. He agreed with the company that although the committeemen didn't initiate the slowdown, they did avoid their responsibility under the contract's no-strike pledge in not trying to stop it. The company tried to identify the leaders but couldn't, he noted. The next best approach, the arbiter reasoned, was to make an example of those who had shirked their responsibility to lead. (Philco Corp., 38 LA 889)

Pay Cut for Slowdown

If incentive employees engage in a slowdown, can they be denied pay guarantees under an incentive plan and paid only for actual output? At least one arbiter has okayed this form of discipline. (American Steel & Wire Co., 6 LA 392)

On the other hand: One umpire said that cutting pay below guaranteed levels was a contract violation and therefore an improper penalty for slowdown. (Jacobs Mfg. Co., 29 LA 512)

Discipline for Post-Strike Offense

One umpire has held that a company could not discipline a worker who acted as a union agent in a claimed violation of a strike-settlement agreement, since the matter was not related to his work performance or job status.

EXAMPLE: After the strike ended, the worker—acting as chairman of the local union—filed charges with the union against a number of workers for scabbing during the strike. Later the chairman was charged by the company with violating the strike-termination agreement, which stated that neither party would take vindictive actions against the other or any worker in connection with the strike. Following an investigation, the company found the worker guilty of the charges and suspended him for 10 days.

Whatever remedy the company had with respect to the asserted violations would lie against the union, the arbiter held, not against the worker in his employment status. It was strictly an intra-union action which conceivably could have been initiated by some member of the union who was not a company employee, he said. (Braniff Airways, 38 LA 82)

Discharge for Strike Misconduct

Can workers be fired for misconduct during strike activities? Violence is the principal charge leveled against strikers for which management feels it may issue termination slips. Violence may cover such varied activities as tossing stink bombs around, attacking supervisors or nonstrikers, throwing stones, and issuing threats from the picket line. Arbitrators generally will consider the evidence on each discharge closely. If the accusation is of the more serious type (such as attacking a supervisor) and the evidence supports the charge, the dismissal may be allowed to stand.

In considering cases involving dismissals for misconduct on a picket line and during a strike, respectively, Arbitrators Clark Kerr and James J. Healy have outlined general criteria which they thought were important These two sets of guiding principles follow:

Kerr—

"(a) How satisfactory is the evidence? Not all evidence is of equal value. Some is more convincing, some less, and some not at all.

"(b) What is the extent of participation? In any mob situation the degree of involvement of the individual in any action taken is important.

"(c) What was the nature of the violence? This has both quantitative and qualitative aspects. Participation in several incidents is more serious than in only one. Some actions are more reprehensible than others. Shouting insults and shoving are of a different order from striking a person.

"(d) Was the violence provoked? To the extent the violence is retaliatory and defensive it is less culpable than if undertaken as an act of aggression.

"(e) Was the violence premeditated or undertaken on the spur of the moment? Premeditated violence is the more inexcusable.

"(f) What will be the impact of the punishment? Discharge is more of a penalty for an old man, than a young one; for a long service employee than a short service employee.

"(g) Was the disciplinary action discriminatory? A company is under some obligation to treat persons similarly situated in a comparable, although not necessarily identical manner. Violence can hardly be said to be the real basis for discharge if other unjustifiable factors enter in.

"(h) What is the general context of the situation?" (Cudahy Packing Co., 11 LA 1138)

Healy—

"(a) Was the alleged misconduct of the aggrieved proved to the complete satisfaction of the arbitrator?

"(b) If the misconduct is proved satisfactorily, was it of such a nature as to warrant discharge?

"(c) If the misconduct is proved, was it the result of certain provocation which mitigates the guilt of the aggrieved?

"(d) Is there evidence that discrimination was a factor in the discharge?

"(e) Was the misconduct of such a nature as to affect employer-employee relationship or was it more appropriately the concern of civil authorities?" (Swift & Co., 12 LA 108)

Amnesty Pledges

When several workers engaged in a wildcat strike, the superintendent promised amnesty to those who began work "without further delay." Of those on strike, 17 did not return until an hour later. They were given one-day suspensions, which they claimed was a violation of the amnesty. The arbiter disagreed, saying that the pledge wasn't a continuing offer to be accepted whenever the workers felt like returning. (Bethlehem Steel Corp., 47 LA 524)

Although an employer's amnesty pledge following a wildcat strike barred discipline for "passive nonviolent participation," it did not bar discharge of two men who tried to promote a secondary boycott. According to the arbiter, the evidence established that they were guilty of conserted misconduct above and beyond actions protected by the amnesty agreement. (Falls Stamping & Welding Co., 48 LA 107)

An employer's blanket offer of reinstatement "without recrimination" after an illegal strike extended to all workers, including the steward who instigated the strike. The arbitrator, however, directed the company to deny back pay as a penalty for her part in the illegal strike. (Strombeck Manufacturing Co., 45 LA 37)

Under union shop agreements, the obligation of workers to join the union is clear, and for this reason grievances under such arrangements are relatively rare. But the lesser forms of union security, such as modified union shop and maintenance of membership, often give rise to special problems—which workers must join, what constitutes union membership, when workers may resign from the union, and the like.

CAUTION—

The Taft Act sharply limits the conditions under which a union may demand the discharge of a worker for failing to join the union or maintain his membership. Even though an arbiter upholds a discharge, NLRB may order the worker's reinstatement with back pay if it finds that his rights under the law have been violated.

Types of Union Security

The union-shop contract requires nonunion new hires to become a member of the union within a prescribed period after initial employment and for nonunion employees to become a member within a prescribed period after the union-shop contract becomes effective. Under the federal Taft Act, the union-shop contract may not require the employer to hire only union members.

The modified union-shop contract limits the membership obligation to new hires, while permitting presently employed workers to continue their nonunion status.

The agency shop permits an employee to refrain from becoming a union member but, if he elects to remain nonunion, he must pay the union an amount equal to the customary initiation fee and periodic dues required of members. Such agreements commonly are adopted in response to state right-to-work laws or to religious scruples of employees.

Maintenance-of-membership contracts require employees who are union members on the effective date of the agreement to retain that membership for the duration of the agreement.

UNION MEMBERSHIP

Application for Membership

Can an employee be considered a union member if he has never signed an application card? Often when a union and a company sign a contract with a maintenance-of-membership, union shop, or other union security provision, the problem comes up of determining which employees were union members at the time the contract was signed.

One arbitrator has laid down the following standards for determining what constitutes union membership:

1. The individual must have signed an official application card showing his intention of joining the union and his desire to have the union act as his representative for collective bargaining.

2. The employee must have paid his first month's union dues.

3. The union must have issued him an official receipt for the first month's dues payment.

4. The union must have furnished him with an official membership card showing that the employee has been accepted for membership.

Only if all these conditions are fulfilled according to the arbitrator, can an employee be considered as having joined the union. *At the same time:* Payment of an *initiation fee* is not necessarily a condition of union membership. The arbitrator observed that unions frequently waive payment of an initiation fee, particularly during an organizing drive. (Bendix Aviation Corp., Pacific Division, 15 LRRM 2650)

Employees Behind in Dues When Contract Is Signed

Granted that a worker was a union member at one time, the question frequently arises whether he was still a member of the union at the time a maintenance-of-membership contract went into effect. If not, he is not bound to keep up his membership in the union unless he rejoins it of his own accord later on.

Most arbitrators who have ruled on this question have based their decisions on the provisions of the constitution or by-laws of the union holding the contract. Ordinarily, the union constitution will provide for automatic suspension of members behind in their dues a certain number of months. When the record of an employee's dues payments shows that he was so far behind at the time the contract went into effect that he was under automatic suspension from the union, the arbitrator will usually hold that he is not bound by the maintenance - of - membership requirement. (Bendix Aviation Corp., Pacific Division, 15 LRRM 2650)

Members in Arrears Carried in Good Standing

Can a union by its action in carrying a delinquent member as a "member in good standing," bar escape of the member from the union at a time when such escape is possible?

This situation usually arises when a membership-maintenance clause is enforceable only against "members in good standing" at a certain date. Arbiters have actually held that the employees must be "members in good standing" and not merely carried as such by the union. (Electrical Workers v. Mae Allport et al., 4 LA 443)

One umpire stated that a union could waive the delinquency of its members when no third party interests were affected. It is proper, he said, for a union to continue to carry members even if they are in arrears in their dues because of illness or financial difficulties, if the members do not object. But when he found that carrying a delinquent member as one in good standing meant depriving him of his right to withdraw from the union under the escape clause, he ruled that the worker did not have to be discharged for not . maintaining membership. (Monsanto Chemical Co., 12 LA 1175)

Signing Membership Application But Not Paying Dues

Is an employee "in good standing" with the union if he has signed a membership application card but has not remitted dues since the signing of the application?

This situation is frequently presented when unions are successful in organizational drives and obtain many membership applications. Some months later when the unions are successful in securing a contract, they find that many of the employees who have signed the applications have failed to keep up their dues. In such cases arbiters generally find that the delinquent employees are not "in good standing" within the meaning of the union's constitution and by-laws and so do not come under the membership-maintenance clause in the contract. (The Randall Co., 8 LA 82)

Company's Failure to Fire Delinquent

Because a company failed to fire a worker who was delinquent in paying his dues, it was forced to grant backpay to a worker who was laid off. The arbiter said that the worker would not have been laid off for lack of work if the company had fired the other employee. (Black, Sivalls, & Bryson, Inc., 42 LA 989)

Dual Union Membership

Can a union withhold membership from workers who belong to a rival union, even though lack of membership is cause for dismissal under a union-shop agreement? One arbitrator said no.

EXAMPLE: Three workers were not members of the union that held bargaining rights at the company where they worked. They arranged with a competing union, of which they were members, to pay their dues to the incumbent. The latter union denied them membership until they disaffiliated with its rival and signed a checkoff agreement with it. The men refused, and the union demanded their discharge under the union-security clause because they wouldn't sign the checkoff form and were tardy in paying their dues.

There is no prohibition against a worker's belonging to two or more unions, the arbiter noted. Although the dues were delinquent, he found that they were paid before the deadline. Since their dues were in order, the umpire ruled that the workers were entitled to membership in the incumbent union and the company had no reason to dismiss them. (Hawaiian Brewing Corp., 35 LA 420)

ESCAPE PERIODS

Premature Resignation Letters

Employees who submit their letters of resignation from union membership prior to the escape period nevertheless may be held to have effectively resigned, particularly where the letters were sent close to the escape period.

EXAMPLE: A maintenance-of-membership agreement provided a 15-day escape period immediately following the anniversary date of the agreement. This was variously interpreted as meaning a 15-day period

beginning November 7 or November 8. Prior to this first anniversary date, 19 employees submitted letters of resignation in the period October 17 through November 5. On November 22, the union informed these employees that their attempted resignations were not effective, since the 15-day escape period ran from November 7 through November 22.

Holding the resignations effective, an arbitrator noted that the employees obviously intended their resignations to become effective on the first possible date. He added that the union was guilty of bad faith in waiting until the last day of the escape period to inform the employees that their resignation letters were invalid. (Carson Mfg. Co., 52 LA 1057)

Absence of Escape Clause

In the absence of an "escape" clause in renewed membership-maintenance agreements, can a worker resign from the union on the date an old contract expires and a new one becomes effective?

Most arbitrators hold that the union-security relationship between parties to the contract is a continuing one which may be interrupted only by formal action of the parties and not by an individual who has benefited by the contract. If the parties do not provide an "escape" period, then none can be implied.

One umpire with this view said that when the parties to a labor contract resort to every known technique to continue their relationship, that continuing character should be recognized and given effect in proceedings such as arbitration. In this case, he said, since it was a collective agreement, no single worker had any power to create an escape period not provided for by the contract. (Monsanto Chemical Co., 12 LA 1175)

Effect of Renewed Contract on Escape Period

In the absence of specific reference to it, is the escape period in an old contract carried forward to the new contract by the terms of a renewal agreement?

Renewal agreements usually provide that all the provisions of the old contract shall be carried forward in the new contract except those specifically modified by the renewal agreement. Arbitrators have held that it is not necessary to provide specifically for the renewal of the escape period as it is renewed with all other provisions. (Fulton Sylphon Co., 7 LA 286)

RESIGNATION FROM UNION

Meaning of Resignation

Under a contract providing for maintenance of membership for union members until they properly resign, what is the meaning of "properly resign" when it is not defined in the contract? In this situation arbitrators often will look at the union's constitution for the proper procedure for resigning from the union. For example, where one union's constitution provided for a 10-day period for resignations, an umpire ruled that workers who had not resigned within this period were still members and so they were subject to the maintenance-of-membership clause of the contract. (Bridgeport Rolling Mills Co., 18 LA 233)

However: Where a union's constitution does not provide for resignation but the labor contract it signs with a firm does have an escape clause, umpires are likely to hold that members can withdraw during the escape period. The agreement a union makes with an employer comes first, they say, regardless of what its constitution provides. (Shell Oil Co., 14 LA 153)

Checkoff Cancellation v. Membership Resignation

Employees who revoke their checkoff authorizations at the time of an escape period in a maintenance-of-membership agreement may be held to be still obligated to pay their union dues, since checkoff cancellation is not the equivalent of resignation from the union.

An arbitrator held this to be the case, even where the agreement specified the same revocation period for both the checkoff and maintenance of membership. (Mack Molding Co., 55 LA 770)

Oral Resignation

Can a union member resign from the union just by giving word-of-mouth notice to his departmental steward? In addition to a strict scrutiny of the constitution and by-laws of the union, the arbiters look to past practice and custom before making their determination.

EXAMPLE: An employee, during a 15-day escape period, verbally informed the chief union steward of his desire to resign from the union. He then refused to pay any further dues. The union requested his discharge for violation of the membership-maintenance clause of the contract.

The arbiter found that under the constitution and by-laws of the union, it was clear that the steward was a designated contact person between the union and its members. Therefore, the employee had a right to tender his resignation to the departmental steward. The umpire further found that neither the constitution and by-laws nor custom and usage in the union required that a resignation be submitted in writing. (Onsrud Machine Works, Inc., 9 LA 375)

Another arbiter has held that "proof of knowledge held by responsible union officers, no matter how received, that a member wishes to drop out of the union" determines whether or not the employee has resigned. He also held that the union's efforts to get the employee to sign a union membership card upon his rehire as a new employee constituted proof of the worker's claim that he had resigned from the union when he left the company. (Chicago Metal Mfg. Co., 9 LA 429)

TRANSFER INTO BARGAINING UNIT

Status of Transferred Workers Under Modified Union Shop

Under a modified union shop, employees who aren't members of the union when the contract goes into effect aren't required to join, but new employees, hired after the effective date of the contract, must become union members after a specified period of time. Under this arrangement, are old employees transferred into the bargaining unit required to join?

At least three arbitrators have ruled that employees transferred into the bargaining unit must be treated like new hires and required to join the union. (Chrysler Corp., 18 LA 664; F. P. Rosback, 19 LA 85; Reliance Electric & Engineering Co., 35 LA 274)

However: Another arbitrator held that an employer was justified in refusing to discharge a salaried employee for refusing to join the union on her return to the bargaining unit, since she could not be considered as a "new hire" under the modified union-shop agreement. The employee had been with the company for nearly 28 years and hadn't been a union member before she was transferred to the salaries supervisory job. (Lord Mfg. Co., 55 LA 1005)

Extension of Modified Union Shop Contract To New Unit

If a master contract containing a modified union shop is extended to cover a new unit, are all employees in the new unit required to join the union on the theory that they were hired after the effective date of the master contract? In this situation, one arbitrator has held, the union-security provision can't be considered retroactive.

EXAMPLE: The union-security clause in the master agreement between a company and a union became effective April 19, 1951. It provided that employees who weren't union members on the effective date didn't have to join, but that all employees hired after that date had to become members within 30 days.

On November 13, 1952, a new unit was brought under the master agreement and the union claimed that all of the workers in it had to join because they were hired after April 19, 1951.

The arbitrator disagreed. For purposes of the new unit, he said, the agreement became effective on November 13, 1952. Hence employees in the unit at that time who weren't union members weren't required to join. (Chrysler Corp., 21 LA 45)

Checkoff

Checkoff is the means of dues collection under four of every five union contracts (more than nine tenths in manufacturing alone). By law, checkoff must be authorized voluntarily by each individual employee, and authorizations cannot be irrevocable for more than one year or the duration of the contract, whichever is the shorter period.

Within this legal framework, various problems may arise. What happens to a checkoff authorization when a worker is transferred out of the bargaining unit? When the union raises its dues and fees, must the company check off the higher amounts? These are the kinds of situations considered in this section.

Effect of Discharge

Where an employee has signed a checkoff authorization which is automatically renewed each year if he fails to revoke it, does the authorization remain effective if his employment is terminated, and then he later returns to work for the company as a new employee? Or will a new authorization be necessary? One arbiter ruled that a worker's discharge ended his checkoff authorization, even though the contract didn't specifically cover the matter. Any other conclusion, he commented, would lead to the "preposterous" result of having a checkoff authorization hanging in a state of suspended animation for a period of several years if a discharged employee didn't think to revoke it. (Link Belt Co., 16 LA 242)

Similarly, an arbitrator held that an employer properly refused to honor an old dues checkoff authorization that had been signed by two employees prior to their termination and subsequent re-employment. (Samsonite Corp. and Rubber Workers, Local 724, 53 LA 1125)

Resignation from Union

Checkoff authorizations are usually irrevocable for the term of the contract or a year, whichever is shorter. Thus, arbiters have ruled that even though a worker resigns from the union at times other than the "escape period," management must continue checking off his dues. (International Shoe Co., 36 LA 867)

Answering one company's contention that continued deductions would violate the Taft Act, which bans company payments to worker representatives except for "payment of membership dues in a labor organization," an umpire said that the requirement was met if the worker was a union member at the time he signed the authorization. (Gillette Motor Transport, Inc., 38 LA 290)

The indication to a company that one wishes to quit the union, even during the escape period, was not sufficient reason to cause the company to discontinue dues check-off. The arbiter ruled that union membership is a matter between the member and the union only. The company should not have acted until after the worker's membership had been terminated. (Yale & Towne Mfg. Co., 41 LA 1073)

However: Another arbitrator disagreed. He reasoned that once a worker effectively resigned from the union, he was no longer a member. Thus, management would violate the law if it continued to make dues deductions from his wages. (C. H. Guenther & Son, Inc., 34 LA 800)

Checkoff Cancellation v. Membership Obligation

Under a maintenance-of-membership contract, cancellation of a checkoff authorization during an "escape period" may not relieve employees of their obligation to pay union dues if they fail to resign from union membership at the same time.

EXAMPLE: A maintenance-of-membership contract provided the same 15-day escape period for the union membership obligation and the checkoff authorization. Three employees revoked their checkoff authorizations during this period, but did nothing about their union membership. An arbitrator held that they were not exempted from paying dues and would be liable to termination under the maintenance-of-membership provision if they failed to make such payments. (Mack Molding Co., 55 LA 770)

Effect of Strike

Under a union-shop agreement, can workers resign and revoke checkoff if the union is on strike and the contract is not in effect? One arbitrator said not. The individual checkoff authorization signed by each worker specified when he could resign, the umpire noted; hence, even though no collective bargaining contract was in effect, the individual membership and checkoff agreements were binding in their own right. (Bethlehem Steel Co., 40 LA 398)

Effect of Decertification

After a union has been decertified, must a company continue paying checked-off contributions to it until the collective bargaining agreement expires? One union claimed that the decertification cancelled only those provisions concerning recognition and representation, while the rest of the contract remained in effect until the normal expiration date. However, the arbiter disagreed. A contract is a bilateral agreement, he pointed out; when the union no longer is able to comply with its contractual obligations as representative of the workers, the company no longer is bound by the contract. (Ferris Sales & Service, Inc., 36 LA 848)

A similar decision was reached when a union that lost a deauthorization election claimed that the voiding of the union-security provision didn't affect the separate checkoff clause.

The arbiter based his decision on a contract-law basis and said that the commitment to pay dues was made in the light of an assumed right of the union to compel membership. Since that assumption turned out to be erroneous, the checkoff authorizations became voidable at the option of the workers. (North Hills Electronics, Inc., 46 LA 789)

Does Promotion out of Unit Cancel Checkoff Authorization?

What is the status of a checkoff authorization after the employee leaves the bargaining unit to become a supervisor? The status of a checkoff authorization by an employee promoted out of the unit may be unlike that of a discharged employee. One arbitrator decided that, instead of being cancelled, the authorization merely remained in a suspended state.

He noted that the authorization cards contained the phrase "future employment" and ruled that this applied to *any* future employment in the unit. To support his decision, he reminded the company that it had a policy of automatically renewing authorizations for other employees who left the unit because of layoff or who returned to the unit within the life of a single contract. (Temco Aircraft Corp., 23 LA 93)

Dues Increase v. Assessment

Suppose a union has a checkoff arrangement calling for the deduction of union dues but not assessments, and then it imposes a levy in addition to regular dues for an indefinite period of time. Can the company refuse to check off the additional amount on the ground that it is an assessment? According to one arbitrator, a company could not refuse to do this.

He found, first of all, that the dues hike was voted by the membership in the form of an amendment to the bylaws, in accordance with the union constitution. Assessments, on the other hand, could be levied by the local executive board without a vote of the membership. Secondly, the additional money was to be used to carry on the regular business of the local, whose treasury had been depleted by a number of strikes, but it was not earmarked specifically as a strike fund, nor was the levy for any set length of time. Finally, the umpire noted that when the union had put similar (but smaller) dues increases into effect in the past, the company hadn't refused to check off the additional amounts. So it couldn't refuse to do so in the present situation, the arbitrator concluded. (Bates Mfg. Co., 24 LA 643; see also Globe-Democrat Publishing Co., 41 LA 65)

However: Where a contract required the checkoff of "regular union dues," an arbitrator held that a company was not required to honor payroll deductions for the amount of union dues, plus an additional $2.00 per month deduction for coverage under the union's insurance plan, which coverage was optional with the employees and subject to change or cancellation at any time. (Southwestern Bell Telephone Co.) 38 LA 393)

Increase in Fees Subject to Checkoff

If fees are subject to checkoff, can you increase the amount of the union initiation fee, once the checkoff agreement has gone into effect? Unless the contract puts a definite limit on the amount of fees to be checked off, the company can do nothing to stop the union from raising it, according to one arbitrator.

EXAMPLE: When a union upped its initiation fee from $5 to $25, the company protested that the fee was "unreasonable and excessive." When it agreed to the union shop and check-off provisions in the contract, the

company argued, it did so with the understanding that the initiation fee was $5; it had never dreamed that the union would hike the fee to $25. Requiring new employees to pay this amount, it said, might hinder its recruiting efforts.

The arbitrator, however, found nothing in the contract to prevent the union from raising the fee; neither the agreement nor the checkoff form, he noted, said what the fee should be. Noting that NLRB had already ruled that the increased fee wasn't "excessive or discriminatory," the arbitrator concluded that the company had no voice in setting the amount of the fee, and that the union was under no obligation not to change it. (Engineering & Research Corp., 23 LA 410)

Escape Period During Negotiations

During a prolonged period of negotiation, six workers revoked their check-off authorizations. Under the terms of the old agreement the workers were not acting within the established escape period. Further, the new agreement was made retroactive, so as to encompass the time in which the authorizations had been revoked. The arbiter said this action was in defiance of the Taft Act, which states that check-off authorizations "shall not be irrevocable (1) for a period of more than one year, or (2) beyond the termination date of the applicable collective agreement." Had the retroactive contract been allowed to apply, the authorizations would have been rendered irrevocable for three years. (Sperry Rand Corp., 44 LA 965)

Many unions oppose incentive pay plans in principle and have succeeded in virtually eliminating them from plants in which they hold bargaining rights. Other unions are on record as favoring incentives—provided they are fair and afford workers an opportunity to increase their earnings in proportion to their production.

Almost all contract clauses dealing with incentives place some limitation on the company's right to revise standards. Arbiters generally have interpreted such provisions to mean that workers' earnings opportunities must be protected when standards are revised, and that changes in conditions must be more than slight to justify revision.

GUIDELINES

Some basic guidelines for establishing incentive pay rates were set forth by a fact-finding board appointed by the Secretary of Labor to resolve a 1946 dispute at International Harvester Co. Here are some of the points made by the board:

▶ "The essential standard should be that the workers affected should have free access to the relevant information so that any injustices in the final result may be corrected through the regular grievance procedure.

▶ Workers should be informed as to the results of time studies, the basis for any company estimates of efficiency of the workers are timed, and the company allowances for such factors as fatigue and personal needs.

▶ Pieceworkers affected by any new rate are entitled to a clear and prompt statement of exactly what the new rate is.

▶ An elementary standard of piecework administration requires that a piece rate, once established, should not be changed unless the relevant conditions of work are subsequently changed or unless an error or oversight was made on establishing the original rate." (International Harvester, Inc., 1 LA 512)

Time Limit on Revision of Incentive Rate

Most contracts dealing with incentive systems provide that management (sometimes with the advice or consent of the union) can revise existing incentive standards or rates, or set up new rates, when there are changes in the content of the job involved. If there is no time limit on the period during which the rate can be changed, is management free to set a new rate at any time after there have been changes in the job?

226

According to most umpires, management has an obligation to revise incentive standards or rates within a "reasonable" time after changes are made in job content. One arbitrator, for example, decided that two years was far more than a reasonable time limit for changing an incentive rate (International Harvester Co., 14 LA 1010; see also Worthington Corp., 34 LA 497). A delay of 13 months after changes were made before establishing a new rate for the job was okayed in another instance, because the arbitrator found that this period of time was necessary to allow a complete restudy of the operation. (Mosaic Tile Co., 16 LA 922)

Overnight notification of a speed-up in the rate of output of a potato-chip bagging machine did not meet the contract's requirements of "reasonable prior notice," according to an arbitrator. A change in rates could occur only if the union was notified sufficiently in advance to permit meaningful discussion. (Daniel W. Mikesell, Inc., 47 LA 986)

Basis for Rate Changes

Where the workload of incentive employees changes, arbitrators in reviewing the incentive rates, may apply the standard of maintenance of prior earnings on the theory that incentive employees should be able to earn as much under the new standard as under the old. (28 LA 259, 26 LA 812, 17 LA 472)

A more nebulous standard requires the maintenance of the same ratio of earnings to effect expended. Use of this standard means that employees receive increased earnings for that part of the increased production that is due to their effort, and management receives the benefit for that part of the production increase that is due to technological improvement. (22 LA 450, 28 LA 129, 10 LA 20) In one case a union objected to an increase in the number of units required and a decrease in the percentage standards on the ground that workers could not earn as much as under the old rates. But an arbiter found that the new method of calcula-

tion would permit workers to earn as much as before. (Timken Roller Bearing Co., 28 LA 259)

Similarly, where another umpire found that greater productivity was the result of machine and engineering changes, he allowed the company to revise the incentive rates. He noted that the stated aim of the incentive agreement was to give workers more money for extra effort above normal. If the rates had remained the same, he reasoned, earnings would have gone up in direct ratio to the increased productivity, even without any extra effort from the workers. He concluded that the rate change did not violate the contract's ban on revisions which lessen the earnings potential of workers. (Libbey-Owens-Ford Glass Fibres Co., 31 LA 662)

Reduction of Rates

Reduction of incentive rates has been allowed where the introduction of new machinery has resulted in increased production without requiring an increase in effort. (11 LA 432, 3 LA 677)

Moreover, reduction of incentive rates has been ordered where employees controlled production on new machines at a very low level. (10 LA 534)

Changing Job Standards During Strike

One arbitrator has ruled that a company violated its contract by revising incentive standards during a strike following the expiration of the previous contract and then putting them into effect after the strike had ended and the new agreement had been signed.

The strike-settling contract, like the pre-strike agreement, said there were to be no changes in incentive standards unless changes were made in the methods of operation. While the stoppage was in progress the firm kept production going after a fashion, but all workers were paid on an hourly basis. Meanwhile, the company's job standards people were told to do some tinkering with certain standards that were considered loose. The tighter standards were made effective when incentive work was resumed a week after the new contract had been signed. The union was told nothing of all this; it became aware of the situation only when workers began complaining about the speed-up.

The umpire conceded that the company could do as it pleased while the union was on strike. But if it meant to make new standards effective during the term of the new agreement, he said, it had to inform the union of its intention during the negotiations over the new contract, so that the parties could negotiate on the basis of full information. By failing to do this, the umpire concluded, the firm violated the agreement. (M. H. Rhodes, Inc., 25 LA 243)

Allowances

The fact-finding board in the International Harvester case gave the following general statement of a standard for allowances to be paid pieceworkers and examples of its application:

"In all cases where allowances are deemed necessary, the pieceworker should be paid his occupational earned rate or his average piecework earning rate, depending on the degree of effort expected and the responsibility placed upon him under the particular conditions which gave rise to the grievance.

"By way of example, it seems obvious to us that, where a worker encounters hard stock, faulty material, or is given erroneous instructions, and is required to continue with the job after calling the situation to the attention of his supervisor, he has every reason to expect to be guaranteed his average piecework earning rate.

"Similarly, where, because of his special skill and aptitude, he is called upon to leave his regular job to perform experimental or other work not a regular part of his assigned duties and which he performs for the convenience of management, he should also receive his average piecework earning rate.

"However, it seems equally obvious that, where a temporary breakdown occurs and he is called upon to perform some other work to occupy his time, which work does not call for anything more than dayrate effort or efficiency, industrial practice generally does not call for the payment of the average piecework earning rate." (International Harvester, Inc., 1 LA 512)

Machine Breakdown

At what rate should incentive workers be paid for periods during which their machines are down for repairs? One arbitrator, ruling on the equities of the situation, agreed with a union that incentive workers should be paid average hourly earnings rather than base rates during periods of machine breakdown. (Pantasote Co., 3 LA 545)

Another arbitrator, however, ruled the other way in interpreting a contract which stated that waiting time caused by machine breakdowns would be paid at the "regular earning rate." The umpire said that the employer need pay only on the basis of the hourly rate and not on the basis of average earnings, as the union contended. (Kensington Steel Co., 13 LA 545)

Temporary Rate for Materials Shortage

Under a contract calling for payment of a specified hourly rate when a shortage of materials "substantially" reduces an employee's output, how far must the employee's production drop before he is entitled to receive that rate?

A union argued that such a provision meant that an employee should get the specified hourly rate whenever a materials shortage caused his production to drop below the point in the incentive range which is on a level with the hourly rate. But an arbitrator ruled that the hourly rate should be paid only when his production drops below the incentive base rate. (Maytag Co., 20 LA 43)

Spoiled Work

If a crew of employees working under a group incentive system have to stop work while one or two members of the crew rework parts which they spoiled, should all the members of the group be paid hourly rates or average earnings?

In one arbitrator's opinion, the rest of the crew shouldn't be penalized for work spoiled by one or two members of the group. The employees responsible for the spoiled work should be paid their hourly rate, the umpire said, but the others should get average earnings for the time they waited while the parts were being reworked. (International Harvester Co., 23 LA 184)

However: One arbiter ruled that under a group incentive plan management was justified in apportioning among all workers in its production line the cost of reprocessing work damaged by two men. The union protested that penalizing all the workers for the mistakes of two was unjust. The arbitrator, however, held that the earnings deduction wasn't really a penalty, but the result of an accurate count of acceptable products. Had the men at fault been made to correct the error, they would have earned less than base wages, a contract violation. Furthermore, he said, the assembly line would have been stopped and the other workers paid only base wages. He pointed out that by continuing to operate, the line made up the reprocessing cost and still earned incentive pay. (Westclox, 34 LA 777)

Built-in Delay Allowances

If allowances for delays are built into the rates under an incentive plan, should workers still be paid their hourly rates for down time? Awards differ on this problem depending upon the circumstances in each case.

In one instance where a crew of incentive workers were held up for an hour and a half because their supervisor hadn't got certain equipment ready for them to use, an arbiter ruled that they were entitled to straight-time pay for the down time. He agreed with the union that such long periods of lost time that were the fault of management were not the kind of delays allowed for the incentive rates. (Bethlehem Steel Co., 29 LA 360)

However: Another umpire turned down a union's claim that incentive workers deserved standard hourly rates for a delay that began in the preceding shift and continued into theirs. The union argued that the incentive plan was not in effect until a crew actually started work. But the arbitrator disagreed, saying that, in the absence of contract language to the contrary, an incentive plan with built-in delay allowances must be considered as covering all delays no matter when they start. (Kaiser Steel Corp., 31 LA 447)

Hourly Workers Assigned to Piecework

If some employees fill in as utility men on piecework operations in addition to their regular jobs at hourly rates, should they be paid their hourly rate or at piece rates for their piecework assignments?

The common complaint of employees who are assigned piecework on a casual or part-time basis is that they are unfamiliar with the work or the machines and, as a result, may not be able to make as much as they would on their regular jobs at their hourly rate. Taking this fact into consideration, one arbitrator has ruled that employees in a "hybrid classification" who do piecework in addition to their hourly-paid work must be paid at least the rate of their hourly scale. He noted that, under the contract, regular pieceworkers were customarily paid at a straight hourly rate or at their piece rate, whichever was greater. In the absence of a contract provisions covering hourly workers assigned to piecework, the arbitrator reasoned, casual pieceworkers should receive the same treatment. The umpire further pointed out that standard practice elsewhere called for hourly rates in such a situation. (John Deere & Co., 21 LA 449)

Job Evaluation

In the absence of an express contractual provision, it is generally recognized that management has the right to establish new job classifications and change existing ones without first bargaining with the union. Some arbitrators have held, however, that a listing of specific classifications in an agreement is enough to prevent the company from unilaterally introducing new ones or tinkering with existing ones.

Even where management has the right to alter its classification system, the union normally may question changes through the grievance procedure.

Many unions regard job evaluation with suspicion and refuse, even when invited, to participate in the evaluation procedure. They view job evaluation as a potential gimmick that can be used by management to either downgrade jobs or get more work for the same money. Other unions, however, have decided that the best course is to seek as much participation as possible in the job evaluation process.

_____**GUIDELINES**_____

Changes in methods of operation unless restricted by the agreement have been held to be properly with the prerogatives of management (6 LA 681, 39 LA 939, 17 LA 268, 46 LA 43).

The right to establish new jobs, eliminate obsolete jobs, or to combine jobs and classifications has been recognized as being a part of management's rights where not expressly limited by the parties' agreement (30 LA 444, 16 LA 955, 25 LA 188, 46 LA 43).

It also has been generally recognized that in the absence of contractual restrictions, management may abolish two job classifications and establish a new classification following a technological change in equipment (19 LA 797, 30 LA 81) or a change in the product (46 LA 43).

On the other hand, an employer's act of recognizing a union has been held to carry with it the obligation to refrain from making major changes in employment conditions and circumstances without consulting with the union (25 LA 611). Such obligation may be *found to exist under the Taft Act, as a well as under the contract.*

Management Right to Change Job Descriptions & Classifications

Does a company have to get the union's permission to change the make-up of a job or classification before putting the change into effect? Even though job classifications, job descriptions, and job evaluation procedure have been agreed on in the past and have become part of the contractual relationship with the union, the company may still have the right to introduce new jobs or take apart existing jobs.

As long as the company pays the established rates and accepts union complaints through the grievance procedure, jobs can be put into effect, described, and evaluated by the company, according to most arbitrators. One, for instance, decided that a company's contract did not obligate it to freeze job titles and duties pending the union's consent to a change. Such a requirement, he said, would place the company in an intolerable position. (Dow Chemical Co., 22 LA 336; see also Diamond Crystal Salt Co., 14 LA 510)

These arbiters, however, also agree that even where the contract specifically gives management the right to establish new or revised job descriptions, the union still retains the right to challenge management's evaluation through the grievance and arbitration machinery. (Emhart Mfg. Co., 23 LA 61; see also John Deere Des Moines Works, 23 LA 206)

On the other hand: Many arbiters believe that management doesn't have the right to change the job classifications which are agreed to in a contract. One ruled that a company could not make a major transfer of job duties from one category to another without the union's consent because it would upset the bargain the parties made when they incorporated the rates and classifications into the contract. (James Vernor Co., 26 LA 415) Another umpire decided that a company had no right to alter existing classifications, even though the contract permitted it to establish new ones. (Faultless Caster Corp., 24 LA 713)

An employer did not have the right, under the management-rights clause of the contract, unilaterally to subdivide a job classification into three classifications. Although the change was made in good faith to eliminate a production bottleneck, management was restricted in its freedom to make such changes by other sections of the contract, according to the arbitrator. Contrary past practices could not justify the action, since the specific contract language governed the situation. (Barcalo Mfg. Co., 31 LA 269)

On the other hand: Under a management-rights clause allowing the employer to establish new or changed job classifications, the past practice of allowing preliminary work of racking parts for plating to be done by skilled platers did not preclude the employer from establishing "racking" as a separate job. The arbiter held that since job descriptions incorporated into the contract failed to list or describe the racking operation at any point, management had a free hand to deal with that job. (General Controls Co., 31 LA 744)

Changes Warranting Job Reclassification

Some contracts require reclassification of jobs in which there have been substantial changes since they were classified and the rates set. How can you determine whether changes in job content are substantial enough to warrant a reclassification?

One arbitrator has held that a union's request for reclassification of a job was valid where certain duties formerly performed by several employees were combined into one job, on the ground that the job required considerably more responsibility and discretion than it did before. (Lockheed Aircraft Corp., 11 LA 490)

The introduction of new-type machines on a certain job doesn't necessarily require reclassification of the job. But if the new machines result in a "material and significant increase" in the skill and labor required for the job, then a rate adjustment is called for. (Hershey Chocolate Corp., 17 LA 268; Morris Bean & Co., 54 LA 418)

Another arbitrator, in denying a union's request for reclassification, said that the job would have to change considerably as to either the duties to be performed or the amount of effort required, and as to the amount of time required, before he would consider it changed substantially enough to call for a revision in the rate. (Central Soya Co., Inc., 20 LA 463)

If a union request for reclassification is turned down by an arbitrator, the union can't keep bringing the matter up again except during contract negotiations, one umpire ruled. He said there was no reason to re-evaluate a job which another arbitrator had ruled was properly classified under a prior contract because the union didn't question the classification during subsequent negotiations, and there had been no material change in the job since the first arbitration decision. (Federal Bearings Co., Inc., 22 LA 721)

Reclassification After Technological Changes

If technological changes decrease the skill requirements for a given job, can it be reclassified into a lower pay bracket? According to one arbitrator, such a reclassification is permissible in the absence of an express contract prohibition. (Marsh Stencil Machine Co., 33 LA 1)

When an employer introduces a new machine substantially different from machines in existing wage rate classifications, he must negotiate with the union over rates to be paid the operators of the new machine, and not merely insert the job in an existing classification (Lockheed-Georgia Co., 48 LA 518)

Factors in Establishing New Rates

When a new job is set up which doesn't fit into the existing classification setup, what factors should be taken into account in establishing the rate for the job?

According to one arbitrator, the following factors should be considered in setting up the rate range for a new job: (1) nature of the duties and responsibilities of the job as compared to other jobs at the plant; (2) existing wage rate structure; and (3) existing method of ingrade rate progression. (Dumont Electric Corp., 13 LA 763) Another arbitrator determined the job rate for a new classification in light of (1) the company's past practice, (2) prevailing practice in comparable plants, and (3) the effect on intraplant wage relationships. (Wetter Numbering Machine Co., 13 LA 177)

Moreover, when two jobs are combined into one, the new job should be evaluated as though it were a completely new job and the rate set accordingly, another umpire has ruled. (Republic Steel Corp., 20 LA 370)

Upgrading under Classification System

What is the measure for telling when a worker is entitled to be upgraded to the next higher job classification? Generally, the test that arbitrators use in solving this kind of problem is whether the worker is actually performing the job duties of the higher classification.

EXAMPLE: Employees classified as specialists third class claimed they should be reclassified to specialists first class because they were qualified to do higher-rated work and they were performing the same job duties as employees with the first-class rating. The arbitrator turned down their arguments because he found that (1) their job duties hadn't changed since they got their third-class ratings (2) there was no practice of upgrading employees merely on the basis of added skill without the addition of more difficult job duties; and (3) the only reason they were performing the same job duties as employees with a first-class rating was that more difficult work, which would have been assigned to the first-class specialists, was not available at the time. (Bethlehem Steel Co., 19 LA 521)

Similarly: An arbitrator held that an employer wasn't obligated to classify "production layout artists" as "creative artists," even if they had the ability to do the work of the higher classification, since they weren't required actually to do this work. An employer isn't required to pay for talent he doesn't use, the arbiter held. (Gill Studies, Inc., 52 LA 506)

Downgrading under Classification System

Can workers be downgraded if it is found that the work they are doing falls within a lower classification? Arbitrators are likely to okay this action if there is a clear showing that the worker is performing lower-rated duties.

EXAMPLE: One company moved an employee to the next higher classification as part of a negotiated plan to eliminate wage inequities. Six years later it discovered that the employee had been performing the duties of his old classification all along, so he was downgraded to his original classification. The union argued that once the employee's classification had been agreed on jointly, it couldn't be changed. The arbitrator decided, however, that the job descriptions were clear enough to show that the employee's duties fitted his old classification and ruled that the company was free to reclassify him (Erie Forge & Steel Corp., 22 LA 551)

However: In another case, an arbitrator decided that six years was too long a period to wait before correcting a classification error. He pointed out that the wrong classification had continued for several years as a direct result of the failure of management representatives to discover and correct the error earlier. The umpire agreed that the company had the right to correct its mistakes, but said that management had more

than reasonable opportunities in the past to make adjustments. He also noted that the employees had a legitimate right to expect that the rates and classifications were the prevailing and correct ones when they went unchanged for six years. (National Tube Co., 7 LA 575)

Moreover: An employer was called down for arbitrarily downgrading three employees on the basis of gradual changes in their duties. This action would have been okay under the contract, the umpire said, except that the employer left six or seven other employees doing similar work in the higher classification. (John Deere Harvester Works, 20 LA 665)

Where Job Overlaps Two Classifications

When employees are performing the job duties of two classifications, should they automatically be paid the rate of the higher job? If the contract states that employees performing the duties of two classifications should be paid the rate of the higher classification, they must be paid the higher rate even if they spend only a small part of their time on the higher-rated-job duties or don't have the skills originally required for the higher job. (Hotpoint Co., 23 LA 562)

In situations where this point wasn't covered in the contract, however, arbitrators have relied on various factors in determining which job rate should apply. One umpire, for example, said employees should get the lower rate because they performed only a few of the duties of the higher job, even though these duties made their jobs as a whole more difficult than those of other employees in the lower classification. (Douglas Aircraft Co., Inc., 18 LA 387)

Another umpire decided that the proper rate for an employee performing the duties of two jobs wasn't the one for the job at which he spent most of his time, but the rate for the job for which he had been trained and was responsible — the higher of the two. (Soule Steel Co., 21 LA 88)

Still another arbiter ruled that workers were not entitled to the pay for a higher classification than their own just because they were voluntarily performing some of the duties of the higher-rated job. (Phelps Dodge Copper Products Corp., 25 LA 64)

Withholding General Increase to Eliminate Red Circle Rates

Most umpires agree than an employer cannot get rid of red circle rates by withholding negotiated general increases. The time and place to do this, they say, is at the bargaining table. Where one company tried to withhold an increase 10 months after discovering that some workers were being overpaid, an umpire said that it had waited too long to correct the error. (Celluplastic Corp., 28 LA 659; See also Big Jack Mfg. Co., 27 LA 858)

Under a contract granting wage increases according to the employees' classifications, former painters who had been reclassified as laborers and permitted to keep their higher painters' wage scales as "red circle" rates within the laborers classification were not entitled to increases negotiated for the painters' classification. The former painters were classified as laborers when the contract was executed and, therefore, were entitled only to increases applicable to laborers. (Bethlehem Steel Co., 31 LA 104)

Effect of Transfer & Promotion on Red Circle Rate

If an employee is transferred to another job within the same classification, can he take his red circle rate with him? Where a red circle rate exists for an employee on a particular job, it's not likely that he can carry the top-plus rate with him in the event that he's transferred, even if he stays within the same classification. One arbitrator ruled that a red circle rate applied only to the job involved and was not the property of the employee to take with him wherever he went.

Likewise, this same umpire held that a worker who is promoted from a red circle rate and later demoted back to the same classification has no right to the red circle padding after demotion. In other words, the promotion has the effect of cancelling the extra red circle amount. (International Harvester Co., 22 LA 674; see also Electra/Midland Corp., 53 LA 694)

Elimination of Classifications

When it comes to eliminating existing job classifications, management may have less freedom than it does in setting up new or revised classifications. Arbitrators sometimes have ruled that where job classifications are included in the contract, the company has no right to abolish any of them without the union's consent as long as the job functions of the classification continue to exist. (Flintkote Co., 41 LA 120)

However: Following what he saw as a modern trend among arbiters to give management more leeway in changing and abolishing jobs, one umpire upheld management's right to abolish job classifications and assign the work to higher-rated jobs. The fact that the classifications were listed in the contract didn't mean they were frozen, he said; they weren't contracted for, but were bases for rates of pay. Hence, the company couldn't have given the duties to lower-rated workers. (Georgia-Pacific Corp., 40 LA 769)

Another arbiter decided that where a larger part of a job's duties had been eliminated, management could abolish the job, even though the contract required it to maintain local working conditions. (Pittsburgh Steel Co., 40 LA 70) Job elimination has also been upheld where duties were reduced or eliminated by extensive changes or automation. (Pittsburgh Steel Co., 40 LA 67; United States Steel Corp., 40 LA 65)

If all the duties of a job classification are eliminated by technological r other changes, what the company can do, one arbitrator suggested, is merely to refrain from assigning any workers to that classification. While it can't formally abolish the classification without union consent, there's nothing to require the company to keep on assigning workers to the job. This action would have the effect of leaving the classification in a dormant state, he pointed out, which might be useful if the job duties of the classification were ever resumed. (Lone Star Steel Co., 23 LA 164)

Grievances concerning overtime work generally fall into one of three categories—(1) challenges of the company's right to require workers to put in overtime, (2) complaints that overtime work has not been distributed properly, and (3) complaints that work has not been paid for at the proper rate.

POINTERS—

► While there have been rulings both ways, arbiters have held more often than not that management can require employees to work overtime if the contract does not expressly limit the length of the workday or workweek. The right must, however, be exercised reasonably.

► If a worker is deprived of overtime work to which he is contractually entitled, umpires often have held, he should be given pay for the missed work. A crack at the next available overtime work isn't enough.

Obligation to Work Overtime

Many cases have come to arbitration over the issue of whether management has the right to compel an employee to work overtime and discipline an employee who refuses overtime. If the issue is not expressly settled in the collective bargaining agreement, arbitrators have generally ruled that management does have that right, provided management has considered legitimate excuses of employees, attempts have been made to find substitute employees who are willing and able to do the work, and sufficient notice has been given to workers needed for overtime.

In a case where the contract stipulated that changes in the work schedule must be mutually agreeable to both the company and the union, the union held that a worker should not have been disciplined for refusing to work overtime since such overtime constituted a change in the work schedule. The arbitrator found, however, that the overtime was for a limited, specified duration and, hence,

not a change which would require union approval. Therefore, management was permitted to require an unwilling employee to work overtime. (McConway & Torley Corp., 55 LA 31)

In another instance, an arbitrator ruled that a statement in the contract that it was the *policy* of the company (as opposed to a requirement for the company) to assign overtime to employees willing to accept it did not deny management its right to compel an employee to work overtime—provided management had exhausted all possibilities of locating willing workers. (General Telephone Co., 53 LA 246)

A provision of an agreement giving the employer sole discretion in scheduling production has been determined to be legitimate basis for management to require overtime. Past practice, even of many years' duration, of relying exclusively on volunteers to work overtime does not constitute a waiver of this right of management. (Colt Firearms Div., 52 LA 493)

It has been found that specifications in the contract of a "normal" workday or "normal" workweek implies that there will occasionally be "abnormal" workdays or workweeks. Such provisions may serve to affirm management's right to require overtime. (Jones & Laughlin Steel Corp., 9 LA 708) However, if contract language definitely and expressly establishes the length of the work week, the arbitrator may uphold an employee's right to refuse overtime. (Connecticut River Mills, Inc., 6 LA 1017)

In general, one arbitrator has stated that the burden is not on the employer to find contractual provision expressly authorizing it to require overtime work; rather, burden is upon the union to point to contractual prohibition against such mandatory assignment. (Seilon, Inc., 51 LA 261) Another arbitrator explained that the underlying theory is that management has retained its inherent right to assign work and overtime. He added, however, that management must be reasonable and fair when demanding overtime. (Van Dorn Co., 48 LA 925)

Equal Distribution of Overtime

Contracts frequently provide for the equal sharing of overtime, with equalization generally limited to employees in the same job classification, in the same department, or on the same shift. Ordinarily, when two or more employees have accumulated the same amount of overtime, the one with the greatest seniority is given the option of the overtime assignment.

In a case where the contract called for equalization of overtime with consideration given to seniority, management scheduled a specific overtime assignment for all first-shift employees and promised to even-up the overtime of second-shift workers within the allotted time period for equalization. When management subsequently failed to do so, second-shift employees with greater seniority than some of the first-shift men filed a grievance which later came to arbitration. The umpire upheld the griev-

ance, stating that under the contract, it was required to cross shift lines if necessary to equalize overtime with consideration to seniority. (Eaton, Yale & Town, Inc., 54 LA 1121)

A collective bargaining agreement required equal distribution of overtime. Management assigned overtime to the employee who had been working on the job in question during regular hours. Another worker who was qualified to do the job and had fewer hours of overtime than the assigned employee filed a grievance. His complaint was upheld. (Vendorlator Manufacturing Co., 53 LA 494)

In another ruling, the arbitrator found that failure of an employee to show up for prior overtime assignments does not justify passing over that employee for a new overtime assignment when the contract specifies that extra-hours work is to be distributed equally. (Grief Bros. Corp., 55 LA 384)

Period in which Overtime Must Be Equalized

Recognizing that it is not always possible to equalize overtime exactly, many contracts specify a permissible spread in the number of overtime hours worked by different employees. One such contract contained a provision that "the Company will distribute available overtime work as equally as possible (within a thirty-six (36) hour limitation) . . ." and further stated that "the employee with the least amount of department overtime will be scheduled first."

An arbitrator interpreted these two provisions to mean that the employer should assign scheduled overtime to the employee with the least amount of departmental overtime credit, but may properly give overtime to an employee whose overtime credit does not exceed that of another worker by 36 hours. He further ruled that when an employee is properly assigned extra-hours work, but his overtime credit increases between the assignment and performance of that overtime, management need not reschedule that overtime for another employee. (National Lead Co., 53 LA 687)

In the absence of a contractual time limit, what is a reasonable length of time in which to equalize overtime assignments? One arbitrator held that four months was not an excessive period of equalization.

One employee complained that a company violated a clause requiring equal distribution of overtime by failing to give him any overtime work during a two-month period when other employees worked as much as 24 hours overtime. In the following two months, his overtime was brought up to that of the other employees. The union claimed he was entitled to pay for overtime missed during the first two months. The arbitrator, however, ruled that four months was a reasonable period in which to equalize overtime, since the contract didn't set any time limit. (North American Aviation, Inc., 17 LA 320)

Avoiding Double-Time Pay

Arbitrators have consistently ruled that management may not assign overtime in such a manner as to avoid paying double-time when such an assignment violates the scheduling of overtime stipulated in the collective bargaining agreement.

For example, a contract called for equal distibution of overtime, and provided for double-time pay for hours worked in excess of 12 in any one day. The employer scheduled a group of workers for overtime and then dismissed them after they had worked a total of 12 hours during the day. Another group of employees, who had accumulated more overtime but were not eligible for double-time pay, were assigned to complete the overtime work. The arbitrator ruled that the employer was not entitled to avoid paying double-time by assigning overtime to workers with more accumulated extra-hours work, even though the contract failed to specify within what time period overtime must be equalized. (Continental Can Co., 52 LA 118)

In two similar situations, the contracts provided for double-time pay for the seventh consecutive day worked and equalization of overtime. Failure to assign extra-hours work to employees with the least amount of accumulated overtime in order to avoid paying double-time constituted a violation of the contract, it was held in both cases. (American Enka Corp., 52 LA 882; U.S. Borax & Chemical Corp., 54 LA 387)

Transferred Employees

In two cases, arbitrators found that, when overtime is to be shared equally throughout a department or work group, employees temporarily transferred to another area are entitled to overtime assignments scheduled in their regular group. As one umpire pointed out, to rule otherwise would mean that management could avoid giving overtime to a particular individual merely by temporarily transferring him prior to assigning overtime. (Massey-Ferguson, Inc., 53 LA 616; Armstrong Cork Co., 54 LA 252)

Qualifications to Perform Overtime Tasks

Certain tasks may require more overtime than others. This may result in a lack of uniformity in the distribution of overtime, due to some employees' inability to perform frequent-overtime tasks. If the contract calls for equalization of overtime, is the company required to train low-overtime employees to perform high-overtime tasks so that overtime can be equalized?

One arbitrator has held that without such a stipulation in the contract, the company need not train employees solely for the purpose of equalizing the distribution of overtime. (Goodyear Aerospace Corp., 51 LA 344)

In another case, however, an arbitration board found that a company was violating a contract that provided for equal distribution of overtime throughout a job classification when that company continually assigned certain overtime work to the same two employees on the grounds that the two employees were the only ones having the necessary experience to perform the work. The arbitrators ordered the company to train the six employees who had been denied overtime so that they could also do the work. (Bridgeport Brass Co., 19 LA 690)

Differences in Proficiency

Differing conclusions have been reached regarding management's discretion in assigning overtime when a certain group of workers are able to perform the overtime task, but are not the most proficient group for that task.

In one instance, the contract called for equal distribution of overtime departmentally. However, it had been company practice to assign maintenance overtime on the basis of special proficiencies of the maintenance workers. The arbitrator ruled that this practice violated the contract, except in cases where the employee having the least overtime was totally unqualified to perform the overtime task. (National Lead Co., 53 LA 687)

On the other hand, another umpire held that it was legitimate to assign overtime for purposes of taking inventory on the basis of ability, despite contractual provision for overtime assignments to be made on a seniority basis. The arbitrator reasoned that special skills are needed for taking inventory, and inventory is totally unrelated to production activities. (Myers Drum Co., 55 LA 1048)

It was the policy of another company not to require female employees to lift more than 50 pounds. Yet it was frequently necessary for women workers to do so during regular hours. When an overtime assignment occured which necessitated lifting of more than 50 pounds, the female workers (who were in line for overtime) were by-passed; and they initiated a grievance. The umpire ruled that management violated the contract, since the women had demonstrated during regular hours that they

were able to perform the work. (Standard Brands, Inc., 54 LA 732)

Overtime by Job Classification

A contract called for overtime work to be performed by the classification of employees who normally perform that type of work. Given such a provision, an arbitrator ruled that it was a violation of the contract for overtime to be assigned to another classification of employees even though the job was to be performed in their work area and they had on occasion performed the particular task. (American Shipbulding Co., 54 LA 1216)

Overtime by Seniority

A small percentage of contracts provide for overtime to be distributed on the basis of seniority. One such contract contained a clause, "Overtime shall be allocated in accordance with departmental seniority unless production would be substantially impaired by strict adherence to this rule."

In one instance under this agreement, management gave an overtime job to an employee from another department who was on hand performing other overtime activities and made no attempt to contact the senior employee in the affected department. The umpire held that management had violated the contract. (Harris Brothers Co., 53 LA 293)

However, management is under no obligation to assign overtime work on the basis of seniority, an arbitrator has decided, if the collective bargaining agreement does not specifically state that seniority rights shall apply to overtime distribution.

A union objected to a company's practice of assigning overtime in a random manner and demanded that senior employees be paid for extrahours work given junior men. The contract said nothing about overtime distribution, but it did contain a clause stating that "seniority rights for employees shall prevail subject to the terms of this agreement." The union contended this meant that seniority would apply in all situations except as limited by the agreement. The company, on the other hand, argued that the clause meant seniority rights would operate only in the manner spelled out in detail in other parts of the contract.

The umpire agreed with the company. In the absence of a provision making seniority applicable to overtime work, the union didn't have cause for complaint. (Crowe-Gulde Cements Co., 30 LA 177)

Probationary Employees

When the contract fails to specify whether probationary employees are to be given overtime, the facts in the individual case will determine the arbitrator's ruling.

A collective bargaining agreement stipulated that overtime was to be distributed equally among employees in a department. When necessary to get additional help from outside the department, overtime was to be given to the senior employee with the least overtime. The contract defined probationary workers as employees.

In a grievance arising under this agreement, the arbitrator ruled that the company acted properly when it assigned a probationary employee in the department to overtime work rather than going outside the department. (Hess & Eisenhardt Co., 53 LA 95)

On the other hand, when the contract calls for overtime to be distributed on a seniority basis, management may not assign overtime to probationary employees (who have no seniority) rather than more senior workers. (National Cash Register, 55 LA 189)

Notifying Employees of Overtime Work Available

To what extent is management obligated to attempt to reach an employee at home whose turn it is to work overtime? Each case must be judged individually.

A contract called for equalization of overtime. The employer called the man with the least overtime at his home to come in for an overtime assignment, but the employee failed to answer the phone. The assignment was properly given to someone else.

Twenty minutes later, however, another overtime assignment became known. The employer assumed that the previously-called employee with the least overtime was still unavailable and failed to try to contact him for the new assignment. The arbitrator ruled that the employer could not assume that the employee had not returned home during the twenty-minute interval and, therefore, violated the contract. (Goodyear Aerospace Corp., 52 LA 1098)

In another case, the contract provided for overtime to be given to the most senior employee classified to do the work. Overtime was necessary for Labor Day, and it was scheduled late in the afternoon of the last working day before the holiday. The most senior employee had been on vacation (his honeymoon), and was not due back until the day after Labor Day. The foreman made no attempt to contact the senior employee and instead assigned the overtime to someone else.

The company argued that it would be unreasonable to have to try to contact the senior employee throughout the holiday weekend. Furthermore should he prove to be unavailable for the overtime assignment on Labor Day, it would be very difficult to get a substitute worker at the last minute. The arbitrator upheld the company's contention and agreed that the overtime was properly assigned to someone else. (Carey Salt Co., 51 LA 1170)

Responsibility for an Error in Assigning Overtime

Arbitrators generally hold that any mistakes management makes when assigning overtime, even if perfectly honest and understandable errors, are management's responsibility; grievants are usually awarded compensation.

Due to a computer error, overtime was improperly assigned to an employee. The umpire concluded that the aggrieved worker must be compensated—despite the fact that he should have been aware of the error and should have called it to management's attention before the scheduled overtime was performed. (Goodyear Aerospace Corp., 54 LA 579)

Remedy for Overtime Missed

The usual remedy awarded when management makes an erroneous overtime assignment is make-up overtime or payment of money the employee would have earned were the overtime properly assigned. Arbitrators are frequently called upon to determine which of the two remedies is appropriate when contracts fail to specify the remedy to be awarded.

Under a contract providing for equal distribution of overtime within the appropriate overtime group in a classification, the employer improperly gave an overtime assignment to an employee from a different classification. The arbitrator ruled for a monetary award—rather than make-up overtime—for the employee who should have been given the assignment. The arbitrator explained that to give the grievant make-up overtime would adversely affect the contractual overtime rights of the other employees in his classification. (Trane Co., 52 LA 144)

In another instance, an employee was mistakenly bypassed for an overtime assignment under a contract stipulating equal distribution of overtime. The assignment was given to another employee in the same overtime group, however. The contract failed to specify any remedy for improper overtime assignments, so the arbitrator imposed an award of make-up overtime for the grievant. He felt that the remedy was appropriate since the bypass occurred within the same overtime equalization roster and no inequities would result from make-up overtime. Furthermore, the bypass was

unintentional, and the employee would suffer no loss of earnings as long as he received the make-up assignment within a reasonable period. (Kaiser Aluminum & Chemical Corp., 54 LA 613)

A contract called for make-up overtime "within a reasonable time" as the remedy for an erroneous overtime assignment where the error was committed unintentionally. In a case arising under this contract, the umpire ruled that "within a reasonable time" was to be interpreted as "at the first opportunity." (Evans Products Co., 48 LA 47)

At another firm, the union and the company had devised a detailed and specific procedure for the assignment of overtime. When the company failed to follow the procedure in making an overtime assignment, to no fault of the grievant, the arbitrator found that the only appropriate remedy was pay for the lost overtime. (Minnesota Mining & Mfg. Co., 48 LA 923)

When the award granted is monetary, arbitrators generally will award pay for missed overtime at the overtime rate rather than at straight-time. For example, a series of grievances came before an arbitrator in which he found that certain employees had been denied their proper opportunity for overtime work. The union argued that the employees should be paid the appropriate premium rates for the hours of work they were denied. The company, however, maintained that they should be paid straight-time rates, saying that the contract specified straight-time as the appropriate rate of pay for any hours not worked. The company also pointed out that it had been established practice at the plant to pay only straight-time in such cases.

Despite the company's past practice, the arbitrator ruled for the union. He said that the most important consideration was that the employees would have been paid at overtime rates if they had worked the hours in question, so he awarded them the "amount of compensation they were denied tne opportunity to earn." (John Deere Ottumwa Works, 20 LA 737)

Definition of "Day" for Overtime Purposes

Where overtime pay is required for all work beyond a designated number of hours a day, the manner in which a day is measured becomes crucial. There are several practices: Some companies use a calendar day, others a 24-hour period following a specified time, and still others recognize the 24-hour period following the start of the particular employee's regular shift.

In one case, several employees who normally worked from 3 p.m. to 11 p.m. were ordered to work from 7 p.m. to 7 a.m. on Monday and Tuesday, resuming their normal work schedule on Wednesday. The contract defined the workday for purposes of computing overtime as "24 consecutive hours commencing with the starting time on an employee's regularly assigned shift."

The union contended that the employees were entitled to overtime pay for the hours worked between 3 p.m. and 7 p.m. on Wednesday. The union argued that the 24-hour period began for these workers at 7 p.m.; hence, 3 p.m. to 7 p.m. Wednesday was the same workday that began Tuesday at 7 p.m. The company countered that the workday began at 3 p.m., the starting time of these employees' regularly assigned shift; and all work performed on Wednesday was to be paid at the straight-time rate. The arbitrator ruled for the company. (Chicago Pneumatic Tool Co., 42 LA 1240)

In another case, a problem arose with the initiation of Daylight Saving Time. The contract required overtime pay for all time worked in excess of eight hours in any one day and defined a day as "24 hours beginning at the time an employee starts work on his regular or assigned schedule." The arbitrator held that the em-

ployees who worked the 7 a.m. to p.m. shift and the 3 p.m. to 11 p.m shift on the Saturday before Dayligh Saving Time went into effect wer entitled to overtime pay for the firs hour worked on those same shifts th following Sunday. He commented tha the contract was very specific i defining a day as 24-hours long, an only 23 hours had elapsed betweer the start of the Saturday shifts and the start of the Sunday shifts. (Neche Butane Products, 49 LA 1195)

Overtime on Holidays

Under a contract that failed t specify the manner of computin compensation for hours worked i excess of eight on premium-pay day such as holidays, an arbitrator foun that employees are entitled to on and one-half times the applicabl premium hourly rate for such hours The contract called for time and one half for overtime work and triple time for holiday work. The arbitrato upheld the union contention that th triple-time holiday pay was the prope base rate to be used for computing overtime on a holiday; hence, over time on a holiday was to be compen sated at four and one-half times th straight-time rate. (Fry's Food Stores 44 LA 431)

Holiday As Time Worked for Overtime Purposes

When contracts are silent on the subject of whether or not an unworked holiday is to be counted as hours worked for purposes of calculating weekly overtime, arbitrators may rule either way.

One company's contract stated tha time and one-half would be paid for all work beyond 40 hours in a week and specified a Monday through Friday workweek. When employees worked a Saturday during a week which included an unworked holiday the union and the company disagreed over whether the employees were entitled to overtime pay for the Saturday work. The company claimed that since the contract didn't specifically say so, holidays need not be counted as time worked.

The umpire ruled, however, that holidays should be counted as time worked. Otherwise, workers would lose pay (the overtime premium) for the sixth day worked because of a holiday. Concluding that the parties meant for workers to enjoy holidays without losing any money, the arbitrator said the company must count holidays as time worked. (Martin Aircraft Tool Co., 25 LA 181)

At least one arbitrator, however, has declared that if the contract is silent on the matter, management need not count an unworked holiday as time worked in figuring when overtime pay starts. The contract stipulated time and one-half pay for work after 40 hours a week. It stated that "hours lost by employees from their regular scheduled shift at the request of the company shall count as time worked for the purpose of computing weekly overtime."

In one week, employees put in a total of 40 hours of actual work, apart from time off on a holiday. The union insisted that the time off on the holiday should be counted as time worked—for a total of 48 hours' work in the week, eight of them compensated at the overtime premium.

The arbitrator decided otherwise. It was not time lost at the request of the company, he said. He considered the unworked holiday comparable to an unworked Sunday, and it should not be viewed as time worked for overtime purposes. (Goodyear Clearwater Mills, 6 LA 117)

Pyramiding of Daily and Weekly Overtime Pay

Collective bargaining agreements generally provide for overtime or premium pay for work in excess of some specified number of hours per day or in excess of some specified number of hours in a week. It is common for these agreements to also contain a clause prohibiting pyramiding of overtime premiums—hours of

daily overtime worked and compensated for cannot be counted again as time worked toward weekly overtime. Problems can arise however, in determining whether certain hours worked, paid for at some premium rate, are in fact overtime hours and consequently cannot be counted toward weekly overtime.

In one such case, the grievant worked 12 hours on his birthday. The contract recognized employees' birthdays as holidays, and provided for time and one-half payment for work done on a holiday. The contract also prohibited pyramiding of overtime premiums.

The grievant was paid time and one-half holiday pay for the first eight hours worked on his birthday, and time and one-half overtime pay for the remaining four hours. The union contended that the first eight hours, the grievant worked should be counted in computing the weekly overtime, since these hours were compensated as holiday work, not overtime work. The arbitrator agreed, rejecting the company's argument that such action would amount to pyramiding. (Hooker Chemical Corp., 50 LA 1091)

A similar situation arose in another case where an employee had been paid time and one-half for the hours she worked on her scheduled day off. The arbitrator ruled she was also entitled to receive overtime pay for the hours worked in excess of 40 during the week, despite the fact that the contract prohibited payment of both daily and weekly overtime for the same hours. The premium pay which the grievant received for her off-day work is analogous to "penalty pay" for Sunday and holiday work, the umpire reasoned, rather than to daily overtime. (Safeway Stores, Inc., 45 LA 244)

Another contract provided for double-time for Sunday work and time and one-half for hours in excess of 40 in a workweek. The contract further prohibited pyramiding of overtime and/or premium pay. Under this agreement, an employee worked Sunday and the following five days. The company paid the worker double-time for the Sunday work, but refused to pay time and one-half for the sixth day, claiming that to do so would be pyramiding of overtime and premium pay. The arbitrator, however, concluded that the double-time pay for Sunday was in fact a penalty against the employer, not premium pay. Consequently, he found that the employee was entitled to time and one-half for the sixth day, and that this would not constitute pyramiding. (Safeway Stores, Inc., 45 LA 1163)

Premium Pay for Weekend Work

Most contracts provide some kind of premium pay for work performed on weekends. Specifically, just over half specify a premium rate for work on Saturday, just under three quarters call for Sunday premium pay, nearly a third provide premium pay for the sixth day of the workweek, and more than a third require payment of a premium for the seventh day.

Arbitration awards in this area provide few general guides for application to the everyday problems confronting union officials. Settlement of disputes over premium pay generally depends on a close reading of complex contract language and its application in the context of the particular bargaining situation.

Sunday Premium

Contracts frequently call for premium pay for work performed on Sundays. For purposes of such provisions, many contracts limit Sunday worktime eligible for premium pay to work begun after some specified hour on Sunday in order to avoid premium payments for work that is part of a Saturday night shift. Without such a limitation, arbitrators will generally hold employers liable for premium pay for all work performed on "Sunday" as defined by the calendar day.

One contract, for example, defined the "workday" as beginning at 7 a.m. and provided for doubletime pay "for all hours worked on Sunday." Third-shift employees regularly scheduled to work from 11 p.m. Saturday until 7 a.m. Sunday claimed that they were entitled to doubletime for all work performed after midnight Saturday night until the end of their shift. The company denied their contention, insisting that the Saturday workday began at 7 a.m. and continued for 24 hours until 7 a.m. Sunday. Hence, all work performed by the third shift employees fell on Saturday, the company claimed.

The arbitrator, however, found that the contract made no such definition

of Sunday. Absent any contractual provision specifically defining the day for overtime or premium pay purposes in some other manner, a day is generally held to mean the calendar day, the umpire explained. He concluded that in this contract "Sunday" meant from midnight Saturday to midnight Sunday and, therefore, awarded third shift employees doubletime pay for all work performed after midnight Saturday. (Trent Engineering Co., 55 LA 1232)

Seventh-day Premium

Rather than specify Sunday as a premium day, some contracts generalize and call for premiums on the seventh day worked. Similar problems can arise in determining when the "seventh day" actually begins.

An employee at one company regularly worked Monday through Friday, beginning at 7:30 a.m. After working his regular week, he was called in at 11:00 p.m. Saturday, and worked until 8:36 a.m. Sunday, with an hour break for a meal.

The contract provided for time and one half for the sixth day worked and doubletime for work on the seventh day. The workday was defined as eight hours. The employer consequently paid the employee time and one half for the sixth day and double-time for only a few minutes on Sunday morning, claiming that the seventh day did not begin until eight hours had been worked on the sixth day.

The arbitrator ruled, however, that the seventh day began at 7:30 Sunday morning since the employee's regular starting time was 7:30 a.m. He ordered that the employee be paid at doubletime rates for all work done after 7:30 a.m. Sunday. (City of Lansing, 53 LA 855)

Pyramiding Premiums

A contract called for time and one half pay for an employee working his first scheduled day off or the sixth day in the workweek, and doubletime for working his second scheduled day off or the seventh day in the workweek. The contract also contained the following clause: "The Company shall not be required to pay overtime twice for the same overtime hours worked."

An employee was scheduled to have Tuesday and Wednesday off. However, he was called in to work Wednesday, his second scheduled day off. He also worked Monday and Thursday through Sunday of that week. He was paid doubletime for Wednesday and straight time the remainder of the week.

The union claimed the employee was entitled to time and one half for Sunday since it was the sixth day worked in the week. The company argued that such payment would be pyramiding, which was prohibited in the contract clause quoted above, as the employee already received a premium for the Wednesday worked and that time could not be counted again.

The arbitrator rejected the company's argument, however. He pointed out that there were two different days involved, and these were not, therefore, "the same overtime hours." He explained that the clause did *not* state that overtime hours worked and compensated for under one provision could not be counted as hours worked for overtime purposes under any other provision. But rather, he said, the clause was intended to prevent paying a double premium in such situations as an employee working the sixth day

in the workweek, that same day also happening to be his first scheduled day off. (Dow Chemical Co., 49 LA 480)

Unworked Days Affecting Premiums

Holidays and other time not worked but paid for may or may not influence the rate of pay on what are normally premium days. Specific contract language is crucial.

EXAMPLE: A contract called for time and one half for all work performed on Saturday. Another provision of the contract provided for "bereavement pay"—pay for up to three days of missed work when an employee attended the funeral of an immediate family member. The contract stipulated that the employee was to be paid bereavement pay for the time he "would have had the opportunity to work" at his "standard hourly wage rate."

An employee under this contract was scheduled to work on Saturday. However, due to a death in his family, he was excused from work that day. The company subsequently paid him eight hours' bereavement pay at the straight-time rate.

The company contended that the "standard hourly wage rate" meant the "straight-time" rate. The union argued that the employee was entitled to eight hours' pay at time and one half, the "standard hourly wage rate" for Saturday. The arbitrator agreed with the union's view and awarded for the grievant. (Marlin-Rockwell Co., 54 LA 99)

EXAMPLE: A contract provided that all work performed on the seventh consecutive day of the employee's workweek was to be paid at doubletime. The contract further stipulated that employees were not to lose pay for worktime lost while serving on jury duty.

An employee was absent from work Monday and Wednesday one week while serving on jury duty, for which he was paid by the company for eight hours each day. He worked Tuesday, Thursday, Friday, Saturday, and Sunday of that week. The company paid the employee at the straight-time rate for Sunday.

The union argued that time spent

on jury duty and compensated for by the company was to be counted as time worked. Thus Sunday was the seventh consecutive day worked in that employee's workweek, and should have been paid at doubletime, the union insisted. But the arbitrator found no provision in the contract stating that time spent on jury duty and compensated for by the company was to be counted as time worked. Absent any such provision, the arbitrator could not sustain the grievance; and he ruled that the employee had been properly paid. (Cabot Corp., 52 LA 575)

In a similar case, another arbitrator also concluded that without specific contractual provision to that effect, pay for jury duty was not to be counted as hours worked when computing overtime. (Coleman Company, Inc., 52 LA 357)

Premium Pay for Shift Work

*IN BRIEF*_____

Clauses providing for payment of a wage differential to employees who work on afternoon or night shifts ordinarily do not give rise to many disputes. Almost all companies requiring night work pay a shift bonus. The rate of payment invariably is specified in the contract, and workers assigned to the particular shift automatically are paid it. Occasionally, however, there may be questions relating to the payment of shift differentials to night watchmen and similar groups or to workers who divide their time between shifts. Under almost three fifths of shift clauses, a larger bonus is paid for the third shift than for the second.

Shift differentials must be included in figuring a worker's overtime rate. This is the law and also the opinion of most umpires.

When Regular Work Schedule Extends Into Another Shift

If portions of employees' regular work schedule fall into two different shifts, are they entitled to a shift premium for any of the hours? One arbitrator held they were not.

Workers who normally worked the evening shift (3 p.m. to 11 p.m.) received a 15-cent premium shift differential. When management unilaterally changed the work schedule for this shift to 11 a.m. to 7 p.m., the employees claimed they were entitled to shift differential for the hours of 3 p.m. to 7 p.m. The arbitrator rejected their contention, stating that the shift differential was only applicable to the eight-hour evening shift, and not to a few hours worked during that time span. (Diamond Shamrock Corp., 55 LA 827)

If a company agrees to pay employees the premium rate required for a shift in which the *majority* of their working hours fall, what rate should be paid an employee who works *exactly* half his time on the day shift and half on the second shift? In one such situation, the arbitrator rejected the employee's claim for a shift premium.

The employee worked regularly from 12:30 to 9 p.m., with a half-hour for lunch between 4:30 and 5. The regular second shift hours began at 4:30 p.m. Therefore, excluding his lunch period, this employee worked exactly half his hours on the day shift and half on the second shift. The arbitrator pointed out that since the lunch period could not be counted as hours worked, the employee could not show that a *majority* of his work time was put in on the second shift and denied his claim for the shift premium. (Canfield Oil Co., 7 LA 322)

Night Premium for Non-Production Workers

Rulings have gone both ways on whether non-production workers on premium-pay shifts are entitled to shift differentials.

Under a contract that provided a shift differential for night work, an arbitrator ruled that the employer violated the contract by denying shift differential to janitors who worked on the night shift. Although janitors had not received the differential prior to this contract and the subject was not mentioned during negotiations, the contract language neglected to specifically exclude janitors from receiving the premium. (Journal-Tribune Publishing Co., 51 LA 606)

On the other hand, it was held in another case that night shift premiums did not apply to watchmen, even though the contract didn't specifically exclude them. The award was based on a past practice of several years of not paying such workers the premium. (John Lucas & Co., 19 LA 344)

In another case, an employer was again not required to pay shift premiums for work at night to charwomen, because they had not received such pay in the six years that they had been covered by the contract. This past practice overrode the fact that the contract made no exceptions to the payment of premium pay for those hours, according to the arbitrator. (Morgan Engineering Co., 33 LA 46)

Inclusion of Shift Premium in Figuring Overtime Pay

If a worker is entitled to a shift premium, his overtime pay must be based on his regular rate plus the shift premium. This is required by the Wage-Hour Law and is also ordered by most arbitrators in settling contract disputes.

A company agreed in its union contract that a bonus of five cents an hour would be paid men working on the second and third shifts. When a employee on a late shift performed overtime work, the company contended that he was entitled only to one and one-half times the *day* rate, while the union argued that he was entitled to one and one-half times the day rate plus five cents.

The arbitrator, in upholding the union view, pointed out that the differential for late-shift work becomes an integral part of the employee's wage. Therefore, he ruled that an employee who worked overtime was entitled to receive compensation for those hours at the rate of one and one-half times his full hourly wage, including the shift premium. (Public Service Electric & Gas Co., 2 LA 2)

Overtime Extending Into a Premium-Pay Shift

Arbitrators generally rule that an employee working a day shift who occasionally is assigned overtime which extends into a premium-pay shift is *not* entitled to have the shift differential included in his overtime pay. However, if the overtime occurs on a regular basis or the contract language suggests that the differential is to be paid, the arbitrator may award the shift premium.

One arbitrator found that employees on the first shift were not entitled to a shift differential for the hour worked after the shift's normal quitting time. He ruled that the shift differential was intended only as additional compensation for second-shift employees who had to give up their socializing time of day. Occasional overtime work performed by the first shift did not alter their status as first-shift employees, and the contract specified that the second shift, not the first, was to receive the differential. (Idal Corrugated Box Co., 46 LA 129)

Under a different contract providing a shift differential for second-shift work, however, another arbitrator held that an employee who *regularly* worked a ten-hour day was entitled to the shift differential for the two hours worked daily on the second shift, in addition to the overtime premium for those two hours. The umpire explained that payment of overtime alone is sufficient for first-shift employees who only *occasionally* work overtime into the second shift. But the additional shift differential must be paid to employees who work overtime into the second shift on a regularly-scheduled basis. (Brighton Electric Steel Casting, 47 LA 518)

Further, where a contract called for shift bonuses for second-and third-shifts for "all work on these shifts," the employer had to include bonuses in the base rate for purposes of computing overtime worked on those shifts by employees regularly assigned to preceding shifts. (Stauffer Chemical Co., 35 LA 529)

In another instance, a case came to arbitration over a company's practice of paying employees who work overtime on their day off on the basis of the shift differential applicable to the shift actually worked rather than on the basis of the shift to which they were regularly assigned.

Employees who regularly worked a premium-pay shift were called in on their day off to work the day shift. The company did not include their usual shift differential when computing the overtime pay for the day shift worked.

The arbitrator upheld this procedure since the practice had been in effect for several years, and the union had not challenged it before. (Bonanza Air Lines, Inc., 44 LA 698)

Reporting & Call-in Pay

*IN BRIEF*_____

More than three quarters of contracts guarantee a minimum payment (usually four hours' pay) to employees who report for work as scheduled. Somewhat fewer agreements—nearly three fifths—provide a work or pay guarantee for workers who are called in to work during their off-duty time.

POINTERS—

▶ A reporting-pay clause probably can't be stretched to cover call-ins for emergency work. There is a clear-cut distinction between reporting pay and call-in pay.

▶ Where a company is relieved of its reporting-pay obligation when it tells a worker not to report, a properly addressed telegram is usually considered proper notice—even if the worker doesn't get it. This may not be true, though, if the contract says workers must "receive" notice not to report.

▶ If work is unavailable through no fault of the company's management nevertheless must notify workers not to report if this is feasible. A failure to give such notice may make the company liable for reporting pay.

Overtime or Call-in

Several problems have arisen over whether specific time worked outside the normal work schedule are to be compensated as overtime or as a call-in. One arbitrator has made the following distinction between overtime and a call-in. Overtime is time worked continuous to the regular work schedule—whether it precedes or follows that shift. Call-in pay, however, is intended to compensate an employee for making a special trip to work; therefore, it is necessary for the employee to be released to leave the workplace immediately after completing an assignment in order for that assignment to qualify as a call-in. (Owens-Illinois, Inc., 55 LA 1121)

Reporting Pay or Call-in

A collective bargaining agreement contained a provision guaranteeing employees a minimum of four hours' work or four hours' pay if called in at some time other than their regular shift or a continuous extension thereof. The contract further provided for a minimum of four hours' work or pay to any employee reporting for work at the start of his normal shift — with certain exceptions, such as when no work is available due to a power failure.

The second shift employees were instructed on Friday afternoon to report for work the following afternoon. Saturday was not a normal workday, but Saturday overtime occurred frequently. A power failure occurred Saturday m o r n i n g. When employees reported for work as instructed, the company told them to go home.

The employees filed a grievance claiming four hours' call-in pay. The company contended that the situation came under the provisions governing reporting pay, and it was therefore not liable for payment to employees because of the power failure exception. The arbitrator upheld the company's view, stating that the reporting pay provisions applied given the established practice of an extended workweek schedule. (General Dynamics Corp., 54 LA 405)

Exceptions to Reporting Pay Requirements

Reporting pay provisions generally list certain situations in which the employer is not required to make reporting payments to employees. These exceptions may be situations where work is unavailable for reasons beyond the company's control or where the employer has given workers prior notice not to report. Arbitrators are frequently called upon to determine if a given situation is truly beyond the company's control or if the company has given employees proper notice not to report.

Some of these situations are discussed below.

Civil Disturbances

A contract guaranteed four hours' reporting or call-in pay, except where employees are denied work for reasons beyond the control of the company. During the civil disturbances following the assassination of Dr. Martin Luther King, the company cancelled their regular evening shift because of a curfew imposed by the governor. Management made reasonable attempts to notify employees through radio announcements, although such notification was not required under the terms of the contract.

The umpire denied reporting pay to employees who came to work, holding that the situation was "a classi-cal illustration of 'other causes beyond the control of the Company.' " (Koppers Co., Inc., 54 LA 408)

Similar civil disorders in another city prompted a city-wide curfew starting at 3 p.m. Several second-shift employees reported for work at 3 p.m., but were sent home. They subsequently claimed four hours' pay under a reporting pay clause requiring such pay for employees sent home for lack of work. The company interpreted "lack of work" to mean absence of the need for the product with adjustments in the work schedule to reduce output. Since this situation did not exist, the umpire rejected the employees' claim for reporting pay. (Lockheed-Georgia, 51 LA 720)

Bomb Threats

A company received a bomb threat. Two previous threats had proved to be hoaxes. Believing this to be another hoax, the company gave employees the option of going home and being paid only for time actually spent on plant premises, or staying and working the entire shift and getting full pay for the time worked. The company said it would not give four hours' reporting pay to employees who elected to go home, under a contractual provision exempting the employer from such reporting pay in case of explosion.

The union later claimed reporting pay, arguing that no explosion actually occurred. The arbitrator denied their grievance, however, He felt that if an actual explosion would exempt the company from reporting pay, the same should hold true for the mere threat of an explosion. Otherwise, "any mischief maker . . . could drive the corporation out of business with threats of one sort and another." (General Cable Corp., 54 LA 696)

Equipment Breakdowns and Power Failures

Arbitrators will look very closely to determine if equipment breakdowns and power failures are, in fact, within the company's control. For example, a contract provided for reporting pay for employees who report for work but find none available, except "if the plant delay results from causes beyond the control of the company." A flue collapsed, necessitating the shutting down of a furnace used in production operations. The union argued that since the flue had not been inspected for three years and proper inspection could have prevented the collapse, the situation was legitimately within the company's control. The umpire agreed and awarded the grievants reporting pay. (Bunker Hill Co., 51 LA 873)

Under another contract requiring reporting pay unless the unavailability of work is due to a major power interruption or equipment breakdown over which the company has no control, the arbitrator awarded reporting pay when a leak in a boiler made work unavailable. The leak occurred following a shutdown and repairs on the boiler, and such leaks were common after boiler shutdowns. Although the leak was beyond the control of the company, the arbitrator said that the company should have foreseen the possibility of the leak and made every effort to discover it in time to notify employees not to report to work. (Rubatex Corp., 52 LA 1270)

However, an arbitrator ruled in another instance that employees who were sent home after a power failure in the main electric feeder line were not entitled to four hours' reporting pay under a contract providing for such payment except where employer "is not able to operate the plant because of reasons beyond its control." The union contended that since the burn-out which precipitated the power failure occurred within the plant, its occurrence was management's responsibility and, therefore, was within its control. The arbitrator accepted the argument that the main feeder line was management's responsibility; but since the power failure could not have been anticipated, it was beyond the company's control. The employees' grievance was

denied. (Erie ARTISAN Corp., 51 LA 850)

Similarly, a power failure due to a malfunction in new equipment was judged to be beyond management's control, exempting that company from payment of four-hours' reporting pay. (E. W. Bliss Co., 55 LA 522)

On the other hand, another company was held liable for reporting pay when a power failure occurred on its premises. A two-inch hole existed in a wall separating the machine room from the turbine room. The hole had been there for three years; the company was aware of it but had made no attempt to seal it.

On the day in question, a water hose flipped out of a tank in the machine room, spraying water through the hole into the turbine room. A power failure resulted, and second-shift employees were sent home. The company insisted that it was not liable for reporting pay claimed by the grievants because the contract exempted the company from such pay when lack of work was due to some accident. The company contended that the spraying of water through the two-inch hole was an accident.

The arbitrator disagreed, however. He admitted the event was unusual, but not unforeseeable, and said that an unusual event is not necessarily an accident. (Mead Corp., 54 LA 1218)

Lack of Heat

When employees reported to work Monday morning, the plant was cold. The oil tank had run out of oil over the weekend. The company had been aware of the oil shortage on Friday, but felt there would be enough to last until Monday. An unexpected, though not uncommon, drop in temperature caused the oil to run out earlier than anticipated. A stand-by gas heater was inoperative.

Employees refused to work due to the lack of heat. A short time after the start of the shift, the company president told employees that the oil shipment was on its way, there would soon be heat, and to either get to work or leave. They all went home. The company did not pay the employees at all that day. The union demanded four hours' reporting pay or at least compensation for the time spent at the plant that morning. The arbitrator awarded payment for time spent in the plant, since the situation was within management's control, but denied four hours' reporting pay on the grounds that there were some equities on the company's side. (Dietz Machine Works, Inc., 52 LA 1023)

Health Hazard

While first-shift employees were at work, a mechanical detector sounded an alarm indicating the presence of unsafe levels of carbon monoxide in the workplace. The employees evacuated the area. Twenty minutes later the company informed the employees that the alarm was a result of a malfunction in the detector, and instructed employees to return to work. Seventeen of them refused to do so, believing conditions were genuinely unsafe; they requested other work for the one hour remaining in their shift. The company said it could not make substitute work available on such short notice.

The 17 employees subsequently filed a grievance requesting the pay they had been denied for the last hour of their shift. Their claim was based on a contract provision stating that employees who report for their normal shift without prior notification not to report will be given eight hours of work.

The umpire found that the employees were justified in refusing to return to work under the circumstances. He further found that the contract failed to limit the company's liability to pay the workers in this situation, and thus awarded each one hour's pay. (Miller Printing Machinery Co., 54 LA 69)

In another case, several employees were suddenly taken ill at work. The company tried to ascertain the cause, but was unable to do so. Upon the advise of the state health department, the company closed the plant two hours after the start of the workday, and paid the employees for the two hours worked.

An arbitrator denied a grievance for four hours' reporting pay, explaining that the company had made every effort to locate and control the cause. Since its efforts failed, the situation was obviously beyond the company's control, and it was therefore not liable for reporting pay under the provisions of the contract. (Lasko Metal Products, Inc., 51 LA 1119)

Anticipation of Poor Attendance

In two cases, companies decided to close down production because they felt that there would be substantial absenteeism due to a snowstorm, making operations inefficient. In both instances, the arbitrators awarded reporting pay to those employees who showed up for work. The decision to shut down because of anticipated absenteeism was within the managements' control, they held. (Westinghouse Electric Corp., 51 LA 298; Muskegon Piston Ring Co., 55 LA 685)

Daylight Saving Time

Under a contract guaranteeing a full day's pay if more than half the shift is worked except when employees are sent home early for reasons beyond management's control, the employees demanded a full eight hours' pay even though they only worked seven hours on the evening that Daylight Saving Time went into effect. Management claimed it was not liable to pay for the last, unworked hour because the institution of Daylight Saving Time was beyond its control.

The arbitrator upheld the union, however. Management could have scheduled the workers for eight hours, even though it would have created confusion at the start of the next shift; and the situation, the umpire held, therefore was not beyond management's control. (Magma Copper Co., 51 LA 9)

Proper Notification

The facts of the individual situation may dictate whether management's attempts to notify employees not to report to work were sufficient to exempt the company from reporting pay.

Following the assassination of Dr. Martin Luther King, severe riots broke out in the city where this plant was located. Concerned for the safety of its employees, the management announced on radio the cancellation of the second shift.

The contract provided for four hours' reporting pay when employees are sent home for lack of work, unless they were notified the night before not to report. Several second shift employees who did not hear the radio announcement reported for work. Along with employees sent home early from the first shift, they requested to be paid four hours' reporting pay. The arbitrator denied their request on the grounds that attempts to notify second-shift employees were reasonable under the extreme circumstances, and there was no "lack of work." Furthermore, the arbitrator held, the company should not have any present or future deterrent placed in its way when confronted with a decision whether to shutdown for the safety of its employees. (Electronic Communications, Inc., 51 LA 692)

In a different case, a severe snowstorm caused management to close the plant. Announcements of the closing were broadcast on four major radio stations. One hundred twelve employees did not hear the announcements, however, and reported for work as usual. They were sent home.

Under a contract provision allowing for at least four hours' straight-time pay to be given any employee who reports for his regular shift without having been instructed to the contrary, the 112 employees claimed four hours' reporting pay. The arbitrator awarded them their grievance since, despite company efforts to notify the employees, they had not been instructed to remain at home. (Niagara Machine & Tool Works, 55 LA 396)

Discipline

If an employee is sent home early for disciplinary reasons, is he entitled to reporting pay? At least two arbitrators have said no.

A little more than an hour after starting work, two employees were sent home for threatening a supervisor, a violation of a company rule. The two employees maintained that they were entitled to four hours' reporting pay under the provisions of the contract. The arbitrator disagreed. Although the contract was not particularly clear on this issue, he felt certain that it was not the intention of the parties, in negotiating the agreement, to protect or reward employees who brought about such a situation. (Unarco Industries, Inc., 55 LA 421)

In another instance, an employee who had a poor attendance record failed to show up for work one day and did not call in his absence. When he reported to work the next day, his foreman stopped him immediately after the employee punched in and asked him why he had been absent. He said he was sick. The foreman did not believe him and suspended him for three days, sending the worker home right away.

The employee filed a grievance requesting four hours' reporting pay for the day he was sent home (but *not* challenging the suspension). The umpire denied the grievance explaining that the foreman could not know of the suspension prior to the employee's reporting to work since he didn't know if the worker's absence was legitimate. Consequently, he could not have given the worker prior notification not to report. Furthermore, the conditions precipitating the foreman's sending the employee home were beyond management's control. (Barber-Greene Co., 53 LA 1244)

Application of Premium Rates

Under a contract providing that double-time rates are to apply for all work in excess of 12 hours in one day, and further providing for a minimum of four hours' pay at time and one-half for call-in, an employee who had already worked 12 hours was called in for another hour and one-half. The company paid him double-time for the one and one-half hours actually worked, but only time and one-half hours for the remaining two and one-half hours of the four-hour call-in guarantee.

The grievant maintained that he was entitled to double-time pay for the entire four-hour period. But the arbitrator held that there was no expressed or implied requirement in the contract that an employee is entitled to the high premium rates for the entire four hours of call-in pay unless he actually works the entire period. The grievance was denied. (General Portland Cement Co., 53 LA 653)

IN BRIEF————————————————————————————

The right to schedule hours of work is listed in nearly a fourth of contracts as one of the rights reserved to management. But even where there is no such listing (over six tenths of contracts do not consider the matter), arbitrators are pretty well agreed that the company may set or change working hours unless the contract says otherwise. It may be required—by law if not by contract—to negotiate with the union, but it probably is not required to obtain union consent before taking action.

POINTERS—

▶ If a contract states what the normal working hours shall be, the company probably can't change the schedule unilaterally.

▶ Even if an agreement is silent on hours schedules, an umpire will turn thumbs down on a schedule change made for the purpose of avoiding premium pay.

▶ A statement of normal working hours does not serve to limit management's right to close the plant on a particular day.

Scheduling Shifts

If a contract is silent on the matter, does the union have a say in installing or changing shift schedules? As long as the contract doesn't limit management's right to schedule shifts, most arbitrators hold, the union's consent is not required.

Where one firm wanted to stagger shifts to allow for continuous operations, the union protested on the ground that there was nothing specific in the contract permitting this. But an umpire ruled that, since the contract didn't prohibit the company from scheduling staggered shifts, it could do so as part of its responsibility for production. (Merck & Co., 1 LA 430)

Another arbiter allowed a company to change hours schedules which were a part of the plant rules but not part of the contract. As long as the company didn't abuse this right to change its rules, it didn't need the union's okay, the umpire said. (Federal Rice Drug Co., 27 LA 123)

However: Where a supplemental agreement granted senior workers preference as to fixed shifts and days off, one arbiter held that management couldn't disregard this and institute rotating shifts on its own hook. The company contended that the supplemental agreement didn't guarantee the continuation of fixed shifts, but merely regulated their administration if the company decided to continue or reinstate them. The umpire pointed out a clause stating that where there was a conflict between the master agreement and the supplemental one, the latter controlled; therefore, eliminating the fixed schedule violated the contract. (Reynolds Metals Co., 35 LA 800)

Contracts Specifying "Normal Week"

Arbitrators have differed on whether a specified "normal week" bars management from changing shift schedules.

In one case, an arbiter okayed the setting up of a seven-day, continuous-shift operation, even though the contract specified an eight-hour day, five-day week, Monday through Friday. Absent language to the contrary, he held, the "normal week" clause shouldn't be interpreted to bar continuous operations; otherwise management would be prevented from introducing new products requiring such methods. (Stanley Works, 39 LA 374)

Another umpire, however, ruled that such a clause was not ambiguous in spelling out a fixed workweek, so management had no right to schedule continuous operations. (Traylor Engineering & Mfg. Div., 36 LA 687)

Hours Schedules for Weekend Work

Do the hours schedules stated in a contract apply to overtime work on the weekend? At least one arbiter has decided that a company doesn't have to pay any attention to the Monday-through-Friday shift hours in assigning work on a weekend.

EXAMPLE: One company called in a first-shift worker to handle a rush job on Sunday. Because of production difficulties, the worker didn't clock out until nearly midnight. The union complained that the first-shift man shouldn't have been allowed to work the second-shift hours.

Rejecting the union's argument, the umpire said it would lead to undesirable rigidity in scheduling overtime if the company had to follow the standard shift hours for weekend work. Such an interpretation would defeat the purpose of overtime work, which is to get the job done quickly, the arbitrator said. (Menasco Mfg. Co., 26 LA 312)

Changing Workweek

Whether or not the company can change the workweek schedule without getting union approval depends upon the wording of the contract.

For instance, one umpire found that a clause setting a regular workweek from Monday through Friday limited the company's right to change its work schedule from Monday through Friday and alternate Saturdays to Tuesday through Saturday and alternate Mondays. Although a different production schedule was needed, the arbiter said, the company had to reach agreement with the union first. (Seamless Rubber Co., 26 LA 758)

Where a contract established Monday through Friday as the basic workweek wherever "possible," an employer did not have the right to institute unilaterally a workweek of Tuesday through Saturday, an arbiter

held. (Norfolk Naval Shipyard, 54 LA 588)

But the fact that a contract said the parties "may negotiate" necessary schedules differing from the standard Monday - through - Friday workweek didn't mean the union's consent was required before changes could be made, another umpire ruled. (Menasco Mfg. Co., 30 LA 465)

Furthermore: Where the management-rights clause of an agreement gave the company the right to schedule work, and where 40 percent of the work force had been on a seven-day workweek for a number of years, the employer was allowed to put the rest of the employees on the same schedule. The umpire held that the company didn't have to get the union's approval to do this. (Celanese Corp. of America, 30 LA 797)

Change in Schedule to Avoid Premium Pay

Even though a company may have the right under its contract to change work schedules, it may be violating the agreement if it makes such changes to get out of paying premium pay.

EXAMPLE: A contract gave a company the right to revise operations in any way within its discretion. Using this right, the company changed a Monday-to-Friday schedule to a Tuesday-to-Saturday one for *one week* in which Monday was a holiday. In this way, employees had to work on Saturday at straight time, instead of at the time-and-one-half rate that would have been in effect had the Monday-to-Friday workweek not been changed. The union protested.

The protest was upheld by an arbitrator. It was clear, he said, that the company had the right to change schedules, but "it is also clear that it was not the intent of the parties that the company should be allowed to abuse this right by changing shifts in order to avoid the payment of legitimate overtime." (Kennecott Copper Corp., Nevada Mines Div., 6 LA 820; see also Menasco Mfg. Co., 30 LA 465; Acme-Newport Steel Co., 35 LA 893)

Change in Schedule to Avoid Contract Benefits

After negotiating a contract granting benefits to part-time employees working 25 hours or more a week, can management limit the working hours of those employees to less than 25 per week? Since the practice of assigning part-time workers to 25 hours or more a week had been in effect for some time, an arbitrator ruled against the reduction. Management pointed out that the contract didn't guarantee 25 hours to part-time workers or prohibit reducing the hours of work of such employees. However, the umpire decided that the contract was negotiated on the assumption that the past practice would continue, so the company was bound by that to continue scheduling hours as before. (Kroger Co., 36 LA 129)

Shutdown on Holiday Eve

If a company thinks that very little work would be done on the day before a holiday, can it shut down over the union's objection? One umpire held that a contract permitting shutdowns for lack of work or "other legitimate reasons" allowed a company to do this.

EXAMPLE: One company scheduled no work on Christmas and New Year's Eves because it was afraid employees would start their holiday celebrations on company time. The union demanded pay for the time lost, relying on a clause stating that the company would maintain an eight-hour day and a 40-hour week.

An umpire pointed out that the contract itself said that the hours-of-work clause wasn't to be construed as a guarantee of any fixed amount of work. Moreover, he said, the agreement had features, such as a reporting-pay clause, that were inconsistent with the idea of a work guarantee. Noting that there was no showing of bad faith on the part of the company, the arbiter decided the shutdown did not violate the contract. (Pittsburgh Screw & Bolt Co., 29 LA 615)

Shutdown After Holiday

Does a contract calling for a regular workweek of Monday through Friday bar an employer from shutting down on the Friday following a Thursday holiday? One arbiter has decided that an occasional shutdown doesn't have

the effect of changing the workweek. (Spartan Aircraft Co., 29 LA 795)

Scheduling Lunch Periods & Rest Periods

If a contract provides lunch and rest periods but doesn't say when they are to be taken, does the union have a say in when they should be scheduled? In one case where the contract didn't schedule the lunch periods, an umpire upheld the union's objection to the company's changing them.

EXAMPLE: The practice at one company had been for employees to eat in four half-hour shifts from 11 a.m. to 1 p.m. Then management decided that five lunch periods would work out better than four, so it changed the lunch schedule to run from 10:45 to 1:15 p.m. When the union claimed this was an unreasonable break with past practice, the company pointed out that the contract, while it provided a half-hour lunch period, said nothing about when it should be taken.

The umpire, though, agreed with the union. The obligation to provide a lunch period implied scheduling at a reasonable time, he said; by custom this meant near the middle of the work shift. In this case, the arbiter decided, past practice had been so consistent that 11 a.m. and 1 p.m. must be regarded as the outside limits for lunch periods. (Bakelite Co., 29 LA 555)

Similarly: Under a contract that didn't limit management's right to schedule rest periods, one arbitrator looked at the company's past practice. He found that the employees had always been given a rest period after three hours' work and decided that this was how the parties must have meant to schedule them. (Rath Packing Co., 21 LA 20)

On the other hand: An arbitrator upheld management's right to stagger rest periods after instituting a continuous operation. Under the contract, times for rest periods were determined by foremen, stewards, and workers in each department. This right, the umpire said, was dependent on the shifts and hours set by the company. When it decided to go on continuous operations, it necessarily followed that rest periods had to be staggered; hence the workers had no cause to complain, he said. (Philco Corp., 40 LA 490)

Working During Paid Lunch Period

If a contract provides for a paid lunch period, can employees be required to work during that time? If some employees are not required to look after any job duties during their meal time, but others are, an arbitrator is likely to rule that this is an unfair practice.

EXAMPLE: A contract provided for a 20-minute lunch period as part of the normal workday paid for by the company. Employees were relieved from all duties during this paid meal period, except for boiler firemen, who were asked to keep watch over their boilers while they ate.

The union asked that relief men be furnished the boiler firemen so that they could eat without disturbance. The company claimed that there was ample time for them to eat and still keep an eye on the boilers.

The arbitrator ruled that the firemen were entitled to relief. Since no exception was made for these employees in the contract, and since they did not receive any extra payment for the additional time spent on the job during their eating time, the arbitrator reasoned that they had to be treated like other employees. (Ford Roofing Products Co., 5 LA 182)

But an arbitrator held that a company was not required to pay employees for their lunch period when they were asked to perform minor tasks of short duration during their lunch period. The contract called for the company to pay for the lunch break if a worker "works straight through without stopping to eat" and called for "up to thirty minutes" for meals which suggested to the arbitrator that uninterrupted meal periods were not intended. (Chevron Oil Co., 52 LA 928)

Coffee Break as Rest Period

Should a coffee break be viewed in the same light as ordinary rest periods? At least one arbitrator has ruled that there is no basis for distinguishing between coffee breaks and ordinary rest periods. Therefore, under a contract specifying that the company would continue its past practices with respect to rest periods, it didn't have the right to eliminate the practice of allowing certain women employees to take a 10-minute coffee break in the morning in addition to their regular two 15-minute rest periods during the day. (International Harvester Co., 21 LA 194)

Paid Washup Time

Where a contract is silent on the subject, can management discontinue paid washup p e r i o d s on its own hook? One arbiter said no. He noted that for many years, workers had been allowed to clean up during working hours. Arbiters usually find unwritten practices involving specific benefits for workers to be binding for the duration of the contract, he said; thus, the practice couldn't be discontinued unilaterally. (Harnischfeger Corp., 40 LA 1329)

However: Another arbiter held that a company could reduce unilaterally two 15-minute wash-up periods per day to two five-minute periods. (Ruralist Press, Inc., 51 LA 549)

Caution: Under the Taft Act, unilateral changes in working conditions may be regarded as a violation of the company's bargaining duty.

Payment for Unrecorded Work

An employee wasn't entitled to pay for "off-the-clock" work which he couldn't prove he had performed. He made no claim to pay until after he resigned from the supermarket at which he was employed. The arbiter refused his claim because he could find no "clear and convincing evidence" that the work actually was performed. (Wrigley Stores, 43 LA 225)

Wage Guarantees & SUB Plans

*IN BRIEF*_____

Weekly and annual guarantees of work or wages are likely to be fertile sources of grievances. One reason for this is that management usually tries to interpret such guarantees as narrowly as possible, since it receives no work in return for payments made in fulfillment of a guarantee.

POINTERS—

▶ A statement of normal working hours generally has been held not to constitute a guarantee of work or pay.

▶ Similarly, a listing of weekly salaries for clerical workers probably doesn't mean the company can't pay pro rata salaries when a reduced workweek is in effect.

Regular Workweek Not a Guarantee

If a contract establishes a regular workweek of so many hours, is this a wage or work guarantee? Most arbitrators agree that such a contract does not guarantee wages or work.

EXAMPLE: A union arguing for a guarantee, relied on two articles of the contract. One provided that the regular workday should be eight hours and the regular workweek 44 hours in six days, Monday through Saturday. The other required the company to maintain standards at least at the levels prevailing when the contract was signed. Putting these two clauses together, the union claimed the company violated the contract when it decided to eliminate Saturday work.

The umpire okayed the company's action on the basis of this reasoning: (1) There was no discussion in negotiations of whether the company was guaranteeing 44 hours' work; had there been any such intention, it would have been stated in explicit contract language. (2) The workweek clause, it appears, was intended merely to set

forth hours of work for purposes of computing overtime. (3) A clause providing four hours' reporting pay implied that there were occasions when a full schedule of work wouldn't be provided; this was inconsistent with the concept of a guarantee. (Consumers Service Co., 29 LA 447; see also International Window Cleaning Co., 10 LA 312)

But: Another arbitrator has held that a contract providing that regular working hours for regular employees shall be "a *full* week of forty hours per week" comprised a guaranteed workweek. (Hampden Sales Assn., Inc., 12 LA 62)

Statement of Weekly Salary

The fact that a contract lists weekly salaries for clerical workers does not mean the company can't pay them pro rata salaries if a reduced workweek is in effect, one umpire has ruled.

EXAMPLE: Protesting a cut in salaries of clerical workers in a steel mill during a period when the workweek was 32 hours instead of 40 hours, a union pointed to a table in the contract listing the "guaranteed salary" of various clerical grades. The union said the company had to pay the "guaranteed salary" w h e t h e r the workweek was one day or five.

The arbitrator, though, thought the union was confusing a guaranteed rate with guaranteed earnings. The "guaranteed salary" is a promise that a salaried worker will be paid at a certain rate, the umpire said, and the contract also made it clear that the rates shown are based on a 40-hour week. The company could cut these rates according to the actual workweek, he said, since the contract didn't specifically say it couldn't. (Bethlehem Steel Co., 26 LA 784)

When Employees Refuse Assigned Work

Can workers be deprived of a weekly guarantee of work or wages if they refuse to do available work which is different from their usual job? Most arbitrators have upheld employers' right to transfer workers to jobs where they are needed in order to make use of them for the guaranteed time. Thus, where a contract gave a 36-hour guarantee for all except those workers who refused to be transferred to available jobs, one arbiter ruled some employees were not eligible for the guaranteed pay because they refused to do some painting which they were assigned to fill in their time. An argument that no "transfer" was involved was rejected. (Boston Sausage & Provision Co., 5 LA 627)

Even where a contract didn't specifically deny the guarantee to employees refusing transfer to available work, an umpire ruled that the guarantee did not apply when employees refused such work. He reasoned that it was clear that the company's guarantee of hours involved a corresponding responsibility on the part of employees to perform the work offered. (Kroger Co., 5 LA 154)

However: Where a prior arbitration award (42 LA 228) interpreted a Supplemental Unemployment B e n e f i t

plan's provisions relating to "lack of work" in terms of plant practice of allowing employees for whom there is no work to decline alternate work, senior employees who declined alternate work when there was not enough alternate work for all of the employees were awarded benefits by an arbiter. Junior workers were also entitled to short-week benefits where the employer failed to exercise his power to "compel acceptance of another job offer," that is, notify an employee of alternate work, order him to accept it, and advise him that refusal to accept such work would result in the loss of benefits. (Pittsburgh Steel Co., 46 LA 774)

Effect of Strike on Guarantee

If one group of employees have a guarantee of hours or wages in their contract and can't work because of a strike by another group, are they entitled to the guarantee? A lot depends on the wording of the guarantee provision. Some arbitrators have said that a clause that just guarantees minimum weekly earnings is not the same as a work guarantee. One umpire ruled that a clause like this didn't require a baking company to pay drivers their weekly wages during a time they couldn't work when the bakers were on strike. The arbiter said that the pay guarantee applied only when the drivers could do work. (Junge Bread Co., et al., 1 LA 569; see also U.S. Steel Corp., 53 LA 550)

Even where a contract contains a specific guarantee of work, one arbitrator has held, the guarantee is suspended when employees can't work because of a walkout by members of the same union under a different contract. He reasoned that all union members must accept responsibility for the actions of any portion of the membership. (Kroger Co., 5 LA 154)

However: In one case an umpire ordered the company to pay the guarantee where (1) the contract clearly guaranteed 40 hours of work in a week, (2) employees had already worked the first day of the week, and (3) they had no work for three days during the week because members of another union were on strike. (Wheatality Baking Corp., 11 LA 526)

Effect of Strike on SUB Eligibility

The extent of a worker's involvement in a strike situation may have some influence on whether he is eligible for SUB payments.

EXAMPLE: Workers who were suspended for engaging in a wildcat strike were not entitled to supplemental unemployment benefits, even though they received state unemployment compensation benefits, one arbiter ruled.

The union argued that, under the SUB agreement, a worker was entitled to benefits, even though laid off by reason of a strike, if he was awarded UC benefits for the same week of layoff. However, the arbiter reasoned that the workers weren't laid off because of a work stoppage, but for disciplinary action connected with a work stoppage. The contract language clearly treated layoffs for disciplinary reasons separately from those resulting from strikes, he added. (Lehigh Portland Cement Co., 37 LA 996)

But: Another arbitrator decided that workers on layoff who were eligible for SUB *before* a strike did not become ineligible when the stoppage began.

EXAMPLE: Following the expiration of the SUB agreement and the beginning of the strike, the company stopped paying SUB to workers who —prior to the strike—had been laid off from the bargaining units which went on strike. It continued the plan in effect for certain workers outside these units. Under the SUB plan's termination provision, the union argued, as long as the plan continued to exist, it had to apply to workers "to whom it had been made applicable."

The umpire agreed. Although the company was free to terminate the *entire* plan upon the expiration of the agreement, it could not terminate

coverage in these units only. Since none of the workers had originally been laid off because of the strike, he reasoned, the continuance of their lay off could not have been a consequence of the strike. The benefit eligibility rule could not be applied as an additional "strike situation" eligibility rule, he concluded. (Allegheny Ludlum Steel Corp., 37 LA 689)

Guarantee Applied to Partial Workweek After Strike

If workers are called back to work after a strike in the middle of the workweek, are they entitled to a full week's pay under a weekly work guarantee? According to one arbitrator the answer is yes. Otherwise a company could not get around the contract simply by withholding work on the first day of a regularly scheduled workweek, the umpire said. (Wilson & Co., Inc., 5 LA 454)

On the other hand: An arbiter ruled that employees were not entitled to short-week benefits under their SUB plan that contained a strike disqualification clause for full weekly benefits. He held that if unemployment resulting from strike disqualified the employees from benefits while "wholly unemployed," it surely disqualified them from benefits while "partially unemployed." (E. J. Lavino & Co., 43 LA 213)

Effect of Layoff on Guarantee

Does a worker lose a weekly hours guarantee if he is laid off before the end of a workweek? Unless the contract says otherwise, a worker coming under the guarantee probably does not lose the amount guaranteed if removed from the payroll by the company during a workweek. Once the employee starts to work he is entitled to a full week's pay. (Keeshin Motor Express Co., Inc., 2 LA 57)

However: One arbitrator made a distinction between employees who were laid off temporarily and those who were permanently terminated. He said that a weekly guarantee provision *did* apply to employees who were laid off during the week with the expectation that they would return when more work was available, but *did not* apply to those whose employment was ended permanently before the end of the workweek. (Walsh, Perini, Groves & Slattery Cos., 21 LA 117)

Exclusions from Guarantee

Most wage guarantees contain language relieving the employer of the obligation to pay the guarantee if work is lost due to certain circumstances. This exclusion may be stated generally in terms of conditions "beyond the employer's control," in which case disputes are almost certain to arise concerning whether in a given situation the loss of work was "beyond the employer's control. Or the exclusion may list specific circumstances under which the guarantee would not be applicable. In such case, arbitrators tend to restrict the exclusion narrowly to the listed circumstances, as the following case illustrates:

An exemption from a weekly wage guarantee for time lost due to causes beyond company control didn't apply where a meat packing company laid off the work force because of disruptive absenteeism. The contract specified exemptions for layoffs due to "flood, fire, power failure, breakdown of plant equipment, or other causes beyond reasonable control of employer." According to the arbitrator, the company was freed from the guarantee only where a layoff was due to "physical" causes such as those listed. The layoff for absenteeism did not fall in this category, so the employer was not relieved of his obligation under the guarantee. (Ohio Natural Casing & Supply Co., 43 LA 883)

Effect of Snowstorm on Guarantee

When a severe snowstorm prevented a large part of the work force from reporting to work, an arbitrator ruled that the workers were entitled to an Automatic Short Week Benefit as provided in the contract. He said that in the past the company had declared workers on layoff in similar situations and should have done so in this instance. He went on to state that the mere fact of a snowstorm did not entitle employees to SUB payments; each storm would have to be appraised on its own "with the test of reasonableness being the decisive criterion." (Kelsey-Hayes Co., 49 LA 666)

On the other hand: Where the contract exempted the employer from SUB liability for time not worked due to an "act of God", workers were not entitled to benefits when a severe snowstorm caused a high degree of absenteeism and forced the suspension of production, resulting in several workers being sent home. As the absenteeism resulted from an "act of God" the employees were not considered on layoff for purposes of SUB payments. (International Harvester Co., 49 LA 892, see also Siouxland Dress Beef Co., 53 LA 9)

Effect of Holiday on Guarantee

Should a holiday be considered a scheduled workday for determining wages under a clause guaranteeing 40 hours' pay for those reporting a certain number of days per week? One arbiter has concluded that it should.

EXAMPLE: A contract guaranteed 40 hours' pay to each man who reported for work, upon request, either five or six days in any week, depending on the department's schedule. Several men reported for four scheduled workdays one week, but each worked less than 32 hours. They were paid for their time on the job plus one unworked holiday. The company maintained that an unworked holiday couldn't be considered a fifth day of work for purposes of the pay guarantee.

The intent of the parties in establishing the 40-hour pay guarantee was to stabilize wages. To accomplish this, the company was to schedule production so workers would qualify for the guarantee, the arbiter said. Therefore, he ruled that the occurrence of a holiday didn't remove the obligation to do so. The men could count the holiday as a day on which they reported for work, he concluded. (Colonial Baking Co., 35 LA 686)

Also: Under an SUB plan providing benefits in an amount equal to 65 percent of after-tax pay when added to state benefit and other "wages" or remuneration, an arbiter ruled that employees laid off for a holiday week were entitled to benefits, even though state benefits plus holiday pay paid by the employer came to more than 65 percent of normal take-home pay. The state unemployment compensation agency defined "wages" for a holiday week as not including holiday pay, and the parties had agreed to apply the agency's definitions, so the employer's contribution did not count, reducing the pay below the 65 percent level. (Pittsburgh Steel Co., 42 LA 228)

However, another arbiter stated that the closing of a plant on Fridays, following Thursday holidays, did not constitute a layoff under the meaning of the SUB plan, and that the employees were not entitled to benefits. (Western Tool, Inc., 42 LA 1064)

Overtime Included in Guarantee

When the contract doesn't specify whether or not a weekly wage guarantee includes overtime pay, should overtime pay be added to employees' regular earnings before applying the minimum guarantee?

At least one arbitrator has ruled that overtime pay should be added to employees' regular wages in calculating gross weekly earnings to which the wage guarantee clause applies. Since the contract clause didn't specify whether or not the guarantee included overtime,

the arbitrator's decision was based on the fact the overtime rate was computed from the daily base rate rather than from the weekly guaranteed rate. If the parties had intended to exclude overtime, the arbitrator said, they would have figured the overtime rate on the basis of the weekly guarantee. (Boller Beverage Co., 19 LA 860)

Eligibility for SUB While Receiving Social Security

If a supplemental unemployment benefits plan disqualifies employees who receive a retirement pension financed wholly or partially by the company, is a worker who is drawing federal social security benefits entitled to payments under the plan?

Interpreting the basic steel SUB plan, one arbitrator ruled that a man can't be considered to be disqualified just because he receives old-age insurance benefits. Even if social security were considered a pension, he added, it couldn't be said to be financed either partially or wholly by the company since it is financed by federal taxes. (Various Steel Companies, 32 LA 529)

Disability Retirement

Where a contract provided for an Income Extension arrangement for use in the event of layoff, a grievant who retired on a disability pension because of a permanent physical disability was not entitled to benefits under the plan. Although income extension aid may be a form of severance pay for employees who are separated through no fault of their own, it is not available to all separated employees, the arbiter noted, but only to those laid off for lack of work or plant closing. (General Electric Co., 49 LA 62)